CREWDOG

A Saga of a Young American

By

JOHN MATT

WATERFORD BOOKS

Hamilton, Virginia

CREWDOG

WATERFORD BOOKS
PO. Box 669
HAMILTON, VIRGINIA 22068

Copyright (c) 1992 by John Matt
All Rights reserved including the right of reproduction
in whole or in part in any form.

Designed by Holly Matt Grody

First Edition
Library of Congress Catalog Card Number 92-60589

Matt, John, date.
    Crewdog
        Includes Index and Bibliography
            1. Military Aviation History 2. 8th AF in WWII
            3. Nuclear testing 4. Weather Reconnaissance
I. Title.

ISBN 1-881429-00-8

Printed in the United States of America

DEDICATION

I must ask:

Why should I dedicate this work to my wife Priscilla
who sometimes mocks my more serious pursuits
and frustrates my paltry genius
by diverting it into mundane and menial chores?

After all, is she not fulfilled enough
with her Shasta daisies and gigantic peonies
and hummingbirds
and her handsome and nobly bred broodmare Thistle Dancer?

I dedicate it to her because I want her to know
I have always been ready to walk through fire for her
if only to retrieve some bauble that amused her:
but to place myself apart from others who have made this same promise,
I claim I am ready to walk through the flames to grasp the prize
then return through that same fire -a round trip, mind you-
to lay the singed trifle at her feet.

CREWDOG

FOREWORD

T HE MEMORY PLAYS TRICKS. This became very obvious when I began to describe events in which I was involved more than twenty, or forty or even -gasp- sixty years ago. When I showed my wife Cris my recounting of our wedding day, which I had remembered as having taken place on a sunny afternoon, she rummaged through her souvenirs and found the invitation which, of course, set the time at 8:00 PM. Since that time, we have occasionally slipped into a routine which reminds me of Hermoine Gingold and Maurice Chevalier singing their way down two different memory lanes together in the film "Gigi."

Fortunately, I had a surprisingly large body of documentation to keep myself straight. Family and school records and pictures, military travel and assignment orders and travel momentoes, along with conversations with family and friends were all used to clarify some of my past's dimmer pictures.

The National Records Center at Suitland, Maryland -part of the National Archives- provided assistance. I was amazed, as I perused World War II combat mission folders to find navigation track charts I had drawn up and turned in to the 392nd Bomb Group intelligence debriefing officer forty-five years before. The Air Force History Office at Bolling Air Force Base near Washington D.C. also helped.

The people at the USAF Air Weather Service History Office at Scott AFB, Illinois were very kind in guiding me through the stacks of records and journals of the several weather reconnaissance squadrons with which I had flown. The Public Affairs Office at Andrews Air Force Base in Maryland -home of the Presidential aircraft- also gave me assistance.

The gracious and knowledgeable ladies of the Purcellville and Rust libraries of Loudon County in Northern Virginia tracked down information and reference books to help me on my long journey into the past.

And then there is John McDonnell, family friend and prize-winning photographer for the Washington Post who put me in touch with his colleague John Ed Bradley, busy with the introduction of his second book, but not too busy to read my bulky tome and offer me encouragement at a crucial time. There are others, and I am indebted to them all.

CREWDOG is the name some military flightcrews have given themselves to show where they think they fit in the military scheme of things.

They don't consider themselves heroes, or cannon-fodder, although they sometimes fit both categories.

CREWDOGS are proud of what they can do and believe they do their best without a lot of interference from the management.

You can't win wars, or go to the moon, or do other great things without them.

CONTENTS

Dedication   i
Foreword   iii
Prologue   ix

BOOK ONE

Chapter 1. The Streets of Gold..1
Chapter 2. The Swaying Palms of Nashville...........................39
Chapter 3. Beyond the Nebulae...54
Chapter 4. The Big Time...78

BOOK TWO

Chapter 5. First Blood...111
Chapter 6. Five Pounds!..124
Chapter 7. Was Ist Das Nuts?..147
Chapter 8. Varsity to V-E Day..173

BOOK THREE

Chapter 9. The Moose are on the Gauges..............................207
Chapter 10. Pull er Up! Pull er Up!.......................................247
Chapter 11. The Gamma Bugs..268
Chapter 12. The King and the Picky Eaters............................289

BOOK FOUR

Chapter 13. H plus Forty-five Minutes....................................321
Chapter 14. Korea: The Unforgettable Forgotten War.............339

BOOK FIVE

Chapter 15. I, John, Take Thee Priscilla..................................357
Chapter 16. You're Holding Her Like a Bomb!.........................384
Chapter 17. Suddenly, the Tallest Thing On Earth..................402

continued next page

BOOK SIX

Chapter 18. Caramba! It's the Samba!......................................431
Chapter 19. There Was No Peace in LaPaz...............................471
Chapter 20. The Presidential Hat..494

Epilogue   501
Bibliography   503
Index   507

PROLOGUE - *The Magic Moment*

THE AUTUMN MORNING WAS SUNNY, with a light breeze blowing off the Hudson into our rapt, mostly young faces. We were watching, fascinated, as an airplane with floats curved around after making a low pass right over our heads and landed in the slightly choppy water just offshore. Its speed died quickly and the pilot, after some difficulties with taxiing, securing of lines and scrambling around by the handlers, got the machine positioned for hauling up the ramp. We all waited impatiently while they got the plane up out of the water, and finally it was done and it sat there before our very eyes like a creature from another world.

The pilot, some dignitaries and most of the crowd moved away from the ramp to dedicate what they were calling the Yonkers Seadrome, which was not much more than the ramp itself and some refueling drums but could turn out to be something someday. It was the 1930's and, after all, there was no way to go but up.

There were just a few other kids on the ramp besides me and I found myself slowly drawn to this red and white painted masterpiece, my twelve year old heart pounding like a dollar-fifty pocket watch. The beautiful creation sat there, the sun glistening on the water droplets which had sprayed on it when its pontoons knifed into the water.

It was a machine endowed with some magic energy which could let it lift itself away from the earth and transport me and my friends to places where the good and the knowable really existed, and where the unknown could be confronted on even terms.

I reached out and brushed my fingers along the fuselage, feeling the barely protruding rivets on its slick surface. The perfect shape of this living machine, the great spreading wings, the rightness of it reached toward me and touched me back, and in that instant, we were one.

From that day to this, the magic of that moment has never left me.

I

BOOK ONE

Previous page: *A tough,determined Japanese aircraft carrier pilot prepares to attack an unsuspecting Pearl Harbor. (ACME Photo)*

Opposite: Flanking the Author, age 7, are brothers Bill, age 9 and George, age 5.

1

THE STREETS OF GOLD

IS IT NORMAL, I have occasionally wondered, to have memories of events that happened when you were very young which were clearer, more tangible than those of the day before yesterday? I can clearly recall, for example, events years earlier than the dedication of the Yonkers Seadrome, like the day my mother took my brother Bill and me up to Getty Square to buy "Lindy" helmets with earflaps and goggles because all the other kids on the block had them. Besides, they were practical, that winter of 1927, for keeping the ears warm and for sleigh riding.

I was just turning four then and it was obvious something great had happened, something which had gotten everybody excited and had changed the world. A man had crossed the ocean and because of it I was trying to emulate the older kids in singing songs like "Lucky Lindy." We got to hear them often because we played them on the crank-up phonograph, usually with the speed set too fast so that the voices came out sounding like R2D2's great grand-pa. We had to stand on a chair to crank the Victrola and change needles and put the trumpet-shaped pickup on to the starting groove of the scratched-up records. The songs were played in between gems like "Just a Gigolo" and my favorite of the time, "Its Three O'clock in the Morning," which is available today only in fossilized form.

Lindbergh's first solo flight across the Atlantic and subsequent flights around the world kept a firm grip on the public imagination. He was not the only one in the public eye however, and larger than life characters like Wiley Post with his black eye patch, Roscoe Turner sporting his robin's-egg blue uniform and waxed mustache, and the ladies like Amelia Earhart and Jaqueline Cochran who took the same risks and were occasionally photographed wearing chic white leather flying clothes.

There were many others and they all kept the news headline writers busy. As I wandered wide-eyed through the joys and hazards which befall a pre-teener in the city I could begin to comprehend, as I learned to read the papers, the magnitude of courage it took for these aviators to do what they did, or tried to do.

The weekly newsreels in the neighborhood movie houses were the source of the more spectacular views and descriptions of the aviation exploits which seemed to occur in a continual stream. Most of the flights were planned to gain publicity needed to get the funding for the more powerful and expensive new aircraft involved, so newsreel cameras on the ground or in the air were focal points in the operations.

This was great when the operation was a success but when they failed, the results were unforgettable. One mental picture which persists to this day is the crash of a GeeBee, a fat, stubby bumblebee-like racing airplane. It is flying a fast, low pass just before the camera when a wing snaps off and the machine rolls and slashes into the ground leaving no visible wreckage except a burning pall of oil smoke.

Record-attempting flights crashing on takeoff, air race disasters and other violent scenes raised up the morbid specters which come with high risk as they still do at Indy or the stock car races, and with the flights of the astronauts. To look at pictures of the famous flyers was to look at people whose days seemed numbered, but who disregarded the countdown out of hand.

Yonkers, New York, which called itself the Terrace City because of its hills was, in the 1920's and 30's a great place to grow up whether you wished to become an aviator, a teller of tales or even do some honest work. Although Yonkers adjoins the Bronx, we insisted on an identity as distinct as possible from New York, and New Yorkers let us know we were welcome to it.

There was at one time a famous comic strip in the New York papers which featured characters called Maggie and Jiggs. Jiggs was a corned- beef and cabbage type who was married to Maggie, a crockery thrower who kept trying without success to teach Jiggs the artful deceptions needed for social climbing.

On one occasion Jiggs was dragooned to impress some innocent boob from out of town with some of the famous New York sights. Atop one of the tall buildings, Jiggs pointed northward and bragged, "This building is so high you can see all the way to Yonkers!" The boob looked at Jiggs and said, "Yonkers? What are they?"

Yes, what the heck was a Yonkers? Three hundred years ago, the Dutch called them jonkheers, the privileged, big-shot burghers who walked around with long, slender canes and big hats and were in charge of settling the area for Holland in the 1600's. They are the same crowd who were diddled out of twenty-six pre-depression dollars worth of valuable trinkets in exchange for the island of Manhattan. The Indian con-men immediately fled, probably to the north around Albany, the state capitol, where cunning and guile thrive today.

Times Square was an easy 30 or 40 minute street car and subway ride, while the ride to Grand Central Station via commuter train was about the same. All of the delights and temptations of the big city were available and convenient, and school trips to the Bronx Zoo, the museums and tourist sights

3

widened our little horizons.

Later in high school, some of us would strike out on unsupervised field trips -otherwise known as playing hookey- to taste the forbidden fruit of 42nd Street. Which burlesque theater should it be this time, the Eltinge or the Republic? After checking the list of performers and studying their artistically depicted qualifications on the posters out front, the dance critic with the most courage that day would screw up his fifteen-year old brass and sidle up to the ticket booth. Casually and with the deepest voice he could manage he would order, "Three please!"

The ticket seller, who could probably estimate our age to the week, usually took the money and gave us the tickets along with an ever so tiny smirk.

My views as to the educational value of these forays remain mixed. We certainly didn't learn much about dancing but we did get training in the female anatomy and how to act reasonably calm while a volcano rages within, an attribute which came in handy several times in later life.

Besides, the girls weren't the only attraction. The comedians who played the other half of the show were no doubt the funniest men alive and the double entendre routines involving baby photographers, hat salesmen and the like would bring more than a mere smile to some of the sterner puritan hearts.

They also sold salt-water taffy in boxes which were guaranteed to contain a valuable surprise and we usually bought one. After all, a box of candy and a fake wrist watch for twenty-five cents wasn't too bad. It was a better deal than the Dutchmen got for Manhattan.

Yonkers, which had grown to approximately 150,000 elevator builders, carpet weavers, sugar refiners, copper cable twisters and commuters to the big city lay well within the sociological blast and overpressure zone of New York and events which took place there sometimes spilled over into our town.

When Mayor LaGuardia cracked down on the rackets, some of the Mafiosi quietly moved north into the Yonkers suburbs to behave, at least at home, like model citizens. When Franklin Roosevelt drove into the big city from his home upriver at Hyde Park, we rushed down one block to Riverdale

Avenue at the sound of approaching sirens to watch the entourage, their wheels bouncing on the cobble stones and trolley tracks, drive through at high speed. FDR drove his small, canvas-topped touring car himself, and we didn't know until much later that his car had to be specially equipped with hand controls because of his handicap.

We were close enough to make quick trips to New York for ticker tape parades, New Year's Eve celebrations, shopping at Macy's, watching the young Frank Sinatra or Benny Goodman at the Paramount and other edifying events.

As close as we were, conscious efforts were made to keep from being swallowed up by the Colossus to the South. We adjoined the Bronx but, somewhat unkindly, referred to that borough as "the dull 20 minute train ride between the city line and Manhattan."

In turn and also somewhat ungenerously, we were referred to as "appleknockers" in honor of orchards which once flourished around Yonkers, and were described as "being so far north that one could ski in the streets in the summertime."

These were the feelings of some people in the Bronx; as for those in Manhattan or Brooklyn, some, like the out-of-town visitor in the Jiggs comic strip, never heard of us or believed we were a strange tribe that lived somewhere between Poughkeepsie and Saskatoon. Everyone knows where Saskatoon is, but to those who haven't heard of Poughkeepsie-that's where the real upstate appleknockers come from.

The antipathy between us and the Bronx took some strange turns, as when Yonkers passed an ordinance declaring it illegal for men or women to wear shorts within the city's boundaries, knowing that all of the flagrantly barelegged hikers and picknickers who passed through this bastion of modesty would be Bronxites. It became an annual ritual to watch for the newsreel coverage of half-clad, guilty parties being issued summonses as they stepped off the ferry across the Hudson from Alpine, New Jersey onto Yonkers sovereign territory.

Believe it or not, we saw nothing strange in this. Perhaps it was actions like these that shamed Mayor LaGuardia into shutting down our beloved New York burlesque houses. But what if the burlesques had also moved north into Yonkers? Well, one of the burlies moved across the river into Newark, New Jersey and the city survived. Although with Newark, in those days, how could you tell if they got damaged or not?

Beefing up the barrier between us and the Bronx may even have been involved in actions by our Board of Education to recruit our teachers from the Ohio area, where speech accents were pure and unsullied by New Yorkese. We didn't know at the time that we were natives being ministered by right-speaking missionaries from Cleveland who would require us to pronounce words like "regular" and "hanger" and "bottle" as they did.

My father's journey to the New World seems a little more complicated than others I have heard about. He came from an area called Galicia which was located near where the present boundaries of Czechoslovakia, Poland and the Ukraine meet.

The Galicia in which he had been born and grew up to young manhood was peopled by Austrians, Poles, Jews and by ethnic Ukrainians like both of my parents-to-be. The area was called an "autonomous crownland" of the Austro-Hungarian Empire, which apparently meant that people were pretty much left to their own devices by Emperor Franz Josef.

Life in the autonomous crownland was apparently pleasant and rewarding enough so that my father intended to build his life there, as he saw things when the 1900's arrived. But to build this life properly, he needed land of his own, apart from that of his family. The way to do this, as shown by other young men before him, was to go to America, where the streets were strewn with carelessly discarded gold ingots, slightly used precious stones and oversized, slightly soiled dollar bills. All of these, of course, could easily be converted into clear title to any number of hectares of land at the foot of the Carpathian hills, and start him on his way to becoming a well-to-do landowner.

The idea of coming to America grew in strength within him until it became irresistible. So he got the fare together and made his way to Trieste, where he boarded a ship for the journey down the Adriatic, through the Strait of Gibraltar and out into the heaving Atlantic toward New York.

My father's plan was to scout out the territory around New York City, find a job which would make him the money he would need, and then return. The coal mines of Pennsylvania were always looking for new recruits, and a number of his friends and relatives had gone there to take up that tough and dangerous job. But he knew he would never get rich digging coal: at five feet-two he would have a tough time making a decent daily quota of anthracite, or even the soft kind.

My father, like the other immigrants, knew that the boast of gilded American pavements was merely a metaphor for the rewards of cleverness or hard work. But as he disembarked from the Ellis Island ferry and looked around in wide-eyed wonder at the giant buildings and had to dodge the impatient, noisy groups of humanity which hurried around him, he might be excused if he took a moment to find a sheltered area, perhaps near the curb behind a lamp post. Then, with a quick glance right and left to make sure no one noticed, he might scrape the pavement with his shoe to confirm what he knew all along, that there was no gold beneath his feet. But then, he might have told himself, that although the sidewalks were paved with nothing more than slate and stone, at least they were paved, which, to someone from the Galician outback, was a big plus.

Now, enter Anna of the Procak family, a handsome, dark-eyed young woman, daughter of a choirmaster back in Galicia. She too took the journey from Trieste a few years after my father to find out where all the young men had gone, and what they were up to.

The Alexander Smith and Son carpet mill in Yonkers, the largest of its kind in the world at the time, needed men and women to work among the whirling bobbins and sliding shuttlecocks of the giant rug looms. Word had gotten around that it seemed to be a good a place to earn the wages needed for survival in this vibrant, scary New World, and both my future parents found jobs there. The hours were long and the wages were low, but hard labor was not involved, and Yonkers was a small, pretty town surrounded by a rural countryside situated in a beautiful setting along the Hudson River.

Middle-Europeans were not the only types of immigrants who came to work at Alexander Smith. A few years before my father arrived in New York and checked the pavement for some tell-tale glitter, a young man, in his late teens like my father, arrived from Ledbury, England. His name was John Masefield and he spent some time working as a bartender's assistant in lower Manhattan in a job which, according to one of my English teachers, required that he clean spittoons. A friend convinced him that life could be better up in the boondocks of Yonkers.

He found a place to live at 8 Maple Street in an area where most of the residents, including my future parents, worked at the carpet factory, a few blocks from our church on Chestnut Street. He was hired as a threader's helper, and his pay quickly jumped from $6.50 to $8.50 per week when his foreman determined that he was a hard worker who took his work seriously.

Masefield had arrived with no inkling in his mind that he might take on a deep interest in poetry, and that he might even become a poet himself. But he began to spend some of his spare time at a book shop on Warburton Avenue, across from the theater where my mother would get to see her first movie.

One day, he bought a book of Chaucer's verses and when he took it home and began to read, it came rushing to him all in a moment, there in his rooms at 8 Maple Street, in the pretty little village of Yonkers, New York, that he should pursue "his birth right" as a poet.

He began to write poetry, first to entertain his friends and himself, then with more serious purpose. By the time he had amassed "two buckets" of it, he burned it all and decided to return to England to do it right. He had been in Yonkers for almost two years, and now he had found the direction his life should take.

Masefield was an international figure when he returned for a sentimental journey in 1933, but displayed no snobbery of any kind and went out of his way to renew acquaintances with some of his old carpet-spinning colleagues.

There is little or no chance he and my father had ever met, but I like to conjure up a vision anyway, of these two young men being thrown together in some minor task at work. The perfectionist Masefield would no doubt be unable to resist correcting my father's halting English. And then, by trifling only slightly with the truth, I could claim that my father had taken English lessons from the man who would become a great Poet Laureate of England.

After my mother-to-be made the trip from Galicia, she joined up with a beautiful hazel-eyed blonde young lady who eventually became my Godmother. I didn't understand what a Godmother was supposed to be, but Mary Lucas certainly looked and acted the role the title conjured up in my mind. We called her Ninotchka, and when she visited us, we all stopped what we were doing and made a big fuss and had a little party.

Mary's visits were made on her day off from her job as a housemaid for a big-time New York architect named Kittredge, who designed some important buildings around the budding Big Apple. She always arrived with a giant box of chocolates and we would have a great time for days afterwards, trying to figure which were the chocolate-covered hazel nuts or filberts, and which might turn out to be a disappointingly gooey creme. Test squeezes, of course, were not allowed.

My future parents met at a pre-World War I version of a singles party. The men and women were all young, marriageable carpet-mill workers from the same general area of Europe and now lived in the same neighborhood in Yonkers. My mother was drawn to this green-eyed, sandy haired little man who had ambitions beyond that of a worker in a rug mill.

It wasn't long before they were married in St. Michaels, the little onion-domed church half-way up the hill on Chestnut Street in Yonkers. It was the same church where my brothers and sisters and I would spend many a fidgety Sunday later on.

Project Landowner was still active in my father's mind when they were married, and my mother was apparently willing to go along. This required, after a few years of marriage, that she pack up most of her belongings and prepare to retrace the long, uncomfortable journey by ship to Trieste and back to Galicia, where, with family assistance and my father's earnings, she would start the process of buying some farmland.

He would remain behind for a while to increase their working capital, and follow later. She would not be travelling alone however, but would take their infant daughter Katherine -little Kasha- with her, and she was excited at the idea of showing off her beautiful new baby to her family.

As my father stood in the cavernous passenger shed and watched his bride make her way up the gangplank with the baby and board the ship, he had no way of knowing that great, world-shattering events were getting ready to transpire, and that it would be quite some time before they would see each other again.

These great events began on a warm Sunday morning on June 28, 1914, as a band of seven assassins mingled with the crowds lining the streets of Sarajevo -a city that is now Capitol of Bosnia, formerly part of the recently splintered Yugoslavia- to welcome Emperor Franz Josef's nephew Archduke Franz Ferdinand, and his wife, Countess Sophie. The Archduke was next in line for the Hapsburg throne, and would rule the Austro-Hungarian empire after Franz Joseph, who was in his eighties, gave it up. Since Galicia was part of this empire, the murder of the heir apparent would, of course, have an effect on its subjects, along with the rest of the empire and, as it turned out, the entire world.

The Archduke had arrived to observe some large-scale maneuvers in the area by the Austrian army. The conspirators were known to the local authorities but were considered just another bunch of youthful crackpots, like many other non-Austrian political groups which proliferated in the ethnically diverse empire. But unlike some of the others, they could see no way to express the nationalistic urges which burned within their souls in the autocratic, repressive regime except in terms of blood and murder.

Assassination Plan A was to throw a bomb at the Archduke's fancy, open car as it passed the police headquarters on the way to the welcoming ceremony at the Town Hall. The bomb was thrown but the driver, who saw the black object arching towards him, accelerated. The device bounced off the folded-back sedan roof behind the Archduke and into the street where it exploded and injured a number of policemen and onlookers.

The bomb-thrower was captured and the Archduke, a stately, mustachioed man of courage who was a trifle on the paunchy side, continued his journey to the Town Hall and paid his respects to the Mayor. It appeared by that time that the threat had now passed, so the royal party boarded the cars and made their way back on the same route to visit the hospital where the injured policemen were being treated.

Before the trip, when Ferdinand had been warned of the possibility of assassination, he fixed his informant with his princely gaze and said, "I do not let myself be kept under a glass cover..." In keeping with this attitude, a police official remarked, "Security measures on June 28 will be in the hands of Providence."

The remaining conspirators, who were said to be atheists and had cut off communications with Providence, were determined to finish their task and fell back on Plan B. As the Archduke's car approached them a second time, this time from the opposite direction, Gavrilo Princip drew his pistol and, from a few feet away, fired two shots. One bullet struck the Countess in the side while the other hit the Archduke in the neck and severed his jugular vein. Both wounds were fatal.

An event like this could have been used by Emperor Franz Josef to round up all of the cranks, nuts and even the honest opposition to remove the irritations which usually beset the almost absolute European monarchs of the time. But the murder of the heir apparent to his throne, a young man he hadn't been too crazy about, was a fortuitous chance to clean up a lot of additional loose ends that had plagued him for a long time.

He now had an excuse to declare war on the small, adjoining country of Serbia which probably had something to do with the assassination and also posed a threat to his empire by playing up to his enemy Czar Nicholas and his millions of Russian troops.

The Emperor's problem was how to declare war on Serbia and limit the ensuing hostilities to just the two of them so that victory could be assured in a short time, even though he knew that Serbia would be a tough nut to crack. But there was a series of interlocking treaties which might come into play if any one of a number of countries declared war and even an Emperor had to act with some caution.

For thirty days, Emperor Franz Josef discussed the matter with the German Emperor, Kaiser Wilhelm. Both of the monarchs would rather avoid a general war, which was possible under the circumstances, but they were surrounded by advisors who looked at war as the best means to cause the German and Austro-Hungarian version of paradise to prevail in Europe and therefore, the world.

In any event, the Germans promised to come to Austria's aid if the Russians -in order to help the Serbs- declared war on Austria.

Meanwhile, America, at this time, was considered to be a significant military power but with no interest in the European power plays. At the time, we still thought that George Washington's advice, given a century and a quarter before, that America should avoid "foreign entanglements," was still a good idea.

So far, we have the Germans and Austrians on one side, and the Serbians and the Russians on the other. But what would the French and the British do? They both had agreements with the Russians and formidable military power but perhaps, thought some of the Germans, who had the most powerful military machine in the world, maybe now was the time to deal with them also, once and for all.

The Austrians drafted an ultimatum for the Serbs, worded in a way which would make it almost impossible for the Serbs to accept, and which would give them forty-eight hours to reply. Both the Emperor and the German Kaiser were still not sure it was the right thing to do, but Franz Josef gave his mutton-chop whiskers a few tugs, signed the ultimatum and sent if forward.

The Serbs actually tried to meet the document's terms but the war machinery was already in motion. Each giant domino started to fall; Emperor Franz Josef declared war on Serbia on behalf of Austria, Russia declared war on Austria, Germany declared war on Russia, France and then Britain declared war on Germany and Austria.

Now, all the high-rollers had bellied up to the playing table, all of them planning on a short war and not envisioning the millions of casualties and widespread destruction that happened in the ensuing long years of carnage.

The well-being of the civilian populations was of little consideration. They were expected to stay out of the line of fire if they could, while the soldiers fought the battles. The civilians were an inconvenient necessity, and would be left to deal with the consequences, like famine, quadruple digit inflation and the sacrifice of their young men.

Meanwhile, back in Galicia, my mother and Katherine were like two sparrows sucked into a hurricane. The area was in the direct path the Russians planned to use for the invasion of Germany, and they found themselves buffeted by the motion of more than a million German and Austrian troops maneuvering through their area into positions just behind the border nearby.

There were thousands upon thousands of infantry soldiers, masses of cavalry, long columns of horse-drawn artillery, endless trains of supply wagons which raised clouds of dust on the unpaved roads. They all moved eastward, toward the Russians, who were involved in the same type of buildup just across the Galician border.

Opposite the Austrians were 1.3 million Russian troops, preparing to move through Galicia on the way to the German heartland to encircle Berlin and make a short war of it.

The Germans, with both eastern and western fronts to deal with, would expect the Austrians to hold off the Russians while they made a massive attack on the other side of their country, on their western front. Their plan, developed by General von Schlieffen, would send a giant army of German troops through neutral Belgium and make a gigantic sweep west and then south in an attempt to encircle Paris and defeat the French quickly. Then they would join their Austrian allies to finish off the Russians.

The winter came, and so did the Russians, all 1.3 million of them and the same thousands of Austrian infantry, cavalry, artillery and supply wagons, minus the great numbers of men and equipment already lost in the Russian attack, came reeling and stumbling back in retreat, followed closely behind by the Czar's army.

My mother described how they had to huddle down on the floor as bullets came punching through the walls of their house during the battle which engulfed them. There were several days while they were in the middle of no-man's-land, with friendly Austrian troops on one side and Russian invaders on the other with artillery arching overhead. Then the Austrians fell back further and the Russians came and the Galicians were suddenly citizens in an occupied country. The Russians, as is usually the case with occupying troops, did not act like candidates for the Good Conduct Medal.

The slaughter on both sides had been monumental, as it had been between the French and the Germans as the Kaiser's troops marched on Paris, with hundreds of thousands of dead and wounded. The newly-developed machine-gun had been introduced into the defenses of both sides, and as attacking troops marched in line across open fields, they were mowed down as they advanced.

Somehow, in the middle of all this, my mother was able to gather up her daughter and flee, to make her way back to Trieste and make the westward journey, never to return.

My parent's initial dreams for themselves and their family had evaporated at Sarajevo, along with the lives of the Archduke and his wife. Now my parents were rejoined after all these harrowing events, and what had seemed like a good idea was now out of the question.

His wife and daughter safely home once more, my father, and I assume he realized how lucky he had been to get his courageous wife and daughter back in one piece, was now forced to change the object of his ambitions from Galician landowner to American businessman. He had become familiar with the saloon business, the type you find in a working class neighborhood: long mahogany bar with a brass foot rail and spittoons, elaborate free lunches including pickled hard-boiled eggs and pig's feet, round tables and spindly chairs, and a booze menu which featured straight shots of whiskey with a small beer chaser. It all sounds so terribly chic.

My father toiled away as a bartender as World War I ended at eleven o'clock on November 11th, 1918, the eleventh hour of the eleventh day of the eleventh month. The Allies ignored the dictum that their armies should be valiant in battle and generous in victory and instead of ending the war to end all wars, let ancient prides and hatreds govern their actions. Instead of building a lasting peace, they merely laid the groundwork for World War II.

Meanwhile, back in America, powerful, well-meaning forces had been at work. The temperance movement which had started out by preaching moderation in the use of alcoholic drinks was seized by people who saw the chance to eliminate them altogether.

The movement, led by a number of church groups, managed to sell the country the idea of amending the Constitution so that the manufacture, importation and selling of alcoholic beverages, except for half-strength beer, was prohibited. The amendment resulted in congressional passage of the Volstead Act, which prescribed prohibition, and the "Great Experiment" was started.

The saloon business, my father along with it, now embarked on an era in which great numbers of ordinary citizens decided they would continue their drinking activities whether it was legal or not. This included party-goers, maintenance drinkers, alcoholics, tired workers getting off shift, politicians, policemen, little old ladies, noble-minded school teachers; all of the same people who use the stuff intelligently today or abuse it with destructive self-indulgence.

Many of the drinking establishments kept right on running, but now they had to take precautions like operating behind an innocent-looking front, such as an ice-cream parlor or a candy store. Access to the illegal saloon was made through doors which only the knowledgeable knew enough to enter, doors which were sometimes fitted with peepholes so that persons of uncertain intent might be turned away.

Where to get the liquor? That was the main question except for the matter of not getting caught, and the problem was solved either by buying the real stuff smuggled across the borders or the shorelines by "rumrunners" or making the stuff

15

yourself. Drinkable alcohol for the do-it-yourselfers was readily available, along with artificial coloring and handy bathtubs.

The years gathered speed and turned into the Roaring Twenties. The Great War was over and the economy seemed to surge forward. Everybody was having a great time even though the celebration of it, when it involved alcohol, was against the law, and celebrate they did.

There were occasional, perfunctory raids by the police who loaded the bartenders and some of the customers into paddywagons and held them for a few hours. My father noted that on the single occasion he was caught in the net, the police made sure that he brought along a bottle of the good stuff for the trip to the station. The station house complement would gather around the holding area for a block party, or I should say, a cell block party.

Somewhere along the line my father, taking seriously the idea that this is the land of opportunity, started his own speak easy business near the main shopping center of town and just a short streetcar ride away from home. It was, to all appearances, a combination ice cream parlor and candy store and I generally spent some time there checking the quality control of the ice cream sandwiches and playing with the cat, only occasionally wondering why I was so lucky to have a father who owned such an establishment.

I didn't really know what a speakeasy was at the time, but I began to notice that groups of customers walked right on through the place and out the rear door into another room. Curiosity finally grasped me by the little hand and took me through the back door and, lo and behold, there were lots of men there laughing and drinking what certainly looked like whiskey.

The tables had little shelves underneath the tops, and if a suspicious-looking person arrived, the patrons would duck their drinks onto the little shelves, twiddling their thumbs and gazing with sudden interest at the ceiling until the peril had passed.

The arrival of the cop on the beat was not cause for too much alarm, since he generally found a table in the corner and was served a drink and was expected to duck it under the table just like anybody else. Of course, he only had to do this if somebody like Chief of Police Quirk showed up to make sure that the speakeasy situation was not getting out of hand.

The Chief, a handsome, silver-haired Irishman with a Barrymore-class profile was chauffeured from his headquarters to scenes of action as a passenger in the sidecar of an elegantly polished, dark maroon Indian motorcycle. Those were the days, when policemen could deter crime by their imposing presence in their immaculate uniforms, and by their readiness to swing that nightstick when the provocation met some vague standard acceptable to the community.

Organized crime was nowhere to be seen, except that a local 3.2-proof brewery was said to be owned by gangster Dutch Schultz, and I presume that much of the smuggled liquor available around town came from The Mob. On one occasion, a high-level gangster on the run from the G-men gave himself up to Walter Winchell, the newspaper columnist, at a rendezvous in front of Proctor's theater right in the middle of town. Otherwise, Yonkers was too far away to have the tommy-gun battles, booze warehouse raids and other acts of violence inflicted on it.

When repeal finally did arrive in 1932, along with the election of Franklin Roosevelt, it came with the strains of "Happy Days Are Here Again" and lots of wild and boozy parties. For saloon owners, the changes were relatively minor, like discarding the peephole door and doing away with the camouflaging operations out front.

The crank-up phonograph we played the Lucky Lindy records on gave way to radio and before every home had one, the have-not kids would group around the street-level window of some considerate neighbor who pointed his radio outward, turned up the volume and let us listen to the World Series and the great prize fights involving Jack Dempsey, Max Schmeling, Gene Tunney and others.

Other advances were going forward and I'm certainly glad they did. Milk wagons, vegetable carts and other vehicles were pulled around the streets by -you guessed it- horses, and I can still see Tony the junk man pull up to the curb, drop the bell-shaped metal anchor which was attached by a line to the

17

horse's halter, then strap the oat-bag around the horse's muzzle.

It was the oats that created some problems which we all took for granted including the slight odor which blended in with the general city atmosphere. The used oats were taken care of by white-coated men with push-brooms and shovels, and trash cans on wheels. They must have been johnny-on-the-spot, since the street was our stickball diamond and I don't remember having to skip over any little obstacles on the way to second base.

Much was made of the improvements by the milk companies when the delivery wagon wheels were changed from metal rims to rubber tires to operate more quietly in the early dawn hours. Soon even this step forward was surpassed when the wagons were replaced by small vans, and an era ended. These onward steps in the march of civilization were brought to naught however, when customers began buying cheaper milk at the new-fangled supermarkets, and home milk deliveries were abandoned.

Supermarkets have become fixtures in our lives: they are a convenient means for buying food at a reasonable price. But they can't begin to compare with the horse-drawn food hawkers for convenience: they came right to your door. Each had a distinctive call which would let the hard-working housewife know that the fruit and vegetable man had arrived, or that the fish peddler was on the street, ready to slice some steaks from one of the fresh fish buried in a mound of ice on his cart. But one by one they disappeared, perhaps to return at a better time.

Other conveniences disappeared too, like the one provided by the scissor man, who pushed his pedal-driven grindstone around and sharpened knives and scissors for a nickel or a dime. And the umbrella man, who carried replacement umbrella ribs around in a quiver, and fixed your brolly on the spot. They not only furnished some needed services but were fascinating to watch; almost as much fun as the occasional one-man band who wandered through the neighborhood, pounding his drum and banging his cymbals while playing two instruments, all at the same time.

The iceman stayed with us for a while, until even the flat-dwellers began to afford refrigerators and central heating.

Depending on the season, he delivered ice or coal in a Model-T wagon. The well-to-do had had refrigerators for some time, but we got along with iceboxes, cooled with blocks of ice placed in one of its compartments.

The iceman would scrape a line with a point of his tongs on the great transparent oblong to mark 25 or 50 pound blocks, then with a tick-tick-tick of his ice-pick he would split it at the right place, scattering shards which we would pick up and suck on. After he placed the ice in the icebox it would, naturally, melt as the day wore on and the water would funnel through a tube into the drip pan below.

The pan needed to be emptied before it overflowed, but every so often a cry would go up, "Meesus, your icebox is leaking! " The guilty party, having recognized the voice of the lady in the apartment below would check her back porch where the icebox was kept, slide the overflowing pan out and toss the water into the alley.

The flat dwellers not yet blessed with central heating had to be satisfied with gas logs or kerosene heaters at one end of the flat and a coal stove in the other, in the kitchen. The iceman delivered the coal for the stove in canvas bags which he and his helpers carried on their backs and dumped into the family storage area in the cellar. The coal was then brought up daily by one of us in the same bucket we used to carry out the ashes. This was done in the dumbwaiter which extended from the cellar to the top floor, with an opening in each kitchen.

Of course, the right way to get the coal upstairs was to put the full bucket on the dumbwaiter and then climb aboard and work the ropes from inside until you got to your own floor. This took some expertise since the dumbwaiter shaft was dark, although you could see the dim outlines of the door openings as you passed them. The risk was worth it; to arrive at the correct place and bang on the door, to have it opened by my mother, who would stand there, arms folded, not too amused. When we later moved into a place with steam heat and a water heater, we could actually feel the lurch of civilization as it shot forward.

The junkman was the last horseman to quit and could be seen creeping along between the rows of Ford Model A's, Chevvys, Hudson Terraplanes, Essex Super Sixes and an occasional long-hooded LaSalle which now lined the curbs. The cow-bells strung on poles amidships on his wagon would clunk in a slow dirge as he looked for a place to drop anchor, the mournful sounds tolling the end of an era.

The march of technology was not always appreciated, how-ever. I can recall when my father took me to Leow's to see Al Jolson in The Jazz Singer -the first "talkie" feature. The film was preceded by an introduction in which Jolson put on his makeup as he described how talking movies worked. He went on and on until, finally, I tugged on my fathers sleeve and said, "Pop, I wish he'd stop talking so we can see the picture!"

Sid Caesar, the famous comedian, was born and grew up in Yonkers and recently described his birthplace, in program notes for a performance at Wolf Trap near Washington as a "rough, industrial town." I never met him even though we went to the same high school, for the simple reason that he was a senior while I was a sophomore and when you are two years apart in school you live on different planets.

Caesar had already attained some celebrity doing funny routines while jerking sodas in an ice cream parlor in his neighborhood, and I do recall seeing him, saxophone case in hand, leaving after school to board the trolley car.

There were some large industries in Yonkers but it seems to me that tree-lined streets and well-kept suburbs made up a good part of the city, and I can't get myself to agree that it was "rough" in those days. It could be that he had been subjected to a music student's ambush, where the poor guy, while trying to pass through a culturally deprived neighborhood, would have his musical instrument case torn from his grasp and tossed around by a gang of envious kids and eventually returned to him.

Our school system was known as "the best in the United States." I believe this was true; we paid our teachers well and respected them, and the Board of Education, which had its heart in the right place, was allowed to operate without a lot of political haggling.

Through some administrative sleight-of-hand, students seemed to wind up where they and their parents wanted them to be. This happened despite a still unresolved culture clash which had been going on for decades, a clash which appeared to involve purveyors of Wasp establishment values and the later arrivals who, though willing, could not embrace these values adequately or quickly enough.

The culture clash was brought home to me on my very first day at Hawthorne Junior High School, in the seventh grade, where those of us who were probably looked at as "the railroad flat crowd" were first mixed with children of middle-class professionals and newly successful merchant princelings. We tried not to seem or act different and after a while it worked as we buckled down to the no-nonsense class-work.

I am sure that most of the better-fixed parents sweated out the effect of all this culture-clashing on the community moral fibre and school grades and especially; who was playing kneesee with whom at the local pizza parlor.

Hawthorne meant the start of the teen years; the longing, secret glances and the moping around, the bursts of silliness and the dragging lassitude, the puppy-love crushes on the immaculate, bewitching, saddle-shoed charmers who could crush thirteen years of budding manhood with a friendly glance at some other young Romeo. As for me, I was too bashful and too protective of my pride lest I be turned down to get into the dating business. In other words I was too chicken, but I knew all that would come soon enough.

How did we ever get any school work done? Lucky for me I was able to get by without making a full-time career of it by doing my studying and homework during recess and at lunchtime or sometimes by coming in a little early.

This fit right in with my first job as a newspaper boy, with the task of delivering the Yonkers Statesman to 80 or 100 flat-dwellers which took an hour or two after school. A little bit of cynicism was added to my psyche at this time as I encountered some of the subterfuges and outright refusals by people to pay their bills although this was, after all, 1937 with the economy not yet revived. The job also meant that I arrived somewhat late at the stickball game or the snowball fight, but such is the price of ambition.

Stickball, swimming, delivering papers, whatever; it all came to a screeching halt on Sunday morning when, no matter what terribly important other things we had to do, we kids were pointed toward St. Michaels Greek Catholic Church and sent forth, along with threats of retaliation from my mother and the Lord if we didn't get there. My brothers and I were given ten cents each for the collection plate, along with another nickel in case they had two collections. With the rites devised somewhere in ancient Byzantium and the sermon in Ukrainian, we did a lot of fidgeting and wool-gathering, unless we had gone to confession the evening before, and were therefore required to take Communion and pay attention to the proceedings.

Confession was a process fraught with peril, bringing us face to face with the evil forces within us, and was therefore put off as often as possible. Once in the confessional, I put myself in the gentle hands of Father Kinash, who was not screened off, but sat on the other side of a prayer stand and nodded quietly as I haltingly listed the monstrous transgressions which I might as well own up to because, I was told, God knew about them anyway.

When I finished my reluctant recitation of meanesses and other self-indulgences, I would drop my gaze and wait for some words of condemnation or at least a sigh of exasperation, but it never came. He announced my penance in such a quiet voice I could barely hear him, then I left to kneel at the side of the altar with other scrubby-cheeked desperadoes.

As I knelt there in the tranquil silence I would absently watch the flickering candles or study the elaborately painted icons. Then my gaze would inevitably be drawn to the large stained glass window behind the altar on which the downward thrust of the Archangel Michael's spear into the writhing, dragon-like form of Lucifer was frozen in lead and glass forever, or as long as God will permit.

By the time I left, my little burden was lightened, but I was too young to know why.

The church also ran a school which my brothers and sisters and I attended for two hours several nights a week. Its main purpose was to keep Ukrainian culture alive in the minds of the new generation and to teach us to read and write the language. After we graduated we immediately began to forget most of what we had learned from Professor Fatiuk, and the squandering of these particular riches is something I regret more and more as the years go by.

Our street -Stanley Avenue- and the few blocks surrounding us was a sort of Noah's Ark of ethnic diversity, with a few examples from just about every corner of Europe and the Near East. Poles, Hungarians, Germans, Irishmen, Frenchmen, Syrians, Persians and others had all arrived in the decade or two before World War I to jump into the Melting Pot.

This great mix prevented our street from becoming an enclave of a particular nationality which, I think, was a lucky development. The adults seemed to be able to communicate and got along while the kids, who also got along most of the time went out of their way not to think or act "ethnically."

It was not always easy as you had to laugh while being laughed at and called a hunkie, but you made up for it by calling the taunter a camel driver, if the name fit, but there was no real meanness in it. You may recall a scene at a hospital in the movie "Deerhunter" in which the doctor asks Nicky if his unusual name was Russian. "No!" he insists, "American!" We all felt that way.

There were a few Jewish families on the block but none of them had kids our age except for Isidore, who showed up one day in farm overalls and high top shoes, a getup which was bound to get attention and require corrective action.

For a few days, he would quietly join the group wherever it happened to gather and politely laugh at the right time and shake his head in despair when appropriate. He was a big, chubby kid but size without the muscles to go with it was not one of the keys to respect so he was generally ignored.

His nice manner finally so enraged one of the regulars that a fist-fight ensued. Surprisingly, he stood his ground, and not only that, he gave as good as he got. From then on, he was one of us for the short time he was there. This meant that he would now be required to trade insult for insult with some degree of talent, and to participate in other ways.

The rewards could be great, like sitting on the curb on a summer evening listening to Joe Dunn as he assumed the accents of Captain Katzenjammer. He told stories that made us laugh so hard our sides ached, until Cop Feeney came zooming around the corner from Highland Avenue to send us scattering toward home.

There were other Jewish people who didn't live in the neighborhood but affected our lives because they ran a lot of the businesses we depended on, like the furniture and clothing stores. Ben Cinnamon ran the pharmacy and we were sent to him when we had something in our eye that had to be removed.

Once my mother gave me a quarter which I offered to Ben when the operation was over but he curled my fingers around the coin and said, "No, give it back to your mother."

And Mr. Friedman's ice cream parlor, the closest to our neighborhood;- now there was a real parlor with a long marble counter and round stools on pedestals that raised and lowered when you turned them. And we never bothered with "two cents plain." It was a fifteen-cent ice cream soda or nothing.

What I mean by a "real parlor" is that he didn't seem to have a speakeasy in the back. One thing he did have was Halvah, which was crushed sesame seeds compressed into oblong blocks which came in a fancy wooden box with mortised corners and a hinged glass lid. I really loved it but it was so rich that after eating just one two-cent chunk I felt like I had swallowed a brick.

The ice cream parlor and pharmacy were down the hill from us on Riverdale Avenue -FDR's route- which also contained Finkelstein's butter and egg store, a fabulous place with rows of glass-fronted iceboxes containing large tubs of fresh butter.

We had a standard order and whenever my sister Kay went there, one of the Finkelsteins, a tall, balding man with metal rimmed glasses would look at my pretty sister and, in a crooning voice, say, "I know what you want!" and he would carve a one-pound edge of sweet butter from the tub and put it in a boat-shaped cardboard dish and the weight would usually be right on.

They also had a coffee grinder which seemed to run all the time and gave out a fragrance you could smell a half-block away. And across the street from them was Weber's bakery which made the best bread in the western hemisphere.

All of these places were within a short walking distance, and a trip down to Finkelstein's for fresh ground coffee and some butter, then to Weber's for quarter rounds of rye and pumpernickel still slightly warm from the oven and we would all be in heaven at breakfast. Such were the hardships and deprivations of tenement life.

And then there was the chicken plucker. Most of the time chickens for our Sunday dinners came from Honcharik's butcher shop down the street but once in a while my mother got the urge for a fresh Kosher chicken and she knew better than to go there without me. We would walk into this small storefront and you could look past the man at the counter through a doorway into a large open area stacked with crates of live chickens.

The man had a large black hat and a beard which fell over a blood-stained white apron and when my mother ordered her chicken, it was always five pounds for roasting. He would walk back to one of the crates and rummage around among the squawking poultry until he found one the right size.

Very deftly, he would tie a piece of rope around its legs, slit its throat, then hang it up over a drum for the blood to drain. In a few minutes he would take the chicken again and dip it into a barrel of steaming hot water for a while, then hang it on another hook for the great moment.

With a blurring flurry of hands, he would start plucking at the feathers so quickly it would seem as though they were disappearing by magic. A few moments more of butchering and the bird was wrapped up and ready to take home.

I don't know what fascinated me about this bloody ritual for I certainly didn't enjoy it. One thing I did know; once I sat down at the dinner table, there was no connection in my mind between the struggling, desperate bird at the market and the splendidly roasted and stuffed chicken that sat before us on Sunday afternoon.

The ethnic mix on our street included some black families who lived in our neighborhood rather than huddling in what I hesitate to call a ghetto near the center of town known as School Street.

Mildred the seamstress lived next door and she seemed to be working all the time whether I brought some work to her or came to collect for the newspaper delivery. Her husband, a big, proud and cheerful man was a chauffeur who owned his own limousine which he parked out front when not on the job. Sometimes when he was simonizing his car he would let us sit in back behind the glass partition and play big shot, with much waving of imaginary cigars and orders for the driver to take us for a ride down South Broadway.

The only black kid who actually lived on the block was Roy, whose family would not let him play with us riff-raff. We heard he could run very fast and on several occasions we went up to his house and yelled for him to come out and join us in getting into shape for Field Day, the annual school athletic competition. When he stuck his head out of the window, which was on the second floor, someone behind him, no doubt his mother, would pull him back in. We never did get to see how fast he could run.

If you were to ask the people in my neighborhood what economic classification they were in, they would not have comprehended the question. Lower class? Who me? Middle class? Well, the middle of what?

As a matter of fact, in our minds, there wasn't any real lower class in this country, only people who might be struggling to make their way up into the mainstream. More accurately, there really weren't any classes at all, except for the genuine upper class, whose pictures were in the rotogravure section of the Sunday papers, usually shown at a party or horse show.

As attractive as they seemed in those sepia-toned news photos they were generally reported in the news section only when they were having difficulties, just as it is done today. Juicy divorce cases, an occasional crime of passion, that sort of thing. And their kids seemed to have nothing to do except stand around in nice clothes and funny haircuts, at least according to the "you're lucky you're poor" movies which we saw every week.

The poor little rich kids situation so affected me that at one time I actually prayed in my nightly prayers that God would never let me become rich. Now just in case He might be listening, I would like to state firmly and unequivocally, that my thinking had not yet matured, and I hadn't anticipated that He would do such a good a job in heeding my prayer.

Having given it much serious further thought, and based on what I have learned since that time, I wouldn't mind at all if I became just a teensy bit wealthy. And I promise not to buy a Mercedes unless the foreign trade balance gets better.

I was in the eighth grade at Hawthorne when something happened that would change my life and my entire attitude:- my father died. This tiny giant with a volcanic temper and steely determination was finally beaten down, the drive within him to be his own man carrying him to a point from which there was no turning back. He died of the type of internal ailments caused by frustration and stress in people who cannot lower their demands even in a losing battle.

John Matishowski, the little big man who wore a black derby hat and chesterfield coat -as any self respecting saloon owner would- was knocked down in his early fifties and we were shattered. I don't know if he got sick because his saloon business was failing, or if the business was failing because he got sick, but suddenly one of the safe places put into kids minds to be there when needed was gone.

It was easy to see that he was getting sicker as the months passed, until finally he couldn't go to work anymore and had to spend a lot of time in bed. Once, I came home from school to find him on his hands and knees on the floor, groaning in pain, as my mother helped him back into bed. A few days later he was taken to the hospital.

My mother sat with him at the hospital as much as she could and still take care of us and one evening around supper time, we could hear her coming up the stairs, then she came up to the door and paused there, on the landing, and we knew she was trying to form her terrible news into some gentle message while trying to control her own grief.

She had had to cope with the news from the doctor all alone at the hospital, and had walked the eight blocks or so back to the house, all alone, trying to find some way to soften the terrible blow. The doorknob finally turned and she walked in, and as she came before all of her kids except for Kay who was still at work, from little Irene, age 4, to Bill, age 15, whatever plan she had made to break the news, along with the composure needed to do it, failed her. She took one look at all those

27

scared little faces and the tears came pouring down her face and all she could do was blurt out, "Your father will never come home again!"

The wake surprised me because so many people were there like Miss Whalen, the principal of our grade school, and others I never saw before. Another thing that surprised me, when I thought about it years later, was that there was no doubt our family would continue to make a go of it. My mother, in her gentle and determined way, took over what was left of the business, which wasn't much. Kay, the oldest child who had started up her own beauty parlor, would later become the principal bread-winner, otherwise who knows what would have happened to us in a day when public aid for such disasters was not yet developed.

Much of the struggle over the next few years was shielded from us kids since my mother was not the type to sit around and count her misfortunes aloud. In fact, we all indulged ourselves in what seemed to be a family trait; to rake through the ashes left behind disasters large and small for some nugget of humor.

But the situation worsened and the nuggets shrunk in size as money got more scarce. Fortunately my job was upgraded from newspaper boy to Western Union messenger; you know-the kids who pedaled around town on bicycles to deliver telegrams in the days before everyone had telephones. It meant a few dollars more for the family kitty and for my own use.

I didn't realize how much my mother depended on those few dollars and one payday I informed her I needed to keep some extra to buy something; I think it was a pair of slacks. I can't forget the crestfallen look on her face, and in a scene that could have been played by Mickey Rooney and Jane Darwell, who was everybody's movie-mom, she said, "I need the money to help with the rent."

I flew into a rage and pulled some bills and coins out of my pocket and threw them down on the floor and started out the door.

And then some feeling overwhelmed me and I looked back and she was on the floor on her hands and knees, picking up the money, looking around to make sure she didn't miss any. I went back and got on my hands and knees too, to help her look, although I must admit it was hard to see beyond that miserable shame.

But there were families around us in even greater difficulty since breadwinners had been laid off and there was no income for them at all. Once, during the Depression's low point, I saw one of the neighborhood families returning home from a store-front food distribution point with cartons and paper sacks of relief food. The father would not look at me; he looked straight ahead as they passed, and I failed to grasp, then, the idea that he was embarrassed.

When I got home, I asked my mother how come we too didn't go to get free food like some of the others and she merely shrugged, continuing to work at the sink, and said, "We don't need to do that."

Why should anyone pass up free food, I thought, so I told her about the people who lived up the street carrying groceries home. She stopped what she was doing for a moment and without looking up, she said, "I guess they were hungry."

I can feel now, very deeply, what my mother must have known; the shame and fear and anger that the man must have felt when he would not look at me. His American Dream was turning to ashes in his very hands, and now the very existence of his family and himself was threatened. He was suddenly unable to ardently and willingly use himself up in his job as he had since he got off the boat, suddenly unable to bring home his hard-earned wages for food and rent and clothing, suddenly shackled by the bonds of charity.

But women sometimes had to become breadwinners too, as in our case. It is because of the ladies in my life; my mother, my sisters, my wife and my daughters that I have developed a strong admiration for the courage of women, not so much the kind used in some personal battle against society's unfairness, but the self-sacrificing courage used to protect one's family. To be this brave: to stand up to life at very difficult moments, to keep strong-minded men closest to them on the road they both know is right and yet refuse to surrender their femininity-what is more difficult than that?

It took a lot of courage to survive and prosper and fortunately, there seemed to be so much of that courage around in those days. Not just in people like the Lindys and the Earharts, but before them, the countless people like my father and mother who left the protection of familiar surroundings and their own way of life to sail, plunge or plod straight into the unknown, to make their fortunes or build new lives.

The reason they put up with it all, I am sure, is that they didn't give much thought to what happened to themselves; they would put up with any uncertainty, any indifference, any contempt, any hardship as long as they created a new future.

And the women; -sometimes even more determined than the men- giving up their youth to work like slaves and worrying day and night and never giving up. That's where I come from. And I'll be proud of them until I die.

One afternoon some years ago, my mother and I sat on a porch overlooking the garden of the house in which she spent her last years. A warm spring sun shone through the newly budding trees which surrounded the place and lit up the artfully planted beds of early blooming flowers.

The slanting sunlight also shone on this brave and gentle lady who had survived wars, depressions, widowhood, and the traumas of emigration. I could see, in her deep brown eyes now tinged with age, that she was content, and as we talked, I suddenly wondered about the dream she and my father once had to build a life back in the old country.

Galicia, of course, no longer existed; one half of it was made part of Poland and the other absorbed into the Soviet Ukraine. But did she miss her childhood home at all? Did she have memories which made her wish that things had worked out differently?

I asked her these questions, and she looked at me with that level, questioning stare of hers for a moment. "My son," she said quietly, "Are you crazy?"

The Hudson River continued to be not so much a playground but a testing ground;- it gave us the means to push the envelope of our curiosity and courage. In winter we sometimes walked out on the ice up to where the stationary ice ended and the moving, boat-sized floes rode by on the tide, grinding against the ice on which we stood and raising the risk of setting us adrift on our own floe.

In the summer we practically lived in or on the water, or at the edge of it, sometimes waiting for one of the excursion boats to pass by so we could dive into the waves caused by their wake. We could recognize which one of a dozen boats was approaching by its silhouette while it was still miles downriver, or by the distinctive sound of its steam whistle as it signaled its approach to the Yonkers dayliner pier.

It became a Sunday morning ritual in summer to stop by the pier on the way home from church to watch the big boats arrive. We would climb the stairs to the second deck of the pavilion and play a noisy game of tag or grasp the pipe railing and hang out over the water until the great, white steamers began to arrive, their many wooden decks packed with people who had already boarded downriver at 125th Street.

There was often a straw-hatted, striped-blazered band on board which played both dance music and the kind you sang to, and the singing and laughter would float across the water as the dayliner approached the pier.

Several of the boats were sidewheelers while the newer ones were screw-driven, and you could hear the signal bells clang as they slowly warped themselves amidst a heaving swirl of water toward the pier where handlers stood by to catch the lines.

The thick hawsers would be dropped around stanchions at the edge of the pier so that the liner could be winched into position and the gangplank laid down. They had names like the Robert Fulton, the Alexander Hamilton, the Peter Stuyvesant- which always made the biggest waves- and the one with my favorite name, the Chauncey DePew.

I only got to ride on dayliners a few times, but had many rides on the "Witchcraft", a rowboat about eight feet long which some of the kids had built. It didn't leak faster than could be accommodated by some leisurely bailing, and we got increasingly brave until one day we found we had actually crossed the mighty Hudson. We knew the river well enough to play the tides against each other; if we departed one hour before high tide, we could cruise upriver for an hour, fool around for an hour while the tide got ready to ebb, then take a leisurely hour with the tide back to where we started. Sometimes we got careless and had to do a lot of rowing against the tide, which could get very strong.

One day my brother George and I and three or four other kids decided we would swim the Hudson, with Witchcraft as an escort. The Hudson off Yonkers is a formidable section of the river, only a few miles from New York harbor and the Atlantic, and deep enough to handle large ocean-going traffic.

At the point we intended to cross it was about a mile wide with the Palisades looming up on one side and the hills of Yonkers on the other. There were several channels and currents we had only heard about and didn't really understand. Moreover, we were, after all, not trained athletes but little kids about fourteen years old and when I say little, I mean that none of us was large for his age.

But it was a perfect day, as I recall, with no wind and plenty of sunshine, so we departed, all of us probably thinking as I did, that we could always hang on to the Witchcraft if we had to. We had timed the tide correctly and as we moved across, we drifted slightly upstream, planning to alight near the Alpine Ferry pier on the New Jersey side. The swimmers pants and keds were carried in the boat along with the ferry return fare, which was a nickel.

The most immediate fear we had was being run down by a ship which did not see us, or perhaps getting caught in its powerful wake, but this did not develop. The other fear which I felt -I don't know about the others- was in swimming in water of unknown depth and inhabited by fearsome creatures.

It was like being suspended by a thread over the middle of a chasm, and if the thread broke, I would sink down into the swirling, suffocating depths and be slowly devoured by crabs and eels, and other dwellers of the ooze.

These fears were respectfully held at bay and we kept on swimming, occasionally yelling to each other for encouragement until we found ourselves in the massive shadow of the Palisades where the cliffs, trees and boulders were now very clearly delineated.

The water was almost like glass and without the pieces of trash and sewage which were always present on the other side. Suddenly, as I was treading water for a moment, something brushed against my foot and I nearly jumped out of my skin.

If I had the Roadrunner's ability to spin my legs and go scooting across the water to the shore I would have been gone. But it happened again, and I realized to my astonishment that my foot was touching the muddy river bottom. This was amazing since we still seemed to have a couple of hundred yards to go.

Someone else yelled, "I hit bottom!" and we kept swimming until the water was only waist high, then we waded, swam and waded until finally we were done, and we marched up to the shore like Columbus landing in the New World.

While all of these things were going on I would occasionally, during a quiet moment and not on purpose, think about my future. I was reading a lot, the "good books" required in school and a lot of pulp magazines like "Flying Aces" and "G-8 and his Battle Aces." G-8 was a flying superman who, along with his pals Bull Martin and Nippy Weston, flew Spads and were always getting captured by the Germans, but always managed to escape to save the entire Allied war effort in the nick of time.

As for my future, there was, of course, not too much to think about. My mind had been made up to pursue aviation when I had touched my first airplane, there at the Yonkers Seadrome, but the question remained;- where do I start? Little did I know that this question would be answered for me in due time.

Meanwhile, I would look up at all passing aircraft with longing, and I had many opportunities to do this since we were within the maneuvering area of many of New York's flight activities. When early passenger aircraft took off from Long Island, their flight path often passed them over our neighborhood and, on certain autumn and winter days, would seem to hang overhead as they fought the not-yet understood jet stream.

The roaring sounds of their laboring engines would cascade down and reverberate among the buildings until finally they would find lesser headwinds and slowly disappear westward, flapping their wings on the way to Chicago.

Now these were Curtiss Condor biplanes, mind you, or "doublewingers" as my young daughter Holly would call them many years later, and to fly on them as passengers surely took the courage of pioneers. No wonder the stewardesses in those days were expected to have some training as a nurse.

Demonstration flights intended to bedazzle New Yorkers also passed overhead, as when Italian Marshall Italo Balbo led his large -for that time- formation of Savoia-Marchetti bombers across the Atlantic to show some Italian muscle.

The great zeppelin Hindenburg passed by us several times on its way to or from Lakehurst, just south of New York, as had the giant dirigibles operated by the U.S. Navy. Once, the ill-fated Hindenburg passed by at a fairly low altitude and we could see every detail including the swastikas on the large, red-painted stabilizers.

The swastika seemed strange as a national symbol and had not yet taken on the ominous significance it would later so we enjoyed the magnificent sight as the monster droned by. What a great adventure it must have been for the fortunate passengers who had just crossed the Atlantic in comfort and luxury. They could now look down on the approaching New York skyline and on the peasants below as someone played Cole Porter on the airship's aluminum piano and they sipped champagne to celebrate the end of their journey.

It so happens that the place from which we usually viewed these activities was where we spent so much of our time; a baseball diamond and swimming area at a park next to the seadrome. Adjoining the diamond to the north, opposite from the seadrome was a loading wharf once part of the Spreckels Sugar Refinery and which was being used more and more by large Japanese ships to pick up scrap metal.

Japan was remote and inscrutable and too far away to worry about but some concerns were beginning to be voiced. One radio commentator predicted that the scrap, which moved to Japan with the speed of a merchant ship, would come back at us with the speed of an artillery shell.

As I think about this a fantasy comes to mind. There in

34

front of our house sits a brand new emerald green Huppmobile with real spoke wheels, a wedding present from our landlady to her new son-in-law. Years quickly pass and the car succumbs to the rough streets, low technology and just plain age and is sold for scrap. It winds up in Whalen's junkyard, where it is sold with the idea it might become another Huppmobile, or even a Pierce Arrow, but instead is loaded on one of the big, wide-prowed Japanese scrap-hauling ships.

The Huppmobile makes its way to Yokohama where it is melted down and, in ingot form, is sent to a munitions factory, perhaps at Hiroshima or Nagasaki, where they had such facilities, and is fashioned into bomb casings, torpedo assemblies, cannon shells and machine gun bullets.

All of these ammunition parts are loaded aboard the Japanese aircraft carrier Hiryu, one of six carriers in the attacking fleet and on the morning of December 7th, 1941 the Huppmobile, or perhaps just the engine block and a couple of fenders, is returned to American soil, to be rammed through the sides of the Arizona, or embedded in the flight line hangar walls at Hickam, or zapped between the eyes of some terrified, not yet fully awake swabby at Pearl trying to play catch-up combat, a seventeen-year old kid who joined the Navy to see the world, a part of you and me.

If one looks at some back copies of Life Magazine for that time -the late 30's- he or she might find pictorial reportage of the U.S. military training maneuvers for our newly increased army in Louisiana. You remember Louisiana; that's where General George Patton told the troops they would no longer be required to shovel horse poop anymore as they were sent off to the real war.

Anyway, during the maneuvers, the soldiers were forced to use stove pipes mounted on boxes to simulate cannons, and packing crates with placards declaring them to be tanks. No wonder the Japanese decided it would be opportune for them to return the Huppmobile, and so they did.

Getting back to the few years before the Japanese attack at Pearl Harbor; we all watched, listened and read about the continual stream of events as they unfolded in Europe: Hitler moving into the adjoining Sudetenland of Czechoslovakia and daring anyone to do something about it; English Prime Minister Chamberlin- the man with the umbrella- and his attempt to buy "peace in our time" from Hitler, and the annexation of Austria by Germany were all part of what seemed to be an inexorable march of events which could only lead either to war or abject surrender by the English and the French.

The French, meanwhile, put her soldiers in underground fortifications called the Maginot Line, using a military philosophy which we kids in high school were told would never work and, of course, it didn't.

Then that absolutely riveting series of events finally happened; the German march on Poland, the ultimatum from Great Britain and then the war itself. We Americans were mere bystanders, militarily speaking, but were certainly heavily involved in many other ways, some of which became evident in my new job at Western Union. I and other messengers had been promoted to inside jobs which required us to take telegrams over the phone, send them out over the teleprinter and sort incoming telegrams for delivery to the various parts of town by the new boys who had replaced us as messengers. The message traffic began to build quickly concerning the conversion to war production in the Yonkers factories, large and small. Even the small hat factory which had somehow squeezed itself between our house and the next tenement beyond had been given an order for Army hats, mainly the wide-brimmed "Yogi Bear" kind.

We began to get long "TWX's", or timed wire messages which concerned orders and shipping notices for military equipment . I could tell right away I would no longer be the vitamin pill I had been while I pumped my bicycle up and down the hills of Yonkers. Now I sat all day in school, and then sat five or six hours in the office after that. My physical decline was actually measurable, since our gym program in high school included Physical Fitness Ratings in which each student had their leg and back strength measured by pulling on a belt attached to a scale called a dynamometer, and by several other ways.

Since height and weight were factored in, I usually scored well because of my small size and once actually found myself second in the entire junior class. We were all lined up according to our score after the tests and I found myself between the football hero and the rest of the jocks, who looked at me with what seemed like suspicion that I had somehow cheated the system. As my typing speed on the teleprinter increased, my Physical Fitness Rating slid downward: it was a poor bargain.

My new job also meant that I would no longer be required to deliver singing telegrams, a task which I dreaded, especially when the birthday person was a schoolmate. The delivery clerk would call the lucky party to make sure they would be at home and, unfortunately, give them time to round up all the relatives and part of the neighborhood. I would arrive, park my bike and march in, hat cradled smartly in my arm and go into my routine. It was torture for me but the people seemed to enjoy the whole idea of a singing telegram and they had a big time, and sometimes even gave me a piece of cake.

Once, I flipped a coin with three or four messengers and lost, so I found myself on the way to deliver a singing birthday message to someone attending a Democrat rally at Vesuvius Hall. Can't you just see it: the waiting functionary escorts me to the microphone on stage as the crowd is quieted and the band, a fairly large one with five or six members, launches into the indispensable song.

I started off about three notes late but finished strong, inspired perhaps by the realization that I hadn't seen anyone I knew. The applause, although partly derisive, was surprisingly loud and as I left, the same functionary escorted me back to the main entrance and pressed a large coin into my sweaty palm.

As soon as I felt it I knew the coin was phony, one of those crude lead copies spawned by the Depression. When I got down to the street I walked to the curb where the bike was parked, raised my arm and threw that clunker down South Broadway as hard as I could.

I graduated from high school in June of that fateful year of 1941 and was offered the job of running a telegraph and Pullman ticket booth for the summer at the Saranac Inn, an expensive and exclusive resort in the Adirondacks. There were guests like William Lyon Phelps, a well known literary figure from Yale who was very friendly and would stop by the booth, dressed in his plus fours for hiking or golfing, to watch me laugh as I read something funny someone had sent him.

There were some of the lesser Rockefellers and other very nice, sometimes haughty people who were fascinating to watch as I became privy to some of the secrets contained in their telegrams.

When I returned at summer's end I was sent on the road again, still at age seventeen, to the Western Union office at Ilion, in upstate New York. Message traffic there had increased dramatically because a large Remington Arms plant was located there. It was there, in a rooming house, that the landlady knocked on my door as I sat around reading the funny papers that first Sunday morning in December, 1941 and told me to "Wake up, the Japanese have attacked us at Pearl Harbor!"

"Pearl Harbor?" I asked myself, as did most Americans. "Where's that?"

Below: *Rescue of seaman from the West Virginia*

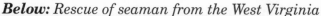

2

THE SWAYING PALMS
OF NASHVILLE

"**O**KAY! OKAY! Everybody fall out in a colyum of bunches, like bananas!"

When the barracks corporal had thrown open the door and stomped down the aisle ten minutes before, turning on lights and yelling "Rise and Shine!..Rise and Shine!" as he went, I just couldn't believe it. My eyes had just closed, I thought, after a long, grinding day of "processing", which meant more physical and medical exams with all the picking and poking and shots and other indignities that went with it.

I had heard a bugle blow, somewhere in the distant darkness but I had thought, "It can't be for us, its not loud enough." And I couldn't believe how cold it was, here in Nashville, Tennessee in March of 1943 and I know I was not the only one who felt betrayed by our ignorant expectations of nice, warm weather here in the "deep" south. On the train ride down, one future aviation cadet, a mean-minded type who couldn't resist taking advantage of the gullibility and ignorance he found himself surrounded with, announced that we would start seeing palm trees about the time we crossed the Tennessee border.

This was greeted with derisive remarks but when this same clown some time later yelled, "Hey, we're crossing the Tennessee border!" everybody sat up and looked. Nothing but wintry desolation could be seen through windows stained by neglect and by coal dust from the steam engine that pulled us.

The train ride had taken forever, a lurching, jolting journey

39

which started out in excitement but slowly dissolved into monotony. We were frequently shunted to a siding to permit passage of more urgent traffic and I imagined a fast train with flat cars loaded with tanks and cannons roaring through, but we never saw them. By the time we got to Nashville, my views concerning train travel were badly warped, and more than off-set the elegant experience I had on the trip to Saranac Inn on which I had dinner in the dining car and retired to a lower berth, all on a deadhead pass furnished by Western Union.

The only difficulty I had on that trip was trying to act like well, hell, I travel like this all the time. It would not be until well after the war that I came to realize again what a great mode of travel it could be.

Meanwhile, we lurched out of our cots and struggled into the unfamiliar feeling, itchy olive drab uniforms which had been issued the day before. Size and fit had priority somewhere behind haircuts and more shots but we were assured we could get them altered in good time. There were some nice, spiffy-looking uniforms waiting for us at flight school, we were told, but here at Nashville, everything was strictly G.I.

Many new recruits in the same predicament will no doubt remember that it was here, at their first station, that the inge-nuity and cruelty of the Axis powers was first revealed to them. The poor condition of newly returned laundry, we were told, was caused by secret enemy tampering with G.I. laundry equipment so that it crunched the buttons from our shirts and blew the pieces through the bottoms of our socks. We tried to conserve our anger until we could confront the enemy directly.

Reluctantly we filed out of the barracks and formed into bunches, like the man said, and then got ourselves lined up into ranks, our breaths steaming out into the cold, dark morn-ing which was yet to show any slight promise of sunrise.

As we lined up I wondered how our adversaries coped with early morning reveille and I was sure they handled it different-ly. In Japan, for example, I could envision the corporal in charge of recruits strutting up the barracks stairs and banging on the door with the hilt of the sword he had been issued when he made private first class. He would yell "Banzai!" and quickly step aside as the door would fly open and the awakened horde, which had gone to bed in full uniform to be prepared for the occasion, would come pouring through, jostling each other to be first to line up.

The Germans, of course, would be somewhat more organized, and as the bugle sounded, each man would step smartly through the waking, dressing and falling out drills, taking no more and no less than the allotted seconds. After being dressed right or left to form into perfect ranks, they would be given the order to "right face" and to march off to the mess hall as their fathers had done and their grandfathers before that, proudly goose-stepping to the familiar strains of the indispensable oom-pah band which had been standing by.

Meanwhile, back in the land of the citizen soldiers, we ran quickly through the roll-call, pausing in the rapid fire-shouts of names and responses only when there was no response, and we came to learn that the absentees were most likely in the hospital with the flu, which had apparently come down with us on the train. After the roll call, we were dismissed until we would again be colyumized to be marched off to the mess hall.

We were given batteries of tests, the same ones we had been given at Governors Island after our applications for aviation cadet training had been accepted. There were eye tests, depth perception tests, hand-eye coordination tests, tests of every kind intended to weed out would-be flyers on whom training would be wasted, and we all sweated them out.

This whole new adventure had started a few months after Pearl Harbor, when I had returned from Ilion and was assigned as a clerk and teletype operator at the Western Union office in New Rochelle, another suburb of New York City.

I had turned eighteen the month after Pearl Harbor and had been wrestling with the idea that I would not wait for the draft, which was taking twenty-year-olds, but would volunteer when the time was right. Aviation cadet training seemed out of the question since candidates had to be twenty-one and have two years of college. But the pull to join the service was very strong as the country now seemed in real, mortal peril, with fears on most people's minds of possible Japanese troop landings in Hawaii or even on the West Coast.

Like a bolt out of the blue, the college requirements were eliminated for both the Air Corps, which was then part of the

41

Army, and the Navy aviation program, and replaced by a college equivalency exam. Since the age eligibility was also lowered to eighteen, it seemed as though they had made the changes just for me.

The time seemed right when the month of March came and I took a morning train, since I was working the night shift then, down to Church Street in lower Manhattan where the aviation recruiting offices were. I couldn't make up my mind whether to go Army or Navy, so I decided that I would walk into whichever came first as I made my way down the street. Bingo!- and it was the Army which would have to deal with me and my ambitions as a flyer. I have occasionally wondered how different my life might have been if I had walked down the street from the other direction.

It wasn't easy to sign up and get on the rolls, not because of the qualifications, but because the Army Air Force was undergoing massive reorganization at the time and, naturally, my first set of paperwork was lost. I had to go through the same routine, tests and all, twice and finally, along with a couple of hundred other guys, I was sworn in. We had been ferried out to a reception center on Governor's Island for the occasion, looking like a bunch of excited, older high school boys on the way out. On our return we looked like sober, very young men who had made a commitment from which there was no turning back.

Back at Western Union, we were continually short of help as the draft took its toll. I was working so much overtime that I was earning more than the manager and, consequently, not able to give too much thought to waiting to be ordered into training. I had no idea when the date might be but was told it would happen when I got orders by special delivery letter, and that the wait could take months.

Nobody made too big a deal about leaving. Three or four of us usually got together in a bar down the street and had some beers, and then wished the guy luck. Those of us whose turn hadn't come yet looked at the departing warriors as disappearing into a sea of uncertainty, swallowed up in the mists like Bogey in Casablanca.

On occasion, one of the departees might make a gesture, like the gung-ho type who had joined the Marines. Along with his usual tasks, he had been in charge of taking down the next days financial column on the phone from Merryle Rukeyser-the father of Louis, the present day TV Wall Street pundit- for forwarding to a New York newspaper.

The new Marine had apparently selected Mr. Rukeyser from a mental list of clients who needed some come-uppance; the more important, the better. And so, on his last day, after he had recorded the column, he let fly with his spleen. Then he hung up the phone, grinning with mischief, and when the satisfaction subsided, he picked up the phone again and dialed the next lucky customer. I overheard only the Marine's end of the exchange, and I got the opinion that he didn't expect to come back to Western Union, one way or the other.

It took another eight months after my paperwork was fixed until the fateful letter came and I greeted it with some pride and apprehension, but mostly with relief. I went through the pre-departure rituals like buying the toiletry kit -everybody did that- and visiting friends and relatives I would not be seeing for some time. And so, in March 1943, I found myself at the Nashville Army Air Force processing and indoctrination center, falling out in colyums like bananas and breathing steam into the frosty mornings.

Nashville lasted four long weeks, most of which we spent under medical quarantine, which was standard Army practice. Here we were, thousands of healthy young men at the peak of the need for female companionship, yet we didn't riot of tear down the fences. Part of our good behavior was due to the bombardment of venereal disease lectures we received, which included some very graphic pictures of the wages of sin.

Our patience may also have been the result of the rumored addition of saltpeter to our food or, more likely, the story that medical treatment in the Army for venereal disease involved the use of "a needle with a propeller on the end of it" inserted into a very tender area. Of course, this was only propaganda, like the posters tacked up here and there which showed a cute sixteen year old bobby-soxer and a big caption on top which read, "She looked clean, but...."

As a further effort in the fight against the wages of sinful sex, the medics insisted on hands-on, no-warning inspections. In the midst of our other activities, we would be summoned, usually in the early morning, to report to the base theater for what was indelicately known as the "short-arm" inspection. Once through the line, we would take a seat in the theater and be subjected to another cinematic anti-sex bombardment.

I was thinking of this particular process the other day and I wondered what would have happened if the well-known traveler from outer space had peered down out of his time warp and had been beamed down into our midst, perhaps next to me. He was a reporter for the Martian Chronicle and was curious, he would say, just what it was that this great crowd of young men, all dressed alike in nothing but G.I. raincoats and shoes were doing all lined up and, one by one, approaching a seated individual up front. He was some sort of high priest, who watched intently as they opened their raincoats and displayed their manly parts to him, and who then nodded and sent them on their way.

What a fantastic scene, what a mysterious ritual! It was certainly something to report back to Mars! And then the spaceman might turn to me and fix me with all three eyes and demand from me the deeper meaning, the true significance of this mind-boggling event. And I, cringing meekly before the force of his intense curiosity would explain that it was merely intended to detect some diseases.

"Diseases? Diseases?" he would cry. Then he would fly into a rage and accuse me of hiding some monstrous earthly secret from him, and as I turned to flee, he would whip out his phaser and zap me right out of my G.I. shoes.

The day of departure for preflight training was rapidly approaching but we had to have a little fun to burn up some of the energy we had built up, so we poured onto buses by the hundreds and took off for Nashville.

Despite the best efforts of the anti-sex propagandists on the base, there is no doubt that there were three things on our minds: young women, girls in their late teens, and other females somewhere in between. But we quickly found out that there weren't that many to go around, and besides, they could pick and choose from officers and non-coms without having to stoop to consorting with raw recruits whose pants didn't fit.

Most of us settled for the idea of a nice dinner, but not

before having some drinks to celebrate. One of our little group scrounged up a pint bottle of Bacardi rum which we passed around and sipped while standing before the sinks and mirrors in a cavernous, white-tiled men's room in the main hotel in town. We were all around nineteen years old and assured each other, between pulls on the straight rum, that we would finish the bottle, have dinner, then look for some real booze, maybe bourbon or some of that white lightning; a whole quart this time.

There were only four of us with one little pint, but it wasn't long before the classic symptoms set in. We were suddenly talking a mile a minute and laughing at any dopey thing that was said. One future flyer, a German kid from Pennsylvania decided to pitch pennies into a brass spittoon near the entrance and challenged us all.

That entertained us for a while, and then a disjointed conversation ensued with regard to retrieving the coins from the mucky bottom of the spittoon and of course, no one was ready to volunteer.

In the meantime one of the troops sidled over to one of the stalls and was unable to disguise the retching sounds as the rum came up faster than it went down. He came out, bleary eyed and pale and trying to act nonchalant. "We heard you making that long distance call," somebody said, "it sounded like a call to..." -and here he strangled his voice- "to Europe!". "To Eyoorup, how are things in Eyooorup?"

We had gotten an awful lot of mileage out of one little pint of rum. It wouldn't be long, perhaps a year or two before some of us babes in the woods would attain world-class boozing status and, in sweating out the next mission, might wind up like a friend of mine who could do a decent job on a whole pint before breakfast.

My name finally appeared on one of the sets of orders which were tacked up daily on the bulletin board and, as expected, I was assigned to pre-flight training at Maxwell Field at Montgomery, Alabama. The center at Nashville was one of those temporary arrangements which has probably been replaced by a housing development, but Maxwell was there long before the war and is still there today as an Air Force

45

base. It was, like another pre-war base at San Antonio, Texas, sort of a West Point of the air with permanent quarters, beautifully landscaped grounds and, of all things, runways and airplanes.

The airplanes were not for us, however, since they were those beautiful AT-6's which looked a little like Japanese Zeros and which were used for advanced training, the step just before graduation. We still had pre-flight, primary and then basic schools to attend and if we made it through those, we would get to the advanced class and if you got that far, you pretty much had it made. Each step after pre-flight training involved you in more complex and powerful aircraft, and by the time you got to the advanced class, a decision had been made whether to assign you to fighters or multi-engined bombers.

We had heard that a West Point-type "class system" was used at Maxwell to teach character and discipline and to weed out those who could not stand stress. Little did I know what all this meant, especially the stress part. There were lower classmen whose character and discipline needed stressing and apparently lots of it, and upperclassmen who had received training in applying stress by being lower classmen.

As we got off the train and were taken by bus to the billeting area, none of us were prepared for the warmth of the welcome we received from the waiting upperclass. "Here they are! Let me at 'em! Let me at 'em" one of them screamed, scratching on the barracks porch screen like a psychotic puma.

Other greetings, which sound a little sophomoric now, mostly a long, drawn out "You'll beee sorreee!" could be heard as we were formed up for another roll call and to get our barracks assignments.

As we were brought to attention before being dismissed, a gang of upperclassmen descended on the formation and strutted up and down the ranks, stopping at some lucky cadet- for that is what we were now- to have his character improved.

We were quickly learning new terminology, like "Suck in that gut, Mister," and "Rack 'em back" and the like. Although it was nice to be called Mister and an elaborate courtesy was used in inter-class dealings, none of it was meant to be pleasant. I almost missed the pure G.I. atmosphere of Nashville, where the only bit of chicken- which is half of a term we learned the first day in the service- we had to put up with was from the barracks corporal. Now, in about one hour's time we came to know what discipline really meant; it crackled in the sunny, spring air and was sucked into our lungs like an ionizing, energizing, threatening radon.

There was no respite anywhere, anytime. Our very first meal and subsequent meals as underclassmen in the great mess hall were "square meals," where we sat ramrod straight on the first six inches of the chair, staring straight ahead, and the movement of the spoon or fork from the plate to our mouths had a square corner in it.

When concentration lagged and the eyeballs started to roam, the reaction was immediate. "You curious, Mister? What are you looking at?" Staring straight ahead again, you say, "The windows, Sir." "Are they clean?" "Yes, Sir." "How many panes in the window?" "I don't know Sir," you say, hoping he'd quit. "Don't know is not a proper answer, Mister! Next time you tell me how many panes there are, understand?" "Yes, sir!" Next time my eyes won't wander.

This harassment failed to dent our appetites. The food wasn't too bad and, instead of trays, we ate from plates, family style, and were required to eat every scrap we put on them. Physical training was the main reason for the appetite, as the first thing we did in the morning was calisthenics, then some more just before lunch, then more before dinner. At some time during the day we would do some jogging and then finish off with some push-ups just in case we had some energy left.

There was also something called "the Burma Road," a miles-long, hilly course which we ran once a week and I vividly recall, one afternoon, as the line of runners ahead jumped up over some obstacle, and when I got there, the obstacle turned out to be a cadet, his face a weird blue, his running, flying, breathing days finished.

Major Bulldog Turner, legendary former linebacker of the Chicago Bears was our battalion commander, a position too stratospheric for us to have regular contact except for an occasional pep talk. He was a big, square-built, imposing presence who wore a Smokey Bear hat and had a habit of slapping his riding crop against his perfectly pressed britches.

47

All of his physical training instructors seemed to be professional athletes who took us to the point of exhaustion, and then just a little further. There haven't been too many times in my life since my bicycle messenger days when I felt as good.

Of course, the good feelings were continually interrupted by upperclassmen who seemed determined to improve my character to perfection, just in case I eventually got to be a four-star general. There was one upperclassman, whose name I shall never forget , who obviously enjoyed the rack-em-backs and the "Did you shave this morning, Mister? Was there a blade in the razor?" routine.

When he racked you he would stare into your eyes with a blue-eyed, unblinking intensity, trying to discern some hidden rages which might match his own. All of the others, however, worked you over as a fellow cadet who might fly in the same airplane with you or on the same mission and I got so I didn't mind it.

I had some help getting to that point, however, by an upperclassman who had noticed that my manner turned ever so slightly belligerent on occasion, especially when my blue-eyed friend took me to task.

We had been dismissed from some formation and he took me aside and stood me at ease. " There's nothing personal in all of this. Can you understand?"

Of course I understood what he was talking about but for some reason I didn't feel the logic of it down in my guts. "We're not racking back your father or your mother or where you come from or how you part your hair. You've got to learn to let all this bounce off you and keep thinking straight no matter what! If you can't do that, you're not going to make it!"

He was back at me again the next morning with a complaint about the shine on my shoes, not Mr. Blue eyes but the good guy, and he acted as though the day before had never happened. But I had started to feel a little different; I was taking the hazing on two levels, shunting the immediate events down some wary, ever-watchful road, and keeping the goal, the quest, the Holy Grail of graduation in some bomb-proof part of my mind. I knew I could make it through Maxwell if I could handle Blue Eyes, and so I did.

There was a lot of class-work where we learned things like aircraft identification, where silhouettes were flashed on a screen first slowly then down to a fraction of a second, and Morse code, which was still used extensively in communications and navigation.

There were courses on "Why we are fighting" which concerned the need to protect our liberty and which seemed superfluous in those grim days. None of it was very difficult but you had to absorb it all in a hurry and there was no time for extra study.

Another thing we did was a lot of close-order drill. If we weren't in class or in physical training, we were drilling, first in squads, then in squadrons, then entire wings. There was a large parade every Saturday morning and I must admit we began to look very smart as those great, perfect rows of thousands of cadets made their moves with precision. The cadet officers -the zebras- with all those stripes on their sleeves, their sabers flashing in the air, would salute the Commander and we would march "eyes right" past the reviewing stand.

We also sang a lot as we marched, songs like "I've got sixpence," and "My eyes are dim, I can not see, I have not brought my specs with me..", and always, "Off we go, into Wild Blue Yonder..."

It was before one of the Saturday morning parades that we were told at the last minute we would be reviewed by an important person. Shoes and belt buckles were given an extra bit of shine and we marched off to the parade ground. As we stood there, lined up and at attention, a great roaring sound began and what seemed like hundreds of basic and advanced training planes began to fly overhead in formation.

At the same time, a shiny jeep started down the line and as it came abreast, I saw with a shock that it was FDR, the President himself. He passed by not more than ten or fifteen feet away and, in his cape and big, grey fedora hat he looked every inch the Commander-in-Chief. He didn't look at the cadets much but seemed absorbed in the overflying planes, pointing at them and nodding to the General next to him to show that he was much impressed. It was a much better view of him than the shadowy image I had seen behind the isinglass

49

window of his car as it sped along Riverdale Avenue years before.

The class-work got more difficult and was dished out at a more rapid rate as the weeks sped by and, given the intense pressure to pass the preflight course, you might think that there would be some cheating. To use some of the academic burglar's tools was made easy, it appeared, since the instructors usually left the classroom during exams. But the honor code was applied with a very heavy hand, and wayward actions were almost totally nipped in the psyche by the constant lectures and references to an officer's honor at every turn. Besides, since each cadet was dishonored if he failed to report violations of the code which he himself observed, every classroom was full of monitors.

Cheating did happen however, and was dealt with dramatically. One midnight, the cadets were all awakened and marched by flashlight down to the parade-ground, and formed into our usual ranks. An officer, his voice booming out across the field, read out the charges of cheating and failure of the code of honor against Aviation Cadet so-and-so, and finished by announcing that he would be immediately removed from our ranks, "and his name shall never be mentioned in the Corps of Aviation Cadets again."

I'm not sure if this was staged for our benefit, but if not, it meant that the poor guy would be on the next train to Jefferson Barracks, Missouri to start at the beginning with basic G.I. training along with those who flunked the course anyway. That incident is as fresh in my mind as if it happened this morning.

One sunny, late spring day we awoke to find that we were now, with our mental attitudes properly stressed and honor intact, upper classmen. The feeling must have been the same as a convict gets when he walks out of the prison gate. We were no longer the rackees, but the rack-em-backers and the feeling of relief was overwhelming and took some time to get over.

We were prepared to dispense our new powers with vigor, and someone even clawed at the barracks porch screen when the new lower classmen arrived, and we all yelled "You'll beee sorreee!" as loud as we could. But the novelty slowly wore away as we began to realize it was not easy being an upperclassman and "stressing" people who were in the same boat with you. We got to believe that the hazing was a necessary evil, but it took some mental effort to work up a feigned, constant, upper-class pose.

Montgomery, Alabama was not too far from Maxwell but we only managed to get there twice. To my northern eyes, it was a quintessentially southern town which lived and breathed slowly and calmly, and though most of her sons were off to the war or getting ready to go and wartime shortages were as bad there as anywhere, it tried to act like nothing was happening worth getting disturbed about. I loved to listen to that beautiful drawl, especially when spoken by the very few pretty girls I managed to get within yards of. It matched the more old-fashioned attitudes, the deceptively different heartbeat of the south and I found myself strangely at home.

Some disturbing notes, however, were the obvious trappings of a rigidly applied segregation; the "Whites Only" signs, the back of the bus business, the general "get out of my way, dammit" attitude.

I must admit the attitude was not much different up North, and although there were no "whites only" signs, there might as well have been. I recall the train ride back from my job at the Saranac Inn, this time by coach, and I noticed that one of the hotel's maintenance men was sitting in the back.

I decided to go for some lunch and stopped to talk with him and then asked him if he would like to come along. "Why don't you go on and maybe I'll join you later," he said. He seemed suddenly uncomfortable and looked away, so I left .

It came as a shock, as I thought about it later, that the man, who had a ruddy complexion not much darker than mine, was sitting where he was and wouldn't come to the dining car because he was acting as he thought a black man should, there, on a train in New York State.

Meanwhile, the countdown was beginning at Maxwell as we slogged our way through the exams and sweated out the grades. Everything came out positive for me and everyone I knew and the day came when, again, we found a set of orders with our names on them tacked to the squadron bulletin board.

I was assigned to a flight school for primary pilot training at Cape Girardeau, Missouri. This course was the first step in actually learning to fly an airplane and would be the first time up in the air for most of us.

We all knew the washout rate at primary was high, and for myself, I took the good news with a little bit of dread, or was it some premonition? Would I get that far and have some critical arrangement of as yet undiscovered deficiencies and lack of relevant experiences combine to wash out my dreams and ground me? I would soon see.

The time came to leave Maxwell and the hundreds of us were lined up in formation, a duffel bag over one shoulder and a suitcase in the other hand. We were marched toward the railroad siding in the hot, sweltering, cloudless morning, already damp with sweat but feeling good enough to sing as we marched. As we passed the Headquarters of the Wing Commander -whose name happened to be Major Brown- somebody broke into a song which Yale men apparently sing to their enemies from Brown University; "What's the color of horseshit? Brown, Brown, Brown!"

Few of us had heard the song before but we sang it with gusto until we realized its implications. Our voices started to trail off but it was too late as a noncom came zooming out of the Headquarters building and ran up to the head of the formation and had us halted.

There was a short discussion, and then the order came, "Double time, with baggage, four times around the Headquarters block!" We were lucky we were in such great shape or I don't see how we could have made it in that hot sun.

When we finished we sort of staggered down to the siding and boarded these soot-stained rail cars which had somehow escaped destruction when the Yankees had burned Atlanta. The cars had been sitting out in the sun and were like ovens as we dragged ourselves in and plopped down on the hard seats. The only cooling we were going to get would be through the windows once we got under way .

I must admit that as beat up as most of us were, we felt we had gotten off easy. To engage in a mass ridicule of a superior officer is a serious thing and certainly could not go unanswered. Besides, no man's name, whoever he is, should be crapped on and it is obvious that the Major, to this day, deserves an apology.

He could have tracked down the ring leaders and made a big deal of it somewhat like General Ben Lear did when some troops marching past him on a stateside Army base golf course yoo-hooed at his short pants.

Instead, we were provided with a lesson that certainly stuck, and we came to realize that if you want to improve discipline, a little bit of suffering goes a long way. However, I also remember that the train finally pulled out and by the time we got a few miles down the track toward Missouri, we began to come out of our stupor and despite our discomfort, started to come back to life .

We were, by this time, well out of earshot of anybody back at Maxwell and somebody in the middle of our car got up, raised his hands like a choir conductor and when he gave the downbeat we all knew exactly what to sing: "What's the color of horseshit? Brown, Brown, Brown!"

You can broil the human spirit in the sun, it seems, and drench it with sweat and stain it with soot and run it around until it can hardly stand, but there's always a little piece of that defiance left unchanged.

3

BEYOND THE NEBULAE

The instructor looked at me across a chasm of uncertainty. He had gotten out of the airplane after we had taxied out to the wind tee and leaned his beefy rump against the big, yellow-painted tetrahedron which had been rotated to show the landing wind direction. Then he studied the ground for a while as I waited for the sign: to go or not to go.

I was in my thirteenth hour of flight training, well past the time I should have soloed, and past the time cadets who had not yet soloed were usually washed out. The trainer quivered and shook slightly as the engine idled and as I looked back at this man who had my future captive in some whim of his judgement. And I waited.

My first flight with this sandy-haired, laid-back southern chub, a man in his middle twenties, took place about a century before. The planes we were to use awed me the first time I saw them, a lot bigger than I expected, PT -for Primary Trainer- 23's built by Fairchild. They were all painted silver, with two seats -one behind the other- with a fixed landing gear and open cockpits. They were solidly built trainers designed to withstand the banging around, mishandling and near crashes which cadets like me subjected them to.

When it was not your turn to fly, you were on "crank duty", which meant you waited by the airplane you would fly later, and when a cadet and instructor climbed in and gave you the sign, you trotted around to the left side just forward of the wing and stuck a large crank into the starter hole.

It took a strong pull and when the cadet in the front seat yelled "Contact", you gave it a turn and the engine roared to life, the propeller whirling around just inches from your left shoulder. Then you had to take out the crank, set it down on the ground so you could pull the chocks from in front of the wheels, then trot alongside the wing tip until the plane was safely clear of the lines of parked airplanes.

The first flight had come after interminable days of classroom work, blackboard drills, lectures on how to use the parachute, the layout and limits of the local flying area, and on and on. I had some advance notice since our names, instructors and flight date and time were posted -where else- on the bulletin board in much the same way George Washington's troops must have found out they were to board the boats and cross the Delaware.

I met my instructor, a civilian like all of those at the school, at the appointed time at flight operations and as we walked out into the bright Missouri sunshine he said, "I'll make the takeoff and fly us around a bit. You just follow me through on the controls. Okay?"

"Yes sir."

We found the right airplane and walked around it a while as he explained about how dangerous a propeller could be, always know where the ground people were and always check the wind tee to know which way the surface wind was blowing.

"You're in the front seat so you get in first. When you climb on to the wing to get on board, make sure you step where it's marked, otherwise you'll put your foot through the wing."

The cranker cranked us up and we taxied to the take-off area. There was no runway, just a large grass patch and the take-off and landing directions were re-oriented each time the wind made a major shift and the wind tee was changed accordingly.

There were all kinds of airplanes milling around, taxiing, taking off, landing, flying around the pattern. Before I knew it I felt the throttle slide forward in my hand as the instructor gave it the gun and we shot forward. The noise and slipstream were overwhelming in the open cockpits and the vibration was enough to make your teeth chatter.

Once we got a little altitude, he throttled back and suddenly it became bearable although the slipstream swept over the small windshield and drummed on the tops of our helmeted heads.

"Look at your compass," he said through the one-way speaking tube." We're heading north and if we want to get back to the field, we have to head back due south. You got that?" he asked.

I gave the intimidating -yet comforting- presence behind me a big nod.

"Don't you ever forget which way the field is or you'll have to put this down in some cornfield one day." Lesson number one.

I actually started to relax a bit, I thought, and when the instructor told me to take the controls, I grabbed the stick with a force strong enough to lift the airplane. I felt him tap the stick so I loosed my death grip, and we went through that for a while; I would tighten my grip and he would make me loosen it.

After a while, he told me to make some turns and of course, as soon as I concentrated on that, my altitude started to porpoise and the instructor said, without impatience, "Coordinate! Coordinate!" It took some time before I could get some coordination going, but it all seemed so clumsy I wondered what the instructor was thinking.

Finally he said, "That's all, let's go back," and as I wobbled my way around to a south heading the field, of course, was nowhere to be seen. I swivelled my head back and saw the instructor holding up his hands, questioningly, as if to say, "Okay, where is it?"

Almost in a panic, I looked alongside the left side, then the right side of the nose until finally, up ahead in the early summer haze I spotted a grassy patch among the cornfields.

"There," I pointed, with the airplane gyrating around like a corkscrew as he grunted through the tube and I felt him take the controls.

It must have been a good guess since that's where we headed and I could feel him push the rudders this way and that and move the stick around with nice, firm movements as we maneuvered around the landing pattern and then landed with a solid thunk. He let me taxi back to the flight line and although I did so only with great difficulty, it was a good sign. I wasn't washed out yet.

The instructor didn't say anything as we walked back to operations, but when we got there he turned to me and, seeing the somewhat dazed look on my face, he said, "That's all there is to flying. You pull the stick back and the houses get smaller. You push it forward, they get bigger."

He watched me smile an uncertain smile, then he left.

It wasn't long before my turns got better and my altitude a little steadier. I even learned to kick in and hold the rudder on takeoff to counteract the engine torque which tried to pull us off our takeoff heading and little by little, got to the point where we were doing some pretty violent maneuvers, like tailspins.

On a couple of flights, we did spin after spin and I wondered if the instructor was trying to "wring" me out, to get something he saw in me out of my system, or to make me quit.

It went like this: throttle way back, pull the stick back as the speed died, then as the wings lost their lift and the airplane stalled, pull the stick all the way back and kick the rudder for a left or right spin and over she would flop and plunge earthward in a great corkscrew, your guts feeling a little strange, the earth spinning around as you looked for a road to help you count the number of turns as it dove toward the ground.

On a three turn spin, just before the end of the third turn, you stopped the turning motion with the rudder and when you were in a straight dive, you "dumped" the stick forward to break the stall and then slowly pulled the stick back, the G forces driving you into the seat until the plane's nose slowly came up and you once again got it straight and level as you added power.

For some reason I never had much difficulty with tailspins and got to do them with some precision. I also did a fair job with "S" turns along a road and other maneuvers intended to teach you how to compensate for the effects of wind on your flight path. But whatever else it was the instructor was trying to do apparently wasn't working to his satisfaction.

I know I still felt somewhat overwhelmed by the whole idea of actual flight. After all, the only vehicle I had ever operated on my own was my Western Union bicycle, and now I was trying to learn to handle a 220 horsepower airplane in a very short time. I began to envy some of the cadets who had come off the farm, where they had learned to run big machines, like tractors, starting at about age twelve and took to flying airplanes like ducks to water.

It didn't take much perception on the instructor's part to sense my feelings for I couldn't hide them, and he may have thought that my confidence in myself was in doubt.

And so it came, on my thirteenth hour of flight time that we had taxied out in the early morning sunlight and made a takeoff and flew around for a while. Then we landed and we taxied over to the wind tee and he got out and walked over to the tee and leaned against it, looking at me.

Finally, he looked at me once more and shook his head. His mind finally made up, he came back to the airplane, climbed in, and I taxied it back to the flight line for the last time. I had gotten that close, but now I was through. My pilot cadet flying career, from first flight to last, was six weeks.

How can I say how much this event wounded me? Even now, after so many years have passed, I still get a little twinge of disappointment that the instructor didn't give me a try. But any damage to my confidence caused by this heavy blow has been erased long ago by subsequent successes in which I could take pride.

It took a number of years before the idea of soloing an airplane once again confronted me and I remember the victory this time with the same immediate clarity as the failure.

I had joined the USAF Aero Club at Washington National Airport while stationed there and as I began my lessons, I was surprised to find I was able to pretty much pick up where I had left off at Cape Girardeau. And by this time, there was nothing about airplanes that could possibly overwhelm me.

The moment came once again when my instructor, Sergeant Magee -old Maggie- gave me the sign. We had been shooting landings at Frederick Airport up in Maryland when he said, "Okay! Taxi over and let me out."

My heart started pounding and I was suddenly a young cadet again and I looked at him. "Maggie, you sure?" He winked and stepped out.

"All it takes is three good landings." Then he reached in back of the seat and took out his jacket and I said, with a smile, "You afraid that might get burned in the crash?"

I got back on the runway and gave it the throttle and as I picked up speed, my senses as alert as they have ever been, I tried to sense the exact moment when the wheels left the ground, and the earth and I had parted.

I felt it and it all came rushing back to me, the instructor at Gape Girardeau sitting on the wind tee and shaking his head and I yelled as loud as I could, "I did it. I did it, God damn it, I did it!" I came around and I must admit I pasted that little Tri-Pacer down just the way I wanted and Maggie, sitting on his jacket by the side of the runway, waved me around again. I did it twice more and I was finished, and I mean, through.

I taxied off the runway and onto the grass and sat there. Here I was, fifteen years after the first time I had tried to solo and I had finally gotten up the nerve to try it again. All that had happened in between; the mounting number of flight hours, bombing missions over Germany, all of this was swept aside as the meaning of the moment sank in; that the bond made at the Yonkers Seadrome when I was a kid and almost severed at Cape Girardeau was once again made whole.

Nothing I had done so far was of real consequence in the idea of this moment, the idea of tentatively, determinedly lifting myself away from the ground where God had intended us to walk and sit and run and be born and die, and to do this for the first time completely on your own with no one to turn to for help, no means to fight off paralyzing panic or some fatal malfunctioning of the mind except your own will.

Now I had done it, and I was to continue on from that moment to press on as a pilot, including the slow, steady building up of the required amount of pilot time, and then finally, after I had left the Air Force, the earning of the "big ticket"; the Air Transport Pilot Certificate with a rating in a transport aircraft, which I got the hardest way of all, at the FAA Academy in Oklahoma City.

Soloing has come easily to many would-be pilots; people of all kinds, the Right Stuff crowd, handicapped people, teen-aged kids, but for a combination of reasons, it did not come to me on my first try. When my instructor looked over at me from the wind tee, he knew that if he let me go, my next flying activities involved all of the most complex aerobatics, and then formation flying, gunnery, and so on, all performed under a pressing time limit.

But it finally did come and the dragon spawned in my mind by that first failure was now slain, that tender spot in my psyche was suddenly gone. I turned the airplane around and taxied back to Maggie a little slowly, because I didn't want him to see how choked up I was.

Of all of the things that could happen to me after I washed out, I least expected to be assigned to Navigation School. My second choice after the pilot course had been for bombardier training and after that, for training as a non-commissioned aerial gunner.

When my name appeared on the bulletin board with an assignment to report to Selman Field at Monroe, Louisiana, for advanced navigation training, I was confused and a little shocked. I knew what a pilot was, and I had a good idea what a bombardier did, but a navigator?

I knew they had to learn to use celestial navigation, both day and night, and this required some understanding of spherical trigonometry and hell, I wasn't too cozy with the flat kind. They also had to learn, I was told, to navigate in arctic and polar areas where magnetic compasses didn't work, and how could anybody do that? And similar mysteries surrounded the means by which a crew would fly for ten or fifteen hours out in the Pacific and try to locate some tiny island like Fred Noonan was unable to do for Amelia Earhart when they both perished.

Strange as it seems, as all of the prospective cadets including myself were taking the motor coordination, intelligence and other tests prior to being selected for flight duty, navigator selectees were required to score higher than pilots.

This doesn't make much sense, since graduate pilots had first call on promotions, girls, whatever. They would be able to order crewmembers like me around to do this and do that, and perhaps grow up to be Colonels.

The idea of seeing the Adjutant to get a change in my assignment crossed my mind but not for long. After all, I wasn't in a very strong position and besides, as a navigator, I still had a chance at getting a commission and I would still have a flying assignment. I had a bird in hand, and the chance of blowing the whole thing and winding up at Jefferson Barracks with subsequent assignment to who knows what dissuaded me. Besides, I didn't have to report to Monroe for three weeks so I would get the chance for some leave at home.

Before I went on leave I decided to give Cape Girardeau one more Saturday night fling. I took the bus into town thinking, on the way, that I should see pretty little Amy with her blue eyes and shiny dark hair, perhaps for the last time.

I had met her, where else, at the drug store soda fountain and I had the gnawing suspicion that if I had asked her to wait for me, she might have considered it, and that scared me.

We had ended our first date in a wild smooching session on the steps of her front porch and she had made me agree that she would save herself for the man she would marry, whether it was me or someone else.

I enjoyed being with her, and who knows what might have developed had I stayed longer but now, as I walked down the main street, I couldn't get up the courage to face her and tell her I had washed out.

I found myself in front of this little beer joint I had avoided in the past, partly because girls like Amy wouldn't be caught dead there. I looked in, then walked in and found an empty booth along the wall and ordered a beer.

The place was long and narrow, with one of those tin ceilings and a couple of fans which stirred the smoky air. I felt some rising excitement as the joint filled with cadets and girls and the noise level rose as the corner jukebox pounded away in the late afternoon.

Somewhere into my second beer I began to focus on a booth across the way in which one cadet was keeping two girls entertained and they seemed to be having a good time. One of the girls caught me gazing their way and she tapped the cadet on the arm and he turned, looked at me for a moment, and waved me over.

Protocol hasn't change much since then, and of course I had to figure out immediately who his girl was. That done, it then became my duty to pay attention to the other one which, I

61

realized right away, was going to be easy.

She was fresh off the farm and looked it, with a tight black dress and a careless hairdo, with her reddish-tinted hair pulled back in a Grecian knot. Guessing her age was difficult; she could have been anywhere from fifteen to twenty. The way she looked directly at me with a level, knowing gaze told me I had to deal with her on equal terms.

And my dear Old Pal, sitting across from me, was already well along on his beery buzz, his words slurring as he told me his name was Harmon and he was from Savannah, a city boy.

"You may not enjoy my company too much," he drawled, "when you realize I'm just a washout, drowning my sorrows."

We were instant buddies when I told him I was in the same boat and we ordered up more beers for us and Cokes for the girls, who, it turned out, had a pint bottle of something which they surreptitiously poured into their drinks.

Harmon and his girl got up to dance and before I knew it I did too, although I hardly knew how yet, especially to the tune of the Dorsey Boogie. The music was pounding on the walls and sending some of the dancers into a frenzy, with bodies sort of flying around so bad I was able to cover up my dancing deficiencies by dodging them.

Then someone put some nickels in and pushed the slow music buttons and I could fake it a lot easier but she looked up at me and laughed and it didn't make a lot of difference.

She kept me at a distance to let me know she wasn't easy, and after a while, she -lets call her Leona- started to get to me, not only the musky, dime-store perfume but her sensuous, small-boned body and heart-shaped face, with those big, wise brown eyes and pouty young mouth.

All of this beauty was pretty well covered up by the farm girl-Saturday night get up she had on, but I knew it was there, and she knew I knew it. When I tried to put my arm around her in the booth, she leaned away and said, "It's too hot. Here, have some of my drink."

Meanwhile, my buddy Harmon was developing a close relationship with his girl Louise, and as the night rocketed on, he suddenly stood up and announced, "We're gonna get a taxi and a pint and go to Lou's friend's fishing shack."

As I stood up to go along, I realized that I was not in full command of all the muscles, neurons and ganglions needed for walking. I seemed to float out of the place behind Leona, noting with satisfaction that she really did have cute legs, not to mention the rest of her, and I began to get my first inkling that maybe all that stuff I had to drink was a tactical blunder.

We drove along a country road for a short while and pulled up to a darkened shack on the bank of what had to be the Mississippi River. Harmon and I did some fumbling around to pay the taxi driver for the ride and the pint, but we got it straightened out and still had enough presence of mind to tell the driver to come back in time so the girls could catch their eleven o'clock bus back to some town across the river.

We went inside and Lou found a lamp and lit it up to show the bare walls of the shack, which had nothing in it but a rough table and a few chairs. There was no way to drink the pint except right out of the bottle, so we all took a swig which, in my case, only made things a little worse.

Harmon and Louise decided it was time to go wading and ran out with Lee and me not too far behind. We all took our shoes off and stomped off into the moon-lit water, sobered only a little by the coolness of it as we splashed around, screeching like lunatics .

I started to yell, "You've got to beat your feet in the Mississippi mud..." as I stamped my feet into the water, but Harmon objected and said "No, No, this isn't the Big Muddy. Look at the moon on the water," he shouted. "It's the Ganges, the Ganges!"

Then Harmon put his arms around Louise from behind, movie musical style, and started to sing in a quavering voice, "Oh I grabbed her by the Ganges..." and I interrupted, "Harmon, girls don't have any Ganges!" so he changed it to "Oh she grabbed me by the Ganges..."

All of this seemed to make Leona mad and she yelled, "What do you mean girls don't have Ganges! How's this for a pair of Ganges!" and she put her hands on her hips and stuck out her promising bosom, but she lost her footing and fell down into the water so we all fell down, still laughing.

I grabbed Leona and pulled her up onto the bank and we sat back on the ground, getting our breath back. And suddenly I had to scramble off to one side as the earth started to go into

63

some sickening gyrations and up came the beer, the whiskey, a little bit of chili we had at the beer joint, and then a little bit extra which must have been my lunch.

Darkness descended slowly, and I could hear people talking for a while and then the lights almost went out, but I fought it off and slowly came back to the land of the living.

Leona was lying down next to me, leaning on an elbow and watching me. She started to laugh, "You cadets. They let you off the base once a week and you come into town with steam coming out of your ears and you drink six beers and you're all finished. You're like little kids."

She was teasing me, just a little. We both lay back and looked at the sky for a while and then the musky perfume and the cute legs got to me again and I drew her over to me. I found those pouty lips and felt the surge of joy as she responded, when all of a sudden her face was lit up in the glare of some lights and I couldn't believe it; it was the damned taxi.

"Can't we just have him wait a while?" I breathed, almost frantically, but I knew I had blown it. There was just enough time to get the girls to the bus and that's all there was to it. We left them at the bus stop after Leona and I had agreed to meet at the same place, same time next Saturday, but we both knew I would be gone and that was the end of it.

Harmon and I got back into the taxi and the driver took us back to the flight school. The guard let the taxi past the gate, which was lucky as he would have seen that we looked like we'd been dragged through a knot-hole.

As we drove toward the barracks, Harmon said, in that wonderful Georgia drawl, "My daddy told me when I left, if I must live it up, pursue only one vice at a time. That's harder to do than I thought."

The gloom descended again as we got out and paid the driver, both of us a little unsteady on our feet. I looked at him and asked, "Harmon, how'd you do?" He smiled one of those innocent half-smiles and said, "Southern gentlemen never tell."

We shook hands and he turned and headed toward the dimly lit entrance of one of the adjoining barracks.

A few days later I left on my first military leave and I looked forward to getting home and seeing the family, but I had to put up with another train ride to get there. The trip was routed via St. Louis and I not only had to stand up for the ten hours it took to get to that city, but I had to stand in an awkward position in the middle of a sardine-packed crowd of G.I.'s who were as miserable as I was.

From St. Louis to New York was a little more comfortable, but not much, and by the time we pulled into Penn Station I had almost forgotten my washout problems. In fact, it got to be a little frustrating after I got home to try to explain what had happened to me. After all, I still wore my fancy Aviation Cadet uniform, which was about halfway in military grandeur between that of an N.C.O. and an officer and caused passersby to stare in curiosity as I walked by.

When I bumped into an acquaintance on the street or in some public place like a bar and tried to explain the significance of being washed out of pilot training I got nowhere so I stopped trying and began to enjoy myself.

What struck me on that first leave was that all the men around my age were in the service and gone somewhere, including my brother Bill, who had become a radio operator on B-25 Mitchell bombers - the kind that raided Tokyo- somewhere in the Pacific, and my bother-in-law Hank Allison- Kay's husband- who was like the oldest brother to us all, was assigned as General MacArthur's staff car driver in Australia.

It was only natural that Hank should find his way into the driver's seat of the General's car. He had driven ambulances in his youth, and had even spent some time as a " 'Drome rider," a daredevil who drove a motorcycle in loop-the-loops around the inside of a globular chain-mesh sphere at carnivals in the New York suburbs.

His grandfather Robert Allison was a mining engineer and inventor from Pennsylvania who bought the first Winton automobile made and thus became the first person to buy a car from a company formed to make and sell autos to the public.

To speed delivery, Allison expedited the manufacture of the car by making some of the parts himself. He apparently took such good care of it that it survives today and can be seen on display at the Smithsonian Museum in Washington.

The love of fine or unusual cars was passed on to Hank and a series of events combined themselves so that he could indulge his desires. First, the Depression caused many well-to-do car owners to get rid of autos they could no longer afford to operate. Second, Hank was able to hold on to his job as a gasoline tanker driver which incidentally permitted him, as one of the job's perks, to keep his personal car supplied with free gas.

When he first met my sister Kay, he was driving an elegant Auburn convertible. Then he found an almost new Cord for sale at a fraction of its original price, and took delight in showing us how the center headlight turned in coordination with the front wheels.

Then came a Chrysler Airflow, the first streamlined car, and then another Chrysler, a long, elegant Imperial touring sedan, one of only a few of its kind made.

We always pestered Hank for rides and I can recall sitting next to him one evening when he took us aboard the Imperial and we cruised down South Broadway, then made our way onto the West Side Drive along the Hudson. One of the kids yelled, "Let's do a hundred miles an hour!" and Hank gave it the gas. The summer night's slipstream came pouring in around the windshield and I looked at the speedometer, which was wavering around ninety, but then Hank had to slack off as we came to some winding curves.

The neighborhood became accustomed to see such magnificent cars parked in front of our homely flat on Jefferson Street, one block down from our previous abode on Stanley Avenue. What would some stranger think, however, as Hank and Kay, a handsome couple, arrived there some sunny Sunday afternoon with the top down, maroon finish burnished to a sparkle.

"Why, they must be some rich people motoring in from the Hamptons," the idiot might muse, "letting us poor people know that even in the depression, the American Dream remains alive!"

There had been other strangers, during the Depression, who didn't care whether a motorist in a fancy car came from the Hamptons or not. It occasionally happened that a pedestrian passing a big Cadillac or Buick stopped at a traffic intersection would lean over and spit on the shiny hood as he passed, then stare defiantly at the driver before he walked on.

Now Hank was putting in his time in Brisbane where there was fear the Japanese would continue southward and invade

Australia too.

And while I fought the Battle of Yonkers, my brother Bill, during one of his relocations in the South Pacific, found himself thrashing around in the open ocean after a Japanese kamikaze plane smashed into the ship transporting him and his outfit and set it ablaze.

The young Japanese pilot, with the transcendental courage of a man who had already consigned his mortal life into the hands of his ancestors, aimed the flying bomb which he flew so that it would slam into the ship's superstructure where the big naval I.D. numerals were painted; where the end numeral in the number 738 gave him two choices so he picked the upper circle of the figure 8 and hit it dead center.

Bill had not accompanied us on our adventure across the Hudson some years before because he had never learned to swim, yet he was able to surmount the natural panic which rose in him as the great swells lifted him and then slid his life-vested form down toward unknown terrors, then lifted him again. After some time, he and some others were picked up by a U.S. Navy torpedo boat, and the skipper, an understanding soul, administered some medicinal rations.

As my leave wound its course, I spent some time learning how to avoid making the mistakes I had made on the shores of the Ganges. I discovered the pleasures of "pub crawling" around the New York area, an endeavor which was a lot of fun in those days because all of the bars, lounges and saloons were all jam-packed and noisy and it was easy to have a good time.

There were girls all over the place, but things were the same as they were back at flight school; there were good girls and there were good time girls. In my case at least, the odds seemed to be firmly stacked on the side of the good girls, which, of course, only added to the mystery and desirability of the females I pursued. Once in a while I would try to pull the old "war is hell" routine, but since I hadn't been there yet it wasn't too effective.

Before I knew it, the three weeks had shot by and I was on my way back to getting ready for the war, which was picking up steam and which, according to my orders, still needed me.

Strangely, the war seemed closer when I was at home because of the food rationing and the war news, all of it bad. Back at the field, they didn't ration the food at the mess hall and we didn't have time to read the papers or listen to the radio.

My new course of training started not with the mysteries of navigation, but with the art of maintaining and shooting all kinds of loud and deadly firearms, especially the 50 calibre machine gun. Navigators were sometimes required to man one of the gunner's positions in the big bombers so we were sent to school to train for an aerial gunner's rating before we started the navigator's course.

The gunnery training took place at Buckingham Field, just outside Fort Myers on the western shore of Florida, across the peninsula from Miami. We were shipped there as soon as we returned to Monroe and I finally found my palm trees and white sand beaches.

The time was late autumn of 1943 and it was the perfect time to be in Florida, for other people but not for us. We didn't get much beach time as there was plenty for us to do on all kinds of firing ranges and in the firearm maintenance training shops.

We started off with lots of skeet shooting on standard skeet ranges, then graduated to flatbed trucks which cruised around an oval course at thirty miles an hour as skeet were popped out at us from unexpected places.

Eventually, we found ourselves in real airplane turrets mounted with 50 caliber machine guns which seemed as big as cannons when we first saw them. The turrets were lined up in a row on the firing range and could be operated as if they were installed in an aircraft. The trick was to fire very short bursts - three or four shots at a time- at moving targets and the idea was to get used to the gunsights and the manipulation of the turret controls while pulling the triggers.

We not only had to learn to shoot, but also had to "detail strip" the machine gun down to its minutest parts, and to identify each part by name. By the time we learned to do this, it wasn't too difficult to "field strip" the same gun, which required us to take the gun apart in less detail, but we had to reassemble them while blindfolded.

I was much impressed by the great size of the 50 calibre

cartridges and the large slug with which they were tipped. There were other weapons in the course, including the Colt 45 pistol which had a kick like a mule and which I didn't learn to handle until years later. We all told each other we could probably do better throwing the gun at somebody rather than trying to shoot him with it.

And then there was the Thompson submachine gun. I don't know exactly why this gun was included but it was certainly a large armful of firepower and I can still remember the instructions; aim at the lower left of the target and let the gun rip its way upward and to the right. I can see why it was a favorite of gangsters and G-men because you sort of "hosed down" the target and it made you feel five times bigger than actual size.

I took the Department of Justice tour in Washington years later and watched as the FBI agent who led the tour give us an exhibition with the big Thompson and he played it like a deadly Stradivarius.

Before we were through with our flexible gunnery training we were given several flights in the back end of an AT-6, the trainer I might have been piloting had I not washed out. It was a 2-seater, and the rear seat was rigged with a swivel-mounted 30-caliber machine gun, which seemed almost like a toy compared to the caliber .50. The idea was to fire at a sleeve target being towed by another airplane flying alongside, an exercise which seemed pretty risky for the pilot of the other airplane.

We heard that some of the target-towing airplanes were piloted by female pilots who liked to strip down to almost nothing because of the heat in the cockpit but they were too far away for us to check out the rumor.

A friend of mine claimed at the time that he met one of the tow target ladies in a hotel lounge and asked her, right out, if it was true that some of them flew missions stripped down to their bra.

"Sonny boy," she said, looking him square in the eye and sticking out her, er, lapels, "I never wear a bra."

It was unusual for anyone to score many hits on the sleeve and no one got more than a few. The air over the Gulf was pretty bumpy and most of the would-be gunners got pretty woozy after a few minutes of bouncing around. Besides, the attempted simulation of combat conditions didn't even come close and everyone knew it, but at least we got the chance to fire the guns at a target in the air.

The course came quickly to an end and it seemed like everyone in our class made it. At the graduation ceremony, some of the cadets managed to have some family members attend to pin their new aerial gunner's wings over their left shirt pocket, but most of us "buddied up" and pinned them on each other. I had forgotten about the wings and it came as a pleasant surprise to be able to wear them and feel as though I was making some headway.

I received another surprise some weeks later back at navigation school when I bumped into some of my former pilot school classmates who had landed at Monroe while making a cross-country training flight and the first thing they noticed were my wings. They hadn't gotten their pilot wings yet but they would, very soon, along with their commissions as Second Lieutenants and their orders for combat, or assignment as instructors, or whatever. The envy surged in me again, but only for a while as I totally submerged myself in the business of becoming a navigator.

The flight navigator course was, as I expected, not an easy one. The difficulties were different from those in the pilot course, where the solution to most problems involved physical moves -the control of the aircraft- and, ultimately, leadership and the accomplishment of the mission.

As a navigator, you had to perform a lot of mental calculations and make decisions as to which information you managed to get was the best to operate on to help the pilot get the airplane to the target and back.

The heart of a navigator's education involved something called dead reckoning. We spent a lot of time fooling around with the gadgets: sextants, driftmeters, radio direction finders and all of the techniques, computation tables, correction factors needed to use them. But these were only designed to help you do your DR, your deduced reckoning.

You could tell the pilot, who in turn could tell the people who wanted to know exactly where the airplane was located with great precision at the time of takeoff, and again at the time of landing, although you might need to ask somebody, on some embarrassing occasion, to confirm the name of your arrival airport.

In between, when you were operating in an area where navigators were needed to determine the position of the airplane, the main weapon in the struggle between precise positioning and operational anarchy was your DR, which had to be backed up and confirmed by information obtained from gadgets or from the use of special techniques.

Dead Reckoning is simple; you get out your map and measure the course, in relation to true north, from departure to destination via all the required checkpoints with a type of protractor called a Weems plotter. Then you apply the forecast wind effects and the varying effects of the earth's magnetic field on your compass, add a little pinch of the error in the compass itself, and your have your compass heading.

Then you measure the distance between your checkpoints as exactly as you can with another indispensable navigator's instrument; a pair of dividers. You've got to be a little careful; on some charts, sixty miles is sixty miles wherever you measure it; on others, you must adjust your dividers to measure sixty miles each time because the distance changes as you move north or south, depending on which mathematic formula was used to construct the chart.

You know what airspeed the pilot intends to indicate on the climb-out and along the various segments of the route as it changes because fuel is being burned off -the speed wants to increase as the airplane gets lighter- and during the descent to destination .

All of these differing speeds are taken into account, along with the way the forecast wind is expected to affect your speed along the ground, and you come up with a series of ETA's and a total flying time.

Once you take off, the main struggle is to determine how far off your planning information is. The first order of business is to get some idea how accurate your instrument read-outs are. Then you launch into the flight-long task of dealing with the flight level wind and temperature information provided by that smooth-talking con-man -the weather forecaster- who has himself been conned by the slippery uncertainties of an inexact science.

Looming over you as you work is the pressure of time; the longer you must go without getting a navigation fix of some kind, the more the positional uncertainty builds. All of this could bring you to the point where you begin to sweat the fuel, and on a long overwater flight, you start to get nervous glances from the pilots and the flight engineer.

It must be a little different aboard ship, perhaps a naval vessel of some kind. I could envision them cruising along at a leisurely 15-knots while the navigator asks the bosun's mate to take the sextant and shoot him a three-star fix. Then, perhaps still dressed in his immaculate uniform, he takes his information to be worked out not in a bouncing, smelly aluminum tube ripping along at several hundred knots, but in the quiet of the bridge where decorum and tranquility prevail.

Maybe, even, they take the sights down to the wardroom and work them up after being fortified by some coffee, or, if they were on a British man-o-war, perhaps with a tot of grog.

And if they were new at the game and screwed up the shots, they could always sneak upstairs, or up the ladder, and get some more. But with us, it would already be too late, because here we are in Tierra del Fuego instead of Monroe, Louisiana.

The night celestial missions were the toughest, and you had to show some progress each time you went out. The airplanes were twin-engined Beechcraft AT-7's, which were used for a lot of things besides training navigators, including hauling lesser big shots and express cargo and who knows what.

Ours were rigged with an astrodome, which was a plexiglass bubble on top of the plane through which we took our sextant shots. Since there were usually three student navigators, it got to be a scramble to use the dome.

Each student had his own desk, next to which was mounted a big, fancy magnetic compass which could be corrected on the basis of star observations. This instrument was considered especially valuable because it was fitted with a cover which looked like a medium-sized salad bowl, and when someone began yelling, "Cup, cup, cup!" during the hot, bouncing ride, one of these was quickly passed to him so that the poor guy's supper could be captured and stashed away, then furtively disposed of after the flight.

It was not enough to be able to capture a star in the bubble of your sextant sight; you had to know which one it was. First we learned the constellations; the Dippers, Orion, Pegasus- all of them, including those over the southern hemisphere. Then we were taught the "pointer system" where stars in constellations which were easy to pick out were used to point toward single stars, like the first two stars in the Big Dipper can be lined up to sight toward Polaris, the North star, which is not bright and is sometimes not easy to locate.

There were times, years later, on a smooth night at high altitude, where the sky was clear and there was no light at all except from the stars themselves and I would capture, say, Sirius and crank it down into the center of my bubble and hold it there for the required one or two minutes, turning the knob to keep it centered as the airplane moved through the night and maybe went through some slight gyration.

I would become mesmerized, peering through the awesome darkness at this brilliant pin-point of light, this mystery of stupefying proportions, seemingly as firmly fixed in its position in the heavens as the mind can comprehend, yet propelled toward somewhere by God's Big Bang.

I would need to do this twice more, using three stars spread around my horizon so that my shooting errors tended to cancel themselves out, and I would have my three-star fix. Each star gave me a line of position, and when the three lines crossed in a very tight little triangle, all of the unknowns; the winds that blew us around, the compass and airspeed errors, the way the pilot flew the heading, all of these were resolved for the moment, and I knew everything I had to know for a while. It was a good feeling.

And sometimes on other nights, when the engines were in quiet long-range cruise and the slipstream just a whisper, I would get lost in the beauty of it and look out into the vastness where there would be no up or down or North or South, just the endless array of stars so bright they hardly winked.

They outshone the myriad, red-lit dials and gauges which were crammed in nice, neat rows any place there was room for them on the darkened flight deck, where the pilots and the flight engineer sat almost unseen in the peaceful half-light, waiting for the longitude lines to slide beneath them.

My friend the Big Dipper was always the place to start in my tour through the universe and the names of each star in the Dipper would run through my head like an incantation; Dhube, Merak, Phecda, Megrez, Alioth, Mizar, Alkaid. And then around the arc of the Dipper's handle to Arcturus, and then several zillion light years over to Spica, and on through the galaxies.

I was in a vehicle firmly held by the earth's gravity, but as I gazed out of the flight deck window I could feel something else pull at me and I would lean forward as some tantalizing flicker of understanding whispered to me from somewhere beyond the interstellar dust and the nebulae. And then some-one would snap on a light, and the feeling would be gone.

Another form of navigation which we had to learn was map reading, which was navigating by observing features on the ground. Rivers, lakes, highways, railroads, cities and towns, mountains; anything which stood out and could be portrayed on a map were available as fixes.

Believe it or not, map reading, or pilotage as it was also called gave some of us more trouble than celestial. For one thing, a lot of towns, railroad and highway intersections and rivers are not that distinctive, and if two rivers, say, which wiggle the same way are overflown, and only one appears on the map, you begin to have a confidence problem.

Many towns look alike from the air, and unless you are low enough to read the name off the water tower, you can't always use them as a fix. Of course, all of this goes up in smoke as soon as you enter clouds for any length of time.

It was a nice, old-fashioned way to navigate and is still be used on occasion by the Cessna or the Piper crowd, but it has now pretty well passed into the exotic. But we had to learn it and learn it well since it could, at times, be the only means of navigation we had, and could help us to help the bombardier pick out the target from a clutter of landmarks.

Toward the end of the course, we were flying missions

which were not limited to one type of navigation, and were allowed to use any means at hand except the radio compass to get to destination within a reasonable time of our estimate. The radio compass, otherwise known as the Automatic Direction Finder (ADF), had a dial with a pointer which pointed at any radio station you tuned in, and it was usually taped over because it made things too easy.

We were finally getting close to the real world, although we had no bombs to drop or guns to shoot and nobody was shooting at us. All of that still seemed remote, but not quite as much as before as the instructors began to describe differences in the operational atmospheres of the different combat theaters.

We were given a questionnaire and asked to state our preference for an assignment after graduation. The choices included combat theaters like the ETO- the European Theater of Operations- which was the big stuff, the Big Time, and the CBI- the China, Burma, India Theater, in addition to assignment as an instructor in a navigation school in the States.

Almost to a man, we completely ignored any sense of reason or logic and based our thinking on all of the romantic notions we had built up in our teen-age minds. Like many others, I picked the CBI because of the exotic promise in those names- China, Burma, India, and the stories we had heard about "flying the Hump" -across the Himalayas- in which our guys flew supplies through the most dangerous terrain, in atrocious weather.

We wouldn't know where we were headed until around graduation time, which I suddenly realized was almost upon us. We had one final flight to make, and the grade we received made up a big portion of our overall score. It was another night flight and four of us would be tested at the same time. We could use any means to navigate and the regular instructors were switched around so we could be looked at with fresh eyes. Any of the instructors had the power to set a man back, or wash him out, or pat him on the head for a job well done. The Lieutenant we got was an unknown quantity, a cherubic, prematurely bald young man who didn't appear tough or easy; just non-committal.

The flight plan was laid out to the south towards the Gulf, over a sea of nothingness where you had to use celestial, and then, to test our ability to use night pilotage, over towns like Natchitoches.

Ah yes, Natchitoches. The name got to roll off our tongue so easily, but only after a good bit of practice. One of our instructors, who came from Mississippi, informed us that the name was invented in retaliation for the naming of one of our northern states "Massatoo...Massatoo..Massatooshitts." He never did get it right.

As it turned out, the night was terrible for navigation, with rough air and broken clouds above us which made celestial almost impossible. Nobody managed to get a three-star fix, and we all had to do with position lines from one or two stars or the moon combined with some guesswork. The radio compass was covered up once more so we all depended on night pilotage to get us home.

Pilotage at night involved a lot of interpretation and imagination, which means there was a lot of guesswork and room for error. You looked at the way the lights below were laid out, especially those which might be strung along the main roads. Then you would conjure up a picture of the way the roads curved and crossed each other and then try to find a similar pattern on the pilotage chart.

A middle-sized town came up underneath us and in the few minutes we had to study it as it slipped by I decided that it was, indeed, Natchitoches and not some other nearby town that looked like it. I used the position to compute my heading and time estimate back to Monroe.

We landed and as far as I could tell, everything had worked out okay for me, but what did the Instructor think? We were debriefed separately and he looked at my navigator's log for a while and put it down and looked at me. "I watched you work up there," he said, "and you did the best with what little you had to work with. You get a good grade from me. Congratulations!"

He got up and shook my hand, and left me sitting there, suddenly no longer tired but a little numb, knowing that nothing but a little bit of paperwork stood between me and the big, real wartime world out here, and I was ready. I was a navigator!

Out of our group of forty cadets, two didn't make it. We didn't know why and we weren't told; they were just gone. All of our ground school classes were finished and one of the instructors said something in his last class that stuck in my mind.

"Right now, all of you know as much about being a navigator as we instructors do, since we just graduated a few classes before you did. The first time you navigate across an ocean to go to combat, you will know a hell of a lot more than we do, and you will still have a lot to learn. Just remember, a lot depends on you guys."

It was time to gulp, and get on with it.

For once, we didn't need to check the bulletin board to find out what came next. Instead, each of us found a large manila envelope on our cot and inside were three separate sets of orders. The first, in a five-line paragraph, wrapped up the entire effort we had undergone at Selman; the doubts, the fears, the good feelings, the grinding study, the mid-air panics, by stating that since the cadets on the following list had completed the course, they were now awarded the aeronautical rating of navigator.

The second order was looked at as the key to heaven, since it offered us commissions as Second Lieutenants in the Army of the United States, and "with our consent," were ordered to active duty in the Air Corps.

The third sort of wrapped things up by saying that since we were navigators and would be officers once we were again sworn in, we were required to "participate in regular and frequent aerial flights." This let the finance office know that we were entitled to flight pay.

The second set of orders also resolved another big unknown since it assigned us -those on the list- to duty with the First Bomber Command, part of the First Air Force at Westover Field, Massachusetts. First, First, First; we learned that this assignment meant we would be assigned to a B-24 Liberator heavy bomber crew for eventual combat missions with the Eighth Air Force over Germany. This was the Big Time. I felt proud and awed.

4

THE BIG TIME

HERE WE WERE, in New England in the spring of 1944, where the weather was perfect for flying or smelling the flowers or being a brand new twenty-year old Second Lieutenant in the Air Corps. But we, all of the hundreds of new Lieutenants: the pilots, bombardiers, navigators, together with the enlisted radio operators, flight engineers and gunners did not come here to smell the flowers but to go to war.

We came here to Westover Field near Springfield, Massachusetts to be rounded up and organized into aircrews and to be trained, in a few short weeks, how to once more do all of the things we had already learned; but now, not on our own but as a crew operating an aircraft that was part of a large formation.

The cadet feeling, the feeling of being a student was suddenly gone and instead of flowers, we smelled the gunpowdery smell of approaching combat. I must admit that being a new Lieutenant was pretty heady stuff, with lots of people suddenly calling us "Sir!", mostly because they had to and that great uniform with the dark green "blouse" and the "pinks," which were the pinkish grey whipcord pants dating back to horse cavalry days. Then there were the shiny brown buckle shoes and the go-to-hell hat which took a lot of time and art to shape into the "fifty-mission crush." It is truly amazing what clothes can do for a person and I, like all the others, began to believe that maybe Congress does actually have the right to designate certain people as "gentlemen."

The sudden freedom we found ourselves with certainly presented us with a bunch of challenges. We were no longer herded into "colyums of bunches" to go to mess or to any other place. We were on our own to show up at training sessions or medical appointments or whatever. We paid for our own clothes and food and could eat wherever we wished, or wherever we could afford. Most of the time, we had complete freedom to leave the base whenever we had the time or inclination. If these freedoms seem like simple pleasures, try being a cadet for a year, or four years as required in the military academies and then let the gates be thrown open.

A good sized pay raise went along with the new title but I noticed, as time went on, that financial problems began to arise, little by little, in this new era. As a cadet, I was paid seventy-five dollars per month. After deducting for my sabotaged laundry, toothpaste, candy bars and other critical necessities, I would take the substantial remainder and split it four ways, one for each weekend and, believe it or not, I never had a money problem. As an officer, my pay was multiplied but, of course, so were my expenses. It seemed that nothing was furnished by Uncle Sam anymore and not only that, my whole lifestyle was jacked up several notches. Fortunately, putting some money in the bank didn't have a big priority with me at the time. I didn't worry about it; like most Second Lieutenants I learned to live from payday to payday. Because of the wartime shortages of most civilian necessities, price controls were applied and that made things a little easier. Of course, what price controls really did was to hold the price on certain things if you could find them to buy.

It goes almost without saying that putting on the uniform of an officer does more than just jazz up the psyche; it marks a very worthwhile accomplishment made under tough conditions. When I think back on it, it was one of the best things I have done in my life. After all, nobody handed me any thing on a platter and I had to reach down deep into all I had learned up to that time and all of the capabilities I had been born with to join with a particular group who had to go through the same wringer I did.

I recall thinking about all of this on my trip to Westover

after being commissioned. The train went through New York and I was given some leave, so I took the opportunity to visit home once more. As we neared the city, I remember imagining my arrival at Grand Central Station, getting off the train and walking down the long platform and out onto the immense, marble floored main concourse, to the big four-sided clock over the information counter where my father and I would meet. And he would suddenly see me in my resplendent uniform, an officer in the U.S. Air Corps, his son who had done something no one in the family had ever done in the old country and he would come to me and grab me, his eyes lit with joy, thinking that maybe the streets had been paved with a certain kind of gold. But then the image would fade, and die away, for after all, he had died seven years before.

The four of us, the officers on the crew; the two pilots, the bombardier and myself as navigator, stood there on the hard-stand and looked at the big Liberator, not knowing quite what to make of her. It was a formidable looking airplane, with its square, boxy shape and not too elegant dual rudders and blunt nose. It had the big fifty caliber machine guns sticking out from every logical place, and looked like it needed every bit of power from its four engines to get it off the ground. It did not have the great, curved tail and sweeping, rounded lines of the B-17 Flying Fortress, which was in combat earlier and was better known than the "Lib".

The four of us had gotten to know a little about each other by this time, and I wondered just how we came to be on the same crew. There may have been some organized, scientific process for putting the flight crews together, but I doubt it. I can picture an assistant operations officer, probably a first lieutenant, and a corporal with large sheets of paper marked off into lined squares. The lieutenant would write a crew number in each box, then the corporal would pick up the roster of aircraft commanders and read them off, and the lieutenant would write each name on the top line in the box. Then would come the roster of the co-pilots, then the navigators, then the bombardiers and so on. After the boxes were filled, the sheets would be taken over to another corporal, a typist, who would type the lists onto a mimeograph master sheet, which would then be installed around the drum of the machine. Then, one of the corporals would press the button and the drum would begin to roll and kick out the printed orders. Once this fool-proof, state of the art crew selection process was complete, one copy would be picked up and posted on the headquarters bulletin board and another in each of the barracks dayrooms, and our fates were sealed. Matching up personalities or personal backgrounds might be used in later wars, but not this one. It worked the other way around; you changed your behavior and came up to speed in your crew position to the extent needed to get along on the crew. It worked just fine.

We had all met for the first time at a large aircrew meeting in the base theater called to get the crewmembers identified to each other and introduced. The crew assignment orders had contained, in addition to names, ranks and crew positions, a seat row number in the theater for each crew. Some seats in our row were already filled when I got there, all of us changing quickly in our minds from green-clad shapes to beings with faces and voices. Other shapes arrived and sat down while someone up front with a microphone orchestrated the proceedings. By the time our row was filled, the names I had read on the orders began to take on identities. We had to sit quietly for a moment as the man up front finished his instructions, then we were able to get up and get together outside as a group to look each other over, and wonder what impression we were making ourselves. We made some small talk and let the moment sink in; we were no longer just names on a list, but people who would get together to plunge into the unknowns of combat.

The main figure, the person who drew the attention of the rest of us was Second Lieutenant John Beder, who would be the captain of t he crew. If a hundred officers had been lined up and I was asked to pick out the crew commanders, John would have been among the first. The job didn't require that you be a trim, solid six-footer but it helped. He had a slightly flattened nose which came from his Golden Glove boxing days back in Indianapolis, and a look in his eye which let you know he was not confused at all about his role as leader of the crew.

Big John Beder was married and twenty-three years old, which automatically set him apart from most of us, who seemed to be twenty or twenty-one and single. However, since there was a general housing shortage around all of the large bases including Westover, Big John's wife remained at home and he had to depend on us for company. Beder had started his military days in the U.S. Army Field Artillery, which, like the cavalry, was just getting out of the horse business. The caissons no longer went rolling along by equine power but were now pulled by truck, or were mounted on vehicles of their own and were called "self-propelled" artillery. In the Air Corps, John Beder could now bombard targets hundreds of miles from home base rather than just over the horizon. He had received his commission in the Artillery and, unlike the rest of us, had undergone pilot training as a student officer rather than as a cadet.

John Samsell, the co-pilot, had a background somewhat like mine. He came from Scranton, Pennsylvania, which could have been my hometown too, if my father hadn't decided that he'd never get rich digging coal and stopped his journey in Yonkers which, of course, was not exactly swimming with Ukrainian millionaires either. He was an inch or two taller and a few pounds heavier than me, with sandy hair; a young man with an already matured outlook, who looked around and made his observations and usually let other people do the talking. Before he entered pilot training he had been an artificer -an old Army term for technical specialist- in Panama. Panama was good duty in those days and Sam probably could have sweated out the war there, but he must have read the same books and seen the same movies the rest of us did, and now here he was.

It was unusual that both pilots had not "come off the street" into the Air Corps like most of us did. As a result, they were not wide-eyed babes in the wood as most of us were, and they already knew their way around the military.

And then there was 2nd Lt. Jack G. Murray, ace bombardier from Atlanta. If he was a babe in the wood he didn't act like one either. He was about John Beder's size and shape, had a shock of blond hair and he was not shy. There wasn't much sense in standing around quietly when you could have a few laughs or maybe needle somebody a little bit, he must have thought. It was obvious from the beginning that Jack did not get his bombardier's wings so that he could sit in the nose turret of tail-end charlie and watch somebody else in the lead airplane do the bombing. He joined the crew ready for business.

We had been standing around admiring the Liberator for a while when a jeep pulled up and Sergeant Jim Morley, the engineer got out. He saluted and we all saluted back, everyone a little self-conscious because of the newness of it all. Morley got the auxiliary power unit going so we could operate some of the gadgets that needed electrical power. Then we climbed on board, up through the bomb bay and into the flight deck. Jack Murray and I marveled at the complexity of it all; the instruments, dials, gauges, knobs, levers, warning placards, control panels and all the other gadgets the pilots and engineer needed to fly the airplane.

Then we found the hatch in the floor behind the pilots' seats and Jack let himself down into the narrow passageway and crawled forward to the nose compartment where the bombardier's station was located. I followed right behind him to where the navigator's position was in this particular model, between the bombardier and the pilots. The airplane had been around a while and had that old airplane smell; the pervasive stink of hydraulic fluid; a little whiff of high octane fuel; stale, spilled coffee; and the elusive, hard to pin down exhalations of bravery and fear.

The navigator's position was sort of an ad hoc arrangement; apparently the original design contemplated the use of a navigator/bombardier rather than a full time navigator and the necessary changes had yet to be made. You couldn't see outside too well, for the original greenhouse nose had been replaced with a turret, and I had to make do with a tiny window on each side plus the limited view through the bomb-sight window. My position had all the right furnishings; a desk about four feet long and maybe sixteen inches wide along the rear of the compartment. Just forward of that, on the right side, was a drift-meter, the usual B-3 with gyro stabilized optics, and up in the ceiling was a standard-sized astrodome with a sextant hook and astrocompass brackets. Mounted on the bulkhead over the desk was a control box similar to one in both pilots' positions for tuning in the radio compass, along with a large dial for reading radio bearings. A small instrument panel with a circular temperature gauge, an altimeter, and compass and airspeed indicators was mounted on the left side halfway between Jack's position and mine.

Near each position were wall-mounted demand-type oxygen regulators with metering valves and flow indicators, with the usual expandable, cloth-covered hoses dangling down in several loops. And finally, at each position was an interphone jack-box with a headset already plugged in. This was to be where I worked, an office that was carried along with me where I would observe and compute and decide and then pass on information to the pilot or the bombardier or the radio operator. It was also the place where I would sweat and freeze, get cramps from the altitude, screw up my sinuses on the descent, benumb my eardrums from all that noise, and sometimes all of these things would happen to me on the same mission.

The sergeants on the crew were all trained as gunners and had taken the same course in flexible gunnery that I did. It was called "flexible" gunnery because the guns were mounted on swivels or in turrets and not bolted down like they are on fighter aircraft. Some of the sergeants had other things to do as their primary job, like Morley, who, as flight engineer, was intimately involved in operating the airplane when it was flying, and was relied on to know about the plane's systems in more detail than the pilots. He was also the go-between between the crew and the maintenance men; the people who, on those dark and misty mission mornings, held your lives in their hands as they worked among the big, finned cylinders, supercharger waste-gates, propeller controls, hydraulic pumps and accumulators, oxygen regulators and all those myriad machines and gadgets that could kill you if they didn't work as advertised. Morley also flew as gunner in the top turret, which was located on top of the fuselage about five feet behind the pilot's seats and just forward of the bomb bays. There was also a hatch on top of the airplane near his turret and Morley would climb up and sit on the edge of it while Beder taxied to the takeoff position. From there, he would get a king-of-the-world view of what was going on and, just in case, keep an eye on wing-tip clearance when we passed another Lib.

Sending messages from airplanes over long distances hadn't been developed very far before World War II and it still had a long way to go when the war started. Ray Murgatroyd, our radio operator, had to use equipment which looked great and was brand new, yet it wasn't much more capable than the radios on the Titanic. Can you imagine going through all that smoky hell as the bombs are dropped, going through a complicated tuning procedure, then unlimbering your Morse code key to send a strike message? It required a steady hand in a situation somewhat like the days when railroad station agents dah-ditted their message from their beleaguered railroad way-stations as Colonel Mosby attacked. Ray was a bright young guy whose freckled face and slight build made him look younger than he was. He got his messages in, and got us the landing weather back home and all the other information we needed to do the job and make it back. Ray was also required to be ready to act as backup waist gunner, and would take over the position if the need arose. When this happened, tuning knobs and frequencies would be forgotten as he scanned the skies for ME-109's and FW-190's. The swivel-mounted waist guns -there was one on each side of the rear fuselage- were manned by Sergeants Merchant and Carr. Carr was a tall, shy, nice-looking guy who, as young as I was, looked young enough to be my kid brother.

The waist gunners had the most demanding shooting job of all. They couldn't just point and shoot like the nose and tail turrets; they had to worry about pursuit curves and deflection, and about a curious, newly recognized ballistics affect which required that they lag their targets rather than lead, as would be natural. And then there was the slipstream, which came pouring through the side windows in great torrents, and which made frostbite a constant threat.

As for the front of the airplane: when a German fighter made a head-on attack at a particular Liberator in a formation, his immediate target would most likely be the nose-turret gunner. Until we became a lead crew, it would be bombardier Jack Murray who manned this turret, and after we became a formation leader, Jack would give up the turret to concentrate on his bombardeering, and an extra navigator would sit there instead.

In the hottest spot of all, the tail gunner's position, which guarded against six o'clock low attacks, was Sergeant Bob Schodrof. His was a lonely position at the tip-end of the fuselage, between the two great vertical stabilizers. He was good-natured enough to squeeze his country-burly frame into those narrow quarters without complaint, and if he ever got woozy as the tail gyrated around during the hours of formation maneuvering, he never let on.

Another gunner who was to watch over six o'clock low attacks and over any other attack from underneath the B-24 did his watching suspended beneath the airplane in the ball turret. I tried sitting in this contraption once or twice during flight and I must admit I got just a little edgy. The turret was kept retracted until some time after take-off, when the gunner squeezed himself into quarters so tight he had to leave his parachute pack outside on the waist floor. Then the ball-shaped apparatus was let down into the slipstream and Sgt. Cal Roever was stuck there until we were pretty much on the let-down near home base and away from any fighter threat.

At some time during our training we had all heard the story about a Flying Fortress ball turret that got jammed in the down position during a mission with the gunner inside and could not be retracted while airborne to let him out. As the fortunes of war would have it, the combat damage which jammed the turret also knocked out two engines and damaged the landing gear so that it could not be lowered, either hydraulically or by manual crank. All of this meant that the gunner would be trapped between the ground moving beneath him and the full weight of the airplane above. The airplane had to land since it was running out of fuel, so the situation was explained to the man. As described by Andy Rooney, the TV commentator, who was there as a correspondent at the time, the gunner "understood what had to be done."

Like so many other things, the gunners assignments would change if we became a lead crew, since the formation lead aircraft carried a radar antenna and dome where the ball turret was usually mounted. There would be a need for one less gunner, so they had to be shuffled around. But for now, Roever joined the other gunners Schodrof, Carr and Merchant and the rest of us to make up a Liberator crew of ten. And if you had called all ten of us "Beder's Innocents," you would not have been wrong.

As we began our operational training in the spring of 1944, it was becoming obvious that the war had gone beyond a turning point and the tide was running in our favor. The Battle of Midway had been fought the year before and the Japanese were beginning to see the handwriting on the wall. But the turning point had yet to be reached in Europe as the German and Russian armies seemed to be stalemated in the east, and the Germans still occupied all of France. The Battle of Britain had ended years before and German bombers no longer attacked London and other cities, nor did they have an invasion force poised in France to head for England. But the Germans now began to attack southern England with V-1 buzz-bombs, which might be called the forerunner of the cruise missile and which carried a powerful, one-ton conventional warhead. Later, the Germans began attacking London with V-2 rockets, and had the Germans developed atomic warheads at the time, the war would have ended differently. Meanwhile, it was U.S. bombers by day and British bombers by night flying deep into the heart of Germany.

The tide of the war might have turned, but that didn't mean fighting in it was getting easier. In fact, the war would very soon reach a level of fury and destruction like nothing this world had ever seen, on the ground, on the oceans and in the air, and we would be right in the middle of it. The Allies had not yet landed in Normandy, so our bombers were over enemy territory as soon as they crossed the channel. We could not know, back at Westover, that southern England was jam-packed with an invasion force which would soon change all that.

The Eighth Air Force, meanwhile, held fast to the idea of daylight precision bombing despite heavy, almost crippling losses in aircraft and crews. The missions were penetrating deeper and deeper into Germany. On March 6th, some weeks before we arrived at Westover, the Eighth flew its first big raid on Berlin and lost 69 bombers, the largest number on one raid. The previous August, Eighth Air Force Liberators had flown the famous low-level bombing mission to the oil field at Ploesti, Romania and out of 102 Liberators dispatched, 30 were shot down. A couple of weeks later, during a raid on the ball-bearing works at Schweinfurt and an aircraft plant at Regensburg, 60 more bombers were lost. "There were so many parachutes in the air at one time it looked like an invasion by paratroops," a friend of mine who had participated and had been shot down, told me later. But despite losses like these, our raids got bigger and bigger until finally the Eighth was sending over 1000 heavy bombers at a time.

I had thought, when I got to Westover, that since the base was close to Yonkers- only a few hours by train- I would be able to get home when I wished. This was not to be, as we were set up for a training mission every other day and in between, I was set up for sessions in the celestial navigation trainer. The CNT was housed in what looked like a large, fat silo containing a dome of accurately reproduced constellations which could be programmed to move as if the platform from which you took your sextant shots was moving at airplane speed. One nice thing about it was that the distance between the required fixes could be obliterated with the turn of a knob so that a six hour mission could be reduced to two.

Early summer arrived at Westover and we did manage to have some fun, mostly swimming at one of the lakes not too far away, and having dinner and a few drinks in Springfield or places close by. A fellow navigator friend of mine, a New England native, somehow managed what seemed to be unbelievable at the time; he drove up one day in his own car. Not only his own car, but it was a sporty 1936 Ford coupe complete with rumble seat.

One reason this seemed like such good fortune was that the girls around Springfield and Chicopee Falls were uniformly great, and there were lots of places to go. Fortunately for us, the dates were usually pretty strong-minded about how far we could go, and how late we could keep them up: in other words, they were "on" to us. Otherwise the next morning's flight could be tougher than it had to be. Besides, as the non-owner of the car, I was invited to take charge of the rumble seat, and as romantic as the idea might sound, romantic it was not. There might be times when the car was doing 10 miles per hour through a neighborhood perfumed by fragrant tree blossoms, with no glaring sun or staring curbsiders, that riding in the rumble seat might be considered pleasant. This never happened that I could remember since it was usually a matter of ducking the bugs or the wind-whipping slipstream or the cold night air that took away the fun. I try very hard not to look at things negatively, but given my experience, I am not surprised that the only rumble seat I have seen recently was a fake that was intended only for show.

Big John had been qualified to take the Liberator without an instructor, so our training as a coordinated aircrew started right away. We began by taking some short cross-country flights and I had to do a lot of map reading to keep our position straight, which kept me busy. There was a sense of feeling each other out since we needed to depend on each other to do the job right. I know that I kept a watchful eye on every landing Big John or Sam made, from "airfield in sight" to touchdown and I'm sure they wondered about me. I found out early on that putting on a confident air, no matter what, was crucial in my relations with the crew. This wasn't always easy, especially on days when you flew mostly in the soup and there was literally nothing to navigate with. Using a lot of hard work and concentration, you "educated your guesses" so that the headings and estimated times of arrival worked out within reason. With luck, they worked out right on the money and that's when you made some points. I had some good fortune on one mission out over the ocean east of Cape Cod where Big John was showing Sam some of the finer points in piloting the Liberator. We flew in circles, and short straight legs, and changed altitudes and generally wandered around about 150 miles off land. There was no way to get a fix of any kind under the circumstances, so I sat back, looking half asleep, but keeping an eye on the navigation instruments. I had reckoned the starting point, and kept a rough calculation of how far we departed from that point. I did manage to get a few drift readings on whitecaps below through the drift meter so I had the wind at our level pinned down.

Then I stood between the pilots' seats to watch them work and wait for them to finish. Finally, Big John looked over his shoulder and said, casually, "Okay, Matt, give me a heading home."

The Boston radiobeacon was too far out for us to pick up, but it was pretty much on course so I gave him a heading and ETA for it, something like 265 degrees and 45 minutes. My lack of hesitation made Big John look around at me once, but he came around to the heading and held it. As we got closer, the radio compass needle started to come around like it should, and even I began to believe the heading was good. By a staggering stroke of luck, the heading took us right over the station within a minute or two and I felt at that moment, over the Boston radiobeacon, that maybe I could relax a little, that I wasn't too much of an unknown quantity to the crew, or to myself.

We started to fly practice bombing missions with bombs packed with sand and small explosive marker charges to show Jack and the pilots how different it was bombing from the Lib compared to the planes they trained in. Then all of a sudden we were flying practice formation flights, complete with simulated attacks by P-47 Thunderbolts who came whistling through the formation and were gone in the flick of an eyelash before anyone could call them out. We were left to wonder if this was the way it was going to be.

Just about the time we were through at Westover, we were informed that our crew had been selected for additional training in "bombing through the clouds" techniques. This was fairly new and had apparently been developed reluctantly since it was not as precise as bombing with an optical bombsight. The need for it came about when bomber crews began reporting that targets were obscured by clouds a high percentage of the time and that missions were being wasted. The procedure substituted radar or radio information for the visual information which would not be available in bad weather, so the accuracy depended on how well the bombardier used his electronics. The winter weather in Europe had been found to be generally worse than predicted, and you had to be ready to bomb through the clouds with some precision or you dumped them uselessly at some jettison point. Once this training was completed, Jack Murray, Big John and Sam were assured of being assigned as a

Path Finder Force (PFF) aircrew which would eventually lead formations to the target, provided they made the grade in combat flying on somebody's wing for a while.

As for me and the rest of the crew, there was no special training to assure us of a lead crew assignment: we had to make the grade in combat to the satisfaction of Big John and the lead squadron commander. When the time came, they would need to have enough confidence in me to navigate a full wing of 90 aircraft and almost 1000 men or sometimes larger formations through the flak alleys and close enough for Jack to see the target, then point the way home.

We took the additional training at Langley Field, near Norfolk in Virginia. Langley was and is another one of those elegant old bases, with immaculately landscaped grounds and permanent quarters of brick and stone. Langley had been the base that Billy Mitchell used when he demonstrated, between the wars, that bombers could sink battleships. He generated a lot of new military thinking and got court-martialed as a reward.

Of course, there just so happened to be some "new construction" barracks at Langley with wood siding and tar paper roofs, out in what was apparently a recently drained marsh. We were quartered there, but at least we had the use of the Officer's Club and the swimming pool and with our schedule, we didn't spend much time in the barracks anyway. As for me, I took the delay with some strange feelings, like a moth who was being irresistibly drawn toward the flame, and is kept away.

Langley lasted only a few weeks and the time went as quickly as it did at Westover. The training primarily involved Jack Murray and the pilots so I only went along so I wouldn't feel left out. In the meantime, about the time we left for Langley, the European war really picked up speed when our side landed on the beaches of Normandy and as we approached the end of our training, our troops were fighting in the hedgerows of France. We got our orders to proceed to Bangor, Maine, which was the staging point for the Atlantic crossing, and we were, after all this time, suddenly on our way.

We went down to the flight line at Langley on a hot day in

August to fill out the flight plan for the trip to Dow. I looked out on the long ramp, at the hundreds of aircraft lined up in straight rows. The heat rose and shimmered from the square miles of concrete and I wondered if I would ever see this place again. We climbed into a jeep and got driven out to the airplane, which turned out to be a brand new, shiny silver, "J" model Liberator. The term "state of the art" wasn't used much in those days, but this was it. All of the improvements found necessary because of combat experiences were built in; better turrets, improved oxygen equipment, upgraded autopilots; the works.

A bomber parked on the ramp on a hot summer day turns into an oven and that day was no different. Our flight suits were soaked with sweat about one minute after we climbed aboard and took our places for the preflight checks. We each had our own checklist to complete, and after I went through mine, I got up out of my seat and stood between the pilots as they went through theirs so I could learn a little. Everything worked nice and slick, and Big John and Sam acted like kids in a toy store as they exercised some gadget that had been improved. The airplane didn't have that spilled coffee and hydraulic fluid stink we had become accustomed to. There were no scratches in the flight deck paint, the warning decals were all unchipped and readable, the windows and plexiglass domes were all diamond clear and un-crazed; it was like sitting in a new car you had just bought.

Morley reported that everything seemed to be ship-shape except for a whiff of high octane fuel odor in the bomb bay, which was a little worrisome, but not that unusual. The flight line crewman had been briefed on the engine starting sequence and he stood by number three engine, which was started first because it had a generator built in, and the crewman scrambled around as the other engines were started. Big John gave the signal to pull the chocks and gave the crewman a "thumbs-up" as we taxied to the run-up hardstand at the head of the takeoff runway. The airplane shook and bounced as each engine was run up to full power, then the checklist was completed. After calling the tower, we swung onto the runway and took off into the sunny, bumpy, Virginia morning.

As we got closer to Dow, Morley, who had been checking on

the fuel odor problem every so often, began to get a little worried as the fumes got stronger each time he went into the bomb bay. The gunners couldn't see any tell-tale plume of gas from the wing trailing edges but that wasn't much comfort. We pressed on and landed without incident at Dow, where we were parked away from other aircraft until the extent of the fuel leak could be determined. Sure enough, one of the fuel cells in the wing had developed a small rupture and would have to be replaced.

Well, at least it was cool at Dow even in August, and we would have plenty of time to get our briefing on the North Atlantic routes and get our survival gear issued. Our next stop would be either Gander Field in the middle of Newfoundland, or further north at Goose Bay in Labrador. Today, a flight to Gander or Goose is like any other flight but in 1944 it was looked at like a trip to the North Pole. Once you left Dow there was no civilization on the way to either place, nothing but several billion pine trees which lined lots of lakes and a few rivers and covered the low hills and an occasional mountain. There were also a couple of places where your magnetic compass became unreliable and sort of wandered around aimlessly for a short time. These effects were caused by large iron deposits around the Seven Islands area which was right on course to Goose. The remoteness of the destinations, the compass problems and the high incidence of poor flying weather caused the route to be treated with caution by those responsible for flight operations on it. The survival briefing, which included a lesson on how to use the flimsy looking survival rifle to kill an attacking bear; -the bullet will merely bounce off his forehead so aim elsewhere- and how to catch fish when you ran out of pemmican bars. We also got a detailed briefing on the rest of the route across the Atlantic to Valley, a U.S. aircraft maintenance base in Wales where we would most likely drop the aircraft off and proceed to our new base by train.

The flying weather, and the way it bunched up the transient aircrews in the pipeline determined whether you went to Goose or Gander, and whether or not you landed enroute at either Greenland or Iceland on the way to Wales. The briefing on Greenland was particularly detailed and raised some con-

cerns because of the forbidding terrain. There were two airfields there which might be used during the crossing:
Narsarsuaq, which was given the code named Bluie West One,
and Sondrestrom Fiord, which was called Bluie West Eight.
Narsarsuaq was situated on the southern tip of Greenland and
was fairly close to the main route, while Sondrestrom was
located further north on the west coast, near the Arctic Circle.
Both places had tricky approaches, especially Sondrestrom,
which was at the end of a long fiord with several kinks in it. It
was easily possible that there would be a low cloud deck just
above the surface of the fiord, which obscured the mountains
on either side. It was like flying through a tunnel until you had
the airfield in sight, which sounds simple, except that there
were other fiord entrances which, as you approached it at the
coast-line, looked like the right one. If you took one of those you
wound up in a blind canyon with no room to turn and fly or
climb out. There wasn't too much likelihood of going to
Sondrestrom except in an emergency, but Narsarsuaq, on the
southern tip of Greenland, was more on course and was frequently used. However, it was possible that landings in
Greenland might be avoided altogether, and we might fly
directly to Keflavik, in Iceland, which had fewer approach problems. We would have to wait and see.

The fuel cell got replaced and we left Dow for Goose Bay.
The weather was overcast but so clear that I could almost
count the pine trees along the way, and I could spot my checkpoints before we came abreast. As usual, we picked a flight
level where the winds were most advantageous and was below
oxygen altitude, generally considered to be ten thousand feet. If
we had several choices, we would pick one that was also reasonably clear of turbulence.

I was especially interested in what would happen to our
magnetic compasses in the Seven Islands area and when we
got there, I was almost disappointed when the main magnetic
compass barely wiggled. However, the standby compass which
was mounted on the windshield between the pilots, called the
whisky compass because the magnetic needle was floated in
alcohol, did swing from side to side ten or fifteen degrees. "But
after all," I told Sam, "it acts almost that bad when somebody

uses the relief tube." "And you're pretty sure that's where the iron is?" asked Big John, just to see if I had an answer. "You can call up the Canadians and tell them to dig right there!"

As we finished our descent over Goose and swept into a circular tactical approach, we looked down on a surprisingly large number of bombers parked all over the airfield. It didn't take too long after landing to find out that the pipeline had been backed up for days, as they were at Gander, due to bad weather all across the North Atlantic. Some crews had been there a week, and the number of transients was so high that they were being billeted on cots in the hangars.

The first night passed, and the next day dawned with no hope of clearing weather on the ocean. The boredom and pent-up anxiety mounted since any facility on the base able to relieve these symptoms even slightly was swamped. Wisely, they closed up the officer's and enlisted men's clubs, thinking that the first time they ran out of anything to eat or drink there would be a riot by the unfortunates in the rear of the line. A mob actually gathered at the entrance to the Officer's Club in the afternoon but it quickly dispersed when the Base Commander showed up. What saved the day was that the aircrews, almost to a man, had packed away a few bottles that had been going away gifts, or had been put aside "in case England ran out of whiskey." "And besides," said one of the pilots as he uncapped a bottle of bourbon, "they only have Scotch whiskey over there." This statement, of course, indicates that the upbringing of some of us had not been fully rounded.

Meals were a problem because of the long chow lines which required us to wait for some time only to find out that we were getting C Rations again, just like yesterday. I imagine an infantryman might read this tale of woe with some exasperation and let us know that he would be happy to have a few drinks of Canadian Club in an airplane hangar and eat C rations at a table instead of a foxhole. Of course, I have no answer for this; all I know is that there wasn't much complaining. We took our little nips of "C.C." and went to stand in line and made jokes about what C rations might be made of.

All of the gloom and boredom quickly disappeared when the weather over the ocean began to clear. When our turn came, we were briefed for a flight from Goose to Meeks Field at Keflavik, in Iceland. As for me, I was disappointed we would be by-passing mysterious and exotic Greenland.

Now, for the first time, the rest of the crew looked at me and wondered if I really knew my stuff. They could do their thing almost anywhere, on any flight; fly the airplane, drop bombs, send and receive messages and nothing changes too much until it comes time to do them in combat. But for the navigator, each long flight was something new, whether it was to cross an ocean or a trackless desert or fly in remote arctic areas. The first time you do any of those things is bound to tighten you up a little and I must admit I was apprehensive. The forecast weather along the route was still not too good and we expected to be in and out of clouds most of the time. I began to wonder if the sun would be visible at all so that I could get some astrocompass bearings to correct the magnetic compass. Not to worry, because we're going anyway.

We took off into a west wind with a full load of gas and as Big John made a climbing turn to our departure heading, I looked down and saw that quite a few of the aircraft were already gone, heading out over the Atlantic just as we were. As we climbed, we bumped around in some low scud for a while, and then we were in between layers as we levelled off at 9000 feet. There were occasional gaps in the undercast and I managed to read the drift and note our crossing point on the coast of Labrador. Suddenly, I knew everything I needed to know for a while and I gave John the heading and ETA to the next reporting point and to the next landmark, which was the southern tip of Greenland.

The astrodome was just in front of the pilot's windshield, and anytime I stuck my head up into it to scan the sky I would get a needling remark from the pilots or Jack Murray, who were sitting around without much to do except sip some coffee. I was able to read enough drift to keep us on course toward Narsarsuaq so I didn't have a lot to worry about.

One thing I had kept in back of my mind was that we should remain on course if we got enough navigational clues to do it, or else, to "lean" to the south of course. If information was sparse, we would not clear the icecap at 9000 feet if we got blown well to the north without our knowledge. We also had to make allowance for the weatherman's warning that barometric pressures around Greenland sometimes got so low that the actual altitude could be a thousand feet or more lower than our altimeter reading.

The weather started to close in on us, with the overcast and undercast merging at times, so there wasn't much I could do except modify the flight plan headings according to what I had observed, and pucker up a little bit. About halfway to Greenland, we tried to contact Ocean Station Baker for a radar fix, but couldn't pick them up. Baker was a U.S. Coast Guard vessel which took weather observations and provided navigational and rescue services. They sat out there week after week in some of the world's worst weather, and I have often wondered how they could keep their minds straight. Then I started to play with the radio compass to try to pick up the radiobeacon at Cape Farewell, at Greenland's southern tip. There was a lot of precipitation static caused by rain droplets flowing around the antenna housing, which blotted out the identification signal. But I could flip on the carrier wave switch and hear a tone on the right frequency which indicated that the station was on the air.

We had been briefed to use any radiobeacon signal with caution since German submarines were suspected of having broadcast signals intended to draw unwary navigators into the icecap. I felt a lot better when the radiocompass needle began to swing around to the front and I could faintly hear the call letters in Morse code through the static, but I still had to keep the German submarine warning in back of my mind. Our tailwind increased as we passed around the south of the low center over Greenland and, as the weatherman promised, the weather got bumpier and cloudier as we proceeded. Everything was quiet on the airplane for a while and the weather started to break a little, and better yet, the radiocompass needle steadied down to five degrees off our left nose, just where it was supposed to be. The ident came in clear and readable as we came closer to Cape Farewell.

The cloud cover developed some large breaks and we were

suddenly treated to the spectacular sight of the tall, jagged, snow-covered mountains of southern Greenland looming up into the clouds above us to our left. Somewhere below us were some hardy souls who cranked out the radio signal on which we homed and as we passed overhead, the radiocompass needle spun around the dial once or twice, then steadied to point behind us. Once again we knew our exact position, but we were not yet out of the woods. We had an even longer leg to fly to get to Iceland, and the undercast was closing in again.

There was rough, mountainous terrain in Iceland too, also higher than our flight level, so I couldn't put my feet up on the navigator's table and "coast" the rest of the way. We pressed on, and by the time we were a couple of hundred miles out of Keflavik, I started to pick up the radiobeacon there. Although German submarine interference with the beacon was even more likely around Iceland than at Greenland, I felt confident enough to announce that we should get ready to let down.

When we got to my ETA for 100 miles out, Big John got his descent clearance and pulled the throttles back without a questioning word, and we dropped down into the undercast.

It turned out the Keflavik radiobeacon was working without the assistance of some U-boat radio operator and we were suddenly crossing the blackened, dark gray lava bed on which Meeks Field was located. All of the tensions which had been built up in us and covered up by the occasional bantering suddenly began to dissipate and we got ready with the business of arriving.

The airfield was on a peninsula on the southwest corner of Iceland which had risen from the depths of the ocean 50 or 60 years before. The volcanic activity was fortunate, since it provided one of the few flat places on the island to build a large airfield. John got his landing clearance and practiced another 360 degree overhead tactical approach, and had to wrestle a bit with a gusty crosswind and short visibility to get the Liberator down. The "Follow Me" jeep met us as we turned off the runway and led us to a remote hardstand where the engines were shut down. Everyone got ready to get off for the ride to Base Operations and then the mess hall except for Morley who, as engineer , had to do a "walkaround" inspection to check the airplane for missing external parts, dripping oil, leaking hydraulic fluid or high octane. Someone would pick him up later.

The scene at Meeks must have looked just as it was up in the Yukon during the gold rush days, with the streets unpaved and the shack -like buildings set down here and there seemingly without much thought. Smoke from the oil-fired heaters of the larger buildings poured out of skinny little smokestacks and was blown off by the constant wind, but a fuel oil odor was left behind to permeate everything.

The aircrew pipeline was backed up again due to poor weather over the British Isles, and all the gathering places including the mess halls and the clubs were jam-packed with bomber crews. After having some supper we went over to the Club where the noise and laughter rose and filled the crowded rooms along with the blue cigarette smoke and the odor of beer. There was no place to hang your hat or heavy flying jacket so we all sat there, overheated and tired, sipping our drinks and trading exaggerated tales about the first leg of the ocean crossing, our excitement refusing to dissipate. There were rumors about one aircrew or another who never showed up at Meeks and perhaps were sitting up on the Greenland icecap, but there was no way we could be sure. Or perhaps they had overshot and plunged on into the ice fields and volcanos of Iceland, whose northern reaches brushed the Arctic Circle. If they did, they might have smashed against the same fog-shrouded mountain that claimed the lives of Lt. General Frank Andrews and his crew as they approached Iceland on a wartime inspection trip.

There were also some wild stories about the secret and forbidden paradise of Reykjavik, not too far to the north, which was said to have good restaurants and lots of Viking maidens, all blonde and over six feet tall. We slowly ran out of steam and made our way outside to wait for a ride to our quarters. The transport turned out to be a big Army six by six, which was okay with us and we clambered up into the back and sat on the slat seats for the long, bumpy ride to our hut.

We couldn't see much because of the low cloud and drizzle, but what we could see, looked like hell frozen over. The crushed-lava perimeter road wound its way around the sea-bottom terrain, and I couldn't help thinking that if the peninsula suddenly sank back into the sea, the fish would be right at home.

As at Goose, we had to sweat out the entire next day for the weather to break, and when the second morning came, we were all alerted and the scramble to leave began. As might be expected, the flight operations briefing room was crowded with navigators drawing up their charts and making up their flight plans. Our destination for this final leg of our trans-Atlantic crossing was, as expected, the Valley airport on the west coast of Wales.

When we were through, we got together with the pilots and got our briefing on the weather and the route. For about the fourth time, we were warned to give Mt. Hekla, a high, active volcano just north of course plenty of leeway on the climb-out, since it had already taken its toll a number of times. Big John, Sam, Jack and I were jeeped out to the hardstand where the rest of the crew were checking their gear. The refueling truck was just leaving and Morley assured us we had the right fuel load, so we got in, the pilots cranked her up and we joined the departure queue. There was an air of excitement as everybody hurried to get off, to get this last leg over with, just in case the weather shut things down again.

Big John made the takeoff into the blustering, drizzly western wind and brought the silver Lib around to a southeastern heading. We were in the soup again and bouncing around heavily before we climbed very high, but we could see some breaks here and there as we climbed along the south coast of the island. I caught a glimpse or two of the ice field near the base of Mt. Hekla, but not the volcano itself, and we appeared to be on course and well clear. We hadn't seen much of Greenland as we passed it, and all we really saw of Iceland was the hunk of recent sea-bottom we landed on. "Well," I thought, "maybe we'll see more of it on the way back." I had my fingers crossed.

This last leg seemed to take forever as we bounced around and the engines droned away. I couldn't do much but sit there and wait for a chance at a drift reading, and play around with the tuning dial of the radiocompass. I also listened to a sound I had become accustomed to; the beat of the propellers as they slowly drifted out of synchronization and had to be goosed back in by one of the pilots by using the RPM controls. Later on, propeller RPMs were controlled and synchronized with each other automatically. But at the time, it was a manual task and took a lot of attention. When a pilot heard the thrumming sound as a propeller started to drift off speed, he would look out of the window on his side and see a blurred shadow where one prop arc overlapped the other. If the two propellers were out of synch the shadow rotated, with the speed of rotation depending on how unsynched they were. The pilot had to merely flick his prop RPM control toggle switch until the shadow stopped rotating and the thrumming sound would stop. There was the problem of getting the two props speeds on one side synchronized with the two on the other side, and this had to be taken care of by teamwork between the pilots.

Occasionally while enroute somewhere, as the crew sat back and waited for the next checkpoint to come up, the tranquility would suddenly be shattered by a quickening Vroom! Vroom! Vroom! as an engine started to do its own thing. Everyone on board scrambled around to determine what was going on until the miscreant prop was identified and either re-synched or feathered and the engine shut down. It was enough to put an extra squiggle in your electrocardiogram.

Meanwhile, the beginning of our great adventure into the real world -our first Atlantic crossing- was drawing to a close. The radiobeacon at Bushmills on the coast of Northern Ireland had been tuned in without difficulty and we homed in on it. Big John got his descent clearance once more and we came down across the northern tip of Ireland, then across the Irish Sea and the Isle of Man and by the time we crossed the English coast we were below the clouds. We spotted the runway at Valley with some trouble since, like most English runways, they tended to blend into the countryside. Another tactical approach and landing and we were there, arriving in the Old World.

From the first moment I laid eyes on the British Isles, my whole concept of the beauty of a countryside, and landscapes, and towns and cities was not exactly changed but given firmer shape in my mind. The British Isles were no longer just mental images of Westminster and Big Ben and the Tower Bridge. Now they were the ground on which we stood and the cool, heavy air of a slightly rainy Welsh afternoon that we breathed, and the green, tranquil countryside that surrounded us.

We looked around us in wide-eyed curiosity, there on the ramp at Valley, a new bunch of tenderfoot Yanks, finished with our first big challenge and ready to take on the next. We were met by a cheerful Tech Sergeant who informed us that we might as well unload everything we owned, since the Lib would remain behind for "European Theater" modifications. He handed Big John a set of orders assigning us to the 576th Bomb Squadron of the 392nd Bomb Group (Heavy) of the 14th Bomb Wing of the Second Air Division of the Eighth Air Force; a jumble of numbers and units which would soon be straight in our minds. The 392nd was located at a small town called Wendling, near Kings Lynn in the eastern bulge of England and we were to leave the next morning by train.

There was the usual reunion of crews at the mess hall at Valley that evening and we all congratulated each other on making it this far. After all, we were really just a bunch of young guys with only several hundred flying hours at the most, yet we climbed into these complicated machines and flew them across a very demanding route in poor flying weather and got them to the other side in large numbers.

"There, I heard her. She actually said it," I said to Sam as we packed our B-4 bags and got ready to catch the train for Wendling, which was about 90 miles north of London.

"She said what?" he asked, as he stuffed his belongings into the zippered pockets of his bag. We both worked our way around a compact, black haired, blue eyed, middle-aged lady who hustled around to clean up the vestiges of our overnight stay at Valley to make it ready for the next crew. "She actually called me Leftenant," I said. "I'd give her a dollar and a kiss on the cheek but she might get the wrong idea."

There were dozens of crews already waiting on the railway station platform in town when we arrived by bus. For the first time since we left Westover, we were able to get all spruced up and into our pinks and greens and shiny shoes and trench coats. The slicked-up non-coms all looked handsome in well-pressed uniforms I hadn't seen them in before, proud of all their many hard-earned sergeants stripes. We certainly looked like an impressive bunch of flyboys.

Part of the train was reserved for us and when it arrived, exactly on time, we clambered aboard, jockeying around for the window seats. We were all suddenly quiet, savoring the moment of our first English train ride as we listened to the "All aboard!" and the slamming of the carriage doors, and then the polite warning toots of the steam engine's whistle.

The engine did some labored chuffing and spun its wheels, then tried again and we were off, away from the shadow of the platform and into the countryside, picking up speed. The train seemed almost like an elegant toy, with everything at half-size; the engine, the cars, the wheels, all on half-size tracks . The carriages were all spotless and the idea of soot, or graffiti or ripped upholstery seemed unthinkable. It was all straight out of an English movie, all polished brass and shiny woodwork. There was no trash along the right of way to spoil the view as we clacked and rolled our way eastward toward the various stops where the crews would begin to disperse as they changed trains for their individual destinations.

During one of the stops we had enough time to get out and get some of the large, thin ham or beef sandwiches which we would get to know and love or hate as time went on, along with mugs of tea. Some were curious enough to experiment with the meat pies and other exotic dishes and the first reactions were, well, mixed. The civilians we came into contact with; the trainmen, other passengers, the people waiting on the platform, all seemed to take us completely for granted. Yanks had been there for some time now, and everybody seemed to be as polite to us as they were to each other. We all tried to be on our best behavior, although the best behavior of a hundred or two young men in their earliest twenties who were headed for combat could get to be a little exuberant.

Our crowd thinned out as we went along and other crews left us for other trains, and as we changed trains too, we were down to just two or three crews, and finally, after another train change, there was just us. We pulled into Wendling station and wrestled with our B-4 bags, our musette bags and duffel bags and hats and coats, and then the train pulled out and we were on a small railway platform in this strange, pretty country, feeling suddenly alone. There were two old-timers sitting on a bench at the far end of the platform, their heads bobbing in conversation as they enjoyed some afternoon sunshine.

The stationmaster came out and directed us to a parking area adjoining the station and, sure enough, there was a trusty old six-by with a G.I. driver waiting for us. We loaded up in the rear and rolled out of the parking area and as we passed fairly close to the two old gents they suddenly stopped talking and looked at us, not with curiosity, but with some feeling I could not fathom in their gaze, and then we were gone down the road. The driver got carried away with all that horsepower and we had to hold on to our seats as he rocketed the big truck around the curves of the winding, narrow road. He slowed down only a little for the guard at the gate, then took off again, and before we knew it, we had arrived at the 392nd Bomb Group Headquarters which was in a square, camouflage painted building in the center of the administrative area.

The Group Commander, Colonel Lorin Johnson was standing there waiting for us as we came over the tail gate and took that long jump down to the ground. He looked young enough to be one of us kids and he probably noted our surprise when we saw the full chickens on his cap and on the shoulders of his leather A-2 jacket. The Colonel was a handsome, medium-sized guy who gave us a Hollywood smile and a firm handshake, and made us think he had been holding up operations until we got there, just the way he did with all the new crews. He looked and acted exactly as a Group Commander should, which also meant you behaved yourself when he was around.

Some of the brass from our new and immediate home, the 576th Bomb Squadron -one of four squadrons in the Group-came out and we all talked for a while. They had the confident, old-pro look of men who were just about finished with their combat tour, and carried no hint of the ultimate doom which would soon befall some of them not long after we got there.

We were handed over to the Adjutant, who had seen hundreds like us and who probably thought we all looked alike by now, and then the supply sergeant, who issued us bedding and folding chairs. As I signed my supply chit I noticed that the item "Officers mattresses" was crossed off and a tick was placed next to "mattresses, three piece."

When I asked the sergeant, "How come?" he shrugged and said, "The cots you're going to put them on are too small for the one piece mattresses." I started to get that old crewdoggy feeling as I had at Goose Bay, when we had been locked out of the Officer's Club, but what the hell, a sack is a sack.

The six-by driver took us to the sergeant's quarters, where our guys were to share a medium-sized hut with another crew. Then they took us to our huts, all painted in British brown-green-black camouflage. We were set up two to a hut, each with corrugated iron sides which curved from floor to ceiling and with just enough room for two cots, two folding chairs, a folding table somebody left behind and one of those- if you'll excuse the expression- goddam stoves. The stove was our only source of heat, and as the winter approached, keeping the thing going got to occupy our minds almost as much as combat. We were allotted one box of coal per week which we lined up for at the fenced-in coal pile behind the latrine on specified days and later on, we made individual sorties to the pile on unspecified days. Can you imagine;- officers and gentlemen sneaking up to a hole in the fence at dusk, looking furtively around as we picked out nice, goose-egg sized lumps and dropped them into sacks which we hid under our coats as we sauntered back to our huts. "But dammit, we're combat men and deserve to be warm," we would think , with just a little tinge of guilt.

Meanwhile, on that first day at Wendling, we dropped off our gear and bedding and had the driver take us to the Officer's Club. It too was painted in British camouflage colors, a low, square building like the Group headquarters, with black-out painted windows. To walk through the door was to be suddenly thrust back in time, to the movie "Dawn Patrol" perhaps, the version with Errol Flynn, with a bunch of young, clean-cut flyboys talking and laughing at the bar at the left of the large rectangular room. There was a big, sooted-up fireplace in the center of the wall across from the main entrance with a couple of flyers sitting on a beat-up couch, sipping and talking. On the right were more beat-up couches and stuffed chairs, with more flyboys, and beyond them, the entrance to the dining room. In the corner behind the stuffed chairs was an old, crank-up victrola and a pile of records which I am sure some interior decorator had thrown in for atmosphere. And if he was really good at his business, he would have included a copy of "It's a Long Way to Tipperary." I looked, but I couldn't find it.

The four of us -Big John, Sam, Jack Murray and I- walked over to the bar, trying not to act too much like new replacements. Big John squeezed in and got us some scotches and Wellington Ales -see how fast we picked things up?- and it didn't take too long to strike up some conversations with people who had been there a while.

Nobody, but nobody wanted to talk about combat missions. The old heads who were well along in their tour had a lot of questions about what things were like back in the States, and gave us a lot of hard, usable information concerning social activities as it involved English girls. It seems that London, with its Piccadilly Commandos was the playground of desperate men and that the classier relationships were made in other places. East Dereham, just beyond Wendling and a little beyond bicycle range, was a good place to start, even this late in the game. Next, there was King's Lynn, a much larger town up next to the Wash where the Yanks had not yet outlived their welcome, at least as far as the companionable young ladies were concerned. And moving up in the world, there was Norwich, the large cathedral city in the center of East Anglia, where the Sampson and Hercules -the Muscles Club- made its home. The Muscles Club was a very large dance hall where females from miles around, aged sixteen to who knows what, came to have fun with young English lads and, when the lads weren't looking, with the Yanks. People drank beers and gin and orange, and as they danced in the intimate darkness they were sometimes caught in the scintillating shafts of white light which radiated from the great, rotating crystal sphere hung from the ceiling.

Even the newer crews, who didn't have a lot of information about social activities, didn't want to talk about combat. They were the ones who taught us how to steal coal, and how to hold on to your own bicycle even though they all looked alike when the club closed. The same problem applied to your hat, which was thrown into the checkroom when you arrived, and we were told that the only crewmen who finished their tour with the same hat they started with were the ones who left ten minutes before the barkeep called "Time Please!" There wasn't much use worrying about it; the only ones who did were those who made a fetish of wearing their own hat.

We slept a little late the next morning, and my first impression when we awoke was that an earthquake was taking place. The metal sides of the hut shook, the stuff on the shelves bounced around, the very ground vibrated with a low, rumbling sound. "What the hell?" I started to say, when Sam, in his usual calm way, said, "The formation is just about together and they're passing overhead." He was right, as he usually was, and we listened as the thunder peaked and then started to diminish as they headed for the coast.

Our first move was to get dressed and hitch a ride to the supply hut, where we bought bicycles that belonged to crewmen who had finished up and departed for home, or to guys who sat in some Stalag, or to guys who were finished with bicycles forever. Then we pedaled down to the Club and showered and had some breakfast, which consisted mostly of "square eggs" which came from the powdered egg can and were made into square omelets. We ate them along with big, thin toasted slices of English bread and G.I. coffee, which was soon to make a tea drinker out of me.

It wouldn't take too long for us to discover that a local farmer set up shop every morning not too far from our site and sold real eggs out of the back of his tiny Morris Minor pickup. The eggs were fresh and sold for sixpence, about a dime in those days, and we would take them back and boil them on top of the stove in our canteen cups. We didn't have too much time to sit around as we had a lot of learning to do, and went through a number of briefings, including tips on how to evade capture if you bail out in enemy territory. We even took mug shots with mussed-up hair and rumpled civilian clothes for use on faked travel cards and were given instructions on how to use the evasion kits which we were to carry on all the missions. They also told us about the bunchers and the splashers -the

British radiobeacons- which were set up for navigating in the local area and could help you find your way home.

Time went quickly as we settled into the routine at Wendling, and the newness of an Eighth Air Force base in wartime England wore off . This gave us more time to think about the reason we came here; -to fly bombing missions. Uppermost in our minds was the big question: how soon would we go on our first trip? We had been at Wendling exactly one week when we got our answer: we were put on alert for a mission the next morning.

II

BOOK TWO

The B-24J
(Courtesy of General Dynamics)

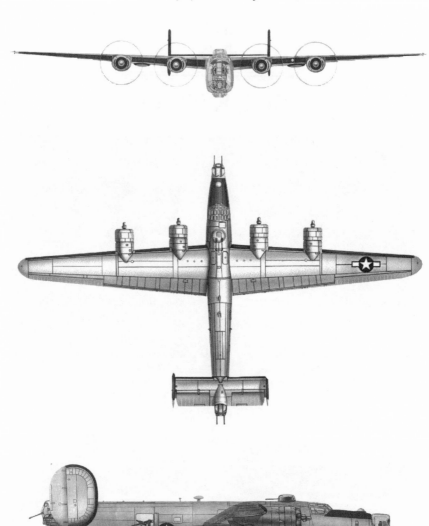

5

FIRST BLOOD

"**G**IVE ME A THIRTY-SECOND COUNTDOWN after this guy ahead goes," said Big John.

We were all a little tense as we moved and stopped, then moved again toward the take-off position. The "go" flare had been fired from the tower and the assembly marker aircraft, first in line at the head of the runway, took off. The queue moved up after each take-off as the loaded, lumbering Liberators nosed down and sent out a squeal each time the brakes were applied. Our turn was next when the Liberator ahead surged forward down the haze-shrouded runway. "Thirty, twenty, ten, nine, eight.. " I counted the seconds as the needle swept around on my hack watch.."three, two, one, go!"

Big John eased the four throttles forward deliberately and the props bit into the misty air and then we too were gone, first reluctantly, then picking up speed so slowly it seemed like forever and finally, we bumped the ground slightly a few times and we were off. Now was a crucial moment because loss of power in an engine on this heavily laden bomber could send us ploughing into the dirt, or stalling out and pranging in head-first; either way was fatal. We sort of held our breath while Sam kept a close eye on the engine gauges as the Liberator slowly dragged itself upward and the big landing wheels tucked themselves in. And then the moment passed us by as the air-speed crept up and suddenly we were up above the haze layer and into the clear.

111

Some of the tension seemed to drop away with the haze and we now had more to do than just wait. We could see the Libs which had taken off before us turning and climbing in a sweeping arc to the left, all chasing the gaudily-painted assembly plane, and we gave chase too.

The formation was already taking form as we slowly gained on the leaders, who flew in climbing assembly circles so that following bombers could catch up. There were so many other bomb groups forming over this one small part of East Anglia that Big John and Sam checked again and again to make sure we were forming on the right leader. As we came closer we could see the 392nd Group tail markings clearly, a black horizontal bar across the center of the silver rudders, so now there was no doubt.

I stood between the pilot seats and watched Big John slowly slide the Lib into position on the right wing of the second "v" in our squadron and then hold it as the formation continued its climbing assembly turn. We were toward the rear of the last of three squadrons in the 392nd Group, so although we were not tail-end Charlie, we were close to it.

All of us re-checked the flimsy again to make sure of what the next signal flare from the leader would mean. Almost all of this gigantic, complex maneuver was performed with minimum radio traffic, from the time of the green "go" flare to the leader's signal flare at the start of the bomb run, since the Germans could monitor most signals if they were passed by radio. Our anchor in the "formating" maneuvering was a radiobeacon called Buncher Five not too far from Wendling, and we would pass over this checkpoint twice, once during the Group assembly, and again at the final assembly altitude of 13,000 feet. There, the Groups would fall into their positions in the 14th Wing as the bomber stream set course for the "coast out" checkpoint, Great Yarmouth.

Because of our aircraft's position on somebody's wing, the navigator in the Group lead aircraft was navigating for us, and my main duty was to "follow" the lead navigator and have an accurate position and heading home at any time if we had to leave the formation. Celestial navigation was not practical on our bombing missions, so my main effort was to keep track of ground checkpoints when I could see them.

I had some time to look around in wide-eyed, excited wonder at all of this massive undertaking which we were part of. Jack Murray had a little more to do since he flew as nose turret gunner and had to make sure, when we reached the target, that the bombs went away, either by Radio Bomb Release - RBR- signal from the lead bombardier which automatically triggered our bomb releases, or by means of his own salvo switch if the RBR hung up. This is the way things would be until -and if- we got to be a lead crew.

When we reached 10,000 feet Big John ordered everyone to get set up on oxygen and I went down to my position in the nose to hook up my oxygen mask and set the mixing valve. Then I re-checked my electrically heated suit and gloves because the air which came streaming through chinks around the front turret would make the temperature inside the airplane same as the outside -minus 32 degrees Centigrade at the bombing altitude. We were not pressurized: no wonder Liberators were often called "whistling shit-houses."

The formation passed over radiobeacon Buncher Five for the last time at the assembly altitude and headed eastward for Great Yarmouth, and began the long, slow climb to the bombing altitude of 23,000 feet. By this time, the 392nd Group had been worked into position as the second of three Groups in the 14th Wing which was formed into a massive, stepped-down "v". The whole 14th Wing had been maneuvered into its place as the second of three wings flying one behind the other in the 2nd Air Division bomber stream. Somehow, the leaders of this operation had gotten over 300 Liberators, loaded with fuel and bombs, each in their assigned slot in their formations, in their desired spot in the sky, on time and on the correct departure heading for the bombing mission.

One of the two B-17 Flying Fortress Divisions -the Third- was not so lucky and the crashing and the dying started early. While forming to bomb the Henschel Motor Works at Kassel earlier in the day, two Forts came together and one of them crashed, but the crew was able to bail out. Another two collided during the assembly near Hitcham and 16 of the 20 or so crewmembers were killed. The formations had to reshuffle positions to fill in the blanks and proceed with the mission as if nothing had happened.

Our Division had also been scheduled to bomb the Henschel works but late intelligence had found a massive buildup of enemy trains at the railroad marshalling yards at Hamm, at the northeast end of the heavily industrialized Ruhr Valley. The trains were intended to supply a new offensive against our armies which were rolling forward in France at this time -October 2nd, 1944, four months after the D-Day landings. The original field order was cancelled and a new one quickly issued calling for an attack on the yards by the 2nd Air Division Liberators.

We came up on Great Yarmouth and as the English coast fell away behind us, there was a rustle of activity aboard as the gunners got ready to test fire their turret and waist guns. The Channel is wide at this point where it enters the North Sea, and when I informed Big John we were sufficiently clear of friendly territory, he gave permission to fire. There were great thudding noises as the gunners let go, firing down toward the water in short bursts, and you could feel the heavy recoil shake the airplane. All the guns checked out okay and were re-safetied for the moment, and everybody sat back again, watchfully waiting.

"How we doin', Matt," said Big John, to break the tense silence, and I could look out and see the enemy-occupied coast clear enough to be able to tell him "we are a little north, maybe 5 or 6 miles." I checked my chart again. "Looks like the leader is trying to get closer to the middle of this flak-free corridor near Ymuiden we've got marked on the flak coverage chart."

There was silence again except for the laboring engines on the climb and the amplified sound of each quickening breath I took through the oxygen system. And then we were on the coast, and somebody was yelling "Flak!" and sure enough, I could look down and see some black puffs far below as they tried to track us. It was our baptism of fire and, at the moment, it didn't look too impressive. The idea of a group of blood-angry people on the ground aiming large cannons at us with the idea of destroying the bombers in which we sat and killing us did not immediately come to mind. Later, perhaps.

The leader passed on the code word to begin dispensing chaff, the bundles of foil strips whose radar reflections painted jagged blips on the enemy radar altitude scopes, and as the flak puffs fell further below, it was obvious that the stuff worked. Apparently, the corridor was not so flak-free after all.

We were across Holland before we knew it, straight across the Zuider Zee just north of Amsterdam, and then the German border came up , the gates to the Fatherland, and time suddenly picked up speed. All of our surroundings: the farmlands and cities below, the skies in which we flew became threatening and it seemed a lot could happen to us, all of it bad, and there wasn't much we could do about it. The leader shot off another flare as we arrived at control point Three and the formation made a ponderous turn to the south, "uncovering" so that the Groups maneuvered from the defensive, massive wing front to the attack formation of a line of Groups headed straight for the I.P., the Initial Point, the start of the bomb run.

We were at the I.P. in what seemed like seconds and altered course a little to the left and this was it, everything we had trained for, everything we had been waiting for. We would bomb by radar because of expected cloud cover, but it seemed less than forecast. We came abeam of Munster, which meant we had three minutes to go and the flak started. The flak we had encountered at the coast had not prepared us for what we now met as we approached the target. A long curtain of black smudges formed itself across the sky before us, raining down shards of steel on the Groups as we pressed on.

And now the clouds below became more scattered, and the marshalling yards at Hamm spread out before us, the largest such yard in Germany, full of rolling stock with military equipment. The flak was becoming more intense as we approached the great sprawl of tracks and waited for the "Bombs Away!" In the middle of all this, Jack called me on interphone and said, "Look at your target chart. Is the leader heading for the right aiming point?" He was only two feet away in his turret, and he looked back at me through the little window, questioningly.

But now we were in the center of the barrage and we could

115

hear muffled pops as the bursts stayed with us and the batteries tracked us. I remember a thought flashing by: what if one of those 88's or 105's came right through the floor where I was standing, when -Blam!- a great black burst of flak exploded right in front of our nose and if it didn't hit Jack it could have scared him to death, but he was okay.

Someone started yelling, "Evasive action! Evasive action!" but the leader paid no attention. Then I began to notice with gathering dread that we had sailed completely beyond the yards and still hadn't dropped our bombs and Jack looked around at me, his look of confusion matching mine. At this point a calm voice cut into my consciousness; it was the leader saying, incredibly, "We're coming around for another run." A black, deadly anger welled up in me as the flak fell away for the time being, and I truly think I could have strangled the possessor of that calm voice if I could get my hands on him. My mind emptied itself of all the epithets I had learned up to now, along with some I had just created. We went around in a great, agonizingly slow circle, back into position for another bomb run. The lead bombardier had not been able to get his radar bombing act together, so here we came again.

We gave the man his second run and it was just as bad as the first time, but we made it and Jack yelled "Bombs away!" as his RBR light came on. Our system had received the drop signal from the leader, and he flicked his toggle switch to make sure ours went too.

We turned off the target toward the east and the flak quickly fell away again. I tried to look out of my left window to see what happened to our first bomb load dropped in anger, but there were too many clouds, too much smoke for me to see, so we would have to wait for the bomb camera photos, provided we got home to see them. The line of attacking Groups proceeded to the Rally Point to the east of the target after all the bombs were dropped. and as the formations turned first northward, then westward toward home, they formed again into the defensive, winged "v" front to prepare for fighter attacks. The course home was laid out to avoid heavy flak concentrations in the area, and to pick up a reverse of the penetration route for the return through Holland.

About this time the whole crew was feeling pretty relieved. Despite facing the German flak twice, no Group aircraft was knocked down and we had reached the target and dropped our bombs. For myself, my fear-driven anger had evaporated at the rally point and I began to feel a little sheepish, and also thankful I hadn't said anything out loud. And how I envied the possessor of that calm voice, who, in the middle of the flak, a man just like me, who could think about an 88 coming through the floor just as I did and disregard it, and get on with the bombing. Could I ever be like that? I made a vow to myself just then, in the middle of my first mission, that I would sure as hell try.

We re-crossed the German border and came abeam of Amsterdam where the slow letdown began. Crewmembers started to unhook oxygen masks and sneak a smoke despite the hazards of smoking on oxygen. Thoughts of getting on the ground and out of the chute harnesses and Mae Wests and heated suits and all the other uncomfortable gear prevailed.

I watched as some of our fighters showed up, some Mustangs, who patrolled above us in lazy, sweeping arcs. Our relative motions gave them a grace and apparent speed which was as unreal as it was beautiful. From somewhere in our formation, from someone who watched the P-51's as I did, a radio voice called out, "Hey, little friend, how about a slow roll?"

One of the fighters above us suddenly swept up into a beautiful, precise roll. In that instant, just as he reached the top, he was struck by a direct flak burst and disappeared in a flash of light. Only pieces remained and they fluttered down toward the green-brown checkerboard earth, glinting in the sunlight as they fell. There was some yelling and scrambling around as we awaited more flak, but our gunners had already been dumping what chaff they had left from the bomb runs and the puffs chased the foil strips down and behind us. The firing had come either from barges or railroad flatcars moved in to cover the often used route we had flown, and would be withdrawn and moved in again some time.

I tried to peer back toward where the Mustang fell and could see nothing, not even a trail of smoke. I have often wondered who that young man was who couldn't resist showing off that great little fighter. Perhaps at some time when he was a teen-aged kid, he had come close to an airplane for the first time, on some sunny afternoon, and reached out and touched it, and the magic reached back and gripped him too and carried him to that point over Holland on that day. Sometimes, even now, when I hear the name "Mustang" I think of this event, the first time I had seen an airplane shot down, this first blood, and no matter what I am doing, a pang of regret strikes my heart.

The intelligence hut was still crowded with aircrews when we got there, even though we were one of the last Liberators to peel off and land and, being new at post-mission procedures on our first mission, it took extra time to get unplugged, unsnapped, unzipped and unloaded. The place was a riot of noise as the flyboys sat around sipping on several ounces of Old Overholt medicinal whiskey, courtesy of Uncle Sam.

The debriefings weren't taking very long because nothing unusual was being reported and when our turn came, this Captain looked at Big John and said, "Notice anything new on this trip?" and all Big John could say was, "This was my first trip. I wouldn't recognize something new if it bit me in the rear end." We all laughed and that was the end of it.

We got up and went into the intelligence library where a sergeant was in charge of the booze, and he asked us each to sign in while he poured a nice, healthy splash into aluminum canteen cups. I noticed the sign-in roster was very long and included names like Napoleon Bonaparte and Adolf Hitler along with real names and I came to find out that the sergeant would pour a whiskey for anyone two or three times, provided the drinker signed the roster each time and didn't use the same name twice.

Morley, Murgatroyd and the gunners took off and the two pilots, Jack Murray and I found seats and sat there sipping the strong liquor, suddenly too drained and tired to move. We were more relieved than anything that we made it through the first one, but also in a slight state of shock. Were they all going to be like this? And it wasn't only the enemy activity, but all the noise and cold, and sucking on oxygen for hours on end from a mask strapped tightly around our faces, and mostly, the weight of all that crap we had to wear the whole trip: the long johns, the heated suit, the flight suit, the Mae West, the chute harness, the big boots. And on the bomb run; the flak vest and helmet, the weight of which really wore you down by the time you got to the rally point. Of course, some of us sat on the flak vest rather than wear it:- first things first.

We sat there, not thinking about anything except finishing the drink and getting a shower and maybe some food. Now had we been more experienced combat men, we might have noticed that something unusual actually did happen, something that didn't quite add up. Why, we should have asked, did the chaff work over the Dutch coast but not on the bomb run? Over Holland the descending tin foil drew the flak bursts like a magnet, but on the bomb run it seemed to have no effect at all, and the bursts stayed with us like a swarm of hornets.

We were also to learn, as time went on, that news concerning our Group's combat losses was not circulated routinely; you usually heard about it over at the Club. For one thing, it often took days to get the loss picture all sorted out since some of the aircraft that did not return with the Group may have landed elsewhere for any number of reasons, or may have made it over the target and most of the way back, only to ditch in the channel or crash land on somebody's farm.

News of losses by other B-24 groups or the B-17 divisions was even more difficult to come by, partly because of security and mostly, I think, because it wouldn't serve much purpose to tell us and let us dwell on it. After all, the bombers were going to go as soon as the next field order came out, no matter what.

As a result there was no way of knowing that on our mission, two Liberators from other Groups were shot down and half of the 296 bombers which made it to the target were damaged by the flak to one extent or another. For these reasons we hadn't heard much about a mission a few days before ours, on the 27th of September involving the 2nd Air Division's attack on the Henschel Motor Works at Kassel, the same target which had been cancelled out for us and replaced by the Hamm rail yards.

Several things transpired to set the stage; first, one of the Liberator Groups, the 445th stationed at Tibenham moved slightly out of the main bomber stream and thus left whatever protection there was in the collective firepower of the massed formation. A heavy snowfall had obscured the ground checkpoints and radar was being used to locate the target. Unfortunately, the radar operator in the group lead aircraft mis-identified the target city and headed the thirty-six plane formation toward Goettingen instead.

Slowly, the group drifted apart from the Liberator bomber stream, separating itself from the train of formations strung along the flight track for sixty miles. The radar bombardier tracked the nebulous blob which he presumed to be his target at Kassel and then it was Bombs Away! and the thousand pounders dropped down into the clouds below.

Next, the U.S. fighter escort was in the area but not, at that moment, very close to the 445th, which was now about ten miles from the other groups.

Finally, a Luftwaffe "Sturmgruppen," a large wolf-pack of heavily armed Focke-Wulfs and Messerschmitts, more than a hundred of them, were in the right place and observed this opportunity and moved in for the kill. They came in from low and behind in waves, their 20 and 30-millimeter cannons blazing, scattering the formation, turning the bomber vulnerability into near helplessness. In the first three minutes, twenty-five of the 445th Libs were shot down. The fury continued as the Mustangs arrived to engage the determined German fighters in a wild battle to try to prevent the Luftwaffe from finishing the massacre.

The Sturmgruppen pilots were no longer conquering aces: they were desperate men who were trying to defend the Fatherland from the catastrophe that had befallen them. They had vowed to steel themselves against the curtain of fifty calibre bullets which the American formations raised against them, to approach so close that their gun-sights were filled, from left-most engine on one side to right- most engine on the other, so that they could not miss. And many of those gunsights were newly designed so that deflections were computed automatically:- just center the target and shoot. They were to find that they worked amazingly well. They poured all that firepower into the bomber formation, and by the time the carnage ended, thirty of the 445th Group's thirty-six Liberators, each with ten crewmembers were shot down, and the remaining few were heavily damaged.

The Tibenham crews must have felt as if they had run into a stone wall in the sky. The few remaining survivors limped home toward friendly bases, with dead and dying crewmembers aboard. Twenty-nine of the German defenders were knocked down, mostly by the Liberator gunners.

The losses further depleted the ranks of experienced Luftwaffe pilots, and those who survived and dodged the Mustangs, looked upon their victory with amazement. It was almost a fluke, but it could happen again if their ground radar control and the concept of the sturmgruppen continued to work.

What would it have been like, I wondered, if that disaster had been inflicted on our group instead, on our first mission, when in the time it takes for a clock's second hand to tick three times around the dial, to have virtually the entire group obliterated; to have Liberators exploding around you or just coming apart, or taking that long, long fall, wrapped in flames, smashing into the ground. To finally make it back to Tibenham alone and thinking you were the only one left, and when the man in the control tower, confused, asks you, "Where is the Group?" and you reply, "I am the Group!" What would it have been like to walk into the half-empty living quarters or clubs or mess halls, everyone stunned and quiet, sitting around feeling lucky and guilty and threatened, contemplating your friends' immediate, short past and your own possibly short future?

Operations officer Jimmy Stewart, no longer an actor but an honest-to-God combat pilot, tried to know what it was like as he debriefed the returning few and could not help but compare the three-minute cataclysm to some of his own tough missions, including the one to Berlin. But the visions of horror were ungraspable: I cannot grasp them today.

But the young crewdogs of Tibenham did not have the time to sit around and grasp horrors. Of the remaining warriors; ten aircrews were picked for the ten Liberators they had left. They awoke in the next morning's darkness and biked down to the flight line to take off on their next mission, keeping a wary eye on the more threatening shadows of doom which now dogged them. There was no corpse-strewn Antietam for them to pass by on their way to their Liberators, just that same old yawning abyss which was always there, wider than before. The target?

121

The same one -Kassel; but this time the Luftwaffe had other things to do.

The organizing of the Sturmgruppen and the tactics they used were logical responses to what had befallen the Luftwaffe since D-Day. The arrival of swarms of Mustangs on the scene and their destruction of a large part of Germany's fighters both in the air and on the ground, along with most of their experienced pilots, caused the Luftwaffe to conserve their planes and men for situations when they could be most effective.

Not only were the Mustangs a superior fighter, they also had the fuel range to escort bombing missions deep into Germany. In the good old days before D-Day, the Luftwaffe Messerschmitt 109's and Focke-Wulf 190's could wait until the escort had to drop off and head back, approach the now unescorted bomber formation from the rear, pick out a likely looking prospect and, almost leisurely, knock out the tail gun, move into the blind spot and then proceed to chop the helpless bomber to pieces.

Mass attacks by German fighters happened in those days too, wiping out entire squadrons at a time, often enough so that the idea of large bomber formations being able to defend themselves adequately using their own fifty calibers became more than suspect. The need for long range Mustangs had become critical.

In that terrible time, before the long range fighters showed up, the Generals must have had some agonizing decisions to make, to back off or to press on whenever disasters occurred, like the periodic bloodbaths inflicted on the hapless "Bloody Hundredth," a Flying Fortress bomb group which the Luftwaffe had chosen to attack with a particular fury, or like losing 60 bombers on one mission to Schweinfurt.

Our own Generals were all combat men: our wing commander; Brigadier General Leon Johnson, who was awarded the Medal of Honor for leading one of the two Liberator groups on the wild and dangerous low-level raid on the Ploesti oil fields, and his boss: Major General "Big Dog" Kepner, commander of the 2nd Air Division -a little guy- who liked to jump into his souped-up Mosquito twin-engined bomber and make sure our formations were nice and tight on the bomb run; and his boss;

Lt. General Jimmy Doolittle, Commanding General of the Eighth Air Force who was awarded the Medal of Honor for leading a group of B-25 Mitchell bombers off the aircraft carrier Hornet to bomb Tokyo that first time.

And somewhere in this aerie of courage and determination was an up-and-coming young general named Curt Lemay, sometimes called "The Cigar" but usually referred to as "Iron-ass Lemay," who had already made his bones many times over, including Regensburg. The target that day was an aircraft plant deep in the heart of Germany, and the unescorted formations being led by Lemay were attacked by fighters which came early and pressed home their attacks for hours. Colonel Bierne Lay, who co-wrote "Twelve O'clock High," watched the battle from a pilot's seat and described how they flew through a rain of airplane parts, bodies and falling crewmembers trying to get their chutes open as they pressed on.

On the other side, the Luftwaffe side, was Adolf "Dolfo" Galland, the brilliant young General of the day fighters. When we arrived in the autumn of 1944, he had just about completed accumulating and dispersing his forces of three thousand fighters, including a growing number of the new ME-262 jets. His plan was to conserve his strength until it could be used for one gigantic, crunching attack which was to be the Great Mother of all air battles. They would brave our Mustangs and Thunderbolts and the curtains of fifty caliber fire from the bombers and try to shoot down five hundred Liberators and Flying Fortresses in one blow. They would take out almost five thousand crewdogs at one time, killed or captured, at a price of perhaps five hundred German fighters, a price he was prepared to pay.

Dolfo, of course, did not inform the people who wrote news reports and compiled statistics concerning his intentions, so they announced to the world that the back of the Luftwaffe had been broken. But the bomber crews, hearing about the 445th at Kassel and other events, referred to the surviving Luftwaffe as "the Spineless Wonders." A little bit of irony there.

6

FIVE POUNDS!

I HADN'T ANTICIPATED THAT MY SERVICES as a solo navigator in combat would be needed quite this soon. After debriefing our first mission to Hamm we all thought, for some reason, we would be off for a day or two and then go again. As it turned out, while we were having dinner that evening at the Mess, we were informed that we were again on alert for the mission the next morning.

They're coming a little fast, I thought, but at the same time feeling that the sooner we got the missions over with, the better. And now, here we were at 23,000 feet, going down the bomb run to a target at Gaggeneau, well into the southern part of Germany, near Karlsruhe. The aiming point was a Daimler Benz plant that made armored vehicles.

Had everything gone according to routine, this probably could have been classed as a milk run since the flak over the target was forecast to be light and inaccurate. There were reports of German fighters massing around Luxembourg on our way down, but the attack never materialized.

It was about this time that during my movements around the nose compartment to look out of the side windows for confirming landmarks through breaks in the clouds, my oxygen hose coupling unsnapped without my knowledge. Normally, there is an immediate, different "smell" when this happens, especially when your altitude is up in the thirties, but at 23,000 feet, the difference is so slight that a busy person might

124

not notice it, and I didn't.

This happened often enough, especially to crewmembers who were not strapped into a seat or a turret, that crews were required, when on oxygen, to check in over interphone at a periodic command from the pilot. I was lucky Big John and Sam took this procedure to heart, and as Sam polled the crew and I missed a call, Jack, in the front turret turned around and saw that I was sitting there at my desk without movement, my head cocked over to one side, my eyes closed.

"Since we had just been told to look for fighters and we would be on the bomb run soon, I didn't figure Matt was just taking a nap," said Jack.

He couldn't leave his turret, so Big John sent Murgatroyd down with a walk-around oxygen bottle to check on me. Murgy later told me that when he came through the tunnel and reached me, he thought I was dead. My face was bluish-gray and I didn't appear to be breathing, but as soon as he plugged my loose hose back into the oxygen system, I came to in a second. A few weeks later one of the squadron tail-gunners was not so lucky: he was already gone when he was checked after missing a call.

With all crewmembers again conscious and breathing, we were just about at the initial point and turning for the bomb run when #3 engine -the inboard engine on the right side- lost power and started to stream smoke. Fiddling with it didn't do any good and Big John told Sam to shut it down and feather the prop.

John decided to press on to the target even though we couldn't keep up the speed and we slowly began to slide out of the formation. We had to make sure we didn't drift underneath another formation and get dropped on, but it looked clear above us. We would not be able to drop on the leader's RBR since we were out of position. Instead, we would have to maneuver over the head of the trail of a smoke marker bomb which dropped with the leader's main load. This smoke bomb popped a few seconds after the bombs went and as it travelled down with the bomb load, it marked it's path so that it would show up in the strike photos.

Jack and I quickly agreed on a procedure to make

allowance for the drift of the marker path caused by the flight level winds, which were substantial. Jack eyeballed the airplane into the calculated position as best as he could by giving headings to Big John and then salvoed the bombs, "with my fingers crossed," as he put it.

We had done the best we could and now here we were, feeling about alone as crewdogs can get. Had we dumped the bombs as soon as the engine quit and concentrated on cutting the turns short to keep up with the formation as they turned for home, we could have stayed with them longer. But they became a slowly disappearing bunch of dots, and then they were gone altogether.

The flight plan hadn't been too far off so the flight level wind forecast appeared to be usable. Besides, it was all I had, as Europe now appeared to be covered with clouds, and I was forced to use dead reckoning without any confirming fixes. If the Germans knew they had a straggler, they ignored the chance and we proceeded unmolested. The threat of flak dropped behind us also, and as we neared my estimate of the French coast crossing we began our letdown. The clouds started to break a little as we got lower, and there were enough holes to let us see that we had crossed the channel and were over England. As we crossed the Thames I could look to the west and see the smoky mass of London, but then we were in the soup again. Fuel began to be a problem, and as I gave Big John a heading for Buncher Five and tuned it in, we dropped lower, less than a thousand feet above the ground, just below the cloud deck.

As the fuel sweat got more intense, Big John spotted an airfield off to the left which wasn't on my map but looked big enough to take us so he turned off and made a straight-in approach. As we crossed the runway threshold red flares started arching up just off to the side, and we all knew Big John was going to have some explaining to do to some RAF base commander. After all, it was just about time for tea, you know, and we hadn't been invited.

As I think again about the events of this second mission, I've got to say that it represents the low point of my performance in combat. Although I helped in getting the bombs off somewhere near the target, and I navigated us back to England, my carelessness in the matter of the oxygen coupling makes me wince when I think about it. As for my navigation, I think it was okay under the circumstances but I didn't feel too good about having to sidle up to a RAF ground crewman after landing and whispering, "Hey chap! What the hell's the name of this airdrome?"

After a scrubbed mission and two days off, we were alerted for our third mission, which was not a charm. The target was Hamburg, which was not only one of the deeper penetrations, it also had the most formidable flak defenses of any target in Germany except for Berlin. It had 300 heavy guns, we were told, 88's, 105's and the big 128's. The 105's seemed big enough, but as for the 128's, I remember sitting there at the briefing thinking they must be as big around as the cannons used to shoot out human cannonballs at the circus.

We were not yet combat-wise enough to have a knowledgeable reaction as the target was revealed to us at the briefing. And luckily, we were not in the same frame of mind as the crews who had been involved in missions like the one to Schweinfurt, some time before, which had made the Generals wonder if the daylight bombing program could withstand such losses. As the crews were being briefed to be sent to Schweinfurt a second time, the briefer finished by wishing them "Good luck, good bombing and good hunting!"

"And good-bye!" yelled someone from the rear. It brought the house down.

Colonel Johnson, our group commander, did the briefing for this one since he would lead the mission as command pilot aboard the group lead Liberator. He didn't tell any jokes, but he was calm, almost nonchalant, and I noted how steady his hand was as he moved his long pointer around the wall map. "We will try something new on this one," he informed us, and then described how we would do the bombing in smaller, six-plane elements for better maneuverability in the flak.

Our group's aiming point was the Heinkel aircraft plant, while the other groups were going after the oil refineries. We were still more than 100 miles away when we could spot the target area because of a column of black oil smoke which had almost reached our level . The lead groups had already dropped their bombs and apparently hit the oil storage tank farm.

We were headed east and about forty miles short of the target when we made an abrupt turn to the south which would look to the Germans like a move first toward Bremen, then Hanover. But we turned east again, then north toward the Initial Point, 30 miles southeast of the target, uncovering from the great vee formation into six-bomber elements as we flew on. Then we were at the I.P. and on the bomb run, and as we looked forward we could see what the sky looked like over a target very heavily defended by flak guns. As we bore down on the run, I didn't see how it was possible to enter that boiling mass of flak bursts and survive, and I could taste that strange, gritty taste of mortal danger in my mouth.

I put on my flak helmet, and took the chance to stick my head up into the astrodome for a quick look back into the windshield at Big John and Sam, as I had often done in the past. What I saw were two flak helmets looking like dark gray turtle shells, each with a pair of eyeballs underneath, looking at all that flak, but determined. And then we were in this storm of flak in a deadly, waiting silence, driving down the bomb run, the Liberators moving up and down slightly in the mass of prop-wash, bomb-bays open, the formation spread slightly so that a wounded, swerving bomber would not take another with him. The lead bombardier had the target in his bombsight and we pressed on, straight as an arrow, the flak bursting all around no matter where you looked, the jagged, tearing fingers of steel reaching for us, and then the bombs were away and the formation made a quick, sharp turn to the right.

We were out of the flak so quickly I felt we had cheated fate and the Germans. The target area, I recalled in all that turmoil, had been obscured not only by the smoke from the conflagration at the refineries, but also by smoke generators which ringed the target and did a pretty good job of denying the visual bombing option. But after our right turn to the east, we turned north and then west toward England, and started the long ride home.

It seemed unbelievable that the entire group made it through the flak, although a third of the aircraft across the target sustained some damage.Our target had been situated toward the edge of the flak coverage, and our quick, six-plane turn to the right got us out of there quickly. However, the large number of such small formations created other problems, and I never saw the idea used again.

Our B-17 colleagues in the 1st Air Division bombed less defended targets in the same general area, and came out about the same. But the 3rd Air Division B-17's had been sent to "Big B"-that most dreaded of all targets, Berlin- where the Germans had promised that a price would have to be paid each time. And pay they did, with 14 Fortresses shot down in a few moments in a mass fighter attack. More than half of the 400 Forts were damaged, some so badly they couldn't make it back home.

And now, we all thought, was time for a little rest, but it was, again, not to be. We were alerted once more for the next day's miss ion and went through the same ritual; early to bed, a fitful sleep, the CQ -Charge of Quarters- looming in the darkness of the hut, his flashlight directed toward the floor as he gently rattled the end of the cot. "Briefing in one hour," he would say, almost in a whisper and he would be gone to the next fitful sleeper. Then a quick shower, and a hardly noticed breakfast of square eggs with toast and the newly discovered tea, followed by a short bicycle ride to the Operations briefing hut.

This time the Ops Officer pulled back the curtain on the big wall chart and ribbon snaked across the channel past Ymuiden, then turned east by southeast deep into the heart of Germany behind the Ruhr Valley. I strained forward and saw that it was Kassel, the site of the 445th massacre.

Our group had two aiming points; the marshalling yards and an adjoining tank works. The flak was forecast to be "moderate," but that word gave me a bit of trouble. "Moderate? Moderate? How can flak be moderate?" I griped under my breath. I guess four missions in six days was making me a little nitpicky about the briefer's terminology.

We came in over Ymuiden again, this time with a wary respect, but nothing happened, not one burst of flak. Was this a good omen? Or had our friends with the flak barges merely been hostage to the tides? We would soon see. Meanwhile, the 1st Air Division flying Fortresses were sent to bomb oil targets again, with a big, augmented group attacking Politz in a very deep penetration beyond Berlin, near the Polish border. Seventeen bombers were shot down by flak and most of the remainder of the 142 aircraft were damaged.

The rest of the 1st Division B-17's attacked another oil target at Ruhland near Dresden and lost three more. The 3rd Division Flying Forts were hit just as hard on another very deep penetration near Dresden where sixteen bombers were shot down by fighters, eight of them from one group.

We pressed on toward Kassel, in the center of Germany, and the first enemy reaction we got was an unexpected encounter with flak in an area between Munster and Osnabruck where no batteries were marked on the flak chart, otherwise we would have avoided it. No one was hit. The I.P. was reached and we made our bomb run into the gathering storm of flak waiting for us. It didn't look anywhere near as bad as Hamburg, but we were in the stuff longer and the bursts were in the midst of the formation. Suddenly, one of the Libs in our group was staggered and he headed in a downward glide, a streamer of smoke and flame coming from his right inboard engine. The streamer became a great sheet of fire and he tried to slip the crippled bomber to the left to keep the flame away. Then he dropped faster, and the fuel tank behind the burning engine exploded and the right wing came off, and the crewdogs' fates were sealed. Next, the lead aircraft slid out of the formation, feathering first one propeller, then another as he turned off and began to lose altitude. But there was no fire, and as he descended, he took up a heading toward the northwest in search of an emergency airfield. The Deputy leader quickly moved into the lead position and completed the bomb run, but the disruption caused by the flak had taken its toll, and the bombing results were only fair.

The subtle, subconscious defenses which arise in a man's mind at such a time arose in mine, and as we headed home, I could picture the falling, burning Liberator in my mind, but that's all it was: a falling, burning airplane. When my mind tried to grope with the idea of what was happening to the crew

130

as the Liberator fell, it shunted the picture aside to be looked at later, or maybe never. After all, they were not us; that navigator was not me; they were in the wrong place at the wrong time, and that would never happen to us. And if we ever got hit, I would be sure to get out and get my chute open and land okay to sneak through the German lines to get back. And who was to say I was wrong?

More than 1400 heavy bombers had been dispatched on this day and 40 of them were lost over the various targets, including an additional two from our wing. A number of other heavily damaged aircraft crash-landed or ditched in the water. And some damaged Forts turning off the Politz target made it to nearby Sweden where they either landed or crash-landed and were interned. The business of landing in Sweden was not looked upon with a lot of favor, although it is obvious that bailing out or crash-landing in Germany was the only other alternative in most cases. The word was passed to us that the actions of any crew heading for Sweden or Switzerland would be closely scrutinized. One thing that didn't help much was a picture that appeared in the Saturday Evening Post magazine showing an interned bomber crew living it up in a Swedish night club.

When we lost the engine at Gaggeneau, the Swiss border was only 70 miles away, something I hadn't realized until many years later. The only thought, in Big John's mind, and in the minds of the rest of the crew at the time, was to get it back home. Getting interned usually meant that the flyers were repatriated after a while under an agreement that they would not again be assigned to combat duties in Europe. However, the agreement did not contain any objection to their assignment to combat in the Pacific. So all you did was to jump from one frying pan into another.

The Swedes and the Swiss let it be known that the landing of damaged bombers in their sovereign territory was a great bother and interfered with their desire to remain neutral at all costs. The Swiss were able to remain aloof from the raging holocaust which surrounded them, concentrating their efforts on making watches and running international banks.

We did bomb Switzerland several times, obviously by accident. Basel, on the northern border and Zurich in the Swiss interior were both bombed by small U.S. formations in the last few months of the war. But is was the bombing of Shaffhausen, a small Swiss city directly on the Swiss border with Germany about six months before we arrived that revealed how precarious the navigational situation could get sometimes, and how a bombing mission could become completely unglued. Combat damage, an error in the flight level wind forecast, poor judgement and navigation equipment inadequate for the task overwhelmed the mission leaders and they bombed an innocent city, this time with a large formation. It was a classic example of desperate human minds trying to force reality to conform with an image, to distort the radar image into something they wanted to see instead of what was really there.

And as for the Swedes, they were able to run factories which provided war materiel to the Germans without fearing any reaction from us involving the use of force. We got away with the same thing supplying the British for a long time when we were supposedly neutral . For a crewdog driving through enemy flak, the idea of business as usual was hard to understand.

We had gotten so accustomed to being put on alert that we didn't think about it any more; we just took it as it came. So, naturally, the Operations Officer surprised us again by telling Big John his crew was on "stand down" for at least a week, and all of a sudden we had all these plans to make: go here, go there, see this, do that. It was amazing how easily we were able to switch our minds from those of young warriors to tourists anxious to collect impressions we might entertain our families with. Of course, we had to survive the warrior phase if the impressions were to be lasting.

The first thing we did was to relearn how to sleep late. And the next was to begin exploring the local countryside outside Wendling. Sam and I would usually get washed up and hop onto our trusty Raleighs and bike on over to see the egg man. We had to pedal back carefully since a spill off the bike with a couple of eggs in each pocket would have been a disaster. After we had been re-acquainted with the joys of genuine eggs we would ride around, looking over the countryside, the birds chirping in the peaceful stillness except when the formations shook the ground on the way to do battle.

Once, the thought of genuine, fresh eggs lured us into a breakfast visit to the permanent party officer's mess, even though we had come to know that crewdogs were not really welcome. The place looked like an Honest-to-God Officer's Mess, with tables set with white table-cloths and upscale tableware. As we entered, I had the feeling of passing through an invisible wall that had erected itself between the flight crews and the permanent party, the people who ran the base and did things like loading the bombs and keeping the Liberators in shape. They actually served real eggs sunny-side-up or poached, or whatever, at least on the day we made our brazen visit.

The Base people had arrived in England early and would stay till the end, which meant several years away from home for many of them. And they often worked in atrocious weather conditions and under great pressure during the very early morning hours, to get the bombers ready to go. But they had their job to do and we had ours and except for some individual friendships, there wasn't much contact between the two groups. They no doubt thought we were irreverent and un-military and perhaps a little arrogant, while we envied their improved living conditions and the air of confidence they had in knowing that they would more than likely be alive to go home when the war ended. Unless, of course, you did things like defuse live bombs.

These feelings sometimes came into play, as when Jim Muldoon, one of our Group's pilots, got involved in a saga involving a mission to Berlin. The flak was very heavy as it always was there and two engines were hit on the bomb run and had to be shut down. He was forced to drop out of formation and into a cloud layer and head for home. As he and his crew proceeded, they broke out of the clouds over Amsterdam just in time to have another engine damaged by flak from the German-held city. They had to drop still lower and jettison all loose equipment. Muldoon and crew were able to limp across the channel and, with about 700 feet of altitude left, spotted what they thought was a runway through the heavy English mists.

133

He made a quick approach and as they touched down, he realized with horror that what they found was about 1000 feet of unfinished runway full of laborers and construction equipment. Muldoon quickly swerved off the concrete onto rough terrain, shedding propellers and an engine, and then breaking into three pieces.

Miraculously, there was no fire and no one on the ground or in the airplane was hurt. They clambered out and after surveying the wreckage of what had been their Liberator, made their way to the construction engineer's office to find a phone. They found the engineer sitting in his somewhat plush office, his tie neatly tucked into his shirt between the second and third buttons as required, and expected that he might congratulate them on their miraculous escape.

Instead, he let Muldoon know he was highly indignant about getting his work interrupted and having his workmen terrified. And as the runway builder surveyed the beat-up, flight suited, fur-booted, unkempt warriors, he let them know how disgusted he was with their un-military appearance.

Muldoon, of course, made sure his pants were pressed and his brass all polished when, courtesy of General Doolittle, he was awarded the Distinguished Flying Cross for his "determination, judgement and skill, resulting in saving the lives of his crew and the workmen on the airfield."

I remember the first bike ride Sam and I took off base because as we pedaled down a country road just outside the gate, we could hear this piping voice, a little boy's voice with a Yorkshire accent singing, "The stars at night, are big and bright, deep in the 'eart of Texas," but he stopped when he saw us come around a curve in the road. We stopped and asked him where he learned the song. "Over at the NCO Club, at the Christmas party." He hesitated for a moment. "Got any gum, chum? he asked.

This was our first encounter with this important question, and these chums not only didn't have any gum, but were also defenseless against what we understood to be question number two, which was; "Got any candy handy?" We hadn't been able to get to the little PX on base for our weekly ration of candy, razor blades and, of course, chewing gum, so we had to disappoint

Tex. From that time on however, we tried to make sure to have some goodies in our pockets on our trips.

The town of Wendling was about as far as you could go by bicycle, and when we went there, we had to keep an eye out for that madman who drove the six-by between the rail station and the base. As we expanded our horizons, we made exploratory trips by bus or train to the large town of East Dereham where they had some small restaurants and a number of pubs. Ah, yes, Pubs. I took my Pub training at the Ploughshare in Beeston, and in several Pubs in East Dereham, pushing aside the overhanging threat of the next mission, whenever that might be, from my mind.

I embarked on a course of study concerning the different brands of beers, mild and bitter, and the ales, both bottled and on tap, and the dark, heavy concoctions like porter and stout. There was gin and orange or gin and lime juice and gin in lots of other ways, but not in Martinis. If I asked for a Martini, the publican would reach for the sweet Martini vermouth and would give me a blank stare if I said "No, a Martini cocktail." My taste buds settled on mild beer, which I could nurse by the "alf pint" for a good half hour as I thought my thoughts or watched the dart game. When I got engaged in conversation, the consumption would speed up as we got into the "It's my turn, No, it's my turn" game, but the beer was warm and a little watery and didn't do much damage.

Later on, I had to learn to deal with the "three o'clock trauma" for the rare occasions when I went into town early in the afternoon. Exactly at three o'clock, the pub-keeper would announce, very loudly, "Time, please, Gentlemen!" and the place would close for a few hours. This quaint exercise in part-time prohibition must have been the result of some compromise with the temperance crowd, to drop a subtle hint that boozing in the early afternoon was, after all, a bit naughty.

When I felt ready for bigger things I made a trip to King's Lynn, a city about twenty miles to the west, on the Wash. Now here was a place with restaurants and hotels and shops, and all of the city bustle I hadn't seen for a while. King's Lynn is where I discovered fish and chips, English style. When I was through sightseeing and pub crawling the restaurants were closed, but there was a tiny little "take-out" stand -although that term hadn't been invented yet- next to the rail station where I was to catch the ten o'clock bus back to the base.

I watched as the lady made a cone out of some sheets of newspaper, dropped in some chips -french fries- then a piece of breaded whitefish, then a few more chips and handed it to me. I was so hungry by this time after smelling the fried potatoes that I inhaled the fish and potatoes and went back to get another. I ate that one just as quickly and as the bus drove up I went over for two more for the road. As the lady handed them to me again, she peered around me to see which bunch of people I was feeding. The whole thing cost only a few shillings and I really liked the taste of them, and I still do. Fish and chips was, or were, one of those things that got me through the war.

It was lucky I didn't stay overnight because when I got back, Sam stirred up from his sleep and told me we all had a three day pass to London. As I stumbled around getting undressed and braving the late evening autumn chill for a foray into the latrine, I couldn't help thinking that maybe I was going to have a little fun before I got my rear end shot off.

The train ride down to London was about 90 miles and four hours and we couldn't help starting to party as soon as the doors of the train were slammed and the whistle tooted. There were two older English businessmen in the compartment and when we pulled the Canadian whiskey out of our musette bags their eyes lit up and they let us know that although they had an attachment to scotch, that all whiskey was good, some was a little better.

By the time we reached Liverpool Street Station, it took a little bit of work to get our concentration re-oriented and to get our new adventure back on the track. We stepped out of the train into the cavernous station, its immaculate trains and tidy platforms in contrast to the bomb-blasted glass panes in the sooty, arching roof. We walked toward the exit amidst the chuffing engines, the bleating whistles and plaintive wails of the trainmen. This was London, the biggest city in the world, the city that Hitler had tried to blitz into submission and failed.

We climbed into the taxi at the head of the rank and told the driver, "The Jules Club on Jermyn Street, near Piccadilly." "I know the place," he said, cheerfully. Everything was perfect; the English taxicab, the pixie of a driver, complete with a white-fringed, shiny bald head and a ready to please attitude.

"Why can't somebody pick this whole thing up and bring it to the States, to New York," I thought, but only for the few seconds. It would be like trying to transplant a part of the Earth's civilization onto the moon. The cabbie quickly surmised we were first-timers in London and proceeded to give us a running account of our trip through town: "We're turning onto Threadneedle Street, and in a moment we'll be passing St. Paul's Church, on the right," and we all looked to see the dusty, looming dome still intact despite the bombing, and after a while; " Now we are driving on Fleet Street, where the newspaper chaps are." We were all silent as we peered around, wide-eyed, and the cabbie continued," We are now entering The Strand, and are approaching Waterloo Bridge which crosses the Thames at this point, and just beyond that, also on the left, is the famous Savoy Hotel."

There was a lot of traffic on the Strand, mostly double-decker busses and other taxicabs, and lots of pedestrians. And then we were in Trafalgar Square and the ponderous weight of British history pressed down on us, here at the center of an empire. The surrounding buildings appeared to have been there forever, or at least since the world began, grimed with the soot of centuries. Lord Nelson, standing atop his lofty victory column ignored our passage through the square and onto that most wonderfully named avenue; Pall Mall.

"I am now turning northward on to Haymarket and in a moment we will make one turn around Piccadilly Circus, at no extra charge, and then to Jermyn Street, which is close by."

Piccadilly Circus was full of traffic and people, which was normal, whether it was five o'clock on Friday afternoon in early October, or almost any other time. The traffic swirled around the statue of Eros, which was heaped with sandbags and boarded up for the duration. It was mounted in the "navel in London's tummy", where newcomers usually got off the underground to start up an evening.

We made the circuit and the cabbie turned off onto a narrow street and after a few blocks he stopped and announced, "The Jules Club, Gentlemen."

It didn't look like much from the outside, or the inside either, we were to find, but it was home for a few days. Sam paid the cabbie because he seemed to have the pounds, shilling and pence figured out, and as we were handed our few pieces of baggage, the driver gave us a sales pitch for a private sightseeing tour of London. When we seemed to show interest, he said, "How about here, on this spot, at nine o'clock tomorrow morning?"

We all looked at each other, and Jack and I said, almost simultaneously, "How about two in the afternoon?" "Done!" he said, his blue eyes twinkling, and he was back in his wonderful little machine, chugging down the street.

Up the stairs and into the Jules Club we went, threading our way through the tiny little lobby to get checked in. The Red Cross ladies who ran the place could spot us as first timers just like the cabbie did and they made us feel right at home. The rooms were tiny and, well, spartan would be a good description; just four walls, a cot like the one I had back at Wendling and a chair. Nothing to put stuff in, or on, no closets, and the crappers and bathtubs down the hall. But after all, who could beat the location, just a few blocks from Piccadilly Circus, and the price; just a couple of bucks, or I should say a few bob, for a place we wouldn't spend much time in anyway.

We got cleaned up and were back downstairs in record time, and checked a wall map of the city to locate the Grosvenor House Hotel in Mayfair, just across Park Lane from Hyde Park. There was an officer's mess there in the Grand Ballroom of this king-sized, world class hotel that was so big it got to be called "Willow Run" after the giant Ford aircraft plant that cranked out Liberators near Detroit. The mess was run cafeteria style, and we were to eat there often because the food wasn't too bad and between the Jules Club and the Grosvenor House, we didn't use up much "fun funds." We saw Glenn Miller play one of his last big band shows at the GH mess one evening later on in our tour, before he was lost on a flight across the Channel. There were generally some Rolls and Bentleys parked out front, almost as many as there usually were in front of the Dorchester two short blocks down Park

Lane. This was Mayfair, where the very rich had their own little Jules Clubs, which were not run by the Red Cross, but by
liveried help who learned their trade in their youth.

The Grosvenor House Hotel help was also dressed in elegant livery, in tail coats and striped vests, with bow ties and
starched wing collars. They carried out their duties with
European perfection, not quite ignoring the hordes of neat,
young bumpkins who descended on them three times a day.
They watched us, but discreetly, their noses held at the standard elevation, a lot of fun to watch back. Like one of the upper
rank help, apparently the assistant head waiter, a little man
with white hair and an elegant bearing who came down the left
side aisle, the first time I noticed, walking with a measured
pace and carrying an eight by ten inch card out ahead of him,
cradled in the fingers of both hands like some fragile work of
art.

The man carefully placed the card on a little holder on the
stage at the front of the ballroom, turned and marched back up
the aisle. I tried to make out what the card had printed on it,
but despite the great eyesight I had in those days, I couldn't
read it from our table. My curiosity grew and by the time we
finished eating, I could wait no longer and walked down the
aisle to the stage to read the sign. It said, "Air Raid Now In
Progress."

Of course, by this time, in the autumn of 1944, the blitz had
ended long ago. The discreet and elegant air raid warning we
had received involved the new means Hitler had devised for
attacking London and other cities. Mass bombing by aircraft
was replaced, on the part of the Germans, by periodic attacks
using V-1 buzz-bombs, which were pilotless flying bombs propelled by pulse-jet engines, and by the intimidating V-2 rocket
bombs. The V-1's announced their arrival with a noise like the
world's biggest chain saw, which froze everyone within earshot
in their tracks. If the pilotless bomb, which flew straight and
level at low altitude like an airplane seemed close by when the
engine stopped, it was time to jump for cover, because the one-
ton warhead had a powerful blast that could knock down buildings.

Once, I was riding in a taxi when the cabbie suddenly

pulled over to the curb and turned the engine off. The heavy droning sound was very clear and I waited for the driver, who was acting like an old hand, to give the word to head for shelter, but we just sat there as the sound started to fade. Then it quit and there was a short silence and then a blast some distance away. The cabbie shook his head slightly, then started up the cab again along with others who had also stopped, and we drove off.

The V-2 rocket bomb was just as powerful, but it arrived without warning. By the time you heard the great double boom caused by the rocket's sonic boom and the bomb blast itself, it was too late. The fusing of the bomb was set not for penetration, but to explode on contact and knock down lots of buildings at a time. Its effects were awesome. However, the attacks were sporadic and the odds against being hit were seemingly favorable enough so that elaborate precautions were not taken. Once, we walked into a pub because there was a lot of singing going on and we wanted to join the celebration. After a moment, a great double blast went off somewhere that shook the tables and rattled the glasses. There was a little bit of swearing and muttering, but the singers hardly missed a beat.

"If you worry about the rockets," said one of the celebrants, beer mug in hand, "You'll spend all of yer time underground!"

One of the dinners we had at the Grosvenor House had to end somewhat abruptly because we found ourselves running late for a performance of a play called "While the Sun Shines," in which a RAF hero and a brash Yank flyboy lock horns over the heart and soul of this beautiful, vacillating English girl. We all laughed pretty hard when the Yank calls his Colonel on the phone and calls him "Spike," although I don't think our English cousins knew why we were laughing. Anyway, the RAF bloke gets the girl, which only seemed right and everyone turned their attention back to the war.

It was too early to go back to the four bare walls of the Jules Club, so we decided to see what Piccadilly Circus was all about. The evening fog had already set in, and as darkness descended, it really got difficult to see your way around, especially when you didn't know the territory in the first place. We passed a newspaper vendor who was hawking the Evening News and when we came close, his voice lowered and he said, "Condoms, boys,condoms?"

This entrepreneur had diversified and also sold "torches" so we bought one of his flashlights to help us navigate. The others eventually peeled off for home as we'd had a long day, but I kept on prowling, some energy within me flaring like a flame finding some unburnt coals. As I walked in the fog, I saw a flashlight snap on, its beam finding a pair of female legs which stopped and turned to face the seeker of truth. I wasn't close enough to hear what she had to say, but I did hear Mr. Torch say, loudly and indignantly, "Five pounds? Are you crazy?" And the flashlight snapped off, the truth revealed.

My unburnt coals ran out, and I too decided to crawl back into the comforting bosom of the Red Cross at the Jules Club. When I got there the snack bar was still open and I devoured a bunch of the thin sandwiches I was getting very attached to, especially the ones made from canned roast beef with a generous coating of mustard that curled the hairs in your nostrils. The only thing they had to drink was some tea, which this wonderful lady convinced me I should try with some canned milk, and when she told me lots of English people drank their tea that way, I decided that perhaps Empire had taken some wrong turns.

The four of us slept late the next morning, and after we awoke and came downstairs, we found a place on one of the back streets to have breakfast. Then we took a walk over to the Marble Arch end of Hyde park, to the Speaker's Corner which was just a few blocks from the Grosvenor House. The soap box orators were in full swing, with perhaps a half dozen small crowds already there on this Saturday noon.

Two or three of the groups were being harangued for their sinful ways by do-it-yourself missionaries, bibles tucked under the left arm, fingers pointed in the air. There were political types too, usually Marxists who were getting a little bit of on-the-job training in agitation and manipulation to be ready for the big day, when their fellow workers would arise, and drag their newly loosened chains down to Buckingham Palace so they could loll around on the royal furniture.

Questions were flung at the speakers by fun-seeking back

benchers, and if some hot retorts were flung back, then the crowd got a little bigger while the fun lasted. On later trips, the biggest crowd surrounded a tall black man wearing some brightly colored plumes in a head band. He called himself a prince, and as he spoke, he would point to two symbols sewn into the cloth of a blue, two-foot square banner mounted on a pole stuck in the ground behind him; a Star of David and a U.S. dollar sign.

"If you align yourselves with these two signs, nothing can harm you," he claimed, "and you will make your way in the world."

There were several promising-looking pubs on our walk back to the Jules Club to meet our cabbie friend for the sightseeing tour, and we stopped in one for the salads and sandwiches that were known as "pub grub," along with some beer.

When we got back to the Jules Club, our man was on the spot, cheerful as ever. The tour took the standard route, one which I have taken several times since, both by taxi and tour bus, but I remember this one. For one thing, the weather had developed into vintage London, with a low overcast and damp, drizzly air along with the threat of fog. It was also wartime London where part of a great battle had taken place directly overhead and in the damaged rows of flats and down in the bomb shelters; and the battle had been won but not the war, not yet. Excitement and dread were still heavy in the air, here, in the city at the center of the world.

We climbed into the taxi and before long found ourselves at the Whispering Gallery under the dome of St. Paul's, at Dicken's Old Curiosity Shop, and standing on the marble crypt covers at Westminster Abbey. It was difficult to believe that the bones of all these great men were here beneath our feet, in a place where the gathered dusts of history covered everything, before the city was sandblasted clean of grime and, to traditionalists who like things a little grimy, some of it charm.

At one point we had the cabbie stop at a pub and had to insist that he have an ale along with us. "Just one while I'm on duty," he agreed, and we found out that he had been a Tommy in France in World War I. All he would say, at first was "That was a tough one to come out alive, or with all your arms and legs," and he fell silent for a moment. Then he brightened again; "But you chaps, flying way up there, way behind the lines into Germany with all that flak. Now that dazzles my imagination! At least I could always duck into my trench unless Fritzie was coming at us, or we were going at him."

Somewhere in our tour we had our picture taken with Big Ben in the background, then the trip was over and the ex-Tommy pulled up to our home away from home and got out of his cab when we did. He came around and shook our hand, each one of us, and wished us luck. He chugged away once more and disappeared into the gathering dusk.

We had a fish dinner at a place that was rumored to have steaks once in a while, but not that night and then we broke up to do our own thing. I was feeling restless and needed to wander around for a while, perhaps to find the girl of my dreams who might be searching through the cat-footed fog to find me, who would not charge me five pounds to tell me how manly and valuable and needed I was. I passed our old buddy the news vendor and got the same sales pitch, and looked at the floozies who tugged my sleeve or made a coy remark or even stepped right in front of me to make sure I saw how gorgeous and desirable they were, or thought they were. I had a few drinks here and there, including the bar downstairs at the Regent Palace Hotel at Piccadilly Circus, which was full of guys like me.

There were some Commandoes there, along with some honest women; WAFS, WAACS and even a SPAR who were all shopping for the future, to become part of Mr. Right's postwar dream. They looked at us, mistresses of all they surveyed, and made their decisions quickly; this guy drinks too much, that guy will look lousy in civvies and ah, but this guy- lets give him a try because of that dimple in his chin.

The odds were just too stiff at that particular bazaar, so I wandered around some more, and found that I had walked all the way up Regent Street and down Oxford Street to the Marble Arch, the boundary marker at the northwest corner of what was coming to be my turf. I gave up my search for whatever it was I was looking for and turned down Park Lane to head back to Jermyn Street. At that moment a bus pulled up to the curb and stopped just ahead of me. I thought it was empty but a young woman got out, and as she stepped onto the sidewalk she glanced up and saw me, then she started to walk

Beder, Murray, Samsell and "the author" in London

down Park Lane also.

From what I had seen in the lights of the bus as it pulled away, she seemed to be about twenty-five and obviously pretty, although, in the dim light, it was only a guess. I didn't really try to overtake her as I didn't want to scare her, but she actually seemed to slow up until I came abreast. I could feel my heart pounding in me as she looked around at me, not startled at all.

"Must you go home?" I heard myself saying. She stopped and I did too as we looked at each other. "Yes, its late," she said in a nice, breathy voice, "Would you like to walk with me?"

What dream is this? Who could believe it? Maybe an 88 actually did come through the floor over Hamburg and I never knew it, and now I was being tested to see if I could withstand the rigors of paradise. As we walked, we talked in fits and starts, mostly about nothing, and then we came to what was obviously her place. She turned up the three stairs to the door, a wide, red-painted door with brass numerals and I came right along with her and she didn't object.

"You can come in for a night cap if you're very quiet," she said in that wonderful voice, and without waiting for an answer, she put the key in the door lock and opened it. The hall light was on and I could see that she was more than pretty, with ash-blonde hair and greenish eyes. When she spoke to me she looked at me earnestly, slightly vulnerable, stoking my fires into conflagration.

"I've been to the cinema," she said as we walked up one flight to her door. "Did you like it?" I asked, thinking that as long as we talked, she wouldn't change her mind and send me, shattered and broken, back to the Red Cross.

"Yes. It was one of yours, with John Wayne. Very inspiring." Dinah was her name, and she worked as a social secretary for someone whose name she didn't mention. Her flat was nicely decorated and as we walked in, she left the hall door slightly ajar. I helped her with her raincoat, and took off my trench coat and hat and laid them on a chair. Dinah sent me into the kitchen where the bottle was and she apologized that there was no ice. I poured two drinks and added a little water and when I came out into her room, she had taken off her shoes, and was sitting on a divan by the window. She patted the seat next to her and I gave her one of the drinks and sat down, still breathing a little hard, not yet certain how to handle this so I didn't blow the whole thing.

I couldn't take my eyes from hers as we talked, and as the irresistible forces of nature drew us closer together, I began to see in her earnest gaze, a hunger, an invitation. Suddenly, I couldn't resist reaching out and drawing her to me and she let me kiss her, the softness and the perfume of her sending me beyond the brink, and I knew right away I didn't have to play it cagey anymore. And when she got up and went over to the hall door and shut it, I didn't care whether I was in heaven or Dinah's place, it was all the same. After she shut the door, she walked towards the bedroom, and I started to follow. She turned around and looked at me, the earnest look still in her eyes, and said, softly, "Oh by the way, the price is five pounds."

The chagrin rose up in me and engulfed me. Then the passion slowly drained until there was nothing left but disappointment and a desire to get out and get some fresh air. I didn't look at her as I went to pick up my coat and hat. Gathering my twenty year old righteousness and my wounded pride, I opened the door, walked into the hall, and went down the stairs.

7

WAS IST DAS NUTS?

T HE WAR WAS STILL THERE when we got back from London. We had gotten four missions in so quickly and so soon after we arrived that they were just a jumbled mass of impressions, not yet sorted out. So when we were alerted, twelve days after our last mission to Kassel, it was like starting over again.

A few days before, the Chief Navigator for our squadron met with a couple of us new replacements at Squadron Headquarters and we biked down to the flight line. A crew chief started up the put-put in one of the Libs to give us electrical power as we climbed up into the bomb bay and went forward to the nose compartment.

"This is the GEE Box," said the man, a First Lieutenant who carried that strange aura of a combat man who had come to grips with the central trauma any fighting man must face -the mortal fear of getting killed- and had transcended it. He reminded me of someone who was recovering from a wound which had done him profound damage, and which he had absorbed and had overcome, for the moment, with quiet pride.

I had seen the GEE Box before, back at Westover, and had even gotten some instruction in its use, in a simulator which used faked signals. Now we could operate the machine in its native habitat, with big, genuine blips sliding across the scope the same way they would on missions. When you could pick up GEE signals without interference, you could fix the position of your aircraft with great accuracy. The accuracy was so good, in

147

fact, that the more experienced navigators were able to guide their pilots to the approach end of a landing runway in very low visibility.

This seemed like the answer to a navigator's prayer, and so it was, but only up to a point. The game of technological cat and mouse was still a little primitive, although it didn't seem so at the time. The mysterious GEE Box involved the use of radio transmissions, so the Germans, quickly perceiving the threat that accurate, all-weather navigation would pose, developed a radio jamming technique that worked. I was to find that I could work the gadget just fine until we approached the enemy coast, and then the powerful, sawtooth jamming signal would blot everything out.

GEE was nice and simple: a master station would broadcast a signal which appeared as a blip on the left end of a scale on a scope -a cathode ray tube- over the navigator's desk. A "slave" station, set perhaps a hundred miles or so on the ground from the master, would receive the same signal, and after a short delay of some millionths of a second, would send out a signal of its own which also appeared on the scope to the right of the master blip.

The distance between the two blips on the scope indicated the time difference, in microseconds, between the arrival of the master and slave signals. The same time difference reading could be found along a line already plotted on a GEE chart, and the navigator merely looked for the right reading on one of the lines on his chart. Get such readings for two different stations and you have a fix.

We were being briefed on the GEE Box because they were now getting enough sets to put them in all the Libs, including Tail-end Charlie aircraft. Now if we could only counteract the German jamming, and then the Germans would counteract that, and so on.

We finished our GEE Box lessons and biked back to the squadron operations hut. The Chief Navigator went over the navigation logs and track charts each of us had kept on our missions. He let us know that he had studied our log sheets, and we appeared to assume that the lead navigator was always right, and that the flight plan winds and estimates could be depended on.

"Always figure that the lead navigator is more screwed up than you are," he said quietly, which was a little surprising, coming from a lead navigator. He may have been thinking about the Gotha mission, eight months earlier, for which the Group had received special recognition. On that mission the German fighters met the bomber formations unusually early - at the Dutch coast- and started their attacks. Perhaps they already knew what the target was; their largest twin-engined fighter factory, situated deep in the German Thuringian heartland. They had, after all, an intelligence system which enabled them to determine, on occasion, the name of the next day's command pilot or the lateness of the mess hall clock, and broadcast the startling facts on Arnhem Annie's program.

The bomber stream had reached the control point at which the Flying Fortress wings altered course for Schweinfurt while two wings of Liberators pressed on toward the initial point for their bomb run on the Gothear Waggonfabrik plant. One wing was being led by the 392nd Group with Colonel Lorin Johnson aboard as command pilot and one of our Chief Navigators, Captain Roy Swangren, as lead navigator. The Colonel's wing would bomb second behind another wing just ahead.

The fighter attacks increased in intensity as the Liberators began to uncover into a line of groups and got ready for the final turn for the target. The Luftwaffe seemed almost frantic and attacked from all directions; they came head-on, or nosed upward from below or curved around to shoot it out with the tail gunners. The Liberator gunners fired back with the same fury at the Focke-Wulfs, Me-109's, rocket-firing Ju-88's, heavily armed Me-110's and 210's; perhaps 150 in all.

As Johnson's wing reached the initial point and turned for the target, he and his crew saw with consternation that the wing up ahead , already on their bomb run, were on a heading which the Colonel's navigator and bombardier were certain would take them to the wrong target. The savage enemy attacks, landmark-obscuring snow on the ground and their squadron-mates being shot down around them must have had their effect on the leading wing. Colonel Johnson's decision had to be immediate: to follow the leading formation to a questionable target and remain within the entire formation's protective fold, or trust his navigator and strike out on their own.

Bombers and fighters were falling around him and flak awaited him up ahead and he must have asked in desperation, "Swangren! Are you sure? Are you sure?" but he took up his navigator's heading.

The bombardiers in the wing did such a destructive job that three months later, on D-day, almost no rebuilding was observed. This plant, which could have provided the Germans with fighter bombers to oppose our landings, lay in ruins. The Gotha outcome was the exact opposite of that which befell the Kassel massacre mission, which happened some time after the attack on Gotha. At Kassel, the command pilot trusted his navigators and lost. It just goes to show you; a lead crew's life was not an easy one.

We were not besieged with such navigational doubts on the way to tear up the railroad tracks at the Mainz marshalling yards, along with the supply and troop trains sitting on them. General Patton was racing forward towards the Rhine so fast that he kept outdistancing his fuel supplies, which had to be ferried to.him by air. A successful mission would certainly aid this great general by denying the German army the troops and equipment they needed for counter-attacks. Meanwhile the Rhine was becoming a more formidable barrier against bombing missions as the Germans pulled their guns out of the territory they were losing and placed them around the Rhine cities and other potential bomber targets along the river.

Mainz is situated about twenty five miles west of Frankfurt, at a point where the Main River branches off from the Rhine. It lay just on the edge of the flak coverage for Frankfurt, and a quick left turn after bombs away kept us out of a lot of trouble. My log shows that we considered the flak we encountered to be light, but accurate. It was with some surprise I learned that half of the attacking Liberators -out of 300- were damaged, including some slight damage to our own, and five were shot down.

On our first missions, all flak was scary; light, moderate, heavy, accurate, inaccurate; it didn't make much difference because it only took one well-placed 88 and we were blown away. Now, the process of battle-hardening was beginning to set in. We could make judgements about the flak amount and accuracy, and whether the chaff was working, all the while looking for the aiming point as we drove down the bomb run, and keeping out a wary eye for the Sturmgruppen. However, we never forgot that all it took was one well-placed 88.

Our confidence was driven up a peg on our next mission, a week later, on which we saw no flak at all. The target was an undefended stretch of the Mitteland canal at the town of Minden, where the waterway is elevated and carried across some obstacles on a viaduct. Our instructions were to bomb either visually or through the clouds, which was unusual for a target which appeared so tiny from 23,000 feet and was considered hard to hit under any conditions.

Somewhere, work was going on in the development of a "smart bomb" which could be steered to some extent by radio signals, but in our part of the war, all we could do was load up hundreds of the dumb kind, and if the target was covered by clouds, dump them out on the shadowy radar image conjured up by the radar operators in the lead aircraft.

The canal was a very important part of the transportation system for the entire northern half of Germany and was used to carry both raw materials and finished war materiel from one side of the country to the other, between the west and east. The British had already knocked out a key north-south segment of the system three weeks before and our task was to finish the job.

This was the first time we were involved in using two-thousand pound bombs, which were fused to penetrate the ground and knock down the strong concrete canal walls and viaduct pilings. The armorers were still winching up the great, monstrous bombs when we got out to the airplane after the briefing. It took only four of them to gross out our bomb load, and each one put such a stress on the shackles that the releases tended to hang up. As a result, a manual cable release was installed in each navigator's compartment as a backup, and my instructions were to pull the handle as close to the bombs away call as possible. Jack Murray would flip an electrical toggle release at the same time.

The target was socked in with no ground in sight at all, and the lead bombardiers, who were using radar information in a bombing procedure called H2X, must have had their hands full picking out their aiming point out of the radar clutter. Suddenly it was Bombs Away! and I gave the red handle a great jerk and down the bombs went, launched either by RBR or Jack Murray's toggle switch or by my hand, it was hard to tell. Our four monsters joined 850 others as each group passed over the viaduct, all eyes straining to see through the impenetrable clouds.

We had to wait several days for the photo recon results to come in to learn that, out of all those bombs, only one hit in exactly the right place, but that's all it took. An eighty-five foot section of the wall collapsed, and a two and a half mile stretch of the canal was drained. A number of other bombs were near-hits which weakened the wall and complicated the repair job for the Germans.

Looking at the mission today, it seems like a bit of overkill to send that many bombers but it was, after all, Germany's most important waterway. And if we had sent one less bomber, who is to say it wouldn't have been the one that did the job? In any event, the Germans did fix it and we had to go after it again later.

The idea of smothering a small but important target with bombs to insure at least a few hits to knock it out came about early in the war after it became obvious that single aircraft bombing individually from high altitude was not practical, at the time. Results, as they involved individual targets within a bombing pattern were spotty and often frustrating. For example, when General Jimmy Doolittle was operating in the Mediterranean before he took over the Eighth Air Force, some of his targets were naval ports sheltering warships and supply vessels. He had great success bombing docks and ports in places like Naples, before the Italians became our "co-belligerents" -what a great word!- and other places involved in Axis operations in North Africa. In one instance, they attacked dock areas in Sardinia with about 100 B-17's and sank the Trieste and damaged the Gorzia, both of them Italian heavy cruisers.

But then, on what he called "the most unsuccessful mission" he ever led, he attacked the harbor at La Spezia, an Italian port near Genoa where two Italian heavy cruisers and the battleship Roma were tied up. Again, about 100 B-17's were involved, carrying large demolition and armor piercing bombs.

The flak was light and the formations were able to make a good bomb run and drop the bombs on the target. As it turned out, one cruiser was untouched altogether, one was damaged, and as for the battleship, one bomb pierced the deck and went right through the bottom without exploding, so little damage was done to it.

Later, after Italy came over to our side, as Lowell Thomas and Edward Jablonski reported in "Doolittle- A Biography," "the Roma pulled out of port and headed for Malta to be turned over to the British. When it neared southern Italy, a single German plane swooped down upon the battleship, dropped two bombs, and sank it." It was later found out that the two bombs were radio-controlled.

John Beder's crew may have been getting battle-hardened at this point, but that didn't prevent us from getting nervous and jerky when the curtain was pulled aside to reveal our target for the 30th of October, 1944. It was Hamburg again, however this time it was not a factory on the edge of town, but the synthetic oil plants in the center of the flak coverage. These plants were among the most jealously protected in Germany. The weather was briefed to be atrocious, and so it was. In fact, the flying weather had been so poor that missions had been scrubbed for the past several days, and this mission to Hamburg seemed to have been scheduled out of desperation.

All of the U.K. and the entire European continent were covered with clouds to one extent or another. We formed with some difficulty and were told to keep an ear cocked for enroute and target weather reports from Mustangs and Mosquito aircraft which were now being routinely sent ahead for reconnaissance. Our course took us across northern Germany and as we progressed, the thick overcast and the undercast began to merge. The First Division Fortresses were the first to run into difficulty and were instructed to head for secondary targets or targets of opportunity. The Third Division Forts were told to abandon the mission altogether and return to their home bases.

Meanwhile, the Libs pressed on and actually reached the initial point some thirty miles southeast of Hamburg when suddenly we were all in the soup and unable to see our wingmates, and the pilots had to slowly, gingerly scatter the formation without any violent maneuvers, our fingers crossed all the while, waiting for someone to come sliding into us. We were strictly on our own, deep in Germany, to get home as best we could, with some discretion as to whether to look for a target or jettison the bombs at the designated jettison point in the North Sea; or, worst of all, bring the damned things back to Wendling.

Big John asked for a heading to regain the planned return course out in the North Sea, and I had some difficulty laying out a course which avoided most of the flak areas on the way to the coast. After fifteen tense minutes, we broke out into the clear, between layers. We were still too new to play it smart, and in a show of cockiness, we decided not to waste the mission. Bremerhaven was almost on course, so we altered heading slightly to the left, knowing we would get some flak, but thinking we would duck into the undercast if fighters found us. The bombs would be dropped on my ETA for the coast.

Since we were not in a lead aircraft and had no radar on board, I had nothing to navigate with except compass, airspeed and flight plan forecast winds. The whole operation seemed a little shaky, and we waited tensely for the ETA to come up. About five minutes to go, Big John told Shodrof in the tail and the waist gunners to report any flak as soon as they saw some.

"Flak?" they yelled. "The sky's been boiling down below and we've been dropping chaff like mad!"

"Lets drop the bombs, John!" I yelled back, realizing that we had arrived early. The flak told us we were over Bremerhaven, or some area close by worth protecting with lots of flak, and therefore, worth bombing. The bombs went and the flak fell behind us as we picked up the flight plan track near Heligoland and headed for home. Jack Murray turned around and looked back at me. "Now that's what I call precision bombing. And I trained for a whole year so I could drop bombs like that."

"Well," I shrugged, "just think, if we hit some submarines down there, the Germans'l think we've got a new gadget."

"Yeah" said Sam, "its called a spit-in-the-wind bombsight!"

As new as we were, we were already aware that a highly

effective bombing mission did not happen automatically, even though we were a bunch of hot shots operating in the big time, or so we were told. It was like trying to stage the performance of a large symphony orchestra each time. First, the music had to be composed by a genius whose work fit into an agreed master plan. Then, the right type and number of players had to be assembled at the right place and the right time with their piccolos and kettle drums, all of them smart enough to read the music and follow the lead of the conductor. And all of this had to be done before an audience which was mad as hell because the players' efforts were certainly not intended for their enjoyment and who lobbed grenades and aimed gunfire at the orchestra with the idea that none of its members should survive the performance.

I was dumb enough to try to make this musical analogy at a concert intermission many years later, and I noticed that a lady in an adjoining group who had overheard it started to get hot under her pretty coiffure. And when the conversation, which probably should have been put on a different track at that point, came to the effect of World War II on the European musical scene, -about which I knew nothing- and I mentioned that one of our crew's targets had been Bayreuth, where one of Germany's hallowed shrines to music was, and is, located, she popped a circuit breaker. "And what did you bomb there," she broke in, her eyes widening in rage, "the schools, or the museums?"

The target at Bayreuth had been an ordinance depot being filled with vehicles and equipment for the protection of the Nazi bigshots,who expected to hide out in the Bavarian "Redoubt" when Germany collapsed. But the eavesdropping lady's anger was too hot for the truth to do any good, and I was starting to get up a little heat myself.

But then I realized that in any performance, whether it be in war or music, no matter what the performance is like, there will always be some critic around to put it down.

We did occasionally perform in a masterful way, where everybody did everything right and we had an extra ration of luck. But generally, the odds were heavily stacked against combat perfection. First, all of us, the pilots, navigators, bombardiers, radiomen and gunners were very young and certainly didn't have any combat experience when we arrived in England. From the beginning, the pilots had to fly airplanes in ways which demanded the utmost concentration all the time, despite the hazards of interfering weather, fighters, flak, fear, fatigue and very complex procedures. Every mission was different; the type of formation, the uncovering maneuver, the target, the type of bombs used, the opposition, the weather, the odds of survival, and which side of bed you got out of before the mission.

Once you got off the ground, you had to live through the formation assembly, which was a dangerous period in the life of a crewdog. With a thousand or more bombers milling around in a relatively confined area, often in marginal weather, collisions were more than likely; they happened just about every mission. They crashed head-on, or slid into each other, or climbed up from below and chewed off a tail; and sometimes a crew bailed out, and sometimes they were unable to. They also had accidents on the bomb run, as they "uncovered" from their enroute configuration into the separate formation elements required for bombing.

The complex maneuver from a wing of perhaps ninety aircraft into a stream of ten-aircraft squadrons, or even elements of six bombers each, between the initial point and the target, with fighters attacking or in heavy flak sometimes required more luck than skill, and the luck wasn't always there. Sometimes the squadrons or six-plane elements bunched up while maneuvering to give their lead bombardier a shot at the target, and one squadron might inadvertently slide under another while approaching the aiming point. If the lower squadron was living right, the higher squadron held its bombs and came around again or brought the bombs back home.

Al Novik and his crew, squadron mates of ours, may have been living right but they got unlucky anyway on a mission to Salzbergen, one of those bad luck targets the Germans were a little extra-sensitive about. Among its treasures, Salzbergen had an oil refinery and a railroad marshalling yard, and it was the oil refinery which we were tasked to put out of action this time.

The target weather forecast called for a 10/10 undercast, in which case all three squadrons would remain in group formation. All would bomb off the group lead bombardier, who would use a blind bombing technique called "GH" which involved somewhat the same principle as the Gee box. In the unlikely event that a visual run could be made, the Groups would uncover into a stream of ten-plane squadrons and the drops would be made off the squadron leaders.

As it turned out, the forecast was right and the target was obscured. Our wing uncovered into three groups and we bore down on the bomb run through moderate flak, and then it was bombs away. All of the group's releases were triggered by the RBR signal and dropped together.

Unfortunately, just about bomb release time, one of the formation elements slid over the top of us, and their bombs rained down around us. A five hundred pound RDX bomb, its nose fuse arming device not yet fully activated, hit Al Novik's left horizontal stabilizer and rudder, and knocked them off the airplane. Without all of his horizontal stabilizer handy to keep his airplane in level flight, Al and his co-pilot, Lt. Jack Graves, suddenly found themselves, their nose-up trim all used up, both hauling back on the wheel to keep the Lib from plunging downward.

Al and Jack were now stuck with the Herculean task of getting their airplane back home even though it took all the muscle they had to keep the Liberator level. Fortunately for Al and his crew, he was built like a linebacker, but he knew his strength wouldn't last forever, and they had a long way to go to get home. They stuck it out, the long minutes, the eternal hours, until finally they were able to let down over East Anglia.

But then, agony of agonies, the returning groups were told that weather over the bases was too poor for landing, and they were ordered to return to the Continent to land:- this happened after part of France had been liberated. There was no way Novik could hack it any longer; not enough gas, not enough strength. As the rest of the group left for France, he pointed his airplane toward the watery dumping ground of The Wash, and ordered his crew to bail out.

Now everyone was gone except for himself and the co-pilot, who held the controls while Al got out of the seat to cinch up his chute harness, then got back in to hold the controls while the co-pilot bailed out. Novik, as he told us later, let go of the wheel and tried to make a dive through the flight deck door and out of the open bomb bay, but when he let go, the Liberator went into a spinning fall, and he was pinned against the ceiling of the flight deck. Not only that, but a fire had developed which began to sweep the flight deck with flames which brushed his face as the uncontrolled bomber swerved around toward the ground.

Suddenly, as if his guardian angel had finally showed up and sent forward a thunderbolt, some part of the airplane came apart and the force which had pinned him let go. He fought his way to the open bomb bay and jumped just a few seconds before the Liberator exploded above him.

He pulled the rip-cord and waited for that big, reassuring jolt of a deploying canopy, but it didn't happen. The chute had dribbled out and a little streamer of nylon whipped in the air above him. He gave the rip-cord another yank, this time with both hands and, with not too much altitude left, got the whole parachute out, while burning wreckage fell all around him. His guardian angel stayed with him and helped him avoid the falling pieces and the flaming carnage they set off on the ground.

Because of Novik, the whole crew got out alive and made it back to Wendling. And since the rest of the Group had been diverted to the Continent, they were the only ones to get back home that day .

Novik's escape seems miraculous, given the number of obstacles he had to overcome, one after the other, to hang on to his life. The real miracle, however, is that this was not the first time his selfless courage was so sorely tested. Just one month before, while trying to bring back his combat-damaged Lib, his fuel gave out and he had to give the bail-out order. Just as he did later, he held the airplane straight and level as the crew jumped and left him alone. On that occasion, he was able to get out of his seat, bound across the flight deck and dive out of the bomb bay to safety. Two of the crew had jumped from the nose-wheel well and apparently hit some part of the plane, and did not make it.

What a feeling it must have been, the first time, as the

next to last man -the co-pilot- climbed out of his seat and left him, his life in his own hands. Now sit yourself in the left seat, the aircraft commander's seat the second time, as the crew bails out one by one, and then the co-pilot looks at you as you try to hold the nose up so that he can make it too, and then he's gone. And there you sit, knowing what was going to happen as soon as you let go the wheel. That's what being the pilot in command is all about.

Al Novik's accident on the bomb run at Salsbergen had a gratifying ending; the entire crew got out of it alive. There were other accidents with their different causes and outcomes, but none of them affected us more than the tragedy which befell our squadron commander, who was returning from a mission which was the last of the required number for several of the crewmembers.

Major Leonard J. Barnes was not one of those celebrating the end of his last mission, since he had already completed one combat tour, and had returned to the 392nd to fly a second. His Chief Navigator, Captain Roy Swangren, the man who had been right when others were wrong at Gotha, would head back to the U.S.A. after a successful mission to Schwabisch-Hall, site of a German jet fighter airfield.

It was customary for aircrews to make some gesture to celebrate during the return of some or all of their number from their final combat trip. Since there was no way you could fly a victory roll, like the fighters do, without the wings coming off, the celebration usually consisted of flying a low pass over the base while firing Very pistol flares as they came across the runway.

And so they approached Wendling, descending as they came, flares shooting out of the flare port in the ceiling of the flight deck. Apparently, the pistol was not seated properly in the port when one of the flares was fired, and it backfired into the flight deck. Such an event was not necessarily fatal, but the fates were determined that Swangren and the others would not beat the odds and finish their tours down to the last, safe landing. One flaming ball of the double flare was being dealt with but the other landed in the bag of yet-to-be-fired flares and there was an explosion which set the front-end afire. Four of

159

the crew were able to bail out, but Barnes, Swangren and five others didn't make it.

What art of language could Colonel Johnson conjure up to explain such agonizingly unnecessary deaths to the crewmembers' families? What was there in Chaplain McDonogh's religious training he might bring to bear on this heavy but seemingly avoidable grief. What can anyone say? If only somebody hadn't inserted the Very pistol into the firing port improperly? If only! If only! If only!

Winter began to close in with a vengeance. Mission after mission was cancelled as frontal weather moved off the North Atlantic and passed over the U.K. and the continent, screwing up operations for a week at a time. We had a trip to Berlin scrubbed as we sat on the ramp waiting for the weather scout's report. Completing a tour quickly was one thing, but finishing it -maybe the hard way- over Berlin was another.

The difficulties were not only with the target weather. Low and middle clouds over East Anglia increased the already high level of danger in the assembling of the formations. Icing threatened the heavily laden bombers on takeoff and in the climb, and demanded lots of character from the mechanics, who had to do a lot of their work out in the open. And cloud layers at enroute and bombing altitudes sometimes prevented formation flying altogether.

We did manage to get some missions in when the weather broke a little; the marshalling yards at Rheine, north of the Ruhr, and the military airfield at Hanau, near Frankfurt. The Luftwaffe had begun to concentrate some of their forces at the airfield and our job was to "posthole" it, to make it impossible to takeoff and land aircraft there, at least for a while.

The target was completely covered with clouds, which meant we had to bomb by radar. The flak was light and inaccurate and it seemed we had a milk run on our hands, except that on our return, we had to thread the needle between heavily defended areas to get home, places like Frankfurt to the south and Koblentz to the north.

The lead navigator's nightmare came true as he shaved things too closely and parts of the formation were put within range of the flak batteries at Koblentz. Someone announced a bomber down as one of the formations behind us received accurate bursts and then we began to get some too. One of the wingmen in our lead squadron up ahead took some damage and slid downward slowly, still under control but in need of an emergency landing. The flak fell behind us and the rest of us got back okay.

As our ground armies made their way across France, there began to be a "victory in sight" feeling expressed in the press, although that didn't have that much effect on our missions;- the flak was still there, and so was the fighter threat and the lousy flying weather. Priorities for the types of targets we were sent to did seem to be changing, however. Targets were being chosen whose destruction would aid in the march across the Continent, like rail yards which handled troops and equipment on their way to impede our ground advance, refineries which supplied fuel to German tanks and aircraft, and airfields which launched fighter bombers against our troops.

Gone were the missions like ball-bearing plants and other "strategic" targets which, when successful, would have an impact which would not be felt for a year or more. There were also missions directly supporting our troops in which we took a direct tactical part in the ground battle, and on which we carried fragmentation bombs to be laid down in carpets on known enemy troop concentrations. This was done around the time of the D-Day landings and on several subsequent occasions. We also attacked road and rail networks directly behind the enemy front lines to prevent the Wehrmacht from making a stand by denying them troop reinforcements and a re-supply of ammunition and equipment.

Because we were bombing pretty close to our own troops, elaborate precautions were set up to make sure we didn't drop short. Exotic-colored friendly flak was fired just below our flight level to show where enemy territory started. We also used an electronic landing system -an SCS-51- which normally pointed a radio beam down a runway for poor weather landings. This time, the beam was set up just behind our lines so that pilots could read a cockpit indicator and determine where the bomb line was. We were briefed on the need to avoid inadvertent and premature toggling, screwed up RBR procedures and other manifestations of Murphy's law;- what can go wrong, will go wrong. The watch-word was; "when in doubt, hold your bombs."

Despite numerous precautions and stern warnings during the briefing, we sometimes hit our own people anyway. At St. Lo during the breakout after our Normandy landings, premature releases -shorts- fell into American positions and killed sixteen G.I.'s. Then, on the next day in the same area, it happened again and 100 of our men were killed, including Lt. General Lesley J. McNair, who was up forward with his troops.

These incidents soured General Eisenhower on the direct tactical use of heavy bombers close to the front lines, but only for a while . He said later that it was impossible to "convince the Army that the battle of St.-Lo had not been won as a result of the support given by the Eighth Air Force."

Strange to say, it was the air Generals who objected to the front line use of heavy bombers, because they wanted to get on with their own set of targets to maintain control of the air. It almost seemed as though there were two wars going on at the same time in the same area. Or perhaps you might make it three wars, since the Royal Air Force generally ignored the directives of the combined bombing program and did their own thing.

The usefulness of troop support missions by heavy bombers was obvious; the field order directing our attack in the Neunkirchen area on November 30th said that "higher headquarters has indicated that the attack of November 27th was extremely successful and it is hoped that [this mission] would have a similar result."

Each of the almost 200 bombers carried 44 100-pound bombs and 2 500 pounders and we got them all in the right area. When we attacked troop concentrations, we were, in effect laying down an airborne artillery barrage, except that our stuff came down almost all at once. The effect must have been horrendous; we were told later that many of the enemy troops who had lived through it were so battered by the tremendous shock of the attack that they lost the will to fight. "Annihilation! Annihilation!" cried one German general who had survived such an attack.

We were even put to work in an attempt to knock out the Verny group of fortresses at Metz, which lay in the path of General Patton's Third Army. This came about when Patton sent his old buddy General Doolittle a jocularly couched note saying that "those low bastards, the Germans gave me my first bloody nose when they compelled us to abandon our attack on Fort Driant...I have requested a revenge bombardment...and that you provide large bombs of the nastiest type, and as many as you can spare, to blow up this damn fort so that it becomes nothing but a hole."

These fortifications were built in the Verdun area during World War I by the French but were modernized by the Germans during their occupation to include, as the field order stated, "the most modern type of gun emplacements." The field order also said;" A successful attack on these positions will be as important as was the reduction of enemy defenses by the Eighth Air Force in July, which permitted the advance of stalled Allied Forces and the consequent liberation of France."

Of course, there was a little bit of hype in the field order, and all of France was not yet liberated, but General Doolittle gave the order so that we could do our bit for the Third Army. The B-17's were operating in the same general area with troop concentration targets on both sides of Metz, and our attack on Fort Driant and the rest of the fortifications was incorporated into the overall mission. With Patton confronting them and the Eighth and Ninth Air Forces on top, the Germans were in a hell of a fix.

Our group had 2000 pounders again, to breach the thick concrete walls of the fortress. We came up on the target with little or no opposition and it was "Bombs Away!" Unfortunately, the balky releases took their toll and many of the bombs had to be released by the manual backup means. The second or two delay in this type of release usually meant the drop was strung out and not too effective. Several of the Libs including ours had a big bomb hung up on one of the shackles, and we had to take them back and jettison them at a designated point in the Channel on the way home.

One unfortunate squadron member had failed to exercise his bomb bay doors periodically on the climb to altitude as required, and when it came time to open them on the bomb run, they were frozen tight. There were times when a crew dropped their load right through closed doors in desperation, but not this time, so they had to abort the release and carry them back to the jettison point. While they circled at a lower altitude and waited for the bomb door mechanism to thaw, they were no doubt very busy trying to think of some plausible story to dazzle the Colonel with.

The results of our group's bombing at Metz were not obvious to us as we turned off the target but we didn't feel they were all that great. We were the first group over the target however, and with a dozen more groups to come, most of them with 2000 pound bombs, it was just a matter of percentages within the impact area.

A short time after the mission, The Eighth Air Force received the following message from General Patton: "This morning I was in the Verny group of forts which, as you will remember, was the No. 1 priority in the bombing attack which you put over on the 9th [of November]. One of the forts was completely removed; I have never seen so many large chunks of concrete in my life. Another fort which we are now occupying as a Command Post for the 5th Division was not hit, but the people were so badly scared that they all left, enabling us to occupy it without firing a shot. The No. 2 priority fort received direct hits and was also occupied without firing.

The Third Army appreciated the magnificent support you gave us. We are now in Metz."

The Third Army and the other allied forces continued their march right up to the gateways into Germany from the west, while the Russians were relatively quiet, and Eisenhower was having difficulty learning when their promised, massive offensive toward the Elbe River would begin. A very tough winter was really beginning to set in, and our missions were getting to be few and far between. For the flyboys, the war seemed to be slowing to a standstill. The continually socked-in airfields, the freezing drizzles, the thick clouds at flight level, the thoroughly obscured targets all combined to just about put us out of action.

We would have thought that the weather would have put the Luftwaffe out of action on the bad days too, but they appeared as determined to do their job as we were. Early in

December, the Group had been part of a mission to Bingen which, because of some scheduling whim, we were not part of. The bombing attack was made even though there were clouds along parts of the bomb run.

As one of our squadrons dropped their bombs, they entered a cloud and were forced to spread the formation, and as they came out the other side, there was a Sturmgruppen waiting for them. Dispersed as the Liberators were, it took only a few minutes for the fifty or so fighters to destroy six of them without much damage to themselves. The Group was able to reform into a tight defensive formation and the fighters broke off the attack, otherwise there could have been another Kassel massacre.

We were soon to find out that other Germans were also not idled by the atrocious weather. Adolf Hitler himself found the parade of low barometric pressure centers across the British Isles and the Continent to be an answer to his prayers -if indeed, he prayed- and made the most of it. In close secrecy, away from the constantly prying eyes of our aerial reconnaissance, he had his High Command make preparations for a massive counterblow that would set us back on our heels.

In an attack he designed himself, the Germans would make a great assault through the Ardennes forest to put themselves back into the war in a commanding position. Planning dispatches were circulated by motorcycle courier, to avoid interception.

As idle as we were, it seemed like a good time to take the train down to London to shake off the base routine blahs and have a little fun. The weather was lousy in London too, but it didn't make much difference and we found the place to be as lively as ever. The Grosvenor House, the downstairs bar at the Regent Palace, a big musical extravaganza of a show, a couple of pubs and then we reluctantly taxicabbed our way back to the Jules Club.

I don't recall much about the show we saw except that it ended with a bang. After what we thought was the last act, there was a pause, and then the doors from the lobby were thrown open and in marched a chorus and a large bagpipe band in kilts, with base drums booming and British flags waving.

Everybody got to their feet and yelled and applauded as they marched down the aisle and onto the stage, led by a teenybopper of a girl. She reached the microphone and started to sing the English marching songs in a big, piercing, thrilling voice, and the place really went wild. Everybody sang along and didn't want to quit, and I think the mostly English audience would have sung all night, but finally the curtain and the lights came down, and we all had to leave.

We had another little surprise, back at the Jules Club, to find a party in progress, so we gave that a little support too. The lady in charge eventually had enough and came around clanging a spoon on the side of a tea kettle, letting us know it was "Time, please!" and we left the lounge for bed. I had made the grievous error of hanging my trench coat and hat in the unattended check room, and although I might have expected that my hat was fair game and would be gone, I was surprised to find it was still there. It was my trench coat that was missing. I retrieved my hat and went upstairs, muttering under my breath and then shrugging; "to hell with it!"

Some time during the night, I was awakened by a sound in my room, and I lifted my head just in time to see a shadowy, departing figure silhouetted in the light of the hallway just as he was closing my door behind him. He was a small, heavy-set guy and it bothered me a little that he didn't appear to be one of us -a military person- but I wasn't awake enough to worry about it so I put my head down and went back to sleep.

When I awoke, I sat on the bed for a moment, thinking that there was something wrong, something missing, and then I remembered my missing trench coat. But no, that wasn't it, there was something else. My musette bag with a change of socks and linen was still there, as were my hat and shoes, and my blouse -my uniform jacket- was draped over the chair next to the bed. But underneath the blouse where I had draped my pants across the top slat of the chair was a blank spot. My pants, along with my wallet, were gone.

To be in the center of London without a trench coat was one thing, but to be there without pants; now that was a novel challenge. I just couldn't believe the situation I was in. There was no closet to look into, but I looked every place else in somewhat of a panic; under the bed, even in the waste basket, but

166

no pants.

Even in a situation like this, I still had to go to the bathroom. After all, it was one of the few things I was dressed for and could afford to do. I sauntered down the hall with a towel wrapped modestly around my waist, trying to act nonchalant as I realized the fix I was in. I found the bathroom and sat on one of Sir John Crapper's great inventions, this one with the word "Deluge" baked into the porcelain in blue lettering, and became lost in my dilemma.

Suddenly, out of the corner of my eye, I spotted the edge of a small bundle of cloth under the adjoining bath tub, which was one of the old-fashioned kind, raised off the floor on short, squatty legs. I reached down and pulled the bundle out, and sure enough it was my pants, my beloved pinks, with the wallet still in the back pocket. Everything was there; my brown, folded AGO card -the officer's I.D. card- pictures, my return ticket to Wendling, everything except a couple of ten-shilling notes I needed for breakfast before returning to the base. I put on those lovely trousers, gave the chain a joyous yank to set off the deluge and left, ready to face the world with newly found confidence. Do "clothes make the man," as the saying goes? It is difficult to say no when you have no pants to wear.

But wait:- the story is not yet over. As I went downstairs with Sam, who was going to buy my breakfast, I passed by the cloakroom, and there, sitting in the attendant's chair, was a young, downy-cheeked second lieutenant -just like me- with a trench coat draped over his arm. As I approached him I could see the play of internal forces on his face; first, he knew I was coming to claim the coat; second, he could see I had no coat with me to give him in return. "You must be Matt," he said, handling me the coat. I had inked my name on the maker's label.

"You didn't see my coat at all?" he continued, resignation on his face. "Nope, sorry," I said, "but at least nobody stole your pants too." He didn't think that was as funny as I did, so I invited him along for breakfast, since Sam was paying for it.

On December 16th, the Germans moved forward with their massive surprise offensive in the Ardennes region of France. This became known as the Battle of the Bulge because of the way their breakthrough was depicted on battle maps in the newspapers. The weather had been so bad that the Wehrmacht had been able to secretly maneuver a great force of three armies including ten Panzer divisions and fourteen infantry divisions into this hilly, heavily forested area and send them, tanks first, crashing through our lines. In a way, we were led into a trap by our own cleverness: in all of the highly secret Ultra dispatches we had been intercepting and decoding, there was no mention of such an offensive, and we were not ready for it.

The plan included saboteurs, German soldiers in American uniforms, paratroops and the dwindling numbers of the German Air Force. The desperation of the Germans was reflected in an incident near Malmedy, when a group of G.I.'s which had been captured were rounded up into an open area and savagely massacred by machine-gun fire. On our side, even the support troops, the cooks, clerks, whatever, were suddenly required to recall their basic training and learn how to use a gun again.

Adolf Hitler's plan had been to launch a blitzkrieg westward through a part of our lines between Luxembourg and Holland which was somewhat lightly held, then turn north toward Antwerp. This Belgian coastal city had been turned by the Allies into the main supply port for our operations in northern Europe, and its loss could stop our continued advance to the Rhine and beyond into Germany until some new arrangement could be made. Not only that, but the capture of Antwerp and Liege, which was on the way, by the Germans could mean that mountains of equipment and tank farms of fuel could fall into their hands, and that would make a whole new ball game.

The blitzkrieg plunged on, twenty, forty, fifty miles beyond the original battle lines on a wide front, and we all began to get a little uneasy. The feeling most of us had was that even though some of the worst fighting was yet to come, victory was a matter of time. Now, we weren't sure, even though both the G.I. and British press played it down.

While all of this was going on, we sat around on alert in the impossible flying weather and sweated it out. The planned ground support targets had to be changed daily as the Germans advanced, and we counterattacked. Finally, on

December 23rd, the weather opened up a little and the Eighth Air Force was able to get some bombers off the ground and make some attacks in marginal conditions in support of our troops.

The big day, however, finally came on December 24th, the day before Christmas, when the weather broke completely, and we were able to put up the most maximum of maximum efforts. Any airplane that had a fair chance of making it to the target and not necessarily all the way back was launched. One group even sent their war weary assembly marker aircraft, barber pole paint job and all, and I wonder what a Luftwaffe fighter pilot would have thought if he had gotten that one in his sights.

The 392nd sent 55 aircraft instead of the usual 30 or so, and whether I looked forward or aft, all I could see were formations of bombers in a giant stream, the biggest of the war to date. The scene could have been lifted from a recruiting poster, with wing after wing of shiny silver warplanes silhouetted against a deep blue winter sky.

Almost 2000 Liberators and Flying Fortresses attacked 36 different targets that day, including rail yards, strategic road crossings, fighter-bomber airfields and concentrations of reserve troops and supplies. Our oversize group was split into two parts, with the first formation attacking road and rail junctions at the town of Ruwer, just behind the southern part of the German bulge, while the second -of which we were a part- was assigned a traffic choke-point just across the Moselle River from Ruwer at Pfalzel. All of our medium bombers and fighter-bombers were turned loose also and it must have seemed to every German soldier in the area that no matter where he went, there seemed to be a bomber or strafing attack headed his way.

As this went on, the men of the U.S. Army's 101st Airborne Division made their place in history when they withstood heavy, desperate attacks and refused to be dislodged from a key road and rail junction in the middle of the German advance, at Bastogne. They held on day after day as we all waited and hoped, and when the Germans sent the 101st Commander, General McAuliffe, a demand for surrender, he sent them the perfect American reply;- "Nuts!"

As Patton made his way toward Bastogne for the rescue,

the Germans withdrew as their entire Blitzkrieg collapsed, taking 120,000 casualties and losing massive amounts of irreplaceable equipment. The Battle of the Bulge was the last large German offensive of the war; from now on they would be on the defensive. Hitler had taken a tremendous gamble and lost.

Did our bombing do any good? Apparently so, as indicated by a number of captured German replacement troops, who were trying to make their way forward not by train or truck, but by bicycle. And when they were taken prisoner, they were already ten days late for the battle.

The Battle of the Ardennes was a truly great victory for Eisenhower and his generals and the American G.I. fighting on the ground. They took on all of the best German regiments and divisions, some with histories of fighting skill and bravery dating far back into their history, and they beat them. And we in the 392nd and all of the other flying groups were proud to play a part.

There is no doubt that our troop support bombings resulted in the saving of large numbers of G.I. lives in the past. Now, the G.I.'s reciprocated in a very large way. By their decisive victory in the Ardennes, which included denial of massive amounts of aviation fuel to the Germans, they virtually eliminated the possibility that Luftwaffe General Galland could mount that great 500 plane massacre of the Eighth Air Force which he had planned for so long.

To this day, in the very rare event when someone uses the expression "Nuts!" in exasperation, I'm tempted to imitate General von Rundstedt, who looked at McAuliffe's reply to his ultimatum, just brought to him by courier from encircled Bastogne, and who said in complete bafflement, "Was ist das Nuts?"

There was still a little bit of 1944 left, so on the 28th of December we were sent to do as much damage as possible to the railyards at Kaiserslautern, in the Saarland where there is a part of Germany on the French side of the Rhine. The Germans would now be preparing to do battle to keep the Allies from reaching the Rhine, and Kaiserslautern would be one of the rail hubs to supply the German defenders.

This was usually a well-defended target, and it appeared

so to me on this occasion, and in my own log, I called the flak "moderate and accurate." The Group diary, reflecting reports from the lead crews, called the flak "meager and very accurate." But the intelligence report, based on the post-mission reports taken from all of the returning aircrews, interviewed as they sipped the Old Overholt, described the flak as follows: "Flak first encountered about 7 or 8 minutes before bombs away, predictor controlled....meager but fairly accurate...Flak next encountered 1 to 2 minutes before bombs away, meager, inaccurate. Flak lasted until 2 minutes after bombs away, moderate but inaccurate, very high or very low and behind, tracking...black and white puffs, some with orange centers."

Then, two paragraphs down, the report continues," One of our aircraft -E #623- is missing. This aircraft, hit by flak 1 or 2 minutes after bombs away, dropped from formation with #2 engine on fire and proceeded under control for about 2 minutes, losing altitude and with fire in the bomb bay. #4 engine caught fire, and the aircraft finally blew up...6 chutes seen."

And further; "B-24, 491st Bomb Group" -part of our Wing- "exploded in mid-air and went down in flames...no chutes seen." The report did not mention another one of our Group's aircraft which had to drop out of formation and land at Woodbridge, a large concrete patch on the way home where pilots with severely damaged aircraft made "controlled crash landings."

Were these aircraft hit by meager or moderate and inaccurate flak bursts? It is possible, of course, that the flak estimates were made somewhere between Old Overholt rations #1 and #2 at the debriefing. It is also possible, although I never tried it, to continue on with rations #3 and #4 and convince yourself that you didn't see any flak at all.

Out of the goodness of his heart, the scheduling man was able to squeeze in one final mission for us on the last day of the year which, for our Group, turned out to be a fiasco. The target was a bridge and railroad crossing at Euskirchen, between the Belgian border and the Rhine, not very far into Germany. On the bomb run, the leader's blind bombing equipment went kaput and couldn't find the target, so the deputy leader took over. The deputy cranked up his own radar bombing equipment, and went looking for another target, taking the Group out of the formation on a solitary mission of our own. It seems like some people never learn.

The new leader found a significant target in his radar about the time an abbreviated Sturmgruppen -there were only fifteen or so fighters- showed up like magic. As we made the run and dropped our bombs, the fighters attacked and did some damage, but no one went down. The pilots had tightened up the formation and the gunners let the Luftwaffe know they would not have an easy time of it, and the attack was broken off.

I have often wondered if the Luftwaffe pilots had as big a New year's Eve party as we did.

8

VARSITY TO VE-DAY

THE SMALL, FLAT, CASKET-SHAPED BOX was lying on my cot when I got back from doing the things I did on bad weather days, like getting a haircut or sitting around the club reading ancient copies of the Illustrated London News. The box was dark blue, and had some sort of document wrapped around it held with a rubber band. I pulled the paper off and opened the box and looked at my first combat decoration;- an Air Medal. Then I picked up the document, and I realized it was the citation. It began with the usual "Under the provisions of Army Regulations...." and then went on to the next paragraph, which started out with "For meritorious achievement...", a phrase which didn't seem to have a very war-like ring to it, but then as I read on, the words, "The courage, coolness and skill displayed by this individual in the face of determined opposition..." jumped up at me, and I thought about that for a while, and I was content. No matter what happened to me for the rest of my life, good or bad, nobody could take this recognition away from me, this moment of realization that I was now firmly part of a group I had always looked at with awe.

By this time in the war, thousands of people like me had gotten this same citation and the same decoration, this sixteen-pointed bronze medal engraved with an eagle diving to the attack, a bolt of lightning grasped in each claw. Some Air Medals have been awarded to people for some action in an airplane -not in wartime- and these are well earned. But most are awarded to the guys who strapped on the gear on cold, damp mornings or sweaty afternoons and climbed into the aluminum tubes, large or small, and, as they advanced the throttles or thrust levers, or got out their maps or bombing tables, or got their guns ready, they may have thought, for a gut-wrenching minute or two, "Oh Jesus, not again!", and then they were gone to do battle. Getting an Air Medal would be nowhere in their thoughts.

But because there is no way to get this medal except by some action in the air, it holds a special place in my mind, and when I see military types from any of the branches, Officer or G.I., with that blue bar with two gold bands on their chest, I know they are part of our crowd:- The Crewdogs.

All of us on John Beder's crew were awarded the Air Medal not once, but several times. If you flew long enough and often enough, you would get it periodically until you got shot down or went home. But you didn't get it by sitting on the ground.

Occasionally I bump into someone who, in an innocent way, seems to think that the aircrews flew missions to get medals; that defeating the enemy was secondary. No one would say this who has been in the position of Big John and Sam and Jack Murray and myself and all the crewmembers, on the last minute or two of the bomb run when we were flying as leader, the Liberator locked on to the cross-hairs in Jack's bomb sight, the great blasts of flak right in front of us and dead level with our eyebrows, every impulse in us demanding that we turn off to protect our lives. And then I would ask this person to stand there on the flight deck and wait for that flak shell to explode up through the floor, and then tell us all we were doing this for a medal.

I still have that first Air Medal. It is getting a little discolored and the ribbon is a little frayed, not because I've ever had the original pinned on. In fact, although the medals were delivered to our huts, we were told that they would be pinned on in a formal ceremony by the Colonel if we happened to be around at the right time, but I never made it.

Winter at Wendling had developed into one of the worst on record. We did a lot of sitting around for days at a time when nothing took off, or we made trips to places like East Dereham or King's Lynn and drank some beer in the pubs. When we did get a mission in, it was generally intended to help the ground forces tidy up the aftermath of the Battle of the Bulge, or to get ready for the Rhine crossings.

On January 8th, 1945 we flew a troop support mission to knock out a road and rail center at a town called Burg Rueland which lay directly in the path to the Ruhr Valley, where the heaviest concentration of German industries was located. The flak was also very heavily concentrated there, which was why the area was referred to as "Happy Valley". Lucky for us, Burg Rueland was well short of the flak defenses and we were able to do the job and return with hardly a scratch.

We had now flown seventeen missions, a number of them tough, a few of them easy, but all of them taking their toll, and raising the odds . We were now a veteran crew, and after landing, we were able to zip through the intelligence debriefing with a few grunts and a shrug. I took my big slug of Old Overholt into the men's room to sip as I washed my face and cleaned up a little, and as I wiped my hands, I found myself studying the face that stared back at me in the mirror.

The down on my cheeks had turned into an honest-to-god stubble, and I could still see the imprint of the oxygen mask over the bridge of my nose and across my cheeks. The flying helmet I had worn for all those hours because it had the interphone headset built into it and also supported my oxygen mask had matted my hair down so tightly that it itched until I could comb it a little. It came to me that I was getting to look a little beat up, not from the oxygen mask marks or the tight helmet or the minus 40 degree cold or the skin-wrinkling dryness of the rarefied air we flew in, but something else. I could see it in my eyes; I was suddenly, since our first mission on the 2nd of October, a lot older. I couldn't quite put my finger on what was changing in me but it didn't bother me that much. I was where I thought I should be, and screw the consequences. It also came to me that in a couple of weeks, I would be twenty-one years old.

A few days after the Burg Rueland mission, Big John came around and announced that we had been selected as a lead crew, as we had expected. There was a lot of additional training to undergo, especially for Big John and Jack Murray. Flying lead would be a big change for me too, since now I would have the responsibility for navigating whatever formation we were leading. Big John had to take another look at everyone on the crew to determine if any changes had to be made, for now was the time to do it, but we all stayed on.

About this same time, Big John was promoted to the exalted rank of First Lieutenant. The whole idea of assigning him as an aircraft commander on a lead crew while remaining a second john would probably have embarrassed even the scrooges at higher headquarters, who acted like they paid for promotions out of their own pockets.

Since we had come to Wendling, we had been required to take part in periodic practice missions, usually three or four hours long, primarily to keep the pilot's formation flying ability at a high level. Now that we were designated as a lead crew, we were taken off the combat mission schedule and given an increased dose of training flights. Big John and Sam were given instruction in how to fly as the formation leader, including procedures for getting a formation together and methods used in uncovering from the enroute, defensive formation to the attack formation for the bomb run, and back again.

As for me, I now had to learn how a lead navigator coordinated his actions with the nose turret navigator and the radar operator. I would now also play a part during the formation assembly procedure since it would be up to me to provide Big John with headings and suggestions for timing maneuvers to get our formation over Buncher Five at exactly the right time. This was necessary so we could be inserted into the bomber stream in the right place to depart England in the prearranged order. A group or wing out of sequence in the bomber stream could result in a massive screw-up of the uncovering maneuver at the Initial Point as the formations split up to head for their assigned targets.

This training routine lasted for more than a month, until February 15th when we flew a practice mission of almost six hours and landed to find out that we were alerted for the next day's mission. The target was Salzbergen, where we were going after the oil again. Between the Eighth Air Force in England

and the Fifteenth Air Force operating from Italy, we were able to make the Germans operate on "starvation" oil rations to the extent that anything they did on the ground or in the air was limited by the fuel consideration. Despite a number of very costly but devastating attacks made by the Eighth and Fifteenth Air Forces on aircraft plants in Germany, aircraft production was as high as ever, but due to lack of fuel, many of them sat on the ground instead of queuing up for the attack and coming at us head-on.

Some of the raids we had made against aircraft plants were intended to hold down production of the new Messerschmitt 262 twin-jet fighter, which had four 30-millimeter cannons and a 100 MPH level flight advantage over the Mustang. As their numbers increased we all began to get a little edgy, even though a Mustang could out-turn it and occasionally catch one in a dive. An ME-262 pilot could bounce a straggling bomber or attack the rear of a formation and be gone so quickly there was no time to shoot back. Some say that if Hitler had put his money into the new jets instead of the V-l and V-2 terror bombs, we might still be fighting the war.

There was another new German fighter, the Messerschmitt 163, a bat-winged model powered by rockets which were used to get the little monster well above our formations. The rockets were then shut off as he dived for the attack and then turned on again to make his getaway.

A somewhat scary story made the rounds about one ME-163 which made an attack on the rear of a formation, then cruised up into the middle of the bombers and sat there. The bomber gunners couldn't shoot without fear of hitting their buddies, but those close to the 163 could clearly see the Luftwaffe pilot as he looked around and nodded as if to say, "now get a load of this, you poor peasants!", and he gave it the needle and blasted off, leaving the bombers, their old-fashioned propellers thrashing away in the thin air, feeling somewhat deprived. However, the ME 163 came along early in the rocket game, and it had a tendency to blow up as it was being fueled.

The selection of bombing targets was carried on at the highest allied military command levels, overseen by Generals

and Air Marshals . But the overall concept on which this selection process was based was decided at the very top, and
required the approval of people like Winston Churchill and
President Roosevelt.

From the war's beginning, the British had come to the conclusion that all bombing should be done at night to avoid the
massive fighter attacks and visually aimed flak barrages which
daylight bombing had to put up with. The British had expected,
when our bomber forces began arriving in England, that we
would put aside our smart-ass notions about daylight precision
bombing and do it the way they did, at night. After all, the
British had been engaged in tit-for-tat bombing of each other's
populations with the Germans, and the disruption of the enemy
workforce and the breaking of his or her morale seemed indispensable to victory. Churchill, whose agreement was needed
before the U.S. could proceed with daylight bombing, had to be
convinced. General Spaatz was sent to point out to him that
with the Americans bombing by day and the RAF bombing by
night, the Germans would be subjected to 'round the clock'
bombing. The phrase had a nice ring to it, so Churchill gave his
approval.

American cities were not being bombed nor were her civilian populations being killed in large numbers and the idea of
our air forces joining the RAF in large-scale "morale" bombings
would have created problems back home and with the U.S.
bomber crews themselves. Our idea was to find specific targets
and destroy them by placing the maximum force of the bomb
loads directly on the target, which was to be primarily military
in nature. Under the RAF concept, hitting a target like an oil
plant or a rail yard in a city they were bombing at night could
happen "fortuitously" when the city itself was the objective.

The massive bombing of Dresden by the RAF on the night
of February 13th, a few days after we had gone to Salzbergen
created a wave of revulsion because of the unusually catastrophic effect it had on the city and the populace. Dresden was
an old center of German culture, and it took some targeting
creativity to find military value in its destruction. Its large population had been increased by more than a half million
refugees, many of whom were forced out of the shelters and
into the streets by the large initial attack with incendiaries,

only to be caught there by the following bombing attacks. A fire-storm developed, a strange phenomenon where all of the fires combine to turn the target into a blast furnace in which the very atmosphere seems to burn.

The next day, the Eighth Air Force sent in several hundred bombers to attack the marshalling yards, and the city was found to be still burning from the night before. The Germans threatened to renounce their adherence to the Geneva Convention and to treat captured flyers as criminals instead of prisoners of war, but it was too late in the war to take such a measure. Despite some hand-wringing and soul searching back in the U.S., plans went forward for dropping the A-bomb, although President Truman and his advisors had to undergo a long and agonizing period trying to decide how to use it to end the war quickly.

Meanwhile, General Lemay, who was sent to the Far East to take over the bombing program could see that we were losing aircraft and crews without getting the Japanese closer to surrender. He embarked on a series of RAF-style fire-bombing raids at night on Japanese cities including spectacular attacks on Tokyo. Japan, after all, had attacked Pearl Harbor and dragged us into the war, but even so, some time after the program began, leaflets were dropped before each raid to warn the residents so that they could get out of the way.

It turned out that we didn't do too much leading on our first lead mission. We were assigned as the deputy to the wing leader, a crew from the 44th Bomb Group "Eight Balls", one of our sister groups in the 14th Wing. Our formation position was to be on his left wing.

The field order specified that bombing was to be performed by GH if the target was obscured, and the Eight Balls had the properly equipped aircraft and crews trained for this technique. Second choice was the use of H2X, or "Mickey" as the radar procedure was called. We had the gear and the trained crew for H2X and would take over the lead if the GH crew could not bomb for some reason, such as complete jamming of the GH signals, or if they were put out of action for any reason, like getting shot down.

A lead or deputy lead bomber really had a gang of people

on board. The usual two pilots, bombardier, flight engineer, radioman, three gunners and I were augmented by the Mickey operator who had a position on the flight deck, and another navigator, who manned the nose turret in place of Jack Murray. The nose navigator provided visual checkpoint fixes to me when he could, and helped Jack identify the target on the bomb run. Jack had the nose compartment to himself, since my position, which faced toward the rear, was moved to the flight deck just behind Big John across from the Mickey man.

The cramped quarters for me and the radar man took some getting used to, especially since we had the big, fat top turret enclosure between us. The turret itself was not fully enclosed, and the various pipes, tubes and wiring protruded out into the right of way and brushed against us as the turret was swung around by the flight engineer. I had only a small window at my right shoulder I could look out of, which meant that suddenly, I couldn't see much of what was going on.

As the Dead Reckoning navigator, I had to depend on the pilotage navigator in the nose turret to read the ground checkpoints for me. When we were in clouds, I could expect that the radar man would give me an occasional radar fix. This arrangement didn't work as well as it could have because it required a degree of coordination which could only come about with some practice. Since the same nose and radar navigators were seldom assigned to our crew on later missions, we had to do the best we could.

As we were approaching the I.P. on this first lead mission, I decided that there were advantages too, in this new arrangement. Being in one of the formation lead aircraft meant that we flew straight and level most of the time, rather than continually jockeying around to stay in close formation. Now, other airplanes jockeyed around to keep position with us.

On this mission, the formation leader was able to make his bomb run, so we continued over the target in the deputy position and dropped our bombs. This was the same mission, described earlier, on which Al Novik had part of the tail knocked from his aircraft but got his crew home.

Operation Clarion had struck some of us as something that the management might think up because they were getting bored with the same old stuff. Day after day, they were sending all those crewdogs into Germany to drop their bombs the same old way, from 22 or 23 thousand feet by the Liberators and somewhat higher by the Forts. This time they would shake people up, both the aircrews and the Germans, by sending us to bomb at 10,000 feet or below. The targets were railroad yards all over Germany which were generally too small to have any significant flak defenses. At that altitude, we would certainly need to tip-toe pretty carefully around the flak concentrations we knew about or it would be a duck shoot, and we would be the ducks.

Because of our altitude, most Germans had never seen our formations except as tiny specks, or at the point of the contrails in wintertime. Now, the thinking apparently went, we would thumb our noses at the Luftwaffe and give the general populace something extra to think about as we flew overhead in perfect formation and dropped our bombs before their very eyes. The group formation was composed of three squadrons, each with ten aircraft; a lead squadron and low and high squadrons. We were leading the low squadron which meant that for the first time Jack would have the chance to show his stuff on the bombsight, as each squadron was bombing individually.

The mission was uneventful as we crossed the Dutch coast at 18,000 feet without any reaction from our friends on the barges, and we stayed at this altitude as we drew even with the Ruhr Valley and then turned south until we were just east of the industrial heart of Germany. Then we turned northeast, further into Germany and began our letdown to 10,000 feet. As we dropped down, the whole pace of the mission seemed to speed up as the terrain moved underneath us at an unaccustomed rate. The lead navigator who was leading our entire wing was having some difficulty in keeping his position straight and we seemed to be changing headings in an uncertain manner. We were too deep into Germany for the GEE signals to reach us, and the hilly terrain in this part of Germany was not well suited for radar navigation. Moreover, large patches of lower stratocumulus clouds hid most of the visual checkpoints on the ground.

As I peered down, a Liberator directly below us suddenly just came apart as I was looking at it. It had taken a direct hit on the first burst from a couple of guns not marked on our flak charts. Both wings, those long, thin Davis airfoils folded up over the top of the airplane and came off, as they had a habit of doing when the Liberator was hit in a certain way and the fuselage plunged on down, bombs, crewmembers and all, and dove into the ground with a great blast. The crew never had a chance. They were pinned flat by the acceleration and waited, during those indescribable seconds of terror, for the hard ground to burst upward to meet them. We took some evasive action and pressed on, our hearts stopped to better hear if our number was also to be called by Mister Eighty-eight, unable to see if some other Libs behind us were hit.

Because of the wing leader navigational problems, we had to give up on the primary target at Nordhausen and head for targets of opportunity. Our group leader split us off from the wing and took us down further, down to 6000 feet and then we drifted still further to almost 5000 feet. It was a curious feeling being down this low in hostile territory, to see all of the details of the countryside; the roads, farm buildings, and streams not as map-like, impersonal terrain features, but close-up, real land touched with the breath of hostile life.

Our group leader found a likely target of opportunity up ahead, a small marshalling yard at Northeim with several strings of freight cars and we tried to uncover into a line of squadrons in the very short time we had. The lead squadron made their drop and we came in right behind them into a great explosion of smoke and flying debris which easily reached up to us a mile above the ground. Jack had to make a very quick run and the bombs hit along the edge of the yard. We didn't get one of those compact, destructive patterns because some of the bombardiers in our squadron had toggled when the lead squadron up ahead dropped and didn't wait for Jack. We didn't obliterate that little railyard as we probably would have if we had stayed up a little higher, but we certainly made a lot of noise.

Three days later, we were assigned to lead our squadron on another mission, a railroad target at Aschaffenburg. The operations planners had apparently gotten Operation Clarion out of their system and we were back to normal with the bombing altitude set for 23,000 feet, and no gimmicks. All of the crew had been promoted to full journeyman grade; all the officers were "Johns" -First Lieutenants- while Morley and Murgatroyd were Tech Sergeants and Roever, Carr and Schodrof at the gunner positions were made Staff Sergeants.

For once, everything fell into place perfectly; weather was not a problem, everyone flew perfect formation, the navigators knew where they were and what the flight level winds were doing, and the bombardiers had lots of time. Enemy activity was negligible as the Germans seemed to be either running out of flak shells, or were pulling their guns deeper into the Reich. Whatever enemy fighters there were to challenge us were swarmed over by the Mustangs and the Thunderbolts and had no time for us.

The bomb bays were just aft of my new position on the flight deck, and as we came down the bomb run, I worked my way around the upper turret well and kneeled down at the entrance to the bays. The doors were already open and I leaned forward, waiting, my oxygen mask and headset plugged into receptacles near the entrance. The big, yellow-banded 500 pound RDX bombs hung in the bays, silent and ominous, filling me with dread, waiting for the bomb-sight to send the bombs away signal to the shackles to let them plunge down like great, dumb beasts when the electrical charge hit the releases. Jack had already performed his ritual of removing the safety wires so that the arming vanes on the nose of the bombs were free to spin off in the slipstream and arm the bombs on their way down.

The enemy terrain slid beneath us and I waited for the flak to blossom and drift by, but none came. And suddenly there was a loud click-click-click and the bombs dropped down, seeming to float under us for a split second as the smoke marker bomb went off with a loud splat. The bombs and smoke marker now fell away with great speed and the big 500-pounders magically shrank in size to tiny dots which sped forward as we continued to the target.

The bright, white plume of the smoke marker pointed its finger at the bomb load, which could no longer be seen, and I waited as the aiming point, the round house near the center of the Aschaffenburg marshalling yard complex moved underneath us. As I watched, a tightly grouped mass of explosions hit the round house dead center and it disappeared in a cloud of smoke.

"I saw a stick of bombs hit the roundhouse," I said to the General and the Colonel who were debriefing us. Big John and Jack had already given their observations not in the intelligence hut, but in the Colonel's office, as befitted a lead crew. Both Johnsons were there; the wing commander and our own group commander, and they nodded as we all looked at a target map laid out on a table.

"Looks like a good piece of work, but we'll need to wait for the strike photos," said the General. We all looked at him as he straightened up and quietly asked Jack Murray and Big John and the other lead crewmembers a few more questions and then we got ready to head for the Old Overholt. It was the first time I had ever said anything to a General. We, the several lead pilots, co-pilots, bombardiers and navigators had been thunder-struck to find him standing next to Colonel Johnson, not only an honest-to-God General, but General Johnson himself, the man from Ploesti, who made it through the savage fury of that low-level raid. He was a tall, immaculate man, with a diplomat's brush mustache, every sandy-colored hair in its prescribed place. He had seemed just slightly pre-occupied during the debriefing, as if he and our group commander had been discussing something portentous when we walked in, and he was still thinking about it. Was it another unusual mission perhaps, one which would make him wonder if the Wendling crewdogs were up to some task he had in mind?

It turned out that what I told the General was wrong. The strike photos showed that it was not just a stick of bombs, but the whole squadron's bomb load that hit the roundhouse. On our very first real lead mission Jack Murray and Big John had gotten everything together and had removed the need to deal with that particular target again. Accurate bombing didn't rate a medal because that was what we were here for, but in this case it did rate a lead crew commendation signed by the General. It meant you could be trusted to lead larger formations and perhaps take on some of the tougher missions which, of course, could be a very mixed blessing.

It was certain that General Johnson already knew about Operation Varsity when he debriefed us, at least in general outline. Looking into those calm blue eyes there was no way of telling what was in store for some of us, that we might have to measure up, to a lesser extent, to some of the challenges he himself had met at Ploesti. As the planners were putting Operation Varsity together, we were sent, three days after Aschaffenburg, to a marshalling yard at a place called Siegen, between Cologne and Frankfurt. And then, three days after that on March 2nd, we went to the synthetic oil plants at Magdeburg, a place which was held in special regard by the crews, mostly involving terror. The Germans always sent up their fighters for this one, and so they did this time, but those that got by the Mustangs found somebody else to attack first and we only had the flak to deal with. The 1st Division lost three Forts, we lost three Liberators and the 3rd Division, which went to Dresden, got involved in a massive fighter battle and lost eight Forts while the Mustangs escorting them knocked down fifty-four of the attackers.

As Varsity moved closer, we went to Stettin, on the Polish coast of Pomerania, just on their border with Germany. For the first time, we were assigned a target requested by the Russians, who asked that the dock areas at the port city be attacked. Large amounts of troops and supplies which were being withdrawn from the Russian front were passing through Stettin for the defense of the Berlin area, just to the south.

The German "pocket" battleship Admiral Scheer was also in port, in addition to transport vessels. We could not see any of these, or the city itself, because of a heavy cloud cover so we were forced to make the drop by H2X. The Russians never did tell us how effective the bombing was, but the British did some photo reconnaissance a few days later and said that we had not wasted our time.

The field order for Operation Varsity did not arrive in the usual way, as a message classified secret on two yards of yellow teleprinter paper. Instead, it was delivered by courier, page

185

after page of orders, assignments, orders of battle, routes, times, etc., etc., in a fancy folder, all stamped Top Secret.

The order began; "Varsity can be considered the most important combined operation since the invasion of France...". It also said that the Allied armies in the north will have crossed the Rhine at three points at zero hour minus six hours by amphibious assault. In airborne operations, the 1st Allied Airborne Army will dispatch 1593 aircraft towing gliders with troops aboard for release in the landing zone, while paratroops would also be dropped. U.S. Air forces and the RAF would neutralize defenses, interdict road and rail traffic and provide close support. Eighth Air Force bombers would be included.

The operation was set for March 24th, and most of the 1700 heavy bombers involved would attack about two dozen airfields in northern Germany within range of the Rhine River. Their task was to crater runways at known jet airfields and to prevent the use of enemy jet aircraft in the area.

Two task groups of 120 Liberators each would also take part but in an unusual way; first, they would drop not bombs but canisters of ammunition and other material to resupply the ground troops during the battle and second, the drop would be made at 400 feet. One task group would drop supplies to American forces and the other to British forces, who were involved in the massive amphibious and airborne crossing.

Soon, we, that is John Beder's crew, would learn that we would lead a formation of thirteen 392nd aircraft as part of the task group re-supplying the British, and that the assault would take place near the town of Wesel, northwest of the Ruhr Valley. Our part in Operation Varsity would require that we be able to find our way, at very low altitude, from our bases in England across the Channel to the Boulogne area, then across France and Belgium to a drop zone measuring 1500 by 2000 yards, just across the Rhine.

We would fly very low to insure surprise and decrease the already high degree of vulnerability we were stuck with. When we found ourselves, a few days after the Stettin mission, with a small formation tearing across French farmland on a practice mission at 50 feet, so low that the altimeter pointer sort of sat on zero, I had to admit, war or not, tough mission or milk run, there was nothing as exhilarating as a legal buzz job. We blasted across the farmlands, sometimes so low it appeared we could drop the gear and wheel along some road that ran along with us, then Big John would ease back on the yoke to slide over a row of trees or a set of wires, then drop back again, skimming across the furrowed sea like 150-knot dolphins. We crossed into Belgium, and came upon a hard-working farmer ploughing his field with a pair of draft horses and Big John tried to give him some distance but the horses reared up and he let them go. Then the farmer furiously picked up a rock or clod of dirt and flung it at us as we cruised by. Imagine yourself in an upper level seat of a double-decker bus screaming along at our speed, and that's the kind of navigation job I was faced with.

The checkpoints blew by us so fast I was only half sure I had the right road or rail intersections, bends in small rivers, small towns with church steeples tall enough to make us turn aside. On we raced until we found our target, a town about the size of Wesel, and Big John pulled the Lib up to 400 feet to simulate the drop, then got the formation back around and down on the deck to head for home. The GEE signals appeared to come in okay at low altitude, but I knew better than to depend on a gadget that could be jammed or crap out, so I concentrated on navigating by reading the landmarks.

The low-level resupply mission to Wesel was to be our 24th mission. We had, by now, gotten ourselves into a mind-set where preflight preparations were routine, although performed with that feeling of dread in back of the mind. This day the feeling of routine was gone and was replaced by something I hadn't felt for a while, the fascination of the moth for the flame. The feeling of dread was still there, but there was excitement too that the invasion of Germany itself was about to start and the war could end soon after.

The risks to us, to John Beder's and to the other Liberator crews were hard to gauge. Low level missions flown into enemy defended areas were not what heavy bombers were designed for. They were slow and not too maneuverable and much too fragile to withstand accurate ground fire. Also, we were prohibited from using our guns to fire back at enemy ground gunners for fear of hitting our own troops. And if we were hit hard, we didn't have much of a chance if we bailed out.

A mission just like ours was flown in support of the British

in Holland the previous September and although the drop had
been made as required, seven Liberators were lost to ground
fire in a few minutes. And earlier in the war when B-26 twin-
engined bombers were being introduced, they were practically
wiped out at low level and had to go to a medium altitude. And
then, of course, there had been the low-level bloodbath at
Ploesti.

The array of enemy firepower facing all aspects of the operation including the glider landings, the paratroop drop and our
resupply mission was somewhat daunting; 375 single-engined
fighters, 260 twin-engined fighters, 40 jet fighters available
and serviceable, with another 675 fighters which could be
employed if they were repositioned to the area in time. The
number of flak guns, both light and heavy, was called "consid-
erable...and additional guns are arriving daily." But the order
continued; "Probably our greatest danger will come from small
arms fire from enemy troops although there is little doubt that
the majority of these will be otherwise engaged at the time."
When I heard this I crossed my fingers and looked skyward for
a moment, because there were 47,000 German troops directly
involved with another possible 60,000 replacements.

Despite all these horrifying numbers, this certainly was
not a suicide mission. The attacks on the airfields and the cra-
tering of the runways was expected to greatly reduce possible
fighter activity. There would also be a massive amount of flak
suppression activity by our fighter-bombers just before the
arrival of the gliders and our arrival 15 minutes later.

As for the enemy troops and their rifles and vehicle-mount-
ed machine-guns, if the ground troops who had made the
amphibious assault and the 40,000 allied airborne and para-
troopers did their part of the job, there would be a large enough
pocket on the German side of the Rhine to permit us to make
the drop and turn while remaining within allied-held territory.
This seemed to be the key to our survival in the relatively
small part we had to play in this great battle.

Now how is a man to think about all of this without slipping around the bend? A general can plan ahead and make
chess-like moves as the battle progresses but the crewdog and
the soldier on the ground must deal with the immediate threat
to himself and his mission. It didn't do much good to strap

yourself into your seat and start thinking, well, if such or such happens I'll do this or that. You had to be ready for anything and take it as it came.

And as for how the generals thought about risk, I'm glad I didn't know of some remarks that had been made by Lt. General Ira Eaker, a former Eighth Air Force commander. While discussing the reticence of ground commanders to make an attack at Cassino in Italy for fear of high casualty rates, he said, partly in understanding their hesitation, that "a ground commander who gets the same casualties that we in the Air Forces take as a matter of course might be criticized and might be called a butcher."

And so it was when we took off at 0930 in the morning and climbed to 3000 feet to form up, which took a whole hour, then we let down to 1000 feet and headed out. Our coastal departure point was near Folkestone, and we got a good view of Dover's white cliffs as we headed across the Channel. As we approached landfall on the French side, the leaders up ahead turned left and headed directly over Boulogne, about 8 miles south of course. To have a large formation of Liberators pass overhead at 1000 feet must have been quite a sight to the citizens of that city, but I thought, Hell, we can show off some other time.

We were still heading southeast when we left Boulogne and held on to that course until we reached a point 20 miles southwest of Lille and then altered course due east. I noted we had gotten nine minutes late, which was not worrisome, since it made us less likely to interfere with the glider landings. If we had gotten early, we would need to kill time somehow before going into the drop zone.

The whole world certainly looked different on this mission. Big John was keeping a 1000 foot reading on the pressure altimeter as the ground rose up to meet us south of Brussels. The terrain was not flat like the countryside we had practiced over, and we were clearing it by five or six hundred feet. The navigation was a lot easier than I had anticipated because the GEE box was working well and I was never in doubt as to our position and our progress. I felt confident enough so that if the other formations took off on a weird heading, I would tell Big

John to wave good-bye to them and take off on our own.

The flight level wind was surprisingly high at about 25 knots blowing into us from the east, and I wondered what problems it would pose for the glider pilots and the paratroops. We reached the final turning point fifteen miles southeast of Brussels and headed northeast on a sixty degree heading with ninety miles to go.

I was free to move around as we had no need to use oxygen so I went up into the nose section to get a better view of the terrain. The tempo picked up as we slowly let down and the ground sped by more quickly. The gunners in the rear were getting ready to dump the bundles of supplies, which were rigged with parachutes and would be dropped through a hatch in the bottom of the waist section. The biggest load, however, was hung up on shackles in the bomb bay and would be toggled out by Jack Murray. The whole drop totaled two and a half tons in each airplane. The sooner we got the stuff out, the sooner we could turn out of there, and we expected the whole drop to be made very quickly.

Now we were coming up on the Initial Point, with the Maas River flashing by, with ten miles to the Rhine, and five more to the drop zone. Big John was getting us down on the deck and we wondered again, as we shot forward, whether the drop zone would be in our hands or theirs. The Rhine was coming up fast and suddenly somebody yelled and a flight of RAF Typhoon fighters came dead at us and then scattered in all directions, barely missing us. They had been on close support and were heading back.

The Rhine flashed by and we came into the fantastic panorama of a big battle in progress, with first row seats suspended a hundred feet above the battleground, heading for the main action at 160 knots. Gliders were everywhere on the ground, some intact, some broken. There were tow planes splattered here and there, still burning. We passed flaming farm buildings on our left, their roofs blown off and columns of bluish smoke rising from them into the haze. There were troops all over the place, some crouching down, some scurrying around.

"Here's the drop zone!" I yelled, about the same time Jack did and Big John pulled the Liberator up and slowed her down to 150 knots, the drop speed. The bomb bay load went out cleanly and the gunners were scrambling to get their bundles out, and then they were all gone and we had done our job. As the parachute-borne canisters floated down I looked forward, to the east, and could see great flashes pretty close by, and columns of smoke rising through the haze left by the smoke-screen of the early morning amphibious crossing.

Big John made his turn and got the formation around to the right and got back down, and we realized with a shock that we were now directly over the battle line, on the German side and we could see the enemy up very close for the first time, firing at us and moving around. We came up on a self-propelled gun, a monstrous thing marked with a black cross, its barrel swivelling along, tracking us, and as we passed overhead there was a big thump as it fired too late and missed us. "E for Easy is going down!" came a shout from the back end but I couldn't see it from where I was. There were calls of distress as Liberators were being hit behind us, big caliber bullets smashing through the thin aluminum into fuel tanks, engines, hydraulic lines, living bone and flesh. The scene on the ground was very confused now, with firing everywhere and tracers flying around, and tanks moving off to our left in the haze and smoke. The noise of our engines seemed amplified, the sound bouncing off the ground just beneath us as we raced on, holding our breath, hearts pumping a mile a minute. But suddenly again, we were flying over our own, over the broken gliders and spilled parachutes, the pock-marked ground, all shrouded in the smoke of war. British paratroops stood around in small groups, unpacking their gear, looking up and waving as we passed, ignoring a small group of German prisoners being marched off somewhere. Big John got a little altitude and we could see the Rhine again, no longer a formidable barrier to be assaulted and, for this mission at least, the boundary of the promised land where we could sit back and see if we were still in one piece.

I clambered back up to the flight deck and stood between Big John and Sam for a while, all three of us talking at the same time about the Germans and the crashed airplanes and gliders, feeling a relief so profound that it drained us and then we were silent, back at a thousand feet indicated, bumping along the countryside like a school of tired whales.

"Twenty airplanes? Twenty goddam airplanes?" some disbelieving, rising voice said at breakfast two days later, as we read the write-up of our mission in the Stars and Stripes. That was the initial report of the toll. Fourteen Liberators out of two hundred-forty had gone down in the target area in all the different ways a mortally wounded bomber can finish its life and the lives of the crewdogs within. The rest comprised a trail of wrecked airplanes and wounded crewmembers at emergency airfields on the route home. We had been directly over the enemy, or within range of his guns for a matter of a few minutes, and that was the price we paid.

E for Easy, piloted by Lt. J. R. Hummel, flying on the wing of the slot man directly behind us had been hit hard by large caliber ground fire and peeled off and away, then dipped down and made a sliding, tearing crash landing in some open ground in the midst of the enemy. Two of the crew had actually bailed out at that low altitude in the few seconds they had; one made it and the other, the navigator, didn't. As Hummel's crew crawled out of the wrecked Liberator, some of the Germans opened fire and a gunner, Sergeant Milchak, was killed instantly. The survivors were rounded up by the Wehrmacht troops, who interrogated them and then treated their wounds and injuries. Four hours later the Germans themselves had to surrender and the Yanks were liberated.

Two other aircraft flying alongside Hummel had to quit the formation due to damage and wounded crewmembers and landed on the Continent. The toll on the gliders and the tow planes was also high as they had to make their releases in the face of the same intense enemy ground fire. Some of the glider troops, dazed by the shock of a hard landing, were slaughtered before they could get out and move forward. And of course there were the paratroops, who started getting killed before they ever hit the ground. They landed right on top of the enemy, who fought back fiercely and then surrendered when they saw that there was no hope.

All of us on Big John's crew had a tough time digesting all of this. We had come through without a scratch, perhaps because the German gunners aiming at us didn't lead us enough and hit people behind us instead. The expectation that most of us had before the mission that the drop zone would be completely in Allied hands had not panned out. A low bluff we had passed over on the way out was expected to be full of Brits, but the Germans had not been dislodged. Well, everything else had been right on; the timing, the right drop area and altitude, the track in and out. And the drop itself couldn't have been much better, with the percentage in the drop zone up in the high nineties. And we hadn't seen one enemy fighter. But Jesus;- twenty airplanes?

There was another percentage figure which we watched out of the corner of our eye, and that was the percentage of aircraft which got off the ground versus those which were lost. On this mission, it came out to around sixteen percent of the Liberators re-supplying the British and at that rate, the Liberator plant at Willow Run would have to crank up production a notch or two. Needless to say, the production of additional crewdogs would also require attention.

Of course, the percentage figure used by the management was reckoned to include aircraft losses versus sorties over a period of time, not just single missions. At one time it hovered around five percent, and when it came down to around three or four percent, the number of missions the aircrews had to fly was increased to thirty for lead crews and thirty-five for non-leads. The chances of coming through a tour unscathed was once as low as one out of three.

Well, as we used to say at the time, we could always see the chaplain and have him punch our ticket.

And how did missions like this affect our morale? Well, there is a great story about an incident described in the biography of General Doolittle by Lowell Thomas and Edward Jablonski involving the "Bloody Hundredth" Bomb Group. This hard luck outfit had been decimated several times and on one occasion, when they had suffered three bad missions in a row, General Doolittle decided to give them a visit to help their morale.

It had been so bad that General "Tooey" Spaatz, his boss, decided to come along to the 100th Base at Thorpe Abbots. The two generals -Spaatz had four stars and Doolittle had three-stopped at the Officer's Club bar for a drink prior to a pep talk they intended to give after dinner. As they discussed their task, a Second Lieutenant, obviously well into happy hour, approached them. The wrenching emotional forces of combat had apparently convinced the young officer that even generals put their buckle shoes on one foot at a time, so he confronted General Doolittle and poked his finger into the three-star chest.

"You think we don't know what you're here for, dontcha?" said the Lieutenant, as remembered by the General.

"Well, I'm here to discuss your problems and express regret that you've had these bad attacks and see what we can do about making things a little better."

By this time Tooey Spaatz, who had traditional ideas as to how Lieutenants talked to Generals, was getting somewhat incensed. But Doolittle remained patient, even when the young flyer again poked his finger into his chest.

"Lemme tell you something, General," he said. "We know what you're here for. You're here to improve our morale and lemme tell you this, if there is anything in this goddam world that will ruin our morale it's a couple of goddam Generals comin' around trying to fix it!"

Instead of yelling for the Group Commander and having the insubordinate young Lieutenant sent home in chains, Doolittle, to his everlasting credit, got his boss down from the ceiling and took the whole thing with some humor. The reason he handled it this way, I am sure, is that three-star General or not, he had never really outgrown his own crewdog mentality which dated back to the days when he flew bombing missions himself, including that first one to Tokyo.

And as for the Lieutenant? Despite his insubordination, he belongs in the Crewdog Hall of Fame.

The same copy of the Stars and Stripes which described the Rhine crossing had some articles about the coming end of the war. "Nazi Resistance Puzzles U.S. -'How Much Longer Now?' they all ask," said one headline. Another article discussed the possibility that the Germans would not formally surrender, and that their troops would withdraw into southern Germany and carry on guerrilla warfare "under fanatical Nazi leadership." There were indications that preparations to do this were already being made, and we would soon take part in dealing with it.

There were some other interesting tidbits in that same day's issue, including: "Broadway is proud of Lt. Commander Eddy Duchin, a famous piano-playing band leader... a hero at Iwo Jima. He helped dynamite coral reefs under fire...Lt. Charles Shea, who used to sell peanuts in Yankee Stadium received a medal for valor awarded by the Bronx for knocking out three machine gun nests in Italy. Incidentally, Shea also received the Congressional Medal of Honor." (Shea Stadium was later named after him.) And finally, there was; "Frank Sinatra set...out last week on a nation-wide tour telling school children the necessity for racial tolerance..."

If the Stars and Stripes reporters had asked us at Wendling about the end of the war, we would have paraphrased a remark Yogi Berra hadn't made yet: it would be over when it was over. They could talk about peace feelers and formal surrenders all they liked, but as long as the Colonel told us to strap on the old Liberator and head east where the well-placed 88's lurked, the war was still on. And as we continued to fly missions, there wasn't much thought that the mission we were on might be the last of the war in Europe.

It certainly didn't feel like the war was about over when, on March 30th, six days after the Rhine crossing we were sent to bomb U-boat pens and maintenance docks at Wilhelmshaven. U-boat pens were among the first targets assigned to Allied bombers in the beginning, and it almost seemed we were starting all over again. The original reason for going after the U-boats was to eliminate the threat they represented to our North Atlantic merchant marine supply line. Since there was no longer any hint of such a threat, we could only look at the briefing map on the wall and shake our heads in wonderment. Fortunately, the fierce defenses of that port city were only a tired and pale shadow by now, but they were still able to knock one of us down over the target. The Forts bombed the same type of targets at Hamburg and lost three more.

Although the enemy ability to mount up some opposition was getting more and more difficult, some of his measures appeared to be beyond desperation. There was the case of the Sonderkommando Elbe, a volunteer group of German fighter pilots who were so fiercely determined to protect the Fatherland that they volunteered to ram their fighters into our bombers.

The tactics they were to use were not exactly in the Japanese Kamikaze style. They were to make an attack from the bomber's twelve o'clock high position by firing as they swooped down, and if the bomber did not go down immediately, they were to continue on, if they were still alive, and try to slash the bomber with one of their wings. The aiming point was to be just forward of the tail with the idea of knocking the bomber's tail off the airplane.

A week after the Wilhelmshaven mission, the Sonderkommando Elbe launched its fighters against the Fortresses and Liberators on their way to attack a number of marshalling yards, depots and airfields deep in northern Germany, on the route to Berlin. Although the Mustangs intercepted many of them, they managed to ram eight bombers and send them down.

The next day the target seemed to make more sense, although not to fans of great music, wherever it might be played. This was the mission to Bayreuth which so incensed the eavesdropping lady at the concert. We were on the lookout for the boys from the Sonderkommando Elbe, but none showed up that day.

The idea of Luftwaffe fighter pilots being in such desperate straits was, by this time, easy to accept. Gone was the time when we visualized them with Nordic blonde hair and icy blue eyes, led by the quintessentially evil Oberst Otto von Preminger, completely invincible in aerial combat unless attacked by Errol Flynn or a young John Wayne. My own mental picture was changed for good during one of our later missions. We had an electronic countermeasures man on board, whose task was to listen in on the German fighter control frequencies to help determine if any new tactics were being used. His position was squeezed in next to mine, and as I watched him fiddle with the knobs on his black box, he looked over at me and nodded, his eyes smiling over his oxygen mask.

"What's up?" I asked over interphone. He listened some

more then he looked at me again.

"These Luftwaffe pilots," he said, shaking his head. "There are a bunch of them circling up ahead, hanging off to one side of the bomber stream. The ground control commander was yelling 'Attack! Attack!' and one of the fighter pilots said, 'Damn it, if you want them attacked so badly why don't you come up here and do it yourself!'"

Had the lady at the concert also known that in addition to Bayreuth, we also launched a mission to Salzburg, another hallowed shrine to music and birthplace of Mozart, she probably would have climbed into one of Sonderkommando Elbe's fighters and come after us. I can see her now in her elegant gown, plastic champagne glass in one hand, finger on the trigger, swooping down on the insensitive barbarians who would put culture at risk, her beautiful eyes wide with rage.

As it happened, the weather was so bad on the way to Salzburg that, determined as we barbarians were, we had to turn around at the I .P. and bring the bombs back after a long eight and one half hours. I am in full sympathy with the idea of preserving the world's cultural heritage, so I would like to describe, for the record, the field order's reasons for the mission: "Reports from ground sources state that...leading party members are retiring into this region, assembling supplies, ordnance and picked soldiers...Excavations not associated with mining or quarrying have been noted. We shall be attacking the main traffic center feeding this area."

Can't you just imagine the Nazi biggies, bereft of the means to skip town because of our final attack on the U-boats at Wilhelmshaven and Hamburg, gathering in the Austrian Alps assuming disguises and forming musical groups to entertain the post-war tourists? There would be orchestras and chamber music ensembles and even some soloists, all dressed in wigs and fake beards and not able to play worth a damn.

But the premier group, the Oops Quartet, to whom all the others bowed and scraped, and who, if you took away the shades and false noses, would look immediately familiar. There would be A. Hitler on the grand piano, "Fats" Goering on the clarinet, J. Goebbels playing the Strad and, in a perfect matching of artist and instrument, H. Himmler on the viola d'amore, which because of its sweet tone, requires the artist to be able to

197

look soulfully skyward as he plays, with only an occasional peek at the music.

The magnificent piano to be played by A. Hitler would be specially constructed for the maestro with a shortened keyboard, for as everyone knew by that time, he was not playing with a full set of keys.

It is impossible for me to depart from the German musical scene without mentioning the daily radio program which brightened our mornings. The anchor-person was a lady we called Arnhem Annie, who was the German version of Tokyo Rose. She reminded us that greedy, cigar smoking war profiteers were stealing our wives and girl friends back home, all of them sitting around with their fingers crossed and hoping that us suckers would get shot down forthwith.

The main feature of the show was Bruno and his Swinging Tigers, who played ricky-ticky American dance music from the 20's and who were so bad that they approached genius. Could it have been, perhaps, the Oops Quartet sneaking in a little practice?

Even though it meant missing the Arnhem Annie broadcast, we departed Wendling on the 14th of April to help the French deal with a remaining pocket of German troops on their soil at the estuary of the Gironde River, near Bordeaux. Our mission was to take out some heavy gun emplacements which had caused us and the rejuvenating French forces to treat the enemy pocket with respect. Once we had destroyed the artillery, another mission would be flown on the next day to the same area, this time with a new type of incendiary bomb made from napalm. The idea was to burn out the German troops since they had been there for a long time and were pretty well dug in.

Since all of France and most of Germany lay between the target and any possible enemy reaction, most of the gunners, guns and ammunition were left behind. We dropped our bombs and Jack Murray did such a great job we got another Lead Crew Commendation from General Johnson.

The incendiary mission was flown the next day and apparently had almost no effect on the Germans, and the French had to go in to get them to surrender the old fashioned way.

It was April 25th, 1945 and spring was upon us and yet the war persisted. Once again we sat in the big briefing hut, looking at a map with a long piece of string marking the proposed route for our mission. Across Holland it went, beyond Frankfurt, beyond Stuttgart, beyond Nurnberg, past Munich, back to the outskirts of Salzburg again. The target was a small railyard at Hallein, not far from Hitler's hideaway at Berchtesgaden, up in the mountains. Only 57 Liberators from our wing would attack this yard, while a larger force of Libs would go to the big railyard at Salzburg itself. Three hundred Forts from the 1st Air Division would bomb the Skoda gun factory and the airfield at Pilsen in nearby Czechoslovakia.

Whatever else the Germans were bringing into the Redoubt area, they had not forgotten to bring in some of their best flak gunners. We frankly did not expect much to happen and as we came down the bomb run and had the target well spotted, I tried to peer through the thin haze over to our right to get a look at Hitler's aerie when Whammo! -the first bursts of flak hit so close I thought we had finally taken that well-placed 88. The Lib lurched off heading about fifteen degrees and Captain Hunsaker, the group command pilot who was with us had to grab on to Big John's seat to stay on his feet. We got straightened up and continued on the bomb run, the flak following us like a swarm of lethal hornets until the bombs were gone and we turned off for the rally point.

It seemed like a miracle that the whole group came out the other end and set course for home. We surmised that some of the flak guns had been placed up in the mountains which ran up to almost 10,000 feet near Hitler's hideaway, which meant that they could reach us at 22,000 feet with accuracy. None of the Libs which had gone to Salzburg were shot down on this day either, but the Fortresses at Pilsen lost 6 airplanes over the target, with 180 others damaged. The Eighth Air Force management had taken it into its head to inform the people at the Skoda works, by dropping leaflets beforehand, that the place would be bombed. This was done to avoid casualties among the workers as much as possible but would also, as the aircrews pointed out, alert the enemy defenses. The defenses, however, had been expected to be meager.

Hallein and Pilsen did turn out to be the last Eighth Air

Force bombing mission of World War II and when the announcement came that there would be no more, I thought of those six Fortress crews over Pilsen. Some of the crews bailed out and made it okay but the others, well, they reminded me of the movie "All Quiet on the Western Front," the original version in which Lew Ayres plays a young German soldier in the first World War who has made it through to the end. And in the closing scene, in the war's last minutes while awaiting the truce, he reaches out from his position in a trench out into no-man's-land for a butterfly and as his fingers are almost there a sniper's shot rings out and his hand falls limp in death.

Not too long after the last mission, I walked into our hut late one morning with my copy of the Stars and Stripes and, as had happened several times before, I found a little, blue casket-shaped box lying on my cot. The spring weather was warming up in East Anglia now and a rare bright sun shone through the window. I took off my jacket and hat and absently dropped them next to the little box which I presumed might hold another Air Medal.

Sam had warmed up the tea pot so I poured some and pulled the folding chair into the sun, put my feet up on my foot locker and picked up my paper. Then the box caught my eye again, for it seemed a little different, and I undid the rubber band which held the citation. The gold-leaf printing on the lid said "Distinguished Flying Cross". My hands, which had gotten to be a little shaky of late quivered a little harder as I took up the citation and looked at it. Sure enough, my name was on it.

My eyes, which weren't tracking right, skipped over the wording: "For extraordinary achievement, while serving as lead navigator on many heavy bombardment missions....superior navigational ability......highest credit upon himself...

I know that many crewmen who deserved the DFC more than I did never lived to collect it. They, like me, didn't come to England just to earn this decoration and perhaps, had they been able to bring it home, it would have stirred up a great surge of pride in them as it did in me, and then would be put away somewhere safely, largely forgotten.

But that wasn't what I was thinking of as I sat in that shaft of spring sunshine. What ran through my mind was that this was the medal that Lindy received just after he soloed across the Atlantic that first time. And now, Big John and Sam and Jack and I had ours.

We had lived to collect it and could take pride in having done our part and perhaps a little extra. Never, on any of our missions, did any of us on the crew give in to the fears which might have paralyzed us in the face of the enemy. Instead, we pressed on each time, and now we could lay claim to a part of the reputation of the Eighth Air Force in World War II; that no mission had been turned away from its target by enemy action.

But the price was staggering. Twenty-six thousand of us were killed in combat out of a force of 340,000. All those earnest, determined, great-looking young guys, lounging around in their leather A-2 jackets and go-to-hell hats were gone, their lives never really started. Even the gung-ho U.S. Marines lost less: some twenty thousand out of a half-million of our best young men. Most of them died hard deaths, some in agonies difficult to imagine. If, some time in the future, this country needs the inspiration to make some great sacrifice, let us think of these men.

The Eighth Air Force had one big job left to do, and that was to get everyone back home as soon as possible. Wendling emptied out quickly as Liberators were ferried back and the Base people and extra flight crews were sent southward by train to make the trip to the U.S. on ships like the Queen Mary. Some navigators like myself were kept behind to join ferry crews for return flights later on.

Every night was "going away party night" at the club and some of them got pretty wild as the pressure relief valves blew. The parties got smaller and smaller and as I awaited my orders, I managed to attend most of them. During the last one, the night before I left, a couple of dozen of us got involved in a project that appeared to involve the destruction of all of the glassware in the bar. Highball glasses, beer glasses, cocktail glasses all flew in a shower toward the big stone fireplace as we would take a sip, stand at attention, make a toast in our best German accent, and let fly. By the time I left, a few remaining diehards were trying to finish the job, but they had tired of using the fireplace as a target and started to aim at the windows. The place really got to be a shambles, but there weren't too many people around the next day to worry about it.

I made one last trip to London, to be there when those brave people celebrated Victory in Europe Day -V.E Day- after six years of war. There were great crowds everywhere, full of joy, gathering around anyone who might climb up on a doorstep or a lamp post to lead some singing. Sobriety was looked upon as an insult to the national pride, and anyone perceived to have a little bit of British reserve left was shamed out of it. A massive, noisy river of humanity made its way around Piccadilly Circus and I was pulled along with it. As we reached the stone arches near the Underground entrance, the one near the Regent Palace Hotel, some Yank raised a G.I. .45 pistol in the air and fired it. The big slug bounced off the stone arch with a ricocheting whine and then flew out over the ducking heads of the crowd. What a hell of a way and time to get killed.

The big question of the day, May 7th, 1945 was when would the official announcement of the war's end be made. Great crowds had surrounded Buckingham Palace and filled Trafalgar Square waiting for the word which, as the late, double daylight saving time twilight ended, still did not come. The German surrender had already been taken by General Bohlen for General Eisenhower in the little red schoolhouse at Reims during the early morning hours. But Churchill's victory message needed coordination with Truman and Stalin and the V-E Day date was set for the next day, May 8th.

London did not wait. Even before darkness fell the crowds got noisier and more boisterous and the first bonfires began to be lit in the streets. I somehow got latched on to a crowd of Yanks who had found some English service women, all of them trim and pretty in their uniforms. In the middle of a lot of yelling and singing and dancing, one of the girls, about five feet tall and as cute as an English girl can be came over to me. She was holding a pint bottle of whiskey and was not too steady on her feet.

"It's about time I met a Yank," she said, "and told him what I thought of him!"

Now whatever brought this on? "And what do you think?" I asked, trying to look completely innocent.

202

She looked at me to see what effect she was having. Suddenly she grinned and said, "I think you Yanks are grrreat!" and she swung the bottle around in an arc. "Just grreat!" and she swung the bottle around again, spilling some of the liquor this time.

"Oops," she said, starting to giggle. "Here you better have some before I spill it all!"

I took a swig which I needed like another hole in my head. We began to hold some inane conversation in the middle of all the noise and excitement, when suddenly she stopped talking in mid-sentence. Her pretty face turned pale and she looked about ready to be sick. I steadied her and guided her over to a low window ledge out of the swirl of the crowd and we sat down. Little by little her head cleared and her tummy settled down. It turned out that, before tonight, she had never had a drink in her life. From what I could see, tonight's booze would probably be her last.

And then she started to cry. "I'm so embarrassed," she wailed, "I so wanted to get drunk like everybody else and have a good time!"

Mustering all of my twenty-one year old wisdom, I got her to stand up and walk a while, then we made our way through the crowd to the big Lyons Corner House which was close by. The place was jam-packed and it took some time to get some tea and sandwiches. The food worked like magic and when she came back from putting herself back together at the ladies room, I suddenly found myself forced to take a new look at the situation. She was not just a pretty, slightly inebriated WAF anymore; she was a pretty, lively young woman, eager to celebrate the big day.

As we walked arm in arm out of the crowded restaurant and joined the smiling, singing, slowly moving river of people outside I couldn't help thinking, "Lose some, win some. If you've got to get into a war, this is certainly the way to finish it."

The next day, the long awaited V-E day, was almost an anti-climax. The crowds were even larger than the day before but were more subdued and probably a little hung over. The biggest mass of people gathered at Trafalgar Square where, at three in the afternoon, Winston Churchill came out on a balcony and declared the peace. I was in the middle of the crowded Square, some distance away from the balcony on which he stood, but not too far to make out the big grin on his face. He waited for the right moment, then lifted his right hand and gave his famous V-for victory salute and the great crowd roared. Then, at nine, the King spoke on radio as everyone in England and millions around the world listened, and the new day had begun.

Wouldn't it be great if, when fifty years have passed since that day, the English take a look at themselves, and consider what might have happened to them, and then pour out into the streets again and light up the bonfires and get a little drunk and disorderly. If they do, I'll certainly be there."

"Oh? How's that again, Dear?" "Er, make that; -my wife and I will be there!

III

BOOK THREE

9

THE MOOSE ARE ON
THE GAUGES

T HE DAY I GOT BACK TO NEW YORK was the day the airplane
hit the Empire State Building. It was July 28, 1945. I had
arrived at Penn Station from Bradley Field in Connecticut and
had to taxi over to Grand Central to finish my train trip to
Yonkers. The cabbie pulled the flag down and looked at me,
asking me where I wanted to go and then he noticed my Air
Corps uniform.

"Hey, did you hear? A B-29 hit the Empire State building!"

"A B-29?" I asked, shocked. Is it still standing?"

Well, it hadn't been a four-engined B-29, but a smaller,
twin-engined B-25 Mitchell, the kind which Jimmy Doolittle
bombed Tokyo with, but a B-25 was bad enough. The pilot had
been unsure of his position flying in low cloud, trying to make
an approach and landing at Newark. This was before radar
directed approach control had been developed and well organized instrument approach procedures had been designed, even
in places like New York.

The pilot saw his doom leap at him in the split second permitted by the few yards of visibility within the clouds which
surrounded him. He instinctively pulled the nose up, but it was
too late for his copilot and himself, and an unlucky passenger
they had on board.

The B-25 hit the building, then the world's tallest, squarely
between the 78th and 79th stories. Most of the bomber pene-

trated into the offices located there like a missile, its fuel exploding, washing rivers of flame through several stories. One engine passed through the building and came out the other side, falling on to the roof of a building below. The other engine also shot forward and hit a bank of elevators, and plunged down into the shaft of one of them.

"Come on, I'll show ya," said the cabbie, and we detoured a few blocks for a good view of the wounded building, a single plume of grey smoke still pouring out from the gaping hole on its face. The excited, good feelings I had about coming home from the wars were pushed aside and that nagging dark feeling came upon me again, one which seemed natural while I was in combat, but which now, suddenly, was more noticeable. The B-25 had blasted a hole eighteen feet wide and twenty feet high where it hit. The two pilots and the passenger were instantly killed along with ten people working in the building. The fire it caused was quickly extinguished but the damage was extensive and it took some time to determine that the building was still structurally safe. Looking up at the smoke, imagining the impact of the airplane crashing through the wall, I couldn't keep the picture of mangled and burning people from flashing into my mind and persisting, though I tried hard to push it all away. "Isn't there any place I can go to get away from people getting smashed up?" I thought, and then the cabbie took off for Grand Central Station.

Arriving home from the war, coming back to people you love and have missed, fills you with feelings unlike any others. There was the overwhelming relief that everybody including yourself was safe and sound, and nobody had changed too much. And the joy that the killing, at least in Europe, was over. And for me and the others on John Beder's crew, no more hauling those deadly bombs up to 23,000 feet and looking for a target to drop them on, the well-placed 88 lurking there in the five-mile high battleground filled with bursting flak and ramming, tearing shards of steel.

There was also something that I still remember acutely to this day; that we were made to feel we were something special and had performed a great service not just for our country but for people everywhere. It started when we got on the train near

Bradley and headed toward New York. People filled the windows of the houses and factories that lined the tracks and waved and smiled as we rode by. The flags and welcome banners they had draped from the upper windows fluttered in the sunshine and gave the scene a festive air. I don't know how many times the people had gone through their routine, but as we rolled down the track and threw kisses back at the women, it seemed heartfelt and genuine and meant specially for each of us.

The idea of being criticized for being in the military was unthinkable as it had been throughout the war. Just after Pearl Harbor when our military situation was very poor and we thought that Hawaii and perhaps even the West coast might be invaded, an anti-war sentiment would cause a person to be marked as disloyal. Men who could not pass the draft physical were looked upon with pity and sometimes with suspicion, and one fellow I knew who didn't make it obviously felt that his life had been ruined.

My mother was there, and so was Kay, and Annie, and Tom and Irene. My brother Bill was still somewhere out in the Pacific but would come home soon. George had joined the Navy and was flying as a crewman in a Grumman TBF torpedo bomber down in Florida, getting his training. Kay's husband Hank Allison was still somewhere in the Philippines but would also be home soon. We gathered at the house that Hank and Kay had built out in the uncrowded suburbs a few years before the war. It was their dream-house, a small place, with enough room around them for big trees and a lawn and some space to raise children. As Kay showed me some of the changes around the place, I found it hard to believe that only a few years had passed since some of my chums and I had helped Hank to clear the weeds and overgrowth so that the foundation markers could be set. Everything that happened before the war had taken on a slightly blurred dimness that exaggerated the amount of time that had passed.

I had thirty days to get back into a normal frame of mind, which shows you how much they knew about the effects of combat in those days. I'm not complaining,- in fact it now seems to me that it was better that we were left alone to work things out, to have our slight tremors or lapses into silence or readiness to booze it, or even our perfectly normal behavior go unnoticed.

Of course, the outward signs of some dents in the psyche usually slowly disappeared or just became normal for some people. But the inner cracks and fissures, the depression which floated in like clouds blotting out a sunny moment for no apparent reason, the quick rages which were mostly kept inside seemed to need some extra effort to be done away with, at least for me.

"How do you feel?" the flight surgeon at Bradley Field had asked me as he had asked the long line of others undergoing "processing."

"A little nervous," I answered -truthfully- but perhaps thinking that's what I had to say to get 30 days at a hotel in Miami or Atlantic City. This gift had been awarded automatically to returnees in the past, but now that there were so many of us, the award was rationed.

In any event, the Doc didn't bite, so instead of going to a hotel on a beach after my leave, I would report to Fort Dix, New Jersey along with thousands of other returnees where we would be sorted out and our futures decided. The war in the Pacific seemed to be reaching its peak with an invasion of the Japanese homeland imminent. In view of the fanatical bravery which the Japanese had already displayed, hundreds of thousands, perhaps a million or two additional casualties on both sides were expected.

As usual, the thirty days leave went by like a shot. It certainly didn't accomplish its purpose of getting my thought processes back in the groove. At first, I spent most of my evenings wandering around the streets of New York, looking for noise and excitement. I saw a Broadway show or two, but most of them were sold out until long after my leave was up, so that was that. I did get to see lots of night club shows, especially the ones with stand-up comic routines. Most of the time I just watched from the bar where I could leave as soon as it was over to catch another show. Sometimes I would get to see three shows in one night, then have a bite to eat somewhere and then wander around some of the landmarks like Rockefeller Center or Times Square.

It was safe to go anywhere, any time as New York's Finest - the Police- still had control of the streets. Usually, when I went into town, I would end the evening by catching the last train to Yonkers from Grand Central at about two AM. After buying my ticket I would walk into the cavernous waiting hall and sit on a bench and read the Daily News. It was almost as peaceful as church. There would be no one there but me and the cleaning women who were usually on their knees slaving away on the marble floor and once in a while one of them at the other end of the hall would let her mop handle drop and you would hear the sharp slap and then, after what seemed like forever, the echo would return.

Once in a while I would meet a girl and have dinner and we would have a nice time but in those days, in New York, if you took a girl out and got a little passionate along the line, they seemed to think you were automatically engaged. A couple of times I had to pass inspection by the entire family before we went out and I got the impression that the old man studied my features very closely so he could track me down if I laid a way-ward hand on his cute daughter. I didn't think it showed that much.

It was from these paranoid poppas that I learned all of the tricks a father should know in protecting his daughters against teen-age predators. I noted the baldly suspicious appraisals, the veiled threats, the bone-crushing handshakes, all intended to communicate messages in behalf of preserving female virtue. When it came my turn to be a paranoid poppa, I worked these guiles with a vengeance, even thinking one time that a hand-some, intelligent young A-student calling on my daughter prob-ably had gone through all the arduous difficulty of making Eagle Scout just to use it as a smoke-screen for his amorous activities. But most of all, if I detected in a young man a sum total of tendencies towards girls which I had in me at that age, a condition obvious only to the eye of an expert, out-he-went!

During that leave I was asked to be best man at the wed-ding of a family friend. The bride was the stepdaughter of my Godmother -Ninotchka- while the groom was a G.I. who had also just come home from the war. It was a very nice church wedding and things went off just great, and one thing it did

211

teach me was that getting married was not necessarily like being put in front of the firing squad. They are still married and have raised a wonderful family and I'm glad I was part of it.

It was during the preparations for the wedding that I began to get an inkling of how much my life had been thrown out of whack by the war. As I looked around me at all of the excited, happy people getting ready to take part in one of life's supreme moments I felt that uneasy feeling of being left behind. They seemed so obviously right in what they were about to do and it shook me.

As I waited for the wedding, I wandered through some of the old neighborhoods and, one afternoon, found myself walking up the stairs of St. Michael's Church. The big doors were open and I took off my uniform cap and walked into the small reception hall. I looked down the center aisle towards the altar and I was a boy again, listening to the choir, fidgeting, waiting for the service to end.

The memories lasted only for a moment for here, in this small church so familiar to me, the anxieties and confusion began to build. I looked beyond the altar and my eyes fell on the big stained-glass window in which St. Michael's spear was still poised over Lucifer's writhing, black-winged form. I waited for the feelings to pass, and for the first time, I clearly realized I had a problem I had to deal with.

"May I Help you?" said a voice off to the right and I was startled for a moment. A priest had come out of the room beside the altar and slowly walked over to me, his eyes searching mine. He was a small man, and wore a black vestment. I didn't know what to say and we both stood there in the aisle before the alter, the banks of votive candles on each side flickering in the afternoon silence.

"You have just come back from the war, I see," he said, glancing at the ribbons on my chest, "Is this your church?"

Finally I was able to gather my thoughts and tell him, somewhat disjointedly, about being Christened and making my first communion at St. Michaels, and about Father Kinash and Professor Fatiuk's school. I fell silent again for a moment, and then I said, "Could you take my confession?"

"Yes, of course," he replied, and he gently grasped my arm

and led me over to the altar steps, in the middle before the center of the altar itself and we both knelt on the red-velveted bottom step.

"You have sins to confess?" he asked after I could not begin, and I looked at him. "When you are in a war, you do some things..." I was able to say, somewhat agitated, and I knew I could say no more.

We both kneeled there, and after a moment, I heard him say, "I will pray to God for your forgiveness," and as I listened to the whispered syllables of his prayer, I raised my eyes and looked again at the great window behind the altar, at St. Michael and his lance and at the writhing Lucifer.

Then he slowly rose to his feet and so did I and we stood facing each other and I could see in the saintly man's eyes that his agitation matched my own. He gently grasped my arm again and said, "I have prayed to God, now you must find some way to feel that forgiveness within yourself. Do you understand?"

"Yes," I replied, but at that time, at that moment, I didn't understand at all.

"One thing was obvious: the world in which I interacted with other people had shrunk in those months of combat. The outer boundaries reached as far as military aviation could stretch, but its inhabitants were limited to my family and crewdogs like me. They were the people I felt comfortable with and held in high regard, and I acted so that they would feel the same way about me. And the world beyond that? Well, to look beyond the boundaries that had been set up in my mind meant that I had to look toward the future, and the desire to do that had been chipped away, a little over Hamburg, perhaps, and a little more while crossing the Rhine, and still more over a little, two-bit target like Hallein...

My leave ended and as I left for Fort Dix, I realized I had acted like a nerd and hadn't paid enough attention to my family. Both my mother and Kay insisted my complexion was turning a little green, and that maybe a little rest at Dix would do me some good. I made some excuses and told them that, for one thing, Fort Dix was only a few hours away and I expected to see them again before any new assignment sent me somewhere else.

My guess was correct, and I had been at Dix for only a short time when the Enola Gay dropped the atomic bomb on Hiroshima and another was delivered to Nagasaki and the war was over. Dix seemed to empty out as we all poured onto buses and went back home, or went someplace to celebrate. Before I knew it, we were down in Times Square by the hundreds of thousands, acting a lot like we did on New year's Eve only a little wilder.

This time the entire war was over, not just one big part of it and that strange attitude most of us had where tomorrow was a hazy pink cloud would soon change. I certainly hadn't given the future much thought and now, the need to do so would flit through my mind and then be gone, although more slowly.

I didn't see any bonfires in Times Square as there were in London, but the joy and relief were the same. Either you acted a little nutty or you laughed at people acting nutty. The liquor flowed in the streets and by early afternoon, some of the crowd already had a good head of steam up, like a small bunch of G.I.s I happened to walk behind near the Astor Hotel. One of them reached out and grabbed a very pretty blonde girl out of the stream of people flowing past and gave her a big smooch. She didn't resist, in fact she cooperated nicely, but the problem was that her boyfriend, a Marine, didn't like it and he pried the G. I. loose and gave him a big shove.

"Hey, the war's over buddy, relax!' said the G.I., but then one of his pals, craving a little excitement, said, loudly, "Hey look! The jarhead's got a ribbon for invading Governor's Island!"

That was too much, and the Marine, figuring that with one Marine and six G.I.s, the odds were in his favor. He made a lot of threatening moves, but the action never got beyond a lot of shoving and pushing despite a helping remark from one of the anxious bystanders, a future fight promoter, who yelled, "Don't just talk! Punch 'em!"

The altercation broke up without much damage and the Marine and his girl walked off. She straightened up his tie and brushed off some non-existent debris from his shoulder, still excited and now obviously proud of her man, proud enough, no doubt, to tell their grandchildren about it when the time came.

"Well, what's next for me?" I thought as I checked back into the reception center at Dix. The idea was beginning to take shape in my mind that I would like to remain in the service and see a lot more of the world.

"Yonkers was a great place to visit, but I wouldn't want to live there," I told my sister Annie once and now I knew it was more than a joke. The war had sort of clipped me from my roots, and now I wanted to go to exotic places and be a world traveler, and staying in the Air Corps could let me do that.

I could also get out and find a civilian job, or more likely, go to school under the G.I. Bill. My problem was I couldn't think of anything I wanted to do more than navigate airplanes, and maybe later, get a pilot's rating somehow. But at least as a navigator, I would always be assured of assignments on international flights, since they didn't need them in domestic operations. Staying in was going to be a problem because a lot of people had the same idea. And as I sat around Fort Dix, waiting for orders to some exotic station, the reduction in forces -the RIFs- started. Most of the officers who got their orders to the separation center were guys who were leaving voluntarily. But there were others who hadn't volunteered and tried to get the orders changed, but it did them no good, and they were gone.

Now my new orders came, tacked up on the good old bulletin board, and I was sent to another reception center at Greensboro, North Carolina. I felt I had dodged a bullet but sweated it out some more as great crowds of officers were RIF'd there too. Once again I outsmarted fate and was transferred again, this time to a pool of navigators at Ellington Field near Houston, Texas, which was a large navigation school.

I had gotten tired of sitting around waiting for orders, so I found a job in a training school which had been set up to keep people occupied. I helped design courses and scheduled classes and I still had time to run into Houston, which was a very lively place. Another big RIF bombshell came out which required that anybody without a job assignment at Ellington be separated from the service, just like that. I had dodged another bullet: my job at the school saved me.

Not long after, the decimated population at Ellington all

got orders, and this time I was sent to Long Beach, California, where survivors like me huddled around, still waiting for orders which might mean a permanent assignment of some kind. When we were not huddling, we took trips into Hollywood where the night life was so expensive that we were all broke halfway to payday. It got so bad that we lined up to volunteer for duty as Officer of the Day, an onerous job which required that you stay up all night to keep an eye on things for the Base Commander. We did it because the O.D. got his meals furnished, and by the last week of the month, we were fighting for the job.

The Douglas aircraft plant was across the field from us and we spent time there looking over some of the new aircraft like the monstrous Globemaster. They were still developing propeller-driven aircraft, and we watched as they ran the taxi tests, where they would run the airplane down the runway almost to takeoff speed, then pull the power off and put on the brakes.

We also watched as a movie company shot some scenes for a film called "The Best Days of Our Lives," with Frederick March, Dana Andrews and Myrna Loy, big stars of the time. March portrayed a banker who was urged, in the story, to take extra risks on loans to returning veterans -a curious notion in today's bank failure climate- while Andrews played a flyboy from the wrong side of the tracks who wanted to marry the banker's daughter. We drove by the filming company one day as they sat around near the terminal building taking a break, and watched as Harold Russell, a recently returned G.I. who had an important part in the movie and who had lost both of his hands, was cheerfully entertaining the group by showing them how well he could use the chromed, hook-shaped grippers that served as replacements. It turned out to be an Academy Award winner.

One more postwar RIF to live through, where half of those at Long Beach were gone -I think they just picked every other name on the roster- and I finally got my assignment. A dozen of us were sent to join a weather reconnaissance flight at Harmon Field in Newfoundland, and for the first time I began to wonder if I had done the right thing. Flying weather reconnaissance sounded great, but Newfoundland?

It came as a bit of a shock to realize that almost a year had passed since coming home from Wendling. I had been "bumming around," being shunted from one base to another, dodging RIF's and scrambling around to get some flying time in. It seemed like a big waste of time during which I hadn't improved myself very much. But then again, the lack of any pressure did give me a chance to unwind a bit , although the waves of anxiety would arise when I awoke in the morning, and would dog me throughout each day.

The choice before me was Newfoundland or civilian life, and I chose Newfoundland. Some of the aura of remoteness and mystery had been removed for me because of my two trips through the area, once on the way to the wars, and again on the way back.

I hadn't seen much on the way over because of the cloudy weather but the return trip was a little different. When the crew had been split up at Wendling, I was sent to a flight crew pool in Wales to await an airplane to ferry back to the States. When my turn came, I drew a C-46 Commando cargo plane, the kind that had been used to drop paratroops on the Rhine crossing.

For a navigator, one airplane is just like another, provided it has enough gear to navigate with. Before the airplane was released to us, a LORAN set was installed. This was an electronic system which worked a lot like the GEE box except that it could be used over long distances, like an ocean crossing.

The pilots were not accustomed to flying with a navigator since the C-46, like most twin-engined aircraft, was generally not used on long, overwater flights. They looked at me like some essential oddity, something they wished they didn't have to bother with.

The return route was just like our trip over, so we took off from Valley and headed northwest for Keflavik in Iceland. This time the weather was only partly cloudy and we got a good view of the volcanos and great ice fields on this island in a corner of the Atlantic. We landed at Keflavik and spent the night, although in the summer this far north there wasn't much of it, and we had to simulate nightfall by drawing the heavy curtains in our hut.

We left for Greenland early the next morning and flew just

above a cloud deck for a while, across the Denmark Strait. The sun was so bright it lit up the cloud-tops and made the pilots reach for their Ray-bans. We were still some distance out when the clouds parted and we came into this clear, unobscured universe where we could see to the end of the world. The massive, mountainous east coast of Greenland hung before us, the high coastal barrier holding the icecap behind it, keeping it from sliding into the sea.

The pilots looked at me with questions in their eyes, not believing we could be so far out of Narsarsuaq, our next stop, and still have this awesome panorama seem so close. I admit I had to double check my work a few times for myself, but I was right and I told them my ETA for the approach was still okay. They shrugged and sat back for after all, what could anybody do but let the ocean and the whitecaps and the island which is like no other, pass below us.

We were all reassured when the pilots raised Bluie West One and got their letdown clearance. We had passed across a small corner of the icecap, which bounced the sun's rays away from it with such strength it was hard to see any of the cap's details. Sure enough, my ETA was pretty much right on.

I was happy to see that the pilots were well aware of all of the difficulties of the approach to this station, and that they were able to put the big Commando down on the first few sections of the PSP -Pierced Steel Planking- runway. The steel planks were laid down and linked together to form a runway because time had not permitted pouring concrete. They made a noise like chains rattling when the landing gear hit them and as we taxied up to Base Operations.

The reason we had left Iceland early was that we could not lay over at Narsarsuaq, but had to continue on to Goose Bay. The place was too small and had very little space for transient crews or ramp space for airplanes. So we had a quick bite and made out our flight plan for our last oceanic leg to Goose. By this time, the pilots and I were old buddies and the trip to Goose and down to Bradley Field went like a breeze. They even let me fly that oversized Gooney Bird for a while.

And now, here I was at Long Beach, one year later, ready to answer both the call of the wild and the demands of Special

Order #77 issued by the 53rd Reconnaissance Squadron, Very Long Range Weather. The Order made me part of the squadron and directed me to report to the squadron's headquarters located at Grenier Field near Manchester, New Hampshire for further assignment to Harmon Field in Newfoundland.

The squadron's aircraft, converted B-17 Flying Fortresses, were located not at Grenier but at forward bases, with a flight of four at Harmon and four at Lajes Field in the Azores. After leaving Long Beach our first stop was at Grenier, where we got some briefings and some training in weather reconnaissance procedures.

All of those placed on the Special Order at Long Beach had not made the trip from California, since some of the married men decided to leave the service when they found out that there were no quarters for families at Harmon. No family quarters usually meant that either the place was so crowded that there was no more room, or that it was out in the boonies and not a fit place for women and kids. Harmon fit into the second category, in 1946, only because the housing, a school and proper medical facilities had not yet been built. Some years later, when it was decided to keep the base as part of our postwar needs in the North Atlantic, everything was put into Harmon to make it a sought-after overseas post, especially by family types who liked the outdoors. When we got there, there was plenty of outdoors and not much else.

The first ride I had in a B-17 modified for weather recon was on our trip as passengers from Grenier to Harmon. I noticed right away that the slipstream didn't whistle through the nose compartment and there seemed to be enough room to move around. All of the armament had been taken out so there were no ports for cheek or waist guns and, of course, no turrets. The nose itself was a big plexiglass picture-window bulge where the weather observer sat, with a small bank of instruments to help him measure and record his readings which were radioed back to Harmon.

The nose was a great place to sit as we winged across the blazing autumn foliage of New Hampshire and a piece of southern Maine. Our flight was not on a direct northeast route to Harmon; instead, we headed due east out over the Atlantic and would turn due north to Newfoundland when the time came. It

turned out that a weather recon airplane seldom went anywhere without taking meteorological observations if it could
mean filling in some blank spots on a weather forecaster's map.

When we reached the coast the pilot slid the "big gas bird"
down to five hundred feet and I had to give up my seat to the
weather man, a meteorologist who was put on regular flight
status for this assignment.

"Well, we've got to give Uncle Sam his money's worth," he
said as he settled into the nose seat and got ready. The routine
observations were not complicated. Every hundred miles, he
would take a barometric pressure reading. Then he would take
a temperature reading to the tenth of a degree on a thermome-
ter which was calibrated against a standard for accuracy and
also took a relative humidity reading by using a psychrometer.
The navigator gave him a flight level wind while the pilot at
the controls gave him some help in reading the amount and
type of cloud cover over the observation point.

The crew navigator had taken a Loran fix and announced
the ETA for the first observation point and when the time came
for the wind reading, I pointed to myself and said "Me?" and he
replied, "Help yourself." The best way to take the wind reading
was on the driftmeter. Drift is the angle between the way the
airplane is pointed and the actual track the wind causes it to
fly. If you read the drift on any heading, and then turn the airplane forty-five degrees on either side of that heading and take
drift readings both times, you get a very accurate wind measurement. If you can't see the surface through the driftmeter,
you calculate the wind in other, less accurate ways.

The navigator moved over and let me get to the driftmeter
which was mounted next to his position. I looked through the
tube and set the grid illumination to my liking, then watched
as the whitecaps slid by, slightly off-angle from the grid. I
turned the knob slowly until they stayed right on the grid and
noted the angle. I asked the pilot for a double drift to the right,
and he turned forty-five degrees to the right and I read the
drift when he levelled on heading. Then forty five degrees on
the other side of our main heading, and I had it. I put the readings on my hand-held E6B computer and read the result, the
first of thousands of double drift readings I would make before
I was through. I would take them over the oceans, over deserts,

ice-caps, glaciers, jungles, any place an airplane can fly.

All of this must sound very primitive to the weather chasers of today, with their rugged Lockheed Hercules turbo-prop airplanes and their computerized, automated gadgets. Well, we had to start somewhere and we did the best we could with what we had. Besides, money for new equipment of any kind right after the war was very hard to come by.

We finished our flight on a north heading and as we crossed the coast of Newfoundland we had to climb up a little to get over a range of low hills near Port-aux-Basques where the ferry from Sydney, Nova Scotia docked. Then the pilot got himself into the traffic pattern and I could look around and see that the rolling, pine and aspen-covered hills and several granite cliffs were close enough to the runways to be a problem, and that a pilot flying an instrument approach better know what he was doing.

The approach was no problem this day as you could see for miles. As we droned down toward the touchdown point, a golden afternoon sun shimmered off breeze-blown St. George's Bay beneath us, and then we were on the ground. I was to find that sunny, warm weather like this would settle in for a week or two at a time in the summer and fall, and you certainly didn't become accustomed to it; you drank it in like champagne whose bubbles would quickly dissipate into thin air.

Albert E. Harmon Field still sits on the southwest corner of the island of Newfoundland, next to the small town of Stephenville. I was there for the last time in the seventies having dinner at the Officer's Club when the TV broadcast was interrupted by the shocking announcement that Uncle Sam would be pulling out of Harmon very soon. It was truly the end of an era, for me and a lot of Air Force flyboys and for the Newfoundlanders in the surrounding communities who had been affected by the base's presence. The announcement had been expected for some time, but everyone held out hope that something would happen to keep Uncle Sam there, but now the hope was gone.

A silence fell over the place and it was obvious that the Newfoundlanders who worked in the club were crushed, their futures now somewhat uncertain. After a few moments, they got back to pouring drinks and waiting on the tables, shrugging off the patrons' concerns, their lives suddenly changed.

The comfortable, well-appointed club I sat in that evening was a lot different from the place I had my first drink in at Harmon in 1946. The original club sat in the same spot, but consisted of two large Nissen huts containing officers quarters and a middle-sized, square building which served as the club itself.

The public part of the club contained a lounge, a bar and the dining room. The officers who ran the base lived there, along with some search and rescue aircrews and the weather recon flyboys who had preceded us. New arrivals had a choice of a room at the club, or a place at the newly built VOQ -the Visiting Officers Quarters- officially known as Harmony Hall. I chose the VOQ along with most of the others because it was a solid, well-heated building with large rooms and decent plumbing.

The four-aircraft unit at Harmon was known as "B" Flight of the 53rd Weather Recon Squadron. Our arrival- the dozen or so crewdogs- was intended to beef up the flight to raise the flying schedule to one per day, seven days per week. It turned out to be a tough schedule for each of us -an eight or ten hour flight every third day- which got to be a grind.

The flying was not easy. The duty meteorologist called the shots: he would examine the day's weather situation map and look for a low center within range, and that's where we would go. Out at 500 feet, bouncing around harder and harder the closer we got to the low center, then we would spiral up through the associated fronts; cold, warm or occluded; until we reached the 700 millibar level -which is around ten thousand feet on the "zeroed out" pressure altimeter- and head back.

We would later fly fixed tracks to fill in some large blank spots on the northern part of the North Atlantic weather map, while our buddies in "C" flight out in the Azores filled in the middle. There would soon be a network of weather recon squadrons in Bermuda, Japan, Guam, Alaska and California, all doing the same thing. The information would all come together at a meteorological center near Washington, D.C. and sent to civil and military users. Before I was through with weather recon, I would have flown with every one of the

222

squadrons, a couple of years with some of them, a couple of missions with the others.

"We're not doing all this to get you guys a perfect flight forecast out of Harmon," said the duty meteorologist. He was defending himself against our irritation that we were flying our brains out and giving them all this data, and yet the forecast for takeoff the next morning would be a complete bust. "If we wanted tactical forecasts for Harmon we'd fly you out to the west of us where the weather comes from."

"Tactical, shmactical," we all thought. Playing a part in synoptic forecasting- those involving large areas covering the entire globe on a daily, repeating basis was great, but we thought that we were entitled to accurate takeoff and landing forecasts at our home base. But after all, what's the difference; no matter what the takeoff weather was, we were going to go anyway.

The summer quickly passed and it wasn't long before the sub-Arctic freeze set in. "Even the moose hate this weather," I said to no one in particular on interphone as we taxied out in the fog and blowing snow. It was four AM and we crept along, trying to find the end of the takeoff runway. I could just imagine the moose in the surrounding pine forests swearing under their breath as they stumbled around in the fog, bumping into trees, tripping over logs, snagging an antler in some branches. Well, that's the way my mind works at four in the morning.

The pilots were really having a tough time seeing ahead. They got the follow-me jeep to come out to lead the way, and the driver finally found the threshold lights for us and sped off, back to his alert shack and his hot coffee and dreams of home. The concrete was slick with ice and the pilots had to do the run-up check on two engines at once, one on each side, to keep from swerving around. Then we sat there for a moment, for all we could see was one runway light, and the pilots needed at least two to see the runway alignment.

The crew at the GCA shack -they worked the Ground Controlled Approach radar landing system- were standing by in case we had to come back for an emergency landing after takeoff. The fog lightened for a moment and suddenly we could see two lights and the dim glow of a third and the engines roared into full power. We had a full fuel load but picked up speed quickly for we had no bombs or guns or ammo or gunners. The runway lights flashed by below us, barely visible in the swirling murk and then we were on our own, hanging in the soup, the pilots watching the dials and gauges, getting up the gear and the flaps.

And then it was a short sweat until we gained enough altitude to clear all of the terrain. I checked the radar altimeter as we climbed over St. George's Bay and it showed we were at a safe height so I gave the pilot the heading for Burgeo on the south coast of Newfoundland, after which we would let down to our usual 500 feet to begin "counting whitecaps."

From the nose, I had a good view of the wing leading edges and reported a thin coat of rime ice, but the pilot decided to let it go until it got to be a bother. We all began to settle down for the long grind, and as I waited for the ETA to come up, I went up to the flight deck where the coffee thermos was and had a cup, along with a little bit of the usual banter.

As I sipped the coffee, I thought about our groping letdown to our 500 foot outbound level, which was made after my guess that we had cleared the hills along the south coast. A radar set for navigation and bad weather penetration should have been considered essential, I thought, but none of our aircraft had them. There must have been thousands of radar sets lying around, radars which could have made it a lot safer for us and improved the quality of our observations, but we had none. I suppose the planners viewed our B-17's as temporary transportation until the full recon system was deployed and bigger and better airplanes came along. But it seemed pretty chintzy to us at the time.

We reached the coast and let down to our operating altitude, expecting to break out, but the soup persisted. As we headed off southeast, out into the Atlantic, I cranked up the Loran, which apparently was going to be my only means of navigation. Until we saw the water, it would also be the only way to calculate the wind speed and direction for the met observations.

The weatherman and I stared out through the plexiglas as the murk swirled around us, leaving a greyish fuzz of frost at the tip end of the nose. Then a hissing noise started and the weather man looked at me. "It's sleet," he said, and looked ahead again, checking his instruments from time to time. The pilot turned on the landing lights for a moment to see how heavy the stuff was and the powerful rays of light were bounced back at us by the stream of ice particles, almost blinding us.

The hours passed, and I was able to read enough Loran signals despite the precipitation static to know we had arrived at the end of the track and we started our climbing spiral up to the 700 millibar level. Halfway up, the composition of the air around us changed and the turbulence started, bouncing us around enough so that I had to tighten my seat belt.

"We're in some cumulus now," the weather man said to the pilot, and the icing gathering on the leading edges turned to the heavier clear ice and the air speed started to fall. The pilot turned on the wing and tail surface de-icing boots and I watched as the rubber linings along the wing leading edges swelled up and fell back, and after a few cycles, the ice began to crack and the chunks disappeared into the slipstream. The prop de-icers also started to work, dispensing de-icing fluid along the prop leading edges and every so often a chunk of ice would come whirling off and wham into the side of the fuselage with a loud bang which would make you jump if you weren't expecting it.

There were other loud noises which made you jump, like when the airplane became one end of a lightning discharge, and there would be a great, loud snapping noise and a blinding flash. We would wait to see what damage, if any, the lightning bolt had caused and it was usually minor.

Once, I was in the weatherman's seat, watching ice build up on the tip of the nose, my face a few inches from the plexiglass when BLAM! a stroke went off. I lurched backward and sat there, blinded and wondering what in hell had happened.

As my sight returned, I heard the pilot calling on interphone to check for damage, and I found some tiny holes drilled through the plexiglass, not at the tip but lower down.

We got so that we didn't worry about lightning too much, except that we had to take precautions so that the radio equipment was not damaged. We found out the hard way that the radioman had better reel in his lead-weighted trailing wire antenna or he might get the top of his transceiver blown off.

By now the precip had stopped and we were caught in an updraft and sucked rapidly upward with a big sighing noise until we topped out, and now it was downdraft time and down we sank and finally, the frontal weather got through playing with us and the air smoothed out again.

The weather man had been as busy as a one-armed paperhanger through all of this, reading his gauges and noting the readings, trying to keep up with the rapid changes we had encountered. Now that we had some smooth going, he would have some time to draw up some curves on the complex profile he had captured in the sounding taken during the climb.

As for me, I made my way to the back end, to the waist section, where the radioman, having been assured by the weatherman that lightning was not expected, was busy sending out our info on his long range liaison radio on the high frequency band. He was using one of those side-action Morse telegraph keys, for on days like this with a lot of radio noise caused by precipitation, the Morse encoded carrier wave cut through the static better than voice transmissions.

I found the hot food locker and pulled out a steaming hot tray, -it was sliced beef today- and despite a slight, lingering trace of my Sunday morning hangover, I ate the whole thing. When I finished, I went back up front to confirm the ETA for the next observation, expecting to see that we were breaking out into the clear, or at least between layers, but the clouds still enveloped us. And that's the way it stayed, all the way back to Burgeo and during the letdown to the GCA pattern altitude.

We had all formed a firm bond of respect for the Harmon GCA crew, who had gotten us down time after time when the moose were bumping into the trees, and without any miscues. GCA is an all-weather landing system peculiar to the military, whose crews have become accustomed to taking instructions from a controller on the ground. Civil aircrews have not embraced it to this day as they do not wish to depend on approach and landing directions from someone outside the airplane; they would rather follow their own on-board gadgets like ILS -the Instrument Landing System- or the newer MLS -the Microwave Landing System.

Although we knew the GCA crew was great, everybody on

the airplane listened to the GCA instructions, trying to detect any hesitation, any hint of lack of confidence as the GCA operator acquired us on his scopes and steered us around to the final approach. Then the main man would get on, announcing himself as the final controller, and he would say," Do not acknowledge any further instructions. If you do not hear a transmission for 30 seconds, climb immediately to 1500 feet and attempt to regain contact."

We never once lost the stream of instructions that followed; the landing gear reminder, the corrections to headings and sink rate which continued even after he announced our arrival at the end of the runway, and then the point at which the wheels should be touching down. It was obvious he always had us pegged within a few feet as he did again on this latest trip, and the threshold lights slid under us in the continuing murk, and we all knew we had it made one more time.

We were turned over to ground control, who told us to taxi to the end of the runway and look for the "Follow Me" jeep, and cautioned us to taxi slowly and not run him down. The weather man spotted him off to one side, blinking the "Follow Me" sign mounted on the back of his jeep, and the pilots turned the B-17 off the runway and fell in behind him. As we got to our parking spot and the pilots shut the engines down, I recall thinking that we had climbed into a large -for the time- airplane, made our takeoff, flown 500 miles out at 500 feet and 500 miles back at 700 millibars, radioed our observations back to the base, arrived back over Harmon and made a safe landing. And never once in that time were we able to see more than a couple of hundred yards outside the airplane.

As the pilots shut down the engines, I could imagine Papa Moose out there in the woods turning to Mama Moose and saying, "What are those morons doing out there on a day like today?"

I have mentioned flying with a small hangover on Sunday morning, but of course we also had, on occasion, Tuesday morning or Thursday morning hangovers. The social activity at Harmon was surprisingly lively as there were plenty of pretty girls who were good company who came from Stephenville or from places nearby like Cornerbrook. They were mostly Irish girls and nice enough to marry, and some of the guys did just that. But at Harmon, there was dancing to the jukebox or just sitting around and acting dopey as you do after swimming through happy hour when drink prices were dropped from the usual twenty-five cents to ten cents: -the stuff was cheaper than water.

There was a long bank of slot machines along one wall of the lounge, and proceeds from the one-armed bandits were used to reduce the prices of meals and drinks in the club. I usually got as happy as any one else at happy hour, but the more I drank, the hungrier I tended to get, and once I had some dinner, that was usually the end of it. And I was also a desperation smoker, either just putting one out or just lighting one up.

Given the climate we had outside, there wasn't much chance for exercise most of the time, or so we told ourselves. For these reasons I was very much out of condition, but there was something else. Mr. Anxiety was still with me and getting more pushy than ever. There were times when this helpless feeling would come over me in waves and I had to fight off the panic, wondering what in hell was wrong. I can remember times when I would wake in the night and my heart would be pounding, and there would be no way I could shut out the noise or the feeling of being drawn toward mortal danger. Sweaty palms were a way of life and so were the shaky hands, which I managed to cover up most of the time. But deep inside me, there was something that told me to sweat this out, sweat this out; one day it will all pass on.

I had lost a lot of my ability to reach out to people, and knew I was drawing into a shell, afraid of acting in some irrational way. If only I could relax, not with booze or some pill a doctor might give me, but by getting back into the frame of mind I had when I was kid swimming across the Hudson; not afraid to be afraid.

I had decided, however, that there was no way I would report my problems to the flight surgeon unless they got worse. If I did, I could kiss my future in the flying business good-bye. And after all, I was always in the real world where I knew I had no problems; it was the incessant worrying about worrying that bothered me.

The concerns also followed me aboard the airplane each

time, but it was different. I felt at home around my flying buddies, my fellow crewdogs, some of whom probably had the same problems I was having. And on the airplane I had to work pretty hard and concentrate on what I was doing, otherwise those feelings of foreboding would come to actuality. But I hadn't seen anything yet. The time would soon come when I would be tested to the core, when I would face the monster eyeball to eyeball.

There are several periods in my life that I have come to consider "the good old days", and despite my anxieties, my time at Harmon and later at Bermuda was one of them. Most of the people I flew with were in their middle twenties, many of them single and raring to go, and all of them very good at their job. Everybody was a well-delineated character, famous for one idiosyncrasy or another. But it was the attitude we all had, the willingness to take risks, the "Crewdogs Against the World" mentality, the readiness to party anywhere, anytime, anyplace, that marked us as a group.

We were not a rough and tough bunch of brawlers. In the years I was with weather recon, I never once saw one flyboy hit another or anybody else. The closest it came was one time in Bermuda, a pilot and a navigator decided to settle things over some difference at the BOQ. They had stripped down to the waist and were getting ready to square off when Larry Connors stepped in between them and said, determinedly, "If you want to punch each other you'll have to hit me first." Larry was too nice a guy to hit, even by accident, so they jumped at the chance to back off.

There were a number of guys like Larry, and Leonard Winstead and some others, who didn't drink or smoke, and when they said "hell" or "damn" they were obviously not comfortable with the terms and used them just to belong. But they partied with the rest and had just as big a time, maybe bigger.

Larry spent his vice ration playing poker and red dog for stakes that scared me when I watched them play. The game at Harmon got to be well known among the crews that flew through there, and often lasted day and night for days at a time.

Larry and Winnie were both fellow navigators, and I admired Winnie too because of his cheerfully positive attitude.

He tried to get us all to play tennis when we later moved down to Bermuda, so we could be as healthy as he was, but it didn't work. They were also both church goers and attended services if they could get there. It didn't seem unusual at all when the chaplain had to be absent from Harmon for a while, and Winstead, without any prior experience, stepped in and led the services each Sunday until the Chaplain got back. And did they try to push off all these noble attributes on us backsliders, sack artists and deadbeats? Yep. Every chance they got.

All those years that Winnie was so cheerful was because he didn't realize he was one of the doomed, this handsome young guy from Hardy, Arkansas with a ready smile. He met his fate one evening on a B-29 Superfortress as the pilot was trying to land at McClellan Air Force Base in California after a long, routine weather recon mission out into the Pacific. They were in an emergency situation as the pilots and flight engineer wrestled with one of those murderous propeller malfunctions. Somewhere in the complex propeller mechanism on one of the engines, some combination of failures had come together and, minute by minute, was dragging the crew closer and closer to the abyss.

They got as far as Roseville, just north of McClellan, when, apparently, the great, long blades on the troubled propeller came into the feathered, edge-on-to-the-wind position. Then they went beyond, by-passing the safety stops into the reverse position. It was like hitting a wall in the air; first the airspeed went, and then the lift , and the great bird dropped flat, almost straight down and smashed into the ground with a crash that shook the ground for miles around. Then the fuel tanks blew and lit up the darkened evening sky.

It seems strange that the aircraft commander on that airplane, Bruce Acebedo was just like Winnie; he didn't drink or smoke and was mannerly to the ladies. They also had a young second lieutenant navigator on board that Winnie was checking out, a Chinese American named August Lam who had that firm yet gentle manner that well-brought up Chinese kids have and who was too young to be anything but pure in heart. All of these men, the whole crew, only wanted to serve people, serve their country, to lead an interesting life, to do good things.

A few days after the crash, Al Elder, who had taken part in the accident investigation came to my office. He and I had both known Winnie for a long time, and he tried to tell me what he looked like in death, that he hadn't been banged up too bad, as if that would help.

"This is the only piece of equipment of his that still looks usable," he said, sadly, handing me Winnie's chronometer. It looked like an old-fashioned pocket watch and had been shock-mounted in a round canister that had protected it. The crystal had been singed a little from the heat, but I wound it up and sure enough it still ran, ticking off the seconds, marking off the even little slices of the day for Al and me, but not for Winnie, not any more.

We were to find that weather recon aircraft were occasionally called upon to support somebody else's project. The first one we became involved in was "Pacusan Dreamboat," an Air Force attempt to set a distance record in a B-29 Superfort. A Navy aircraft, a P2V twin-engined Neptune called the "Truculent Turtle" had just set a record by flying, without refueling, from Perth, Australia to Columbus, Ohio, where their fuel finally ran out. The distance was 11,250 statute miles. The "Dreamboat" plan was to fly from Honolulu, over the North Magnetic Pole to Khartoum, in Egypt, a flight which would exceed the Navy distance by 20 miles.

Our task was to drop our regular tracks and fly to the U.S.-operated Sondrestrom Fiord Airfield, about halfway up the west coast of Greenland. After a crew rest and refueling, we would fly a course which paralleled part of Dreamboat's proposed track from Sondy, eastward over the icecap to Iceland, taking our usual met observations.

The de-icing equipment on Dreamboat had been removed from the B-29 to save weight and improve the wing and tail streamlining, so they couldn't fly through ice-inducing cloud layers. They were stuck with a minimum flight level of well over 10,000 feet to clear the ice cap, and any climb they were forced to make because of clouds would increase their fuel consumption. So they had to wait around in Honolulu, poor guys, until our reports and those of our Alaskan colleagues showed that the route and planned flight level looked good.

231

And wait they did. We flew the track week after week until Colonel Irvine, the Dreamboat commander finally decided to go under less than ideal conditions. The weather recon flight found a clear level for him just above the ice-cap and saved him some fuel, but he had already been flying higher than planned and it was not enough. After more than thirty-nine hours his gas ran out short of Khartoum and he was forced to land at Cairo. The Truculent Turtle and the U.S. Navy had prevailed.

Our job had not been easy. Sondy is situated at the end of a long, winding fiord and, like Narssarsuag to the south, was closely surrounded by steep mountains. It was no place to play around in lousy weather. Like most places in the arctic and polar areas, it was subject to "phase conditions" or white-outs;-sudden snow squalls and very high winds which came pouring down off the cap and which could shut the place down in the space of minutes.

If two places on a base were more than a certain distance apart, a "phase shack" equipped with rations and a heater was set down between them, and if a "Phase One" condition started to blow, anybody on foot or in a vehicle with any sense who was near a phase shack ducked in and sat it out, usually for a few hours, sometimes for days.

The chill factor reached the "exposed flesh freezes instantly" category and visibility went down to absolute zero and there is no way you can find your way. Years later when I was on a crew passing through Harmon, where phase conditions were very rare, one of the pilots and I were making our way down to the flight line on foot when the snow started to blow very hard and we could hardly see. We were about halfway between our quarters and the "O" club and when I asked the pilot "Which way?" he said, "There's no hot-buttered rum back at the quarters! " Good advance planning, since it was only nine o'clock in the morning.

We spent three days at the club, sleeping on the bare floor, since the sleeping quarters there had been renovated out of existence years before. Electrical power was out on the entire base, so we all pitched in to cook some of the chef's suggestions over canned Sterno. We shared the chores along with a hangdog contingent of G.I. guard-house dwellers evacuated from next door because of the power failure.

After the second day, I said to my friend, "If we had gone to the quarters we'd be sleeping in a bed instead of on this damn floor. Was this worth your hot-buttered rum?" He looked at me calmly for a moment. "You're damn right," he said finally, taking a sip and smacking his lips as the storm raged outside.

It turned out that the people trapped in the quarters envied us the whole time. Although they had beds to sleep in, their food consisted of emergency rations eaten cold out of little tin cans. They didn't feel any better when they found out that even the guard house prisoners ate better than they did.

The first trip we made to Sondy for Dreamboat was flown in pretty good weather and we found the right fiord and landed on the snow-packed runway without difficulty. The place looked deserted and nobody came out to guide us in so the pilot taxied over to the ramshackle tower and shut the engines down. Finally, a forlorn-looking figure in padded pants and a parka came out of a shack next to the tower and trudged over to us on the packed snow. He came around to the pilot's side and looked up at him through bleary blood-shot eyes. "You got any whiskey Mister?" was the way he welcomed us to Sondrestrom.

As primitive as the place was in most respects, the quarters weren't too bad except that they were grossly overheated, just like all G.I. quarters in the arctic. The heater thermostats were hidden to keep them from being tampered with, so when the temperature inside went up, somebody would open some windows, even when it was minus twenty outside, and the thermostat would drive the temperature up even higher. The other problem was that there was a detached, central latrine serving several sets of quarters. The latrine building was about fifty feet away from the quarters, and you had to race along the duckboards out in the open through the frigid air to take your shower or whatever. After a few such trips, you tended to want to take a short cut if you got an urge, and as you stepped out the door, there, just off the duckboard path would be this big, commanding sign which said, "Do not urinate here!"

Arctic flying was not a routine exercise, so the G.I. map-makers had tended to ignore the area, and the right navigational maps were hard to come by. There are a number of ways you can construct a map, and the one we needed this far north was a polar stereographic projection, in which the map-maker views the North Pole as the center of the world.

Someone found a single copy of such a projection in a dusty drawer, but it did not stretch far enough south to cover our track from Sondy to Keflavik. We were forced to use something we learned in navigation school and never thought we'd use;- map construction. By extending the longitude and latitude grid to the south and free-forming some of the major terrain features, we got what we needed. We made additional copies by tracing the original on thin paper, up against a window, and the first time I used my copy, I had my fingers crossed until we picked up the Keflavik radiobeacon.

The winter wore on at Harmon and we all got to know each other, the guys who got there first and the newcomers. The only difference between us was that the original crowd had finished their flight training about the time the war was ending and had not seen combat, while us new people were the war-weary type, with lots of missions, Purple Hearts, DFC's, tics and shakes.

It was amazing how many of the later arrivals had been shot down and spent time in a Stalag or a Japanese POW camp. About five minutes into happy hour we would start hearing stories about outsmarting the Goo-goos, -the German camp guards- and what they did with the dirt from the tunnels they had been digging. They were all funny stories, and the tellers even managed to work some humor into their descriptions of why and how they bailed out and got captured. Generally, they had been knocked down in the big, bloody raids on places like Schweinfurt or Regensburg or Berlin.

It didn't take long before the differences were levelled out, because it was the flying ability of each crewmember that counted. And if the pilots were only pretty good when they got there, they got to be very good in a hurry or they weren't going to survive. They had to overcome more problems on a normally bad day than most pilots had to deal with all winter. I had a good idea at the time how great some of them were, but as my years in the Air Force marched on, I would always look back and think that a number of them were the best I had flown with. They had to be or I wouldn't be here to tell my story.

Our visits to Iceland as part of the Dreamboat Project put us in contact with some of the first "Yankee go home!" incidents we had to deal with. First of all, the city of Reykjavik was not a collection of tar-paper shacks and igloos, peopled by denizens of the North who paddled to work in kayaks. When we took our first hour-long ride up the bumpy road from the Keflavik airfield and got off the in one of the main squares, it was like stepping into the set of a Sonja Henie movie. It was a miniaturized European metropolis, picked up from Denmark and set down near the Arctic Circle.

Reykjavik, even in the forties, had theaters, restaurants, hotels, museums, a university, hospitals, churches, a good harbor and the national Parliament. It was, and still is, laid out with that Nordic sense of order and tidiness, and it was into this neat and tidy ambience that we intruded our usually cocky, noisy, irreverent attitudes. We certainly never meant any harm in our seeming lack of respect and in our determination to have a good time, but after having been stuck with our unwanted presence for a few years, the Icelanders must have thought that we created enough damage just by being ourselves.

They are a fiercely independent people who had just gotten their freedom from Denmark a few years before and some of them looked at our base at Keflavik as a beachhead for a foreign invasion. There were some Icelanders who leaned toward communism, and who wanted us out and the Russians in, and who wanted to run things when the Russians came. As for the U.S., we certainly wanted to hold on to the base for its strategic location involving submarine activities and as an aircraft refueling stop. To have the Soviets come in with military privileges would have been a disaster.

The Icelanders did eventually have their Russian romance as we were invited off the island and the Russians came, but that was long ago and it didn't last long. While we were there, our military people at Keflavik had a pretty rough time of it, virtually imprisoned on the base, and the price they and their families had to pay so that young Icelanders could be insulated from the jitterbug mentality was high.

One of the first things we learned about Icelandic culture is that they love to party, and I mean party! We had been told that the Borg Hotel was a lively place so we went there to check it out. Four or five of us sat down to an elegant dinner, the only diners in the place, wondering if we had been conned, waiting for something to happen. When we asked for some highballs, the waiter came back with some ice and mixers, along with a half bottle of American whiskey. It turned out you could buy a half or a whole bottle instead of individual drinks, so we took the half bottle for a start. It got to be about nine o'clock and we heard the band start tuning up, and suddenly the double door entrance to the adjoining ballroom opened and people started to pour in. Before we knew it, the place was filled with people, laughter and music, so we moved in and found a table. There were a number of amazingly pretty girls who were friendly and ready to dance with us; blondes, brunettes and redheads. Vikings were in their bloodlines, along with a bunch of frisky Irish monks who sailed across from Ireland hundreds of years ago and apparently did more than just sit around and play the harp.

Almost everybody spoke excellent English with just a slight accent so we could talk while we danced, at least to begin with, when Wham!- an elbow banged into my ribs and I looked around to see this large Viking floating past us, an innocent smirk on his face, and then Bang!, it happened again. I looked at the girl, questioningly.

"If you want to dance, it's something you have to put up with," she said, apologetically, so I shrugged and pressed on. I made up my mind to tell myself it was all accidental, but it wasn't long before I fell into a defensive dancing mode, which meant I took a quick peek behind me when I sensed a Viking approaching.

The real trouble almost started when we were all back at our table in between dances. Someone at the next table tugged on my sleeve with more urgency than he really needed, and when I looked around, this bulky guy in a leather coat said, distinctly, "Yankee Go Home!"

A few minutes later, he did it again, somewhat more forcefully and when I ignored him, he grabbed my arm and just about pulled me out of my chair. I jumped up, ready to do battle, but my buddies grabbed me while another Icelander got himself between our table and the arm jerker. After a while, Mr. Leather Coat left and we all got back to the business at hand. We danced a lot more and laughed at each other's funny stories and smoked up a storm, and then the chandeliers were blinking to tell us the party was over.

As we came up to the hat check booth to get our parkas, the Icelander who had gotten between me and the man from the leftist Welcome Wagon came over to me and I didn't know what to expect.

"I want to tell you what happened...." he said. "I know damn well what happened..." "No, no, you must understand what I have to tell you. That fellow who pulled your sleeve came here to create an incident so he can write about it in his newspaper column."

I should have shown some appreciation for the trouble he was taking to tell me. He started to leave, then hesitated; "You must not fight no matter how much they provoke you. Please remember that."

His advice was remembered by me and all of our troops, as we never had incident worthy of being written up in a pro-communist newspaper column. We got to know what situations to avoid and actually made an effort to be on good behavior most of the time except late at night when we tried to have as much fun as the Icelanders.

I didn't get to know and appreciate that unusually beautiful country and its great people until much later, when I was part of an FAA crew doing some work calibrating landing systems there. As civilians, we were treated so differently I thought we had landed on the wrong island. It certainly was much easier to make friendships.

Our job in Iceland with the FAA took us to every part of the country, and we spent a lot of time confirming the alignment of their air traffic control radars, checking and setting the ILS systems at both the Keflavik and Reykjavik airports, and aligning the navigational aids around the island. Had Iceland changed much almost twenty years after that guy grabbed me by the sleeve? I never did get the chance to check the Borg Hotel to find out, to see if Mr. Leather Coat was still scanning the crowd for some likely subjects for his column, for after all, we were all staid, solid married men by this time. Now, doesn't that just break your heart?

However, I did get the chance to make some clinical observations on one FAA trip to Akureyri, on the northern part of the island where we spent some time assisting in the installation of a new navaid. The man at the hotel desk suggested we stop in at a certain night club and when one of our guys asked him to pronounce the name of it again, the man said, "Oh, just tell the taxi driver to take you to the Bucket of Blood." Oh?

Akureyri is almost right on the Arctic Circle and there is no way there could be lots of excitement that far north, I thought, as we paid the driver. We opened the entrance door and looked up this long, double flight of stairs covered with a fancy red carpet just in time to see two burly men heave an aggressive acting customer from the top landing. The poor guy hit about the middle of the upper flight of stairs, bounced and came to rest on the middle landing. The impact altered the man's attitude immediately, and he got to his feet, looked up at the baleful gazes of the bouncers, then turned and staggered down the rest of the stairs.

"Gentlemen," I said, "do you think we ought to go into this place?" But they were already gone, running up the stairs and into the club so fast I could hardly keep up.

Keflavik was not a U.S. base anymore but was run by NATO. Even so an occasional Russian airplane landed there, and one time after we ourselves had landed and walked toward the air terminal, we found a Soviet Tupolev Bear reconnaissance bomber sitting on the ramp. It was parked directly in our path, deserted and without a guard, so we walked up to it and then underneath the monster. It had that long body and great wings and bomber nose and all those contra-rotating propellers on its four big turbo-prop engines. When we got to the terminal, I asked John Steinmetz, the trip commander, what he thought and he shrugged. "Looks to me like it's made out of hammered-out beer cans," he said.

Project Dreamboat had ended, back there in 1946, and we settled back into our synoptic weather track routine, grinding out the observations at 500 feet outbound, 700 millibars back, spiralling up through the fronts which drove the ocean surface into a froth. But word was circulating in "B" Flight that we would be gone from Harmon soon, and that the Flights at Harmon and the Azores and also "A" Flight, now located at Morrison Field near West Palm Beach, Florida would be consolidated at Bermuda.

As the planning progressed and spring approached, the pattern of our flight activities changed. We began to combine some logistics flights with our recon missions and found ourselves crew-resting on the beaches of Bermuda and Palm Beach, or eating king-sized langouste in the Azores. We were doing some pretty fancy crewdogging, living about as well as first lieutenants and non-coms ever do, although all the flying and then playing around when we should have been resting was hard on the body.

The Azores are a bunch of Portuguese islands about a thousand miles this side of Lisbon, generally the same latitude as Washington D .C. They are actually the tip-ends of the Mid-Atlantic Ridge that happen to be high enough to stick up out of the water. Mt. Pico, for example, on another island about seventy miles to the west of our base, is a great looming dark mountain that sweeps dramatically out of the water. It served us as a landmark which could be seen from a great distance unless it was obscured by clouds. When measured from its 7615 foot peak down to its ocean-bottom base, it is a bigger mountain than Mt. Everest.

On my first trip to Lajes Field, a U.S.-run base on the island of Terceira where "C" Flight was located, our track passed directly over Pico, and we just barely cleared the top of the cone and looked down at the lava bed within. There was a plume of volcanic steam which floated up from it and streamed downwind.

One of the first things you had to do at Lajes was to walk just outside the gate to find the small house of the man who made Wellington boots, the kind that come up about halfway to the knee. He made them from goat-skin and cured the hides in urine, also from the goat -I hope- and when they got wet everyone looked around to see who or what was causing that strange odor. But they were very comfortable and just right for walking or flying or whatever a man wants to do with his boots on. We were still part of the Army and wore brown shoes with our uniforms, but the boots came out somewhat on the red side. However, when they were shined up they really looked great.

I guess there weren't enough goats to go around to make shoes for everybody because bare feet were the order of the day except for the people in the towns. Occasionally, you could see a man dressed in a dark pin-stripe suit and black hat, with an umbrella hooked over one arm, carrying his shoes as he walked. To be able to maintain an air of dignity while unshod seemed to me to be, if you'll forgive me just this once, a difficult feat.

We once took a trip by jeep to the other side of the island to the large town of Angra do Heroismo and wandered around the parks and down the ancient, crooked streets before finding a restaurant overlooking the ocean. It also overlooked a mountainous rock which stuck up out of the water just offshore which had formed a natural shelter for German U-boats where they could be refueled while shielded from curious eyes. The Germans had apparently moved in and made a deal with the Portuguese which could not be refused, but they behaved themselves and there didn't seem to be a lot of horror stories floating around. It was not unusual for a passerby on a country road to wave to you and wish you "Gut Tag!"

Later on, the British moved in and then the U.S. replaced them as the war was ending. The Azoreans were always polite and genuinely friendly, probably because they all had relatives back in the States. They also put up with some bratty behavior from us, like the times we would land at Lajes at two or three in the morning and take a jeep into the town of Praia da Vitoria just outside the base and bang on the shutters of this restaurant we had gotten to know.

We probably woke half the town before the sleepy-eyed proprietor would come down from his upstairs sleeping quarters to start up the stove and get out the Mateus rose or the Grandjo wine or the Monte Crasto Portuguese champagne. We usually had steak and eggs, and all of this didn't cost a lot of money, which was lucky, since we had to do it all on our lieutenant's pay.

By the time the sun came up the proprietor would have gone back to bed while we sagged in our chairs groggy with fatigue and time zone lag and all the wine and food. The man who was still coherent enough to continue telling lies about his exploits as a flyboy or as a Casanova was usually appointed to drive the jeep back to the base, an event which could be the most dangerous part of our trip.

There were also bull-fights, over at Angra, the Portuguese kind where the bull is not killed, but compared with the kind back in the old country, they were not big time. It's not that they weren't dangerous, like when a bullfighter, -an American- jumped behind the barrier after his turn with the cape and forgot to duck when the bull, who had been trying the whole time to jump out of the ring, tried a jump right where the bullfighter was standing with his upper body above the barrier. The man, who was fairly tall and thin, was sort of squashed against the rail and had to be carried off on a stretcher.

They also ran bulls through the streets to give the local boys and men a chance to show their macho, which they had plenty of. The bulls would go plunging down the narrow cobble-stoned streets, scared and mad as hell, outrunning and trampling the young guys who didn't make it to a doorway or up over a wall. The bulls could reverse direction on a dime and come back up the street with electrifying speed, their heads down and deadly-looking horns at the ready, looking for a body to spear and throw up into the air. Nobody seemed to get killed and everybody had an exciting time. After I saw it the first time, I didn't feel sorry for the bulls anymore; they seemed to be able to take care of themselves.

Mostly though, the Azores are a peaceful group of islands with a very temperate climate and a sense of the ancient. Columbus had stopped there to take on provisions for his crazy journey, just another bunch of transients who better pay cash on the barrel-head because they were on their way westward to drop off the end of the world.

The Azoreans permitted their citizens to work on government projects, like road-building, in lieu of paying their taxes, which sounds like a great idea. It is a fertile and friendly place where the serenity is occasionally broken when the people threaten to secede from Portugal and become part of the United States.

Some of the Azoreans have felt the urge to follow

Columbus to the New World strongly enough to stow away in our westbound transport aircraft, which used Lajes as a refueling stop. One of the waiters in the Officer's Club, a big, balding guy was one of these, and on his first stowaway attempt, according to the story, he made the trip across the ocean okay. He then waited until the airplane was deserted and -probably with some help- sneaked off and made his way from the flight line, through the streets of McGuire Air Force Base in New Jersey, to the main gate.

He could have walked right out into town and been gone, but made the mistake of stopping to ask the military guard, in halting English, "Which way is California?" The story sounds too good to be true.

The Azoreans and the Portuguese in general are a wonderful people and it was a pleasure to be involved with them later on in international aviation meetings. They are the type of people who, had the world gone mad some time before the Russian perestroika, would have been there to pick up the pieces and in their intelligent and deliberate way, help put them back together again.

The spring of 1947 arrived very slowly and reluctantly as it usually does at Harmon, and it was almost over before we got the orders to move down to Kindley Field, Bermuda. Kindley was one of the bases -British at the time- on which The U.S. obtained 99-year leases in trade for a number of over-age U.S. Navy destroyers. The swap was made prior to Pearl Harbor to dodge our neutrality laws, which prevented the sale or donation of war goods to the belligerents on either side. It almost seems like a model for the Iran-contra deal, except that there were no powerful political forces arrayed against it.

Our orders directed us to move to Kindley in July, so we had plenty of time to begin round-robin flights between Harmon, Lajes, Morrison Field in Florida and Bermuda to gather up the equipment and people we needed to start up operations as a full squadron at Bermuda. On one occasion, we sent three airplanes from Bermuda to Lajes at the same time, with only one designated to make weather observations.

I was on one airplane that didn't need to take the readings, so I challenged the navigator on the other unemployed aircraft to make the 1885 nautical mile trip to Lajes without using any navigation equipment. We agreed on one use of the astrocompass for one bearing on the sun just after takeoff to get the main aircraft magnetic compass correction. No driftmeter, no sextant, no Loran box, nothing except our eyeball readings of the winds as indicated by the whitecaps and wave swells on the ocean below. We would have to make mental guesses as to what corrections to apply to the surface wind readings to make them valid at our altitude.

We took off about twenty minutes apart so we could fly out of sight of each other. I asked the skeptical but trusting pilot to get down to three or four hundred feet to reduce the need for corrections for altitude, and he agreed "as long as we didn't get into any clouds." There was no chance of this as we were going right up the middle of a big Bermuda High, nothing but sunshine and seagulls and feeling free as a bird.

About halfway over the wind quit altogether; zero drift, no head or tail wind, not the slightest bump of turbulence, we sat there like kings of the sky, sailing along, no longer men in a machine, but just part of this beautiful planet. A leaping school of fish, a whole cloud of them, would break the surface and we looked at them in wonder, curious as to what made them jump. We were always on the lookout for whales and saw them once in a while, but not this time; they were all down somewhere beneath us in the awesome depths marked four thousand fathoms and more.

There had been other trips, a little different, with lots of surface wind, and I could watch the velocity build up as we bounced along. Then just ahead I could see a line of cumulus across our track, and just underneath was a squall line, sharp as a knife, marking where one mass of air was smacking into another, the whitecaps on either side of the line moving in abruptly different directions. When we hit the line there was a violent wrench and we were knocked about fifteen degrees off heading, the same way the flak did to us at Hallein.

The navigation challenge had been a piece of cake from the start, and when the outermost island of Flores rose on the horizon, the pilot called me on interphone and said, "If you're through playing around, give me your ETA for Lajes so I can give them a call." He climbed up a little, just enough to do a sedate buzz job along the shores of the islands of Flores and

243

Sao Jorge, past the brooding hulk of Pico; and then he got into the pattern at Lajes. We were soon on the ground and at the club, a little bushed by now, sipping the Mateus and devouring baskets of great little Portuguese rolls and butter as we waited for our food. What a life!

Now, suddenly, it was July, 1947 and it was time for Bermuda. We found ourselves moved into a different way of life, where the regulations were actually enforced in detail, and we were given to understand that as far as our behavior was concerned, on and especially off the base, we had better "straighten up and fly right."

That was easier said than done, for after all, most of Bermuda was devoted to the pleasures of tourism, and it was not against regulations to have fun like the tourists did. Most of us were not on the ground for a long enough period of time to do justice to an additional ground job, so the few days between trips were free. So play we did, sitting on the beach, making the rounds of the Elbow Beach Club, the Princess, the Bermudiana and other hotels to check on the new arrivals that came in on PanAm or British Airways or the cruise ships.

Aside from G.I. vehicles, there were only two full size cars on the island: one for the British Governor General and the other for the Kindley base commander. The others were tiny Austins, Fords, Sunbeam Talbots and other English cars suitable for the narrow, winding Bermuda roads which were designed with horse carriages in mind. Some of the more affluent crewdogs bought cars, while the peasants like me bought motorbikes which we souped up a bit by shaving the cylinder head. The locals usually used a French-made motorbike which had such a tiny engine that it could barely make the 20-MPH speed limit going downhill. The thing I bought was a little different; it was really nothing more than a motorized, heavy duty bicycle and I could get up a fine head of speed, but I had to tinker with it after every couple of trips to town.

The combination of narrow, winding roads, blind curves, and high stone walls running alongside made for a hazardous situation, and it got to most of us sooner or later. The speed limit for cars was rigidly enforced, and at one time the local newspaper reported that a young G.I. had been sentenced to a day in jail for being clocked at 21 MPH, one mile more than the island limit. But surveillance of motorbikes was more difficult, so the U.S. Navy, which occupied the other end of the island, prohibited their people from riding motorbikes altogether after the accident situation got out of hand. One of the walls even claimed an Astronaut later on, and ruined both an arm and his career in space.

Mix all of this up with a little bit of alcohol and things could get a little hairy. One morning Gus Thompson was driving his Austin to work from his house in St. George when he met a horse carriage -a taxi- coming the other way around a curve on the wrong side of the road. Gus stopped, but the carriage kept on coming and swerved at the last minute so the horse was not hurt, but the wheel of the carriage jumped onto his front fender and ran along his running board, knocking off his door handles before it landed back on the road.

The carriage driver was not hurt either as his bloodstream was filled with a muscle relaxant called Screech in Newfoundland and Black Death in Bermuda. It was a privately distilled concoction that turned a persons eyeballs shocking pink and cured dandruff "from the inside."

The other part of Bermuda, the non-tourist part, was peopled by wealthy or well-to-do Britishers, who lived in gorgeous, beautifully landscaped homes and "cottages" and who kept to themselves. We occasionally saw some of them at lunch time at the 21 Club which was located upstairs in a building overlooking the main wharf. It was a favorite spot of ours and we usually made a stop there any time we went to Hamilton, Bermuda's big town.

As we settled down in Bermuda, we were dragged firmly back into the military fold, some of us even wearing British-style knee-high stockings and short pants, although not during the Saturday morning inspections-in-ranks.

The presence of families forced our attitudes and behavior into a more civilized track, but only most of the time. We could still carouse a bit on occasion, but the flying was the thing, and playing Bermuda tourist, as pleasant as it was, had to take a back seat. Besides, we had something new to deal with; the hurricane season was approaching. We thought we had gone through some rough flying situations out of Harmon, but we had only seen the beginning.

10

PULL ER UP! PULL ER UP!

"**W**E'RE GOING TO HIT THE WATER!" yelled Gus Thompson and the engines roared into full power as we were being sucked down, foot by foot toward the wildly heaving seas. We both tried to hang on as we looked at the radar altimeter dial, staring with growing terror as the two blips closed toward zero altitude. "Pull 'er up! Pull 'er up! somebody was yelling on interphone as the giant waves roiled around us, the great sheets of spray flying across our nose almost at our level. We could feel the great force of the wind as it gripped us and I wondered how the pilots could cope with it.

Our nose was up in the air as the props dug in, pounding away out of synch and it looked like the end of us when all of a sudden the massive downdraft let us go and we plunged upward and the pilots grabbed and pulled and pushed and twisted the controls and levers all at once, yanking the power back and somehow setting us back to straight and level. Gus Thompson and I both sat back for a moment, limp as rags, and I am sure the rest of the crew felt the same, all amazed we were still in the air. Gus's meteorological computers, pencils, pads, graphs and tables were all over the floor in his position in the nose, while I had to look around for my stuff too.

The pilots, Bertram Henry Martens -otherwise known as B. Henry- and Frank Carden got the airplane up just below the base of the scud again, around six hundred feet, although there was no hope of maintaining any constant altitude for long. We

247

had to be able to see the sea surface, as terrifying a sight as it was, to find our way into the eye of this monster.

"I never thought I would be reporting waves classified as phenomenal, but that's what they are!" yelled Gus, and I agreed. We had been knocked off our heading and we got back on as things settled down a little.

I had to set up another probable course into the eye, aligned at right angles to the wind direction when it had reached gale force, coming from our left. I had cinched up my seat belt so tight that I had to loosen it to lean over my drift meter to get a reading. We were bouncing around so hard I could only make a rough stab at it, and the drift appeared to be approaching forty-five degrees -the end of the scale.

"Wind's roughly 120 knots, from 180 degrees," I announced, hanging on to the driftmeter, trying to keep my voice even as I was jolted in my seat. "Roughly is right!" said some clown on interphone and I asked for another ten degree correction to the left. The scud started to lower and the blinding rain showers started once more.

As the rain became a torrent, a new problem arose as the heavy streams of water washing across the cooling fins of the radial engines dragged the cylinder head temperatures down to a dangerous level. If they got too low, we would begin to lose power at a time when we needed all we could get, especially if we hit another downdraft.

We were in a "Chinese bind". The pilots could try to raise the head temperatures by applying more power, but that would make us go faster and put more water over the cooling fins. B. Henry came up with the idea, there in the middle of a hurricane, to increase the power, and at the same time, drop some flaps to slow down the airspeed. But now we wallowed along in a poor configuration for very turbulent air, the airspeed well below normal and we all sweated even more than before.

We were all thinking: we had been on the edge of disaster, and now we could quit flying any second. But the procedure worked and the head temperatures levelled off. Either chance or the guardian angels stepped in as we broke into the clear for a moment and the pilots were able to get the flaps up, and get the airspeed back to normal. The rain had slowed, but then we could feel the savage grip of the winds again as the hurricane swallowed us whole.

Gus and I could only hang on again as the pilots fought to hold the heading, and it seemed that keeping the airplane straight and level by flying on the gauges was a matter of luck. We peered forward, looking past our wide-eyed, expectant reflections in the plexiglass for a glimpse of the surface to confirm that we were still right side up. Suddenly, the noise, the rain, the hammering turbulence all quit at once and we were in the eye.

There wasn't much time to exult, that first time, since we weren't completely sure how we had got where we were, and we knew we would have to get back out. But after a few minutes, we began to sit back a little and look around us, at the uncertain, heaving sea, with waves coming from all directions, and at the high dome of clouds above us.

"I'll be off heading," said B. Henry, obvious relief in his voice, as he began to circle around, taking care to stay clear of the wall cloud surrounding the eye. I had to do my best to come up with some sort of reported eye position and maximum wind estimate, but in view of the monstrous winds and the erratic headings we had flown, I had to do some educated guessing. Meanwhile, Gus was scrambling to get his temperature and barometric pressure readings, along with descriptions of the state of the sea and the cloud coverage so that all of our information could be sent to the Hurricane Center at Miami.

When we had left Bermuda, we were briefed that a "disturbance" had been reported by a ship several hundred miles northeast of Antigua. We had no way of knowing what we would find when we got there, and were left pretty much on our own as to what to do when we arrived on the scene. After all, we had Gus Thompson on board, and he knew as much as anyone back in Bermuda as to what data would be helpful in tracking the storm if there was one.

Like mountain climbers who have had a dangerous ascent to the top and could now face just as much peril coming back down, we got ready to exit the eye. All of us; B. Henry and Frank in the pilot's seats, Tom Thrower the engineer, and the radioman and Gus and I cinched up our Mae Wests a little tighter as Bert took up a south heading, with forty five degrees added for the drift we knew would be there, and we ploughed into the wall once more.

We were swallowed up again, the turbulence not quite so hammering, the rain not quite so torrential, the gut muscles not quite so constricted. This time, we were not heading into the unknown, but trying to find our way out. There would be a time, after we landed, to talk about what had happened, and what we did right or did wrong. But now we pressed on in silence out of the monsters backside and breathed a little easier each time the turbulence lessened, or I got a lower wind reading, or the clouds started to break so that we could see glimpses of sunshine.

We headed for Antigua, beat to a pulp and dripping with sweat and the rain that had leaked around the edge of the plexiglass. As we approached the island, we agreed that it was not far enough away from the hurricane and some weird turn in its path might trap us on the ground during the night. So we decided to continue on to Beane Field on St. Lucia, several hundred miles further south and we flew there in the bright sunshine, over an undisturbed sea.

"But that's not supposed to happen!" said Gus Thompson. "The book says that down-drafts do not extend down to the surface!"

We were sitting at the hotel bar, hunched over our beers, speaking quietly and still in a little bit of shock. And then there was the problem of too-low cylinder head temperatures: was there a better way to handle that? But mostly we talked about the northeast quadrant problem. It was generally accepted that as a storm moved up hurricane alley toward Florida, the movement of the eye piled up the weather at the right, front quadrant, where the circling winds met the resisting atmosphere ahead of it.

The northeast quadrant was to be avoided, we were told, but this was easier said than done. No radar, intermittent sightings, and all the rain and turbulence made it difficult to keep from being swept around by rapidly increasing hurricane force winds. Lack of experience didn't help either, and although B. Henry had flown a hurricane before, he had to depend on me to keep us on the correct track, and I had had only one lesson so far. However, we had been successful, and "discovered" a major, expanding hurricane which was given the name George. We were also able to start the plot of its track toward the Bahamas and Florida so that people could be alerted to the approaching dangers.

The morning came, and it was time for lesson number two. I don't know how the others slept, but I tossed and turned for a while then dropped off into a slumber so deep I felt drugged when the wake-up man banged on my door. We had some breakfast and headed out to the airplane, everyone making certain to appear casually optimistic.

This time we would not be caught by surprise: we knew what we were headed for. Gus and the pilots and I had discussed our strategy, and decided to approach from the south, and do everything we could to keep from being blown off the track we set up. George was estimated to have moved several hundred miles during the night to a point about two hundred miles northeast of Puerto Rico, and as we tracked northward across Antigua and then turned northwest toward the Virgin Islands, we started our descent to the usual 500 foot altitude and got to work.

When we arrived at the Virgin Islands, we turned north again and set our course for the eye. The surface winds picked up rapidly: thirty knots, forty knots, fifty knots, and, quickly, sixty-five knots. This time, all of our equipment had been tied down and checked, and Gus and I made sure that the tools of our trade, the dividers, computers, charts and curves were taped down so they would not fly around in the rough air.

We were hitting the gale force winds sooner than we expected and we began to know that the monster was still growing. The drift readings quickly passed twenty-five degrees. And then came those damned rains, not just in showers and sheets, but like a stream from a gigantic firehose. The airplane shivered and shook as the water battered us and then it would quit for a moment and we could look down on the boiling sea. The wind blew the tops from the waves and laid them out in long, frothy streaks so that the green water was barely visible. The drift was increasing so quickly it was almost impossible to keep up with it: by the time I was able to get a drift reading and give the pilot a ten-degree left correction it had already changed ten more.

It was obvious we were being blown around in that deadly spiral and penetration from the south was out of the question. Gus leaned toward me and yelled, "Are we going to hit that northwest quadrant?" and all I could do was nod and pick up the interphone mike and tell the pilots. "Let's turn off and try it again," I suggested.

"Give me a new heading," said B. Henry and we turned right, toward the northeast and out of there. "Let's go ahead and box it and take another look as we pass south of the eye," said Frank Carden, who had been commander of our flight detachment at Newfoundland. "We can decide on another penetration attempt when we get there."

We had reached a point where the wind had dropped to about sixty knots, and we turned onto the first leg of a four-sided box around the eye. With all of that wind on our tail, we really went zooming along as we proceeded to the first turning point. We reached it and continued on, and had flown three legs as we approached a point south of the eye, the point from which we could try another penetration. We now had a fairly good estimate of the geographic position of George's eye, but could only guess at the maximum wind speed around the eye itself. It must have been approaching 130 knots as we had made our turn right up next to the eye, and we could assume it wasn't going to go much higher than that.

We were all silent for a moment as the pilots decided what to do. We took another look at the rear end of this massive beast roaring and smashing its way toward Florida, and then one of the pilots said, "The hell with it. Let's try it again tomorrow."

Well, it didn't happen tomorrow. Apparently the squadron back in Bermuda decided that perhaps another crew could also use some on-the-job training, so another B-17, positioned at Miami, was dispatched and another set of crewdogs graduated, as we did, on their first try and made a successful penetration.

After sitting around Borinquen all day, we were pretty anxious to get one final try at George over with and get back to Bermuda. As we departed again the next morning, I kept running what I had learned over and over again in my mind: you can't just read drift and adjust the heading for it. You've got to anticipate! Anticipate! When the drift reaches twenty degrees,

252

correct for thirty degrees. It was a simple navigational problem that was encountered all the time, only with larger numbers.

We bored in once more, coming up from the south, heading into the eye which had moved as if on rails, now at a point northwest of Puerto Rico. I not only anticipated, I over-anticipated and we stayed on our desired track. The rain was lighter and so was the turbulence, south of the eye. But the wind was there, all of it, and we were already off the scale when we were swallowed up once more.

For just a moment, George shook us, then soaked us and terrified us, then we were in. The rain quit and we could hear the engines once more, and the overcast above us was just a thin haze. It had been so easy this time, even though the hurricane was bigger and more violent than ever. But there were no downdrafts, and no low cylinder head temperatures, and no northwest quadrant.

After we toured the eye for a while, Gus said to the pilot, "I've seen all I want to of this bugger. Let's go home!"

After we had exited to the southeast, back toward Puerto Rico, we gave George some leeway and came around to a heading for Bermuda. I thought, almost absently, that penetrating hurricanes wasn't the best way to calm the beasts of panic and anxiety that lurked with in me. But strangely, I didn't get bothered much by my goblins and gremlins while on these missions: on the way into the eye I had too much to concentrate on and on the way out, my mind was occupied with the feelings you get when you do your job in spite of some possible mortal perils.

In any event, in the relief of the moment, I felt cocky enough to lean over to Gus and say, "Well, that hurricane's not a virgin any more!"

Gus, who was working on his report for the radioman, took the dead, two-inch stogie from his mouth as he looked at me, some sudden wisdom in his eyes. "Neither are we," he said.

The hurricane forecasters at the Miami Hurricane Center no doubt hoped that George's westward movement would slow and the great storm would "recurve" toward the northeast and head out over the North Atlantic, but this was not to be. It pounded it's way on almost a straight line toward Florida and hit that state with full force, killing fifty people despite the forewarning and the precautions they had taken. It also caused one hundred million 1947 dollars in damage, which made it one of the most violent storms of it's time.

Back in 1928, a similar storm in the same general area killed more than 2000 people. There had been no system for tracking storms and warning people in the directly threatened areas and they were trapped and drowned where they lived. They could only look at the signs of the approaching storm without any knowledge of its path or strength as they had many times before and say, "I'll run for it when the time comes." Many of them couldn't run fast enough.

Hurricanes and typhoons had been reconnoitered since World War II. The experiences that other crews had had before us had been recorded somewhere, but the reports were written for meteorologists. If anyone had developed a standard procedure for penetrating an eye, none of us had seen it, so we would have to write one of our own.

We had all read, somewhere, about the first intentional flight into a hurricane's eye by Colonel Joe Duckworth and a young navigator, Lieutenant Ralph O'Hair four years earlier than our trip, in 1943. They did it in a two-seat, single-engined AT-6 trainer in a hurricane which had crossed the Texas coast and had reached a point over land between Galveston and Houston.

Duckworth knew better than to ask for authorization to make the flight since he certainly would have been turned down. And as commander of the Air Corps Instrument Flying Instructor's school at Bryan, Texas, he could certainly not make the excuse that he had flown into the eye by accident: few pilots knew more about flying in bad weather than he did. In fact, you might say that if anyone should have known better than to do such a thing, it was Duckworth. But like Lindbergh before him and Chuck Yeager afterward, he was drawn to that part of the world that was still flat so he could sidle up to the edge and look down into the abyss.

There was no abyss, only some wild turbulence which bounced the dinky little airplane around from time to time, and lots of heavy rain, but in the eye, there was relative calm and open sky. Duckworth and O'Hair made the short flight back to Bryan without difficulty and were met by a weather officer named Lieutenant William Jones-Burdick. The meteorologist made the mistake of expressing disappointment about having been left behind on the historic flight, so Duckworth said, "Okay, hop in and we'll go back through and have another look." So off they went, and took another look.

Word of Duckworth's unauthorized feat had gotten around Bryan Field and some B-25 pilots, who figured that if someone could fly into a hurricane's eye in an AT-6, it would make more sense to do it in a larger, twin-engined airplane, and so they also joined the list. Of course, making unauthorized flights doesn't equate with military disobedience, but it comes close. The Air Corps gave Duckworth the Air Medal anyway.

As we left Hurricane George behind us, I began to think to myself, "Why did we do it?" On the first flight we were caught by surprise; we hadn't known what to expect but had succeeded, almost as if by accident. But we had come within a few knots of airspeed and a few feet of altitude of being dragged down into a terrifying death.

And yet we went out again the next day. Of course, you can drown in your own bathtub. But the idea of coming down on the water and somehow living through the impact and then fighting, hopelessly, to stay alive, the harsh, choking seawater filling your lungs, knowing that you would finally be dragged down to the bottom of one of the deepest parts of the sea -8000 fathoms straight down- might have daunted Ulysses. Any man on the crew could have feigned some illness, or just refused to go, but we all went, willing to plunge into one of nature's most terrifying cauldrons to do what needed to be done to help protect people, and not be counted a coward.

When we returned to Bermuda, a hurricane alert which had been called while we were gone was downgraded for the time being. If the storm had recurved while we were tracking it, it could have passed near or over the island. Such an event had not happened since the '20s, when a hurricane came by and ripped off the roof of the St. George Hotel and generally tore up the place.

Later on, we were to undergo a number of hurricane alerts and on several of these occasions were required to evacuate our aircraft to safe havens in the U.S. to protect them. There were touching scenes as the brave flyboys strapped on their Mae Wests and climbed into the aircraft departing for the safety of the mainland, leaving the wives and children to huddle together in the shelters on the base as the storm approached.

Finally a hurricane or two actually passed over Bermuda, and, of course, we had provided ample prior notification. Damage was not extensive and nobody was hurt, and most people on the island expressed their thanks for our efforts. A substantial number of the locals, however, let it be known that had it not been for the meddling with nature by the hurricane hunters, storms would have continued to avoid the island.

On one such occasion I was forced to stay behind because the airplane I was scheduled to navigate for evacuation didn't check out. It had to be tied down and its wings sandbagged to spoil the lift which high winds might create, and had to be reoriented once or twice by tug as the wind direction shifted. The center of the storm actually passed directly overhead and the meteorologists who watched it on their ground radar were surprised to find that it had two eyes. The winds got up to 80 or 90 knots and I could say, with the arrogance of an old hand, "Well, its not a very big storm."

One observer, obviously an amateur scientist, decided to step out of the door of the operations building into the winds which were blowing at their peak. His purpose was to check the claim of the makers of his cigarette lighter that "It Works in a Hurricane!" The experiment failed when the winds filled out his raincoat like a sail and flattened him against an adjoining building. The idiot, his experiment abandoned and his hat headed east at ninety knots, half-crawled his way back to the operations building. I had to pound on the door for quite a while before they let me back in.

The Gods of Chance, who had some input into the flight scheduling department, apparently thought I hadn't had enough hurricane exposure during my first encounter, so when the next big storm came by a month later, it was my turn again. We had a different set of pilots: George Kougias was the aircraft commander and Charlie "Cumulonimbus" Jones was co-pilot. Both of them were married men who had been able to bring their wives and kids with them to Bermuda.

John Chambliss Mays was the flying meteorologist, an elegantly uniformed and groomed Texan who looked disdainfully at those who didn't at least try to have a little class and who was, like others I have described, not long for this world. John Mays liked to have a good time without getting involved in the uncouth partying some of us got involved in. He did all of the right things in Bermuda: he rented a nice house, bought a car and socialized with nice people. He met a beautiful young lady on the island and married her, getting a real start in life at a time when the threatening shadows of risk and uncertainty might have given him pause.

He met his end, there in Bermuda, sitting in the greenhouse nose of a B-29 trying to make an approach while having trouble with an engine. It was early evening and people on the base were on their way to the clubs or the mess halls or having dinner at home, or standing in line at the base theater, getting ready to end the day. Many of them could see the big Superfort as it passed overhead to begin its approach. As it came back around and headed for the runway, it staggered into a stall and crashed into the ocean. The fuel on board exploded and the flames lit up the sky and reflected on the pink stucco walls of the base buildings. They lit up the faces of the uncomprehending bystanders, some of them wives and children of those on board. There were some survivors, but John Mays was not one of them.

We were not in a Superfort, back then in October of 1947 when my second hurricane reared its ugly head, but still flogging around at 500 feet in a B-17. Once more, the task was to check out a maritime report of an atmospheric disturbance near Jamaica. Luckily, all we found was a disturbance, although we knew all of the conditions were right so that this could be a good sized storm some day, like maybe tomorrow.

We spent the night at Coolidge Field on Antigua and returned the next day to find that the disturbance had changed to a good-sized commotion of 70 or 80 knots. We penetrated the eye without difficulty and then headed for MacDill Field at Tampa, Florida for our crew rest and to discuss the next step with the meteorological nabobs who were stationed there. There wasn't too much discussion; the task was to penetrate the eye one more time so that the hurricane watchers would have accurate information for issuing the final alert bulletins before the storm crossed the coast of Florida.

This time we found all of the familiar features we had grown to know and love: the monstrous turbulence, the torrents of rain battering against the plexiglas nose, the almost sideways flight into the eye. One hundred-twenty knots was our wind estimate as we punched through and just as we entered the eye there was a quick, heavy lurch and some of us thought we heard something snap. We held our collective breath for a moment, but we were still flying, this time in an eye with blue sky and bright sunshine and fairly calm seas.

When we got back to MacDill, the first thing that Kougie did was to walk around the B-17 to look at the left wing root, where the wing entered the fuselage. Sure enough he found some popped rivets and damaged fairing, all of which made us wonder what effect the big lurch had had on the main wing spar. Kougias looked it over for a while, then decided it didn't look that bad, and we got ready to return to Bermuda. We noticed that this time, he didn't delegate the ceremonial tire kick to C.B. Jones, but gave the left gear a gentle nudge with his own toe to placate the gods in charge of mechanical design and reliability.

Apparently there was nothing wrong with the wing spar - the wings stayed on- and we were able to make the return to Kindley without event. Word about the slight damage had already reached there, and a small crowd of family members and squadron mates was there to greet us.

We hadn't been in Bermuda very long before a lot of changes began to take place. The buildup of the squadron went forward with new people and new airplanes arriving as the months passed. In between hurricane missions, we flew trips to Kelly Field in Texas to pick up B-29 Superforts to ferry back to Bermuda. The airplanes were modified for weather recon use, with armaments removed and special meteorological equipment installed.

All of the pilots were undergoing training and getting checked out in these bigger, somewhat newer aircraft. Some of the flight mechanics who flew with us on the B-17's were being upgraded to the position of flight engineer, who operated some of the system controls at a panel of their own located just behind the pilots. But most of the FE's were new arrivals who were already trained, including both officers and upper grade non-coms.

"This looks just like the control room of the Hindenberg!" said someone sitting in the pilot's seat of a B-29 for the first time. To climb out of a B-17 and into a B-29, the airplane used to drop the A-bombs on Hiroshima, was a little overwhelming. The flight deck extended from a bulkhead just in front of the large bomb bays, forward past the flight engineer's and pilot's stations, and still further forward to include the plexiglass greenhouse nose itself.

The bomb bays were modified to carry large fuel tanks for our long range flights. A long, narrow tunnel extended over the bomb bays and connected the flight deck with the rear compartment where the radar and radio operators, scanners and the dropsonde operator toiled. The two scanners, who doubled as relief crewmembers, rode in large plexiglass blisters which bulged out of the waist of the airplane. They kept an eye out for oil or fuel leaks, smoking engines or other non-scheduled events. The dropsonde man was involved with a device normally called a radiosonde which was launched from the ground by balloon.

As used on the airplane, the dropsonde man didn't send his gadget aloft; he dropped it through an air lock during the high altitude leg and let it descend by parachute. It was easy to tell when he made his drop because the change in pressure would suck on your ears as the air lock opened and closed. As it floated downward, the dropsonde sensed certain conditions in the atmosphere it passed through and automatically transmitted its findings which were recorded on board.

The engine and slipstream noise levels were a lot lower too, not only because pressurized compartments tend to keep sound out, but because the engines were further away from us on the longer wing. Up front, our working positions were well forward of the airplane's center of rotation, and it took some time getting used to the wider gyrations of the Superfort in turbulence or on a final approach in gusty winds.

We all presumed we were getting the pick of the war-weary

259

B-29 fleet, but they were, nevertheless, war-weary. There seemed to be an overly large number of reasons for an engine to fail in flight and we were to run through the list until some modifications were made and we got some operating experience. There were also difficulties with the propeller controls, and when we had a certain type of failure, there ensued a scary situation in which the great sixteen and a half foot propeller decides to do its own thing.

The prop overspeeds with a great roaring noise, out of control, unable to be feathered, ready to plunge the flight into a completely unpredictable course of events. The pilot slows the airplane down and hopefully the prop RPM slows down too and he might get to nurse it home that way. Or it might freeze in the unfeathered position, suddenly loading the airplane down with a great drag which had to be dealt with. Or it might keep winding up and come off the shaft, possibly knocking the adjoining prop out of action or slicing into the fuselage.

There was some discussion of a procedure that had apparently been successfully used, in which the pilot dived the airplane and then pulled up the nose abruptly. If things worked right, the overspeeding prop, it's shaft heated and weakened by the beyond-limits RPM' s, would come off and describe an arc, first dipping below and ahead of the B-29, then rising up and shooting over the top, still spinning like mad, well away from the aircraft.

On one occasion, a Superfort just departed from Yokota Air Base near Tokyo developed this problem. The crew tried all of the tricks without success and as the overspeed and the vibration got worse, the crew feared the wing would fail, so they bailed out. The airplane, still on autopilot, was headed south and crashed harmlessly into the sea near Oshima while the crew, after being picked up on land south of Tokyo, headed for the Officer and NCO clubs.

Word of the incident hadn't gotten around as some of us walked into the Club dining room. The pilots, navigator and weather man were sitting at a table in their flying suits, which was unusual, and drinking French 75's, which were usually reserved for Sunday brunch. On closer examination we could see that some of them had a contusion here or there and that a couple of red parachute rip-cord handles were propped up against the flower arrangement on the table. They were still high on being alive after a very close call and were having a great time. More than anything, they were celebrating the fact that they had been able to bail out over land rather than a thousand miles out over the ocean.

The replacement of B-17's with B-29's meant a lot of changes would happen, most of it good, some of it bad. It flew a lot faster and could carry more fuel, so we could cover a lot more ocean on each mission. The missions also got longer and more of a grind: fourteen hour trips were common and sixteen hour missions were not unusual.

The big thing for me was the radar. In the B-17 we were like a bunch of blind men feeling our way around in a cage full of tigers. Now, at least we could tiptoe around the beasts to some extent. It also made sense, in the B-29, to fly higher and our two basic altitudes were raised from 500 feet out and 10,000 feet back to 1500 feet out and 18,280 feet back. The latter altitude was the height of the 500 millibar level -one of the heights at which weather forecasts are computed.

The Superfort's ability to fly high was occasionally used to try to fly over the top of a hurricane, sometimes without success. A few days after we had made our first eye penetration, one of our newly assigned B-29's was sent from Bermuda to fly into the storm at a high level. They were to investigate conditions in the atmosphere around the storm to help determine what steered a hurricane on a particular course.

Mack Eastburn, one of the first of our pilots to be checked out, took the big airplane up to 40,000 feet when the engines started to backfire violently and he had to descend. They estimated that when they reached the top, the big cumulus around the eye went up another 20,000 feet above them.

It is probably just as well we didn't know at the time we may have been flying under a cloud eleven or twelve miles high and were being tossed around by forces powerful enough to create a cloud of that height. But such clouds were not always there. While making a low-level penetration of a storm which was so puny we disdainfully entered from the north side, we found 80 knot winds, and when we departed to the south, we

261

couldn't find winds that exceeded 30 knots. We climbed to 10,000 feet completely in the clear and passed over the eye again and found some swelling cumulus but no thunderheads.

The 1947 hurricane season wore on, and enough big storms were hatched west of Cape Verde and sent along the hurricane turnpike toward the U.S. east coast or the Caribbean area to keep us busy. I managed to become involved in six or seven forays into the eyes of hurricanes before January rolled around - the end of the storm season- in addition to a number of false alarms and threats that never developed.

Winter in Bermuda was pretty easy to take, and I can recall trying for a suntan around Christmas time. An occasional rainy, windy spell would come along and we might get a little uncomfortable in the unheated Bachelor Quarters, but a single blanket over the sheets took care of that. And no more hurricanes for a while: that was a relief to us all.

Very quickly, most of the old, reliable B-17's were gone to the boneyard or the smelters to be re-fashioned into pots and pans and percolators. One or two of the big gas birds were kept for administrative and logistics flights to the stateside headquarters or maintenance depots. However, they were soon replaced by a C-54 cargo airplane which had the needed capacity to haul replacement B-29 engines around.

When the spring arrived and we had no hurricanes to chase, we got into a routine of flying fixed tracks to the northeast and east of Bermuda. The east track was an exercise in pure monotony, twelve hundred miles in a straight line across the becalmed, glassy water of the Bermuda triangle and across the Sargasso Sea, where we observed an occasional patch of floating seaweed. It all looked the same to us: "bags and bags of sweet frig all," as the British say, with only an occasional ship to buzz in a non-threatening way.

We didn't buzz every ship. Once, not long after takeoff, we came upon a formation of ships the radar man had spotted, a circle of blips with a large blob in the center. We dropped below the four tenths fair weather cumulus to take a look and as we

262

approached, we could see it was a U.S. Navy aircraft carrier task force sailing southeast, probably toward Roosevelt Roads. The surrounding escort destroyers and cruisers moved around slightly in their perimeter positions while the giant carrier sailed serenely on, slicing through the sea without effort, a picture of great, silent power. We turned off and let it have plenty of room, giving it full possession of the ocean it so obviously owned.

On another occasion, a ship being buzzed blinkered a message, read by the radio operator, asking the crew to come up on a common radio frequency. When contact was made, the ship's captain advised that he was having difficulty with his steering mechanism, and asked for help in getting some spare parts. Kougias, who happened to be aircraft commander that day said, "Why not?"

An arrangement was made to have the parts air expressed to Bermuda, and a day or two later, they were dropped alongside the ship by parachute from the reconnoitering B-29. The ship's crew fished the floating container out of the water and the repairs were made.

The Superfort was a long-legged airplane: it could fly high and fast for long distances. Because of these characteristics, plus our ability to make detailed in-flight weather observations, we were asked to support an interesting project in the same way we had supported the Pacusan Dreamboat non-stop flight from Honolulu to Egypt. The project was called Fox Able One and involved the first trans-Atlantic crossing of U.S. jet fighters from the U.S. to Europe.

The Cold War was at one of its peaks, and the flight was intended, among other things, to flex some muscle by showing how quickly and easily we could get some fighters to a European scene of action.

The British Royal Air Force would do the same thing in reverse, although the significance of flying numbers of fighters from Europe to the U.S. was not explained. Perhaps it was intended to explore the logistic possibilities available in the event Canada invaded the United States.

We should explain to the British that Canadians already do periodically invade the United States, penetrating as far

263

south as Florida in the wintertime, while Americans counterattack in the summer. The only opposing forces each invading army usually encounters are the thin grey lines of customs and immigration inspectors at the border.

The flight of the fighters was to begin at Selfridge Field in Michigan, the home of the 56th Fighter Group, and was to end at Furstenfeldbruck Air Base near Munich, Germany. This U.S. base was one of those closest to the Iron Curtain, and the significance of the flight would not be lost on the Soviets.

Lt. Col. Dave Schilling, commander of the 56th, was one of the top U.S. fighter aces of World War II, with 22 1/2 victories. He was a very hyper guy with energy buzzing around him like St. Elmo's fire, always raring to go. If you had some idea to solve a problem you had better show results real fast otherwise his efforts would have swirled around you to get things done some other way.

Our B-29 crew included some of those who had penetrated into the eye of hurricane George; Frank Carden, B. Henry Martens and Gus Thompson. And to that illustrious group was added Don Ketcham who, like Frank Carden, had attained celebrity status in weather recon; everybody knew who they were and what great pilots they were. Don would later take his talents to the Boeing Company where he would show airplane buyers how a big jet should be flown.

We began our planning and experimented in the air with some possibly useful tactics like formation flight within clouds with assistance from our radar, which Schilling thought was too risky. As he worked on the operation, there was no way he or anyone else could know that he too, some years later, would join the select few who had an Air Force Base named in his honor. Smokey Hill Air Force at Salina, Kansas was given his name because of his great war record and his impact on U.S. fighter capabilities after he was killed in an auto crash in England.

Schilling was a hands on group commander, which meant that he would lead the mission. He had people around him who were with him over Germany when they brutalized the Luftwaffe, and they all worked well together. In the air, they took their job as fighter pilots very seriously; on the ground, they weren't serious about much of anything. After watching them in action for a while, we began to realize we still had a few things to learn about having a big time.

The oceanic part of the route was right through our old stomping grounds, from Goose Bay in Labrador to Narsarssuaq on the southern tip of Greenland; to Keflavik, Iceland; to Stornoway in Scotland. The main thing the Lt. Colonel wanted from us was to take off from each departure point as the jets waited on the ground, observe the cloud cover along the route for the leg, and especially, to observe and report the landing weather at destination. If it looked okay, we were to give him the go-ahead.

"I want you to tell me you can see the landing runway from your altitude before I go," he said.

Just to make sure we got it right, he located an Air Force meteorologist who had once been an F-80 pilot, Major L. J. Pickett and had us take him along to look at the weather as a fighter pilot would. And to make sure Pickett got it right, Schilling had his Chief of Operations, Lt. Col. "Dingy" Dunham fly with us too. Schilling paid a lot of attention to the weather because they had only one shot at Narsarssuag and Keflavik. Once they got there, they wouldn't have much fuel left, and there was no place else to go.

Another task of ours, once we had sighted destination and the jets had scrambled, was to reverse course for one third of the leg, turn around and head once more for destination. As we turned we would activate a directional radiobeacon we carried on board which the fighters could use for homing as we headed toward destination.

There were sixteen F-80 Lockheed Shooting Star jet fighters in the crossing, piloted mostly by young samurai who hadn't yet come to realize, deep in their souls, the finality of that last, smashing, burning impact that awaited some of them. They were led by thirty-ish flight leaders, who, by this time, knew what the score was and had made a choice. Between the quick, final blow, and gumming hamburgers in some old folks home, they had concluded, somewhere in their psyche, that quicker was better.

The trip across the ocean started with a lot of razzle-dazzle and came to a screeching halt at Goose Bay. For some reason, we were ordered to halt at Goose until the RAF Dehaviland Vampire jets arrived from England. Somehow we got diddled by the Brits out of the honor of making the first jet fighter crossing of the Atlantic.

Moreover, the delay turned into a five-day wait for the weather to clear and Schilling finally got launched. The procedures we had worked out and rehearsed worked pretty well and everybody got across. There was only one close call, on the leg from Iceland to Scotland, when the ventilation system on one of the jets quit and the cockpit temperature got very high. The pilot, like all of the others, was wearing his rubber water survival suit and his body temperature got to the point where he began to feel woozy. But he toughed it out and got down all right.

There was no way the flight could pass through the United Kingdom without having all the Yanks attend a big reception in London. It was at the Savoy, I'll have you know, and all of the upper hierarchy of the RAF and the USAF were there. But of all the people I saw there that night, the only one I clearly remember was comedienne Martha Raye, who lit up the whole room with that big smile.

Schilling and his troops had apparently been pre-entertained by the lower RAF echelons at Odiham, where the Lockheeds were parked. It may have been that they had just discovered jet lag and were experimenting with scotch whisky as an antidote. I have observed and even participated in such experiments myself and, of course, when you get up the next day, you don't know if you feel lousy from the jet lag or the antidote.

As I looked at some of our fine young men rocking back on their heels and trying to string three coherent words together, I couldn't help marvel at some of the RAF types, both young and old, at the way they were able to handle their liquor. No matter how much they put away they seemed, as I had observed on several occasions, to remain coherent, mannerly and amusing, right up to the time they fell down and were carried off by an attendant apparently trained for that purpose.

With some difficulty, Schilling and his pilots survived the reception and continued their trip to Furstenfeldbruck. There was, of course, another reception after they arrived, this time an afternoon affair on the lawn at the Officer's Club. It was hosted by the Base Commander and some of the organizations assigned to the field, including a B-29 reconnaissance squadron which did some technical snooping along the East German border.

Everyone was having a fine time until a great roar of engines filled the air, and a black-painted B-29 just cleared a line of trees and headed straight toward us. We scattered across the lawn as he thundered on, shaking the ground, just high enough to clear a squat chimney atop the officer's quarters. We had to admit that it was a pretty fair buzz job, although the timing and location were a bit questionable.

A couple of Schilling's fighter pilots took the incident as a challenge, and rushed by jeep down to the flight line where they found an F-80 with enough fuel in it. One of the pilots got off and had his revenge; however, even though he didn't clear the officer's quarters chimney by very much either, it just wasn't as impressive.

We managed to make the return flight back to Selfridge without losing a pilot, or running over a pedestrian.

11

THE GAMMA BUGS

IT WAS ABOUT THIS TIME -the middle of 1948- that we became more and more involved in a secondary mission which was to become of utmost importance: the search for radioactive dust particles floating in the atmosphere which could have been the result of nuclear explosions. Weather recon squadrons were being strategically placed to intercept weather systems which would affect areas of U.S. interest as they circulated around the world. This placement would also work out well to intercept residual clouds of radioactive debris floating along with the weather systems.

At this time, the U.S., with some British participation, was the only country known to be making and testing atomic weapons. It was assumed that the U.S.S.R. would one day build such bombs, perhaps by 1953, but the watch was on, just in case. The key area in this monitoring arrangement was the Pacific Ocean off the Kuriles. This was where radioactive debris from a Soviet bomb test was most likely to be detected since it was generally downwind from the Soviet Union. The recon squadron at Eielson Air Force Base in central Alaska took frequent samples along a line which lay across the most likely path of contaminated air. A new squadron would be placed in Japan, near Tokyo, and the monitoring tracks of the Alaska, Tokyo and Guam squadrons would be aligned to stretch from the Equator to the Pole.

The method developed for taking air samples was simple.

A metal enclosure roughly three feet square and capable of withstanding the forces of the slipstream was installed on top of the fuselage of the B-29's about midway between the wings and the tail. There were two intakes which directed outside air against paper filters which were mounted in holders and slid into place by the dropsonde man. The filters were changed periodically along the route, marked with position, altitude and other information, and stored in safe containers for analysis on the ground.

We took samples just about any time we were in the air; recon missions, ferry flights, administrative or logistics trips; we sniffed at everything like a bunch of hounds. As we were building that long picket line across the western Pacific, we flew another north-south line in the eastern Pacific from McClellan Air Force Base near Sacramento, California. And in addition to the new squadron at Tokyo, another would soon be placed at Honolulu for additional coverage. Even so, there were important gaps to be filled, especially to the south of the U.S.S.R. It was possible that if the wind circulation was in that direction, the Soviets could detonate a bomb and it could go undetected.

There were, of course, seismic and other means for detecting large explosions. But when the device was set off above ground, air sampling could not only give firm proof that the event happened, but could also furnish evidence of the engineering prowess with which the bomb was designed.

During this time we had an occasional false alarm which sent us scrambling to chase hot spots that weren't there. We also tracked dust clouds from our own tests which could be identified as such in the air sampling labs. As a result, the monotony of the daily weather recon grind was sometimes broken when two or three airplanes were sent on non-routine missions with some time spent away from home.

One morning, several crews were called to a classified briefing for a flight which would depart in a few days. It was so classified they refused to tell us where we were going, only that we would be gone for a week and that we would be given a sealed package of orders and the necessary navigation maps. The three B-29's were to be fully loaded with fuel.

We played the classified bit to the hilt. After takeoff from

Bermuda, we flew a course toward the U.S. as we opened the tightly sealed package, which was marked SECRET. Then we dropped down to 100 feet or so until we were out of Bermuda radar range, then swung toward the newly discovered destination: Tripoli in Libya, North Africa.

We would refuel at Lajes in the Azores and proceed to Wheelus Airfield, a U.S. base just outside Tripoli. This was before Khadafi's time, and before we had removed all of our World War II forces from North Africa. The flight from the Azores to Tripoli took about eleven hours, through the Strait of Gibraltar, across Algeria and Tunisia, then southeastward to Wheelus.

As we crossed the Tunisian coast and turned toward Tripoli at eighteen thousand feet, we found what seemed to be a dark, purplish-brown cloud bank looming ahead of us. We were to discover that it was not a cloud bank, but the leading edge of the seasonal sand storm which boiled up all along the coast of North Africa and sat there midway across the Mediterranean, a zillion tons of Algerian, Tunisian, Libyan and Egyptian sand particles flung upward by the winds and floating to the north because there was nothing to hold them down.

As we let down, the shoreline became discernible, first on the radar, then as a hazy, straight line separating the lead-colored sea from the sandy terrain and rocky outcroppings which we could see up ahead. Then Tripoli began to take shape, a cream-colored mirage of minaretted Moorish buildings floating midway between the sand-laden sky and the sea. It looked like an inviting place to visit and I hoped we would have the time. But that would have to wait; we landed in the sunset, too tired to do more than get some dinner and go to bed.

The next morning we awoke at the transient quarters to find ourselves in this strange world of sand and hazy sunshine. We found some breakfast and then took a walk down to the flight line to check on the maintenance status of the airplanes. The heat had not yet come up and the air was heavy and cool, with sort of an ancient, musty smell to it. The sand had stopped blowing but it was forecast to start up again before noon, but I had the feeling that nobody would notice it but us.

The B-29's were ready to go so we were set up to fly a couple of tracks out in the Mediterranean during the next few days. Another crew was given the honor of the first mission, so we had a day to ourselves, and knowing that wherever the U.S. builds a base in this world, there is a G.I. bus from that base to the nearest city. We found it and took the ride to Tripoli.

From a distance Tripoli had looked like some shining jewel, its courtyard walls hiding some tempting and mysterious Arabian delights. Tripoli might have been like that in the past, perhaps when the Italians had occupied the place. But now as we walked around we could see that the courtyard walls hid a lot of grime and disrepair, especially in the old part of the city. We prowled through the narrow streets, taking it all in; the tinkers in their private alleys hammering away on metal plates, squatting in the shade and ignoring the acrid smoke and noise which filled the air; young but not too enticing looking women flipping up their veil as we passed, giving us the age-old high sign; stumbling into what turned out to be part of a mosque and fortunately not encountering any of the believers who might exercise their right to spit on an encroaching infidel.

It finally got to be too much; not the mysteries of North Africa, but the walking, which had taken the whole day. We made it back to the main part of town and found a cafe with tables out on the sidewalk and ordered some beer, a word which the waiter understood immediately. He brought some bottles of good German beer which were nice and cold and suddenly we were back on familiar ground. If you can buy a bottle of no-nonsense beer, why, western civilization can't be too far away.

When our turn came for a mission, we flew a track roughly due east from Tripoli, passing midway between Tobruk and the island of Crete. We continued across the Mediterranean and made our turn just short of Beirut and headed back toward Tripoli. By the time we started our letdown into Wheelus the wind was already blowing pretty hard and so was the sand.

All of a sudden we had a bit of a problem. The flight had been a long one, about ten hours, and if the visibility got too poor, we had to think about an alternate landing airfield that was open and within our fuel range. The tower quoted a half-mile visibility as he cleared us for an ADF -Automatic Direction Finder- approach based on the radiobeacon. In this type of

271

approach, tracking signals to the approach end of the runway are not provided by the radiobeacon as it is on an ILS precision approach: the pilot only knows the direction of the beacon and must do some ad hoc maneuvering to find the end of the runway.

We dropped down into the yellowish murk with the sun dead ahead, glaring dully through the sandy haze just enough to cut forward visibility down to zero. The coast stood out clearly on the radar as we crossed it but after that there were no further landmarks that I or the radar operator could make out. With only a few minutes to go to the runway, the ADF needle finally steadied enough for the approach. Down we dropped still further, and we all started to sweat, trying to make out the ground before it came up and banged us in the nose. The radar altimeter was no good to us here, over uneven terrain.

The weather man up front spotted the runway and yelled, "There it is, over to the right!" and the pilot tried to wheel the big Superfort around but we couldn't get there in time. He shoved the four throttles forward and we had to go around.

"John, I'm going to backtrack to the northeast about five minutes. When I turn back around, give me a heading to the field again. The ADF needle is swinging too much for me to follow it that far out."

Wheelus Airfield was lost in the radar ground clutter so we were stuck with the ADF approach. I was able to get an approximate fix where the wavering radiobeacon bearing crossed the coastline as I saw it on the radar, so I crossed my fingers and gave him the heading. As we settled on our approach heading, the ADF homing needle swung around badly for a minute or two as we headed back, then steadied. Down we dropped again into the dull blinding glare of the sun, this time with a little more desperation, every eye alert on the flight instruments and engine gauges or scanning for a glimpse of the ground.

Again the weather man yelled, "There it is, off to the right!" and the pilot horsed the airplane around into an almost vertical bank. We waited for that shuddering stall but he had enough airspeed to keep control and came out of his turn and banked left again to line up with the runway for his landing.

"Gear down, flaps down, coming down," crooned the co-pilot

and the wheels banged down on the runway numbers as if the pilots had planned it that way all the time.

We flew our small allotment of missions and got ready to return home. Someone had found a halfway decent restaurant in Tripoli where they served Italian food and three or four of us went there to celebrate the end of our mission and our departure for Bermuda in the morning. Along with the Italian food, I had some gritty-tasting Chianti which didn't seem too bad after about the third sip. For dessert I had some big strawberries which were covered with a cream sauce and a generous helping of pathogenic bacteria which the proprietor threw in for free. We had been warned against eating uncooked foods off the base but I was twenty-four years old by this time and there wasn't much you could tell me.

The stuff hit me about halfway between Tripoli and Gibraltar on our way back to the refueling stop in the Azores. Fortunately, the B -29 was large enough to have a potty but it didn't take long before there was nothing left in me that I could give up. Then I started to burn up in great, cycling flames of fever and I laid my head on my desk, trying to regenerate some of the strength that had completely deserted me.

Luckily the navigation on this leg was easy and with some help from the radar operator, who had some navigation training but little experience, we were able to come abeam of Gibraltar with full knowledge of our position. Then I made myself sit up and take a Loran fix once in a while on the remaining 1000 long, endless miles to the Azores, so long and endless it seemed as though the airplane creeped through the air like a fly through molasses. Finally we were on our letdown to Lajes and I stretched out on the nosewheel door as the pilots looked back at me wondering what was wrong.

The next thing I became conscious of was that I was laid out on a bed and that several strange figures hovered over me, watching me closely. I was in a hospital room and one of the figures -all of whom were wearing surgical masks- had apparently given me a shot of some kind. They nodded and talked with each other, and one of them fiddled with an intravenous bottle and tube which was hooked into my left forearm. Then they moved me into a room by myself and left me.

273

"Damn it Lieutenant, its only two days since you almost died on us and now you're agitating to get out of here. Just you relax and enjoy it!" The doctor, who was a Captain, seemed a little bent out of shape as he pulled the stethoscope from his ears and left the room.

The medics had met the airplane with an ambulance and when the pilots described my symptoms and told them we had just arrived from North Africa, the first conclusion they jumped to was the likelihood of smallpox. They soon found out it wasn't smallpox, but in my tortured body, one bug was as bad another if it could kill me.

They had been taking a blood pressure reading once an hour, that first night in the Lajes dispensary and some time in the early hours, as someone pumped up the arm band, the doctor and his assistants realized they had a touch-and-go case on their hands. That's when my blood pressure started to slide toward zero, and that's when they gave me the adrenalin, "which brought you back like magic," the medic later told me.

I was still a little wobbly when they finally let me, their only customer, go after the third day. I took the shuttle bus down to the Post Exchange cafeteria to get some coffee and a doughnut when I realized I only had about eleven cents in my pocket. There was no way the crew could wait around Lajes until I recovered, so they found a replacement navigator and took off. They had dropped off my B-4 bag with my clothes but my wallet with money, I.D. card and a set of travel orders were still in my flight jacket pocket in the airplane, which had made the trip back to Bermuda without me.

So I left the cafeteria and went over to the base finance office for an advance on my pay, a gimmick which wandering lieutenants often used to keep from starving. The finance clerk looked at me as I if was some kind of a nut when I told him I didn't have any travel orders, or even my I.D. card, that they were in my flight jacket, etc.

"No orders, no I.D., no advance," was the answer I got. "Maybe if you see the Base Commander, he might authorize it." The way he accentuated the word "might" gave me the idea that the Base Commander might also send me back to the dispensary and put me in the room with the padding on the walls.

I walked back across the street and went into the PX cafeteria again trying to decide whether to have the coffee or the doughnut since I couldn't afford both. Not only that: I had to decide what I was going to do about getting in touch with the squadron, and getting back to Bermuda without orders to present to flight operations.

The PX coffee wasn't too bad and I sat there, enjoying a fantasy of revenge against the Base Commander and his entire staff. I pictured myself leaning against the PX entrance with my hat outstretched for alms, a couple of artful rips in my trousers, perhaps leaning on a crutch I would borrow from that crabby Captain at the dispensary. Wouldn't that be novel: a homeless First Lieutenant?

My problems evaporated in an instant, because who should come walking into the cafeteria but Jocko Vercelli, an old navigating buddy of mine who had escaped the clutches of weather recon and was now in the somewhat more genteel air transport business. First, he bought me a doughnut, then he loaned me twenty dollars, and then he went down with me to the air terminal and fixed me up with a ride to Bermuda as an extra crewmember. Of course, I would have done the same for him. Well, I'm not too sure about the twenty dollars.

It turned out that our sniffing along the Mediterranean was in vain and when I got back to Bermuda, the flying schedule was changed back to routine weather recon flights for all crews. Of course, it never stayed that way for long and special tasks kept coming along. For example, there was part of an air-sea rescue squadron also stationed at Bermuda and we were called on to assist them in searches whenever an airplane was lost at sea. A British airline once lost two passenger airplanes about a week apart on flights from Bermuda to the U.S. We searched for both of them and never found a trace.

Then the French lost a big flying boat full of passengers on the long flight from Dakar, Senegal in Africa to the Caribbean area. One of our crews found pieces of it -it was an old airplane made partly of wood- floating off the coast o f Senegal. A tramp steamer Captain who was directed to the burned and charred remnants reported encountering sharks so huge he could hardly believe their size.

We got a nice letter from the French Ambassador to the U.S. which was endorsed by General George C. Marshall, who had become Secretary of State. But besides the sharks, what sticks in my mind was that when we were flying out of Dakar for the search, the French furnished our flight lunches which included a bottle of wine for each man. No, monsieur, we drank coffee instead.

And now came the time for me to leave Bermuda on permanent reassignment. Including my time at Newfoundland, I had been overseas for three years and was eligible for rotation back to the States. They had been three of the longest years of my life and when the Adjutant asked me if I intended to extend my stay overseas in Beautiful Bermuda, I didn't think about it very long. I was ready to come back home.

It really wasn't the hurricanes, or the long missions or the people I worked for or anything associated with the job itself. After all, the new assignment cooked up for me was in another weather recon squadron, located at Fairfield-Suisun Air Force Base near San Francisco, where much of the flying would be the same. But my home base would be in the United States, not on a tiny island. And I would be in California near Sacramento and San Francisco which, for a single guy, seemed like a very good move. My new job at Fairfield was as Chief Navigator, which I viewed with a little bit of apprehension. I wanted to keep a full flying schedule, flying in my turn and leaping off any time a special mission came along. So all the new job meant was that I would be a crewdog with an added administrative burden. As the time passed, this attitude was to cause me a few problems.

The base at Fairfield-Suisun -pronounced like "too soon"- was given the name of two towns nearby, and was soon to become Travis Air Force Base, named after the Colonel who commanded the base soon after I arrived. He was the very model of an American Air Force Colonel; handsome, smart, brave and patriotic to the marrow. His ancestors dated back to Colonel Travis of Texas and the Alamo, a man born for leadership because his leadership was instinctively accepted.

When he arrived he convened a meeting of all officers at the base theater and announced his basic operating principle; if you were an administrator, carry out the commanders orders: if you were part of a flight crew, whether it was transport or rescue or recon, accomplish your missions exactly as required. After that, your time was your own to enjoy. What better news could a crewdog hear? Here was a man who knew what the military flying business was all about, a man who could fly any airplane on the field.

It was too good to be true. It wasn't very long before the base was taken from the Military Air Transport Command and given to the bomber boys, the Strategic Air Command. Colonel Travis was kept on as the commander, but he had to undergo a dramatic transformation if he was to become part of SAC. The laid-back daily routine was gone. A SAC wing arrived and the fire-breathing atmosphere of General Curtis Lemay -whose rear-end was no longer made of iron but of tempered steel- prevailed. Everything that happened at Fairfield-Suisun was intended to keep the bomber wing in the highest state of readiness in the event the cold war turned hot.

The transformation of Colonel Travis was immediate and complete. He knew that General Lemay intended to keep his commanders terrified, and that this terror was to be passed on to the crewdogs and the maintenance crews. Before, he had made it a point to fraternize with the crowd at coffee time at the PX cafeteria. After, he set up a rigidly timed fifteen-minute coffee break, complete with a starting and ending whistle. On one occasion he actually chased a dawdling coffee drinker through a window as the laggard tried to escape after the back-to-work whistle had sounded.

The coffee shop incident is only one example of what the Colonel had to do to keep from getting fired and disgraced himself. The main score that was kept on him was the performance of the bomb wing in operational readiness tests. He apparently scored well for he stayed on and was promoted to Brigadier General at a time when commanders who felt smug when they went to bed late and exhausted found out at breakfast time that they had been fired.

He stayed on, that is, until one day he took off in one of his B-29 bombers loaded with bombs and fuel and pranged right there at the runway's end at Fairfield-Suisun which was, not much later, renamed Travis Air Force Base. That's what it usually takes to get an Air Force Base named after you. In the case of a SAC base, the process was especially difficult.

An even more difficult time of it was had by Brigadier General Richard E. Ellsworth. The boyishly handsome flyer had had a long involvement with the Air Weather Service, dating all the way back to World War II when he commanded a squadron supporting the dangerous "Over the Hump" supply flights across the Himalayas. I had seen him during his occasional visits to our weather recon bases later on, and he certainly didn't appear to be the fire-breathing warrior type.

But fire-breather he turned out to be, at least after General Lemay got him in his steely grasp, and transformed him the same way he had changed General Travis. Ellsworth, in 1956, was assigned as a SAC wing commander at Rapid City Air Force Base in South Dakota. The wing operated the SAC mainstay bomber, the giant Consolidated B-36, which had been conceived and built with global operations in mind. The '50's were also a time when a struggle ensued in the Pentagon between those who wished to provide for national security by building a radar-equipped, interceptor armed defense line around the North American continent, and those who demanded we put our money in to a powerful, upgraded bomber fleet. The bombers would be used as the force behind what would later become the concept of mutually assured destruction: if an enemy planned an attack on the U.S., but knew he risked a good chance of being bombed back into square one, he would not attack in the first place.

The radar chain was built, and the bomber boys were, of course, not happy since they could foresee a slow withdrawal behind a radar-monitored Maginot Line, and an increased threat to our security. Ellsworth conceived a plan for a dramatic demonstration of the new picket line's inability to guard North American shores. There were some known weak spots, and he planned to fly one of his B-36's -in person- through one of them, proceed into America's heartland and simulate the bombing and obliteration of one of our cities.

He positioned his big bomber at Lajes Field in the Azores and when a strong weather front was forecast to move across the line of radars in New England and eastern Canada, he departed on a blind flight plan. The young General kept his altitude very low, and as he crossed the shoreline, he hoped that even if the radar could reach him at his treetop altitude the returns would be confused by the buildups in the front.

But there, just past Nut Cove in southeast Newfoundland, stood a mist-shrouded, rocky outcropping looking as it had since the last glacier receded, but now it would have its appearance altered as the B-36 slammed into it. The giant mass of machinery, all six engines grinding away, wings full of fuel, fuselage filled with twenty-two crewdogs smashed into the rocks and trees and scattered itself into an instant graveyard. Rapid City AFB became Ellsworth AFB, but the Maginot Line question was not resolved until a short time later when Sputnick came along, and there was suddenly no line to hide behind.

And did any of us crewdogs entertain thoughts of somehow getting an Air Force base named after us? Not Hardly. But then again there was McConnell AFB in Kansas, named after Captain Joseph McConnell, who had been an Eighth Air Force Liberator navigator just like me. However, he had come back from World War II and had taken pilot training, and then went on to become the leading fighter ace in the Korean War. After that, he joined the Right Stuff Association at Edwards Air Force Base in California as a test pilot. He met his end at Edwards as he was engaged in the hazardous occupation of pushing the envelope.

At Travis, it could have been that the weather recon crews, who did not have to come to work every day in their flying suits and be ready to take off on a one-way mission, were considered a bad influence around the SAC crews. More likely, SAC needed the ramp and hangar space so we were shoved aside and the entire squadron transferred to McClellan Air Force Base about 40 miles to the east, just outside Sacramento, California.

If you must be shoved aside, McClellan was certainly a great place to land because it was, we quickly learned, a garden spot. McClellan was an air depot, a place where they made major modifications to aircraft and performed heavy maintenance, like complete aircraft and engine overhauls. There were perhaps ten thousand civilian employees there but only a few dozen military people who worked in the depot headquarters.

To leave the "war is imminent" SAC atmosphere at Travis and enter the peaceful, quiet world of McClellan was like walking out of the storm and into the sunshine. Since I didn't have a home life to occupy me, I could spend most of my time running my navigation section, or flying or playing around. But at McClellan I began to catch myself, on occasion, envying the married guys who seemed to have life pretty well put together. They were raising families and flying, and did not need to act like the would-be aviation playboy of the western world.

Our new emphasis on sampling the air for radioactivity changed our operational routine somewhat. We still flew the long tracks out in the Pacific, usually up towards the Aleutians, taking the usual weather observations and sniffing the air for those tell-tale particles. Once in a while the flight would be directed to continue on to Alaska from the far end of the track to close a gap created when the Tokyo squadron aborted a mission. Our flight would land at Eielson Air Force Base near Fairbanks where another of our squadrons flew regular tracks to the North Pole. After a day's rest, we would return to McClellan. Somehow, I talked my new squadron commander into letting me take one of the Alaska flights as an extra man, to be dropped off there for some cross-training in polar navigation.

There had been some discussion within the operations section about setting up a pool of polar-qualified navigators at McClellan so that there would be no limits on where we could go. At the time, only crews with navigators trained in the art of polar navigation operated in that never-never land where, for a number of reasons, ordinary navigation procedures cannot be used.

It was easily possible to get yourself into a position where you completely lost the handle on your direction of flight and had no way to regain it. And if your fuel held out and you came up on some land sticking up out of the ice floes, it just might be October Revolution Island, or even Bolshevik Island, both of which lie just before the North Siberian Lowland on the wrong side of the Arctic Ocean.

The idea of flying along without knowing which direction your nose was pointed, and whether the airplane was flying in a straight line or a large arc is a terrifying thought. A year before, one of the SAC recon crews, who also operated in the polar area, got themselves in this predicament and were forced to land on a frozen lake in Greenland, more than 2000 miles from destination. I read a report, some years later, of a civil transport navigator who found himself in such a fix over arctic Canada. They emerged from a cloud bank and as the sun came up over the horizon, he was surprised that it was dead ahead, "because it should have been directly behind us." They kept scanning the radio compass dial and finally were able to tune in Norman Wells on the Mackenzie River and make a safe landing.

Generally, the Air Force does make an effort to keep things simple, but polar navigation successfully resisted the attempt. For one thing, measuring direction relative to true north is made impossible because the meridians used for the measurement all come to a point at the Pole. That problem was overcome by printing a "polar grid overlay" on the polar navigation charts. This provided an entirely new means for measuring direction, at least to those who could somehow absorb it in their minds and use it in flight with confidence. Understanding the procedure was made difficult by a statement in the opening paragraph of the study guide we used, and which began, "Along the 180 degree meridian on polar charts, true south is the direction of grid north...."

Once you got by that hurdle, you were given hours of instruction on how to determine direction and fly a heading without a magnetic compass, since they worked poorly or not at all. You learned all the things that happened to gyros, the ones in the autopilots and those in the compass systems. The gyros began to build up errors in heading as soon as they were turned on because they can't be built perfectly, and because of apparent forces on them as they move from one earth position to another, and because those positions are on an earth that is rotating on its axis.

I would get my training by undergoing a ground course, and then taking a flight as one of the three navigators assigned to each of these missions, which were flown to the Pole every other day.

Chuck Massey, my old buddy, was in charge of navigation training there and he seemed perfectly willing to give me the visiting fireman treatment and get me checked out as one of the "Pole Cats." He had become accustomed to such visits although most of them involved people who merely wanted to deadhead up to the Pole just to say they had been there. One visitor was Charles Augustus Lindbergh himself, certainly not in the visiting fireman category, whose curiosity had been aroused by the idea of a squadron which was able to fly to the North Pole as a matter of routine.

Lindbergh was met by General Gaffney, who was the Commanding General of the Air Force elements in the area. As the baggage was being loaded aboard the staff car for the trip to the VIP quarters, Lindy said, apologetically, "If you don't mind, I'd like to stay in the flight crew's quarters and learn things first hand."

The quarters were set up two to a room, and he moved into Chuck Massey's oversized accommodations and bunked there for his entire stay. The whole idea of it boggles the mind; to have Lindbergh himself in their midst and brief him about the squadron's polar navigation procedures and then send him on a trip to show him how it was done. And of course Chuck, a big, easy-going Texan could handle it easy as pie.

Lindy certainly should have been impressed by Chuck and the people in the large navigation section. They could speak the astronomical jive and played around with new ideas like trying to get the bearing of the sun when the sun was below the horizon by determining which way the sunlight was polarized. This was important since, at certain times of the year, most of a fifteen or sixteen hour mission could be in twilight when no stars were visible, and a bearing on the sun would be the only directional information you had.

The easiest time to navigate was on a clear night when you could see the stars and take all of the fixes you needed. Flying in full daylight in clear skies was not as easy, since there was less celestial information available. Then came the difficulties presented by the spring or autumn twilight. But the worst time of all was at any season when you got into a long, continuous cloud bank and you couldn't see the sky and were therefore unable to get celestial information. In this case, reading drift on open leads in the ice floes by radar might be all you had for a long time.

The cloud banks consisted of ice particles which slid along the outside antennas and created radio noise which drowned out the few available Loran signals and completely swamped the high frequency radio communications. When this happened and there was no telling how far the clouds extended, the orders were to turn around and come back.

Everything depended on the crew's ability to determine how much the steering gyros were drifting early in the flight so they could compensate for it and fly an accurate heading. The gyros in the autopilots and in the main compass system, the Bendix N-1, were all rated against celestial bearings and the gyro with the least drift was used to steer by. The N-1 could also sense magnetic direction but this function was uncoupled during the long portions of the flight when the magnetic lines of force were nearly vertical, which meant that the compass needle wanted to point up or down rather than indicate direction, and therefore became useless.

Lindy completed his ground training and after some frigid weather fits and starts, he got his trip to the Pole. In doing so, he was able to observe some of the monstrous hardships the air and ground crews overcame as a matter of daily routine; minus forty degree temperatures, blowing snow and ice crystals, frozen engines, continual darkness, metal too cold to touch; the list was long.

The mission aircraft didn't check out and the backup was too cold to start. Everybody buckled down and got things defrosted and fixed and after the usual superhuman effort, the backup Superfortress finally departed. Lindbergh's pilot for the trip was none other than Royal Connell, who, with Massey as navigator, had flown the first weather recon flight over the Pole. Roy's flying ability was exceeded only by his prowess at Gin Rummy. I had innocently fallen into his clutches once, at Sacramento, when, apologetically and with Irish charm, he plucked my feathers like a kosher chicken. I never won a hand, and I came to believe that he could either read my mind, or had x-ray vision, or both, and I am not a dumb card player. After all, my street education had required that I become proficient in such esoteric card games as double-deck pinochle.

A few days later, Roy showed up wearing an expensive sport jacket, obviously one I had bought for him.

"John," he said, " I happen to have a little time, and I wonder if you would like to play a few hands."

"Not only no, but hell no," I said, trying to be polite. He shrugged, trying to hide his disappointment, knowing that financing new slacks for his sport coat would not come from me.

All of this makes me wonder, when Roy took Lindy around the Northern Horn, did they only discuss the myriad technical details involved in getting a B-29 off the ground and up to the Pole, or did Roy just happen to have an old, beat-up deck of cards? It was a 3500-mile, sixteen hour trip, and a game of gin could help pass the time.

And as the big bird descended on the way back on a heading to Aklavik for the final turn to Eielson, as the condensed, frozen breath and body steam began to melt from the ceiling and drip down on the crew and the new Pole Cat, did a blitzed and dazed Lindy pull out his wallet to settle up? If he did, and Roy finally got that new pair of slacks to go with his fancy sport coat, at least I can say I was in great company.

For some reason, General Gaffney didn't meet the airplane when I arrived. Well, that saved me the trouble of telling the staff car driver I would prefer to stay with the crews, especially since there was no staff car either, just the usual Air Force blue "six-pack ," an oversized pick-up truck with a six-passenger cab which served as the crewdog flight-line limo.

My ground training took several days, which gave me the chance to make a couple of trips to Fairbanks to see the sights and to observe how Alaskans entertained themselves. Some of the prices just about knocked my hat off, like three or four dollars for a hamburger -this was May of 1949- and everything else was just as high. One night we wound up in a steamy, jam-packed club of some kind out in the boondocks where everybody drank lots of beer and sang at the top of their lungs, especially a song called "Squaws Along the Yukon," an anthem to the unrequited desire which plagued the lives of the lonely out-backers. The big subject of conversation was the Tenana River lottery, which paid off a very large sum if you had the ticket stamped with the date and time closest to the moment of the first spring break in the winter ice jam on that river, near Fairbanks.

My flight came up on the schedule and I was assigned as third navigator, the one who had to make the sun bearing computations for the alignment of the astrocompass and maybe shoot a sunline with the sextant if we got the chance and, also, to get the coffee. The weather forecast was a little shaky, with some cirrus along the flight path, perhaps enough to give us some problems.

The pilots made their takeoff into a bright arctic morning and there was no hint of high cloud as we came around and headed north, toward Point Barrow. We would then head straight for the Pole at the 500 millibar level, or 18,280 feet on the pressure altimeter. Our return would be made at the same level, but to avoid duplication of weather observations, we would aim for a point well east of Barrow to spread the area of coverage, and then head for Eielson.

As we climbed, the Brooks range spread before us, a great barrier of ice-covered, jagged stone, mile after hundreds of miles of frozen emptiness reaching up to eight and nine thousand feet. Looking down on this pristine, beautiful stretch of snow and ice-locked desolation, I suddenly felt the safety and comfort which the Boeing put between us and the hostile ground beneath us. The engines sang their powerful song as we climbed, our subconscious ear on the alert for the first missed beat, but they ran smoothly and we were reassured.

We levelled off and arrived over Barrow, then set off across the Beaufort Sea, flying over an endless expanse of pack ice which stretched to all horizons. We were headed toward a goal which great explorers like Peary and Amundsen and Byrd had expended so much of their souls to reach. Now I was going there, with people from a squadron who went there every other day, awed by the idea of it only when some difficulty arose.

Everyone breathed a small sigh of relief when the First Navigator announced he had been able to get his first few astrocompass checks and that the drift of the main steering gyro appeared small. The three of us fell into a routine and I noticed that former Liberator pilot Bill Aldrich, the aircraft commander, peered back at us over his shoulder every so often. He must have been looking for any hint of a navigation problem, any trace of a lack of confidence in our movements which might show up before we got too far along, but we put on a good act and after a while he seemed to relax.

We passed the 80 degree North latitude line, making about 240 knots when the first inkling of difficulty showed up. "My HF is getting swamped by noise," said the radio operator, "What's going on out there?"

We all looked forward, and sure enough, the slightest wisps of greyish cloud were passing over us, just above our level. "We'll keep an eye on it," promised Aldrich.

It got so that keeping an eye on it became very easy to do because the stuff got more dense, little by little, until finally, the sun disappeared from view. I could see the pilots shaking their heads as they looked forward, and Bill said, "If we don't break out by the next observation, we'll have to turn around."

I certainly didn't like the idea of sitting in the soup without any means to check on our gyro heading for any length of time, but to get this far and not get to the Pole would be a great disappointment for me. Time seemed to be on hold as we sat there in our big cocoon, the ice particles slithering over the nose, the wings, the radio antennas. We could no longer navigate or talk to the outside world, and to continue under these conditions was just asking for it.

"All right, we're coming around," said Bill, and he started a slow, careful turn, no more than a quarter needle width on the turn indicator. Turning an airplane put forces on the tiny gyros which could change their drift rates as they whirled around at thousands of RPMs in their instrument cases, and Bill did not want to induce any more change in the rate than necessary. Too steep a turn had been the cause of the SAC recon's wayward journey to Greenland.

We had gotten to 85 degrees North latitude, 300 miles from the North Pole when we turned. And now, still in the soup, I had that feeling again that we were suspended by a thin string which could snap if our gyros decided to screw up and we were sent on an unknown heading. After he finished his turn, Bill turned in his seat and looked at me, an apologetic look on his face.

"Sorry, John. We'll have to get you to the Pole some other time."

It had taken Admiral Peary twenty years of trying before he made his trip to the Pole, and, until weather recon came along, there had been twenty-nine attempts with only six successes. Now, the polar crewdogs tried it every other day and made it most of the time. One of them, Sergeant James Boswood, made the journey more than fifty times.

The polar navigation problem disappeared for most people, about twenty years later, when inertial navigation systems came along. They had been developed for NASA's Apollo program which put Man on the moon, and for navigating our Intercontinental Ballistic Missiles on journeys which, if the deterrence concept worked right, would never be taken.

I hadn't made it to the North Pole the first time, but now, some years later, I had another chance, after inertial systems had come into common use. We took off from Andrews Air Force Base, just outside Washington D.C. in an Air Force Boeing jet called the Speckled Trout, the airplane assigned to transport the Chairman of the Joint Chiefs of Staff. The airplane spent most of its time as a test bed for new systems of interest to the Air Force, and on this trip, I went along to help evaluate some of them.

The Boeing had three different pairs of inertials and a new long-range radionavigation system which used Very Low Frequency (VLF) radio signals from U.S. Navy communications stations around the world. The wavelengths of the signals were so long they weren't too far from the audible sound spectrum, and because of this, they had the characteristic of hugging the earth and travelling very long distances. Moreover, there were enough stations around the world that world-wide coverage was foreseen.

I was, by this time, an FAA inspector who specialized in long-range navigation systems. I would take this chance to gain some knowledge of the new radionavigation system in the event a civil air carrier might want to use it in arctic or polar areas. I would also get to see whether one of the newer pairs of inertials -LTN-72's made by Litton- would operate satisfactorily after start-up and alignment on the ground as far north as Thule in northern Greenland, our departure point. A pair of these systems would later be installed aboard Air Force One.

Flying toward the North Pole in the Speckled Trout compared to making the ride in a B-29 was like climbing out of a big, old touring sedan and into a new Fleetwood Cadillac. The big jet had that VIP Never-Dull shine as befits the aircraft used by the Chairman of the Joint Chiefs of Staff, and had amenities like crew bunks and a microwave oven. I noticed that the aircrew meals had improved greatly over the years but still had some way to go. A good corned-beef on rye with a Polish pickle would have been a large step for mankind.

The 850-mile flight from Thule to the Pole was made in brilliant sunshine from start to finish, but with the gadgets we had on board, we would have been unconcerned whether it was day, twilight or night, or whether we were in or out of the clouds. There was a slight haze lying atop the ice-pack below but not enough to hide all that nothingness from view.

We all watched as the digital position readouts on the six inertials and the VLF system silently flipped upward; 89:30 North, 89:40, 89:50. The end-of-leg alert lights had all flicked on about the same time to warn of a turn coming up and now they all began to flash at the 30 seconds-to-go mark.

Suddenly, we were there, at 90 degrees North latitude, with all of the systems reading out within fractions of a mile on this comparatively short flight. As we passed over the Pole, the latitude readouts began to drop off as they should, all except for the VLF system. To the great chagrin and embarrassment of the VLF system designer who was on board with us, the latitude readout kept climbing; 90:30, 91:00 and on up.

"Hey! That machine's going straight up to the moon!" some insensitive soul cracked as the designer shook his head. He knew instantly what software changes he had to make and it did turn out to be a good system. But for the rest of the flight, he had to carry the burden of his genius with some humility and a defensive smile.

12

THE KING AND THE PICKY EATERS

T HE SUPERFORTRESS plowed through the radioactive hot spot, the snapping, crackling, popping nuclear debris swirling around the fuselage and over the wings, and pouring into the cabin and engine air intakes. The poisonous air also hissed through the slots in the WB -29's "bug catcher," -the three-foot square air sampler mounted on top of the fuselage- and left invisible traces of tell-tale isotopes on the big sheets of filter paper.

Lt. Bob Johnson and his crew had no means on board to tell them they were flying through the airborne remains of the first Soviet atomic explosion, and would not know they had done so for some time. They suspected what might be happening, however, since the Alaska weather recon squadron had been placed on alert, with weather reconnaissance and air sampling mission priorities raised from routine to "must fly." Flights that were aborted would need to be made up without delay.

Most alerts in the past had been scheduled to coincide with detonations of our own at the Enewetak or Nevada proving grounds. This one was different: -the office in the Pentagon which issued alerts had received a number of indications involving intelligence reports and seismic readings that a large explosion may have taken place in the U.S.S.R. Now, air sampling was needed to ascertain if the disturbance may have involved an A-bomb and, if so, to collect some of the airborne debris for laboratory analysis. Such alerts had been called before, but nothing came of them.

Johnson's trip had begun like any other mission and then turned into one of those sagas which he and the other crewmembers would remember for the rest of their lives. They had flown the outbound leg from Fairbanks, Alaska to Yokota Air Base near Tokyo and after a crew rest, got ready to return to Fairbanks. The route between Alaska and Japan crossed the flow of upper level winds which blew over the Soviet heartland and out into the Pacific Ocean. If debris from a Russian bomb entered the upper atmosphere, there was a good chance that it might be intercepted on this route.

While Johnson and his crew slept, a typhoon had crossed onto the main Japanese island of Honshu and was approaching the Tokyo/Yokota area from the south. Because the typhoon's eye was bearing down on them, the crew was awakened an hour early and was forced to hurry the preflight procedures so they wouldn't get trapped on the ground. Yokota was already in near darkness and under a low ceiling of heavy cloud and gusting sheets of heavy rain.

Bob Johnson taxied the Superfort through the truly crummy flying weather, the kind that made you wonder why you stayed in the business. All of the crew: the pilots, both navigators -one of them just happened to be my old buddy Chuck Massey- the weather observer, the flight engineer, the radio operator, the scanners; all they could think about at this time was, "let's get up and away from here and maybe -just maybe- come back at a better time.

The pilots poured the coals to the big bird, not able to see very much in the mist and heavy rain showers, using some extra muscle to keep the airplane straight in the swirling gusts. They got off and climbed up out of the low scud, thinking that perhaps they had it made when BLAM!- a loud explosion on the right side rocked the airplane and the scanner could see a plume of flame trail from number three engine.

"Fire coming out of Number Three!" he yelled on interphone, waiting for it to blow again but the engineer cut off the fuel and the flame quickly shrank in size and then died. The death of the engine had been immediately evident on the gauges, and the pilots and the engineer got it shut down and feathered the propeller.

What a hell of a fix! In the middle of a typhoon, heavy as hell with an engine out; what's a pilot to do? Johnson decided that since he was still very close to Yokota, with its long, wide runways, ground-controlled approach system -GCA- and all of the emergency paraphernalia, he would try to sneak it past Mother Nature and get it down on the ground.

The GCA man got him lined up for an approach and down he came, trying to control all of the wild gyrations and looking for the runway threshold lights. The lights didn't show up at flare-out time and GCA began to lose radar contact intermittently in the very heavy rain, so the pilots rammed home the go-around power and thought -somewhat tentatively- let's try it one more time.

Down they came once more and still no threshold lights in sight, and Johnson came to realize that they would have to go elsewhere. He had twice gotten the order to "Pull up and go around!" at the last moment, an order very rarely issued by GCA. The tower advised that Misawa, another U.S. airbase 350 miles northeast on the island of Hokkaido, was unaffected by the typhoon and had good weather, so that would be their new destination.

Now came a new set of problems. They had to get some altitude to clear the terrain, but with their heavy fuel load and an engine out , they would have to proceed with patience and a close eye on the air speed. It seemed to take forever, even with the throttles almost fully forward, to get the gear and the flaps up, to get a little more airspeed and some rate of climb. But in Johnson's mind; in the mind of the copilot and the engineer and everyone on board, the question loomed: "What if we lose another engine?"

There is no way the Superfort would be able to maintain level flight; they still had most of their takeoff fuel, in the wing tanks and in the four auxiliary tanks in the bomb bays. "So we better be ready to bail out," everyone thought as they ran the bail out procedure through their minds.

But Bob Johnson knew there was another possibility, an "instant fix," a procedure which had first popped into his mind when the engine exploded. He thought about it again as he looked at the red-decaled, safety-wired toggle switch on the control pedestal marked "Salvo." It would be so easy to just reach over, snap the wire and toggle it and in a flash, the bomb bay doors would pop open and the four volkswagen-sized tanks would plunge down, tearing hose connections, wiring and supporting straps apart as they left. The Superfort would instantly shed ten tons of weight and most of their problems.

Unfortunately, a decision to use the Salvo switch was not that easy. The vision of four big tanks full of fuel landing in the middle of some town or city below them somewhere in the murk would make even a desperate aircraft commander pause, and Johnson pushed it out of his mind. They sweated it out, and stayed with it, and after two hours, they got to Misawa and made the engine-out landing. Bob Johnson and his crew waited on the ground until the next day's inbound flight from Alaska was diverted there and the airplane turned over to them to finish their mission.

As a consequence of this somewhat terrifying series of events, fate decreed that Johnson's flight, on September 3, 1949 between Misawa and Fairbanks would be credited with the timely discovery of the Soviet's new atomic capabilities, and with obtaining some analyzable evidence of the scientific and engineering prowess which had been used.

The discovery, in the western world, was cataclysmic, and would cause consternation in the White House and panic in the Pentagon. The Russians were thought to have needed three or four more years but now, overnight, fundamental military and geopolitical policies would need revision to cope with the new situation.

Soviet technology, with a very large assist from their espionage activities, had paid off. The Russian A-bomb explosion had, in one blinding flash, altered the global balance of power. If they could proceed directly to development of the more powerful H-bomb before we could, the balance would be altered still further, and the free world would be in mortal danger. Those of us who flew the tracks each day and sampled the air didn't think of the situation in such lofty terms. But after that flight on September 3rd, and the consequent announcement of the Soviet explosion, we all took the sampling job more seriously.

The radioactive evidence brought back on the September 3rd flight triggered extra sampling flights by all of the weather recon squadrons; Guam, Alaska, Bermuda and our own in California. There was an effort made to coordinate the flights so that the radioactive cloud could be tracked as it moved eastward. The exposed filter papers were rushed to the laboratories by courier for an analysis which was complicated by the need to pick out " their" isotopes from ours. With people like scientist J. Robert Oppenheimer involved, firm, correct conclusions were reached, and President Truman announced the bad news.

After September 3rd, the activities of the weather recon squadrons were not the same. We continued to fly the routine tracks toward Alaska, but now found ourselves flying more special tracks, sometimes to Eielson, sometimes on a long track deep into the central Pacific, with a turn to the south and a landing at Hickam Air Force Base near Honolulu. Suddenly, the air sampling effort took priority.

Meanwhile, the 375th up in Alaska fought the grinding cold and all the other problems that come with the polar and arctic territory. They also had to worry about the possibility that attacks by Soviet fighters might be made to discourage our air sampling efforts as they prepared to make a bomb test they didn't want sampled. An attack by a MIG-15 against a U.S. aircraft did occur but the Russian was driven off by return fire. This happened in the spring of 1953, six months before a weather recon aircraft sniffed out the first evidence of a successful hydrogen bomb explosion by the Soviets. It had taken them four years to make the step up from A-bombs to H-bombs.

Looking back on what the Alaska weather recon people were able to do and the conditions they had to overcome both in the air and on the ground, I can only say that this country owes them a lot. In true crewdog style, they didn't look for medals or recognition from higher up, which was just as well, because there wasn't any and it didn't make any difference. Like the hurricane hunters and the typhoon trackers, they were heroes every day.

It was on a fine spring morning in 1950 when we suddenly

became aware of a plan to place a flight of three B-29's at Dhahran Airfield in Saudi Arabia to be operated by crews from our squadron. We were to close the gap to the south of the U.S.S.R. which was not being monitored by routine air sampling missions. Rumors sprang up concerning the need to fly tracks closer to the Soviet Union and one of them involved a reported rocket testing range near the Caspian Sea.

The rumor held that our monitoring was needed to see if the Russians were somehow combining their development of new rockets with the further development of their A-bomb. At this time, -early 1950- nobody had nuclear missiles and nuclear bombs had to be delivered by airplane or some other means.

The plan moved ahead swiftly and in April, some of us found ourselves sent to the air depot at Tinker Air Force Base in Oklahoma City to pick up additional aircraft. These were the original model B-29's which were still equipped with gun turrets but had been modified by adding weather recon and air sampling gear. Although the turrets were operational, no guns were installed.

By the end of the month we were ready to go and the Superforts headed out on a familiar route; Westover AFB in Massachusetts, Lages in the Azores, Wheelus Air Base at Tripoli in Libya. We had to spend an extra day at Wheelus because of a minor maintenance problem, and although I did go into town for more sightseeing, I had my meals on the base. I even avoided the strawberry jam at breakfast, even though it came from the good old U.S.A.

Departure morning came and we went down to Base Operations and filled out our flight plan and clearance and walked out to the flight line. There was a familiar scene; engine stands were pulled up to number two engine and the crew chief and a couple of mechanics stood on them and seemed to be putting the finishing touches to their repairs. The cowling sections were handed up and fastened, the stands were pulled away, everyone pitched in to pull the props through, fingers were crossed all around and we climbed in. The pilots and the engineer started her up, and everything checked out just fine.

As we continued our journey eastward across the Mediterranean, we weren't certain whether we might ruffle some diplomatic or military feathers by crossing the coast at

Beirut and then proceeding over Syrian and Jordanian territory directly to Dhahran. Up to now, we generally crossed just
about any border we pleased, except for those around communist countries, and nobody complained. But things were changing and countries were beginning to require overflight clearances, with scheduled border crossing times. Our problem on
this trip was that we weren't certain who owned which piece of
territory and how angry they might get when we violated their
sovereignty.

Well, we passed over Beirut and over Damascus in Syria
and over a piece of Jordan and nothing happened, so we
pressed on. If we were to try that now, we would have Israeli F-
16's, Syrian Migs and whatever interceptor the Jordanians are
flying these days all trying to get a piece of us. We crossed into
the northwest corner of Saudi Arabia and turned a little to the
south to pick up the Trans Arabian oil pipeline, which ran
across the Arabian peninsula from Sidon on the Mediterranean
to Ras Tanura, on the Persian Gulf near Dhahran.

We dropped down a little to look at the terrain, which was
covered with that yellowish, sandy haze we would become
familiar with. The pipeline gave us good guidance as it went in
a fairly straight line to the Dhahran area. This was fortunate,
for there wasn't much else to navigate by.

As we got lower, we started to take a good bouncing around
in turbulence caused by the rising, sun-heated air. The constant hammering really got to us after a while and we were to
find out that that's the way things are over the desert. It was a
relief to report " 30 miles out" of Dhahran and get our approach
and landing instructions, and then get on the ground.

Here we were, in the spring of 1950, not the least bit surprised that we sat on the shores of the Persian Gulf, ready to
fly tracks over this sun-blasted land of rock outcrops and sand
dunes that stretched beyond the horizons. Just a few weeks
before, we were flying routine flights out of California, or special flights to Alaska, or Honolulu, sometimes to Japan or back
the other way, to Europe. Now we would fly over a Martian
landscape seemingly devoid of signs of life, except for the
pipeline and places associated with it, like Qaisumah and
Umm Rudhuma and Badanah. New places to go, new things to

see, new people to try to get to understand. Except for being underpaid, and no promotions, and being overworked, and not appreciated by the management, flying slightly dangerous airplanes and getting sandbagged by an occasional plate of bad strawberries, it really was a hell of a life.

However, along with the downside items in the crewdog's life just enumerated, you might as well throw in the living conditions at Dhahran. It seemed romantic, at first, to live in a tent among the sand dunes, but that feeling ended the very first morning as the sun came up and then the sand started to blow. The big particles bounced off after imparting a little sting, but the powdery stuff clung to your eyebrows and lashes and the hair on your arms and legs and put a gritty taste in your mouth.

And then there was the sun's heat. The temperature, we learned, was measured three ways during the day; shaded air-which is the usual way- then out in the naked sunlight, and finally, the ground surface temperature, measured by a probe stuck into the sand. Shaded temperatures over 100 degrees were normal for the time we were there, while the un-shaded readings out on the ramp were ten to thirty degrees higher. The probe stuck in the sand at noon usually came out reading about 150 degrees.

Our headquarters were set up in some G.I. tents which were designed with double ceilings to keep us cool as we wrote reports and did some planning. The problem was that we had to keep the tent sides closed because of the blowing sand, and it seemed to me it was always cooler outside than in. In fact, we had to rearrange our workday to extend from sunrise to about ten-thirty AM, when thermometers hung on the tent poles passed 100 degrees.

On one occasion I went back to the headquarters tent after lunch to pick up a portable typewriter. The tent flap had been kept closed to keep the sand out, and when I pulled it back and stepped into the tent, the heat was unbelievable. I drew a breath of air that was like fire and my eyes began to swim and I came to realize that I had better move quickly or I would have a problem. I stepped back outside for a moment to cool down, then I made a dash inside to grab the typewriter and managed to get back out without taking a breath.

It wasn't long before we realized that the only way to stay cool was to find an air conditioned place and spend as much time there as you could manage. We found there were some empty rooms in the barracks and told the base commander we wouldn't mind bunking six people in a single room just to get the air conditioning.

I somehow got assigned to a room at the end of the building where the air conditioning compressor was mounted up on stilts just outside my wall. I had gotten so I could half-sleep standing up in crowded trains, or take a snooze lying on the vibrating, bare-metal nose wheel door of a B-29, and in other such places, so the air conditioner, which was about six inches from my ear was just another challenge. Every so often the droning noise would cause me to become partly awake in the night, and once, as I lay there on the upper bunk, I half dreamed I was in a noisy, open-cockpit biplane on a long, never-ending journey across the desert to places like London and Paris, and Yonkers, and other great cities of the world.

It took five days for us to get our flying act together, and we were back in action, bouncing along over the desert, the pilots trying to hold 10,000 feet in the turbulence. Among the dunes and wadis I found Al Qaysumah where the pipeline began to parallel the course we wanted. Then I waited for Rafha to come up and remembered we were briefed to stay south of it because the Iraq border was just on the other side.

We climbed and doubled back to Dhahran, then kept heading east, toward Karachi, Pakistan. The navigation on this leg was easy, since we could position ourselves accurately along the shoreline on the radar. Over Bahrein Island and the north tip of Qatar, then across the Persian Gulf to the Trucial Coast at Sharjah, into the Gulf of Oman and, with Muscat on our right, into the Arabian Sea.

When we reached a point just off Karachi, we turned and headed back on the same track. The air wasn't as bouncy as it was over the desert and I had the time to sit there and muse over what it must be like on the ground at Muscat, or across the water over in the mountains of Iran. And was the briefing officer joking when he told us that red-headed men were in great demand around Sharja for breeding purposes, whether they were willing or not? One of the red-headed guys pulled his hat down tight over his head and laughed, a little too loud.

It had been a fourteen hour trip. We landed and got our postflight duties squared away; the chutes, Mae Wests and oxygen masks packed away in the parachute bags, the weather log dropped off and the duty meteorologist debriefed, the sampling filters packed away somewhere, and so on.

We showered at the BOQ and trudged over to the Officer's Club for that first cold beer. We had a full bar at Dhahran, operated with Italian help and with the uneasy approval of the teetotalling Moslem authorities. They kept a wary eye on the operation to make sure their own people were not somehow drawn into the snares of alcohol.

To drink in that climate wasn't much fun anyway. I can recall making the mistake of having two Martinis instead of one before dinner, and then stepping out into the cauldron of heat outside for the hundred yard walk to the mess hall. By the time we got there, I felt as though I had been clubbed on the head.

The full bar was not long for this world. Our weather recon contingent had been there for four months and had returned to McClellan when an unfortunate incident happened back at Dhahran. One of the base G.I.'s -a medic- got into a boozy argument with a taxi driver as he tried to depart ARAMCO, the Arabian American Oil Company compound, to return to the base. The people at Dhahran all went to ARAMCO occasionally because they had such things as a restaurant, cinema and bowling alley there.

The altercation started to get violent about the time the Airport Director of Dhahran Airfield, a Saudi Major, was leaving, and he got in between the two men to stop the proceedings. The G.I. reportedly turned on him and punched him around a bit, and an international incident was started.

General O'Keefe immediately shut down the bars at Dhahran until an investigation could be made and confined everyone to the base to insure that no new fuel could be added to the fire. In the meantime, the unfortunate G.I. was readied for his court-martial. This was the situation which prevailed when Colonel Whitfield, our Group Commander, arrived to see if weather recon operations being performed by our replacements were being affected. I came along as his navigator and as I walked into the Officer's Club, I found that the bar was boarded up and an alcohol-free gloom had settled on the place.

Not long after we left, prohibition was repealed, but the only drinks available to celebrate with were wine and beer. A short time later, alcohol was once again banished, this time on a country-wide basis. The cause was another incident, this time involving one of the King's sons, a nineteen-year old. The young prince, his mind addled by liquor he drank at a party at a British diplomat's house in Jeddah, angrily left after an argument and returned with a gun. He began to shoot wildly, and one of the bullets struck the diplomat, who was shielding his wife. The Englishman was killed and, so the story went, the surviving wife was offered a large sum of money in lieu of the separation of the King's son from his head. She took the money, which seems wise, but the King's son was nevertheless sentenced to prison.

For those who couldn't resist the temptation, the administration of Koranic punishment could be viewed on certain Islamic sabbath days in the town square at Dhahran as the wielder of the sword of justice swiftly and without hatred or anger, chopped off the right hand of a thief, or the right hand and one of the feet of a thief who had been caught and had escaped; and, occasionally, a head. I once asked the barracks boy, who spoke English, whether a thief with one hand might steal again. "A thief is a thief," he said. "With one hand he can steal only half as much." And he laughed in a way that I could not tell if he meant it as a joke.

The harsh punishments obviously deterred crime, for there was very little of it that we heard about. Striking each other, for example, is a serious matter as the court-martialed G.I. was to find. I once watched how two Yemeni laborers were able to deal with a confrontation between themselves without inviting the swift and sure punishment they knew could await them. They were digging a hole in the terminal floor to repair some plumbing and became so furious with each other that they began to yell at the top of their lungs, disregarding the people staring at them.

Then they drew up about five feet apart and started to spit at each other. First one, and then the other took aim, and the gobs flew through the air, mostly missing the mark. Then they ran dry and the force of their anger was spent as they both squatted on the ground, their wiry-muscled chests heaving, their eyes downcast. After a moment, they looked at each other, and I thought they might start up again, but first one of them nodded, then the other, and it was over.

For one man to strike another was not always prohibited. We had landed at Jeddah to refuel and were standing near the nosewheel talking with an airport official as the refueler pulled the hoses around and climbed up on the wing. The official was dressed in riding britches and waved his riding crop around as he talked. The refueler came down and walked over to us with some question and he interrupted the official as he was speaking. The man in the britches half turned toward the man and hit him, hard, across the side of the head with the crop. The poor refueler covered his face with his hands and staggered off, while the man with the crop continued his conversation as if nothing had happened. I guess he was a member of the privileged class.

Hanging around the air conditioned club wasn't all there was to do at Dhahran. We had a swimming pool which we used a lot, and there was a standard G.I. base movie theater which played a new film every other day. It was in the theater that I began to realize that Arabs, who helped fill every seat in the place, thought about a lot of things the same way we did. I could look around me and see that they were caught up in the same emotions we were as the story unfolded, and they laughed at the same things we did.

One time it was different however. The film was, of all things, "Tales of the Arabian Nights," and there were murmurs of appreciation from some of the Arabs as they looked at the authentically dressed characters, sipping coffee from the authentic little cups, saying all the right things.

But then it came time for the female star, Maureen O'Hara to show up, and she came wheeling down this lush, green oasis path dressed in gauzy little nothings, seated on the neck of a large, trumpeting elephant. It wasn't the gauzy costume, or the overly lush oasis greenery that brought the Arabs, laughing, to their feet. It was the elephant, and the idea that the movie-makers could be so ignorant as to present the idea that such animals roamed the desert. After they laughed and shook their heads for a while, they sat down and resumed watching, eating their popcorn and sipping their Cokes, just like they do in Massachusetts and Natchitoches.

Christian religious services were also available, if you wanted to be real sneaky about it. The services were illegal, or I should say they were not permitted in the agreement we had with the Saudis for use of the base. So when a chaplain came on board, he was assigned as an administrative officer and did not carry the usual religious insignia over his breast pocket.

The Chaplain's room was sort of a religious speakeasy; when you walked in there was no sign of clerical paraphernalia of any kind. But with the flick of his wrist and the sleight of his hand, the covert chaplain could convert an innocent-looking flattened box standing against one wall into an instant altar. One day the barracks boy, who apparently had been briefed to look for tell-tale signs of Christian crusading, used some of his own sleight of hand and uncovered the secret altar. There wasn't much of a fuss; the Saudi co-commander told the American co-commander, who told the chaplain he had twenty-four hours to pack up his altar and get out. Fortunately, there was a flight out the next day.

Weather recon was not the only type of flying that went on at Dhahran. The U.S. Ambassador to Saudi Arabia, J. Rives Childs kept his C-47 Gooney Bird there, and when the Ambassador wasn't on one of his infrequent trips, it was used to haul supplies and people around.

I got to know Captain Jack Womack, the Ambassador's air attache and pilot and his navigator, Lieutenant B. B. McKinney, both of whom had been there for some time. I let them know I would be happy and even anxious to fly along on their trips anytime, anywhere, whenever I was free. I was also to get to know "Radio Willy" Williams, who was Womack's radio operator. He was not to be confused with "Radar Willy," an FAA air traffic controller at Chicago's Midway Airport, the world's busiest. The Chicago Radar Willy was known far and wide by our country's civil airline pilots for his ability to direct bad weather approach operations like a symphony conductor, working with efficiency, safety and an occasional touch of tension-breaking humor as the big airliners worked their way down the stack.

The Radio Willy I got to know was one of those indispensable people who got things done because they knew everybody and everything it was necessary to know. If Willy was around, everything was under control. He was a short, chubby, alert sergeant who laughed a lot and was very fast with a come-back.

B.B. McKinney had been there for some time and had seen enough of the Middle East, but I and some of the others in our flight were getting to feel cooped up on the base and he was perfectly willing to let us fly in his place. There were one or two trips a week to Asmara, in Eritrea, just across the Red Sea from Yemen, slightly north of the horn of Africa. The city was situated on a cool plateau, about 7000 feet high and had markets where we picked up fresh vegetables and fruit and other provisions.

To get there, we flew southwest across the Arabian peninsula, just skirting the northern edge of the Rub al Khali -the Empty Quarter- the world's largest sand desert where even a suited-up astronaut might hesitate to tread. Then we crossed the Red Sea down near the southwest corner of the peninsula, remembering that even Moses had to wait until the Sea was parted, while we zipped over it in a few minutes without a lot of fuss.

Once across, the ground rose up to meet us and we had to climb a little to get a better view of honest-to-God trees and plains of green grass, with herds of livestock roaming around the outskirts of the thatched-roofed, wattle-hut villages. When we landed, the supply sergeants went into the market while Radio Willy found us a taxi and we drove around this surprising, pleasant small city of Asmara none of us had heard of before.

The Italians had built it well, with wide avenues, municipal buildings and villas which fit in with the lush, green surroundings. Willy also took us on a mandatory visit to a shirt shop on the main avenue, not to look at shirts, but to gaze on this absolutely stunning salesgirl. She was about eighteen with classic, chiseled features, a clear, slightly bronzed complexion and big, hazel eyes that didn't avoid your gaze but looked at you steadily with a little bit of defiance. Every so often she would give her lovely chestnut hair a shake and lift her hand up to smooth it down, her ivory bracelets clicking together, and then she would walk over to get more shirts, all of us staring at her like bumpkins.

She had let it be known that although one of the tribal chiefs outside the city was pursuing her, she was open to offers from a suitable American to marry her and take her away from all this. Here, in this dusty little shirt shop, she held us spellbound, radiating desire warmer than the desert sun as she laid out shirts which we had a tough time concentrating on.

The image of her wheeling a baby carriage down Jefferson Street forced its way into my mind for a moment. Even in this tender condition, I could foresee her presence inexorably drawing the innocent and naive neighborhood into inchoate, violent confrontations as the mill workers, street sweepers, butchers and bakers all responded to primordial urges beyond their control and thrust me aside as I tried to shield her. "She must be mine!" they would cry.

To get us both some respite, I would take her to Loew's Theater in Yonkers, an elegant art deco movie house decorated with Persian rugs and landscape paintings, to see "White Cargo." Hedy Lamarr, at the height of her fame, is starring as a bombshell native girl and in her memorable entry scene, she suddenly confronts Walter Pidgeon, the hero.

"Who are you?" he asks, and the big screen is filled with that gorgeous makeup-darkened face and half naked body and those big, smouldering eyes and says, proudly and for all posterity, "I am Tondelayo!"

I feel the Princess of Asmara tense next to me, and then she jumps to her feet in the darkened silence and yells, "No, no, you fools ." And she places her hand on her heaving bosom and declares, in a rising, clear voice that carries across the staring rows of heads, "She is an imposter! I am Tondelayo!" And then, amidst the startled hubub we rise from our seats and walk grandly down the aisle and into the street where the royal streetcar awaited. Yonkers would have gone up in smoke!

Radio Willy then took us to buy something no visitor to

Asmara was permitted to leave without; a set of salad bowls made from the wood of olive trees. Most people back at Dhahran had a set or two which they would bring back home with them, and they were even sold in the small post exchange, but buying them in Asmara where they were made was the thing to do.

It was a short taxi ride to the salad bowl merchants house. We walked into a high-walled courtyard and were greeted by the merchant, a small, old and pleasant gray-haired Italian. He didn't speak much English, but that didn't make much difference with Radio Willy around. He knew enough Italian, Arabic and hand waving to actually hold a conversation.

We sat around a large table in the courtyard, examining the salad bowls and enjoying the cool air and the surrounding greenery. The man brought out some Strega, and we sipped it in the pleasant half-shade of some spreading, small-leafed trees, thinking that we better enjoy this while we can, for in a few hours, we would be back in the land that shade forgot.

Back at the airport, we noticed some armed World War II Spitfires with Royal Air Force markings on the ramp. It seems the RAF was still fighting a leftover part of World War II around Asmara, flying their beloved Spits which were rigged for ground strafing. The British had defeated the Italians in this area during World War II and now some of them had been kept behind to hold the lid on the tribal turmoils which kept erupting.

Asmara was connected with a road which wound down through the steep edge of the plateau, down to Massawa on the Red Sea. Most of the city's supplies like fuel oil and gasoline came up this road, which was under constant ambush by rebellious Shiftis and if the road was shut down, the place could not operate.

"Yes," the operations man said, "the RAF boys take off most days around lunch time to shoot up the Shiftis, then they come back just in time for tea." Now if you must go to war, I thought, you might as well do it with a little bit of propriety.

There were other places to buy provisions, and I managed to get to Teheran a few times. It was a large city and not as much fun as Asmara, but it had an atmosphere all of its own.

Usually when we landed there, we were given the use of a weapons carrier, a sort of military pickup truck which could carry four people in a tight squeeze in the cab. On one trip, the Shah himself was scheduled to leave town for the airport an hour after we intended to depart. At such times, the Iranian army stationed foot soldiers about ten feet apart on both sides of the road for half the distance to the airport. The rest of the way was guarded by horse-mounted troops about thirty feet apart, also on both sides of the road.

We picked up our cargo in town, which happened to be a load of watermelons and cantaloupes and headed back to the airport, down the troop-lined road. Because of the small truck cab, and because there were six of us, we tossed coins for the ride up front, and Radio Willy and I lost. At this point, we didn't know about the troops lining the road.

There was no other vehicle on the road but ours and we sailed on, with Willy and I sitting on a crate just behind the cab with our feet resting on top of the watermelons, suddenly embarrassed by our predicament. There was no hiding from the startled gazes of the lined-up soldiers, so we sat up nice and straight, as if the melons were a great prize, and we had been honored to escort them on their journey. Every so often one of the soldiers, only ten or fifteen feet away as we passed, saw that I was an officer, and made a confused, half-hearted effort to present arms. There was no way we were going to salute back so we stared straight back down the road, models of military demeanor. We finally got to the horsemen and the situation was eased, for all they did was stare down at us with the usual disdain of a man on horseback peering at unmounted mortals. Disdain or not, I'm sure some of them must have thought, "An American officer sitting atop our magnificent melons, preparing the way for our leader's departure. What will the ShahinShah think of next?"

Now, of course, I don't flip coins for any damn thing.

By one of those strange coincidences that happens if you get around a lot, we crossed the path of the Shah during his trip to England to look at fighter airplanes for his air force. As we built up the flying time on our Superforts, one of them had come due for an extensive inspection which had to be made at a large maintenance depot. The closest such place was at Burtonwood, in England, and so off we went, telling those left behind that as much as it grieved us to leave Dhahran, "somebody had to clean up the spills and throw-ups of life," and we were willing to go all the way to England to do it.

Burtonwood had been one of the primary maintenance depots operated by the U.S. forces during World War II and although it still did work on USAF aircraft, it was now back in the hands of the British. As we waited there for the inspection and some repairs to be completed, we got word that the Shah of Iran would be landing and that all officers, including the few Yanks who happened to be there were invited to attend a lunch being given by the Royal Air Force.

The Shah landed right on time and the sitting crowd of about a hundred or so officers jumped to attention as he strode into the mess with some retainers. He was not a large man, and was dressed in a very natty, light blue uniform with lots of ornate braid. The big shots took their places at the head table while we, as transient foreigners were situated in the last row of tables. Well, at least they were nice enough to invite us.

On our return to Dhahran, we were asked to take some passengers back with us. They turned out to be several young Saudis who were attending Sandhurst, the British West Point. Since the passengers were in the rear, we didn't get to talk to them much because of the long, hard-to-negotiate tunnel which separated them from those of us in front. As we headed back south across the Mediterranean, the pilot asked me to crawl back to see how they were doing. They were immaculately dressed in their British style uniforms and stood at the waist windows, looking down at the sea and the coastlines with an anxious curiosity.

"We would like to know exactly when we cross over into our country. Could you tell us this please?"

I said I certainly would and crawled back to check on the exact ETA for crossing the Jordanian border into Saudi Arabia. As it was about to happen, I crawled back once more and stood before them, staring down at my watch. When the second hand crept around to the right minute, I raised my arm and brought it down.

"Now," I said to them, "we are over Saudi Arabia!" My intent was to be lighthearted about it but the force of their emotion surprised me as they grabbed each others' arms and looked down at the moonscape, at At Turayf just across the border, and Badanah and Ad Duwayd along the pipeline. They shouted to each other and tears of joy came into their eyes for they had been gone for a long time. Now they would soon be on the ground among the fathers and mothers who raised them and with people who would renew their pride as Arabs and as children of Islam.

General O'Keefe apparently thought it was a good idea to break the isolation of his staff at Dhahran once in a while, so he put them aboard the Gooney Bird and sent them to Manama on Bahrein Island a few times each month. We went along too when we could, just to see the place and to get away from the blowing sand for a few hours. The flight took only a few minutes, and we spent the time looking down at the barely submerged sand bars and the pastel blue sweeps of deeper water which separated Bahrein Island from the Arabian Peninsula, trying to spot sharks or other large fish.

The flight would be over before we knew it and after the short ride into town, we would begin some aimless wandering along the old, dusty streets and through the markets. Before long, we would give in to one of the gang of bright-eyed young boys who hounded us as we walked and gave him a couple of Riyals to be our guide.

"I find you best price!" he declared, "Sandals, wallet; all kinds leather. You speak!"

In between markets we passed an old beggar on the street and as he approached, the guide boy started to shoo him away, as part of hi s job. But the man looked beat up as if he'd been in a street fight so a couple of us called him over to hand him some coins. As he came close, I looked at him and realized he had only part of a nose, that it seemed to have been worn right off his face. The idea that he was about to get some money had lit up his face in a wrinkled smile and when I handed him the Riyal, he did not grasp it, but held up both hands and sort of wiped it from my fingers. The realization hit me that this was a leper, for he had fingers missing from his hands and had to

307

hold the coin by pressing his palms together. Those leprous hands had touched mine and I wondered if I should be alarmed, but I could only look at this poor man and wonder how he could still smile.

I made several more trips to Bahrain after that, and each time this same old beggar would be waiting for us somewhere, his crippled hands down in the folds of his ragged robe, a rheumy-eyed, smile on his face. Then I would give him a couple of dollars and his face would really light up and he would back away, nodding his head and then stand there as we left, the bills pressed between his palms.

More than anything, it was that smile that got to me. Here was a man who had been saddled with one of life's heaviest burdens. He was an outcast who had to deal with the effects of his terrible disease every waking moment. But when I looked into that worn-away, surrealist caricature of a face, I looked past the smile and saw no self-pity in his eyes, just a hardness which told me he did not need pity from me. He was a bunch of sores covered with rags but he smiled, and behind the smile I could see the strength of a man who believed he would soon enter the gateway to paradise. Surely, here was another of God's miracles, the miracle of faith, and it beat me down; it transformed the patronizing pity I had felt into a humility that still affects me.

Bahrain was a place you could do anything your little heart desired, whether it was to smoke a pipe of opium, dally with a good-time girl or buy all kinds of wondrous goods. Rhinoceros horn aphrodisiacs, various essences of strange lizards and snakes for aches and pains; you name it and it was for sale somewhere.

I could imagine the Flight Surgeon back at McClellan, in the course of one of the tough annual flight physicals we had to undergo, looking through a microscope at samples of body fluids of someone who got carried away in one of the shops at Manama. He would scratch his head, wondering what those strange looking animals were. But we played it smart: we looked at things, and listened to the sales pitches, but all we bought were sandals and pith helmets and the like, because we didn't want to bring those strange animals home with us.

We were sitting around the club after dinner one evening when Jack Womack began to talk about a trip he had to make the next morning . His mission was to pick up our Ambassador in the Gooney Bird, fly him across the peninsula to Jiddah to pick up the British Ambassador and then bring them to Riyadh in the center of Saudi Arabia to visit the King. There was a discussion of the various etiquettes which might be required if the crew was invited to the royal dinner.

"Make sure you use your right hand," said one veteran of several tribal banquets. "And if they serve goat's eyeballs, you're going to have to pop one in your mouth and act like you think they're just great."

Jack's navigator, who must have been a picky eater, started to squirm a little. "When you toss it down," someone continued, "must you stare at it eyeball to eyeball?"

"Well," answered the sage, "just make sure you don't point it at the King."

It was at this point that McKinney turned to me and offered me the trip. I consider myself a picky eater too, but I wasn't going to refuse a trip to visit the King of Saudi Arabia, goat's eyeballs or not. In fact, in my mind's eye, I had some idea that I could pick up this, er, royal delicacy and palm it like a magician and simulate tossing it into my mouth and chewing on thin air as I dropped it onto the floor. I could then flick it away from me with my foot for the sweep-up man to find and enjoy after the party was over.

As we departed Dhahran, Ambassador Childs said, "I want the crew to do what I do, to go where I go, and enjoy the visit. I trust Jack has told you not to wear uniforms, and I hope you have brought civilian clothes." In fact, Jack had told us about the civvies and we all showed up in slacks and sport shirts, which was the only type of civilian clothes we had brought with us. The Ambassador himself wore the same garb during the entire trip, in contrast to the British Ambassador, who wore a seersucker suit, starched shirt, necktie and pith helmet.

When we landed at Riyadh, we were led to an ornate tent pitched alongside the runway, a tent obviously not for goatherds, but for Bedouin royalty. It was large and cool, and elegantly carpeted. At first I thought we were being greeted by the King himself, but it was his son Prince Faisal, the second in line. He was very tall and quietly regal and shook each visitor's hand without changing his somewhat mournful expression. He had some polite chit-chat with the two ambassadors as we stood around on the soft carpets, trying to take our cue from the others and tossing off the little cups of green coffee, one after the other, the way they did.

After a while we all left the tent and climbed into some cars to go see the King. The palace wasn't too far from the airport, and we were dropped off in the courtyard of this great, grey, royal-looking pile of stone with a long, crenelated roof line. We walked up a path to the palace entrance, the Prince and the ambassadors in front, then the pilots, then Radio Willy and me.

The path was flanked on the left side by concrete grillwork about eight feet high, and we could hear females murmuring behind the wall as we walked by. The murmuring, along with an occasional giggle as we proceeded was the only evidence of a female presence we were to encounter at Riyadh.

We were ushered into a large, ornately decorated room and there was King ibn Saud himself, standing before a throne-like chair, waiting for us. He was surrounded by a retinue of about a dozen people, half of them in British-style officer's uniforms, plus four or five bodyguards who were armed with curved scimitars.

The King was dressed in a conservative, brown robe of lightweight material and was wearing a white head scarf with a golden double head-cord. One by one, we were presented to this legend, tall as his brother and every inch a king. I could feel the bones through the soft flesh of his hand when I shook it, his grip now gentled after seventy hard years of his warrior's life. The king gave no sign that the severe arthritis in his legs, which would soon force him into a wheelchair, gave him pain.

He nodded slightly to each of us, and as we moved on, I stood off to one side and peered back at this figure of strength, and then looked at the scene around me, a scene that could have sprung from some daydream I had as a boy. I had expected to be awed by all of this, and I was. But after a few moments, I was able to relax and turn my awe into curiosity, for there was an air of friendliness in the room. There was a complete lack of pomposity on the part of the Arabs, including the King, and the pitch of conversation rose along with a lot of laughter.

One particular surprise was the lack of servility with which the King's retainers approached him, as if he was just a little more equal among equals. This really came home to me when I realized that the driver of our car was there too, looking as if he felt right at home, but I found out afterward that this social ease came to him because he was one of the King's younger sons.

The reception didn't last long and as we left, Ambassador Childs told us that, as expected, we were invited back to the palace to dine with the King the next day, after the sun went down. The problem of the goat's eyeballs rose in my mind for a moment, but then I thought; well, I got myself here, I'm glad I'm here and there's no way I'm going to do anything that will embarrass the Ambassador. So pass the damned plate!

We got back into the cars and left for the guest house and as we passed a massive set of wooden fortress gates, Willy, who knew some of the history, pointed to a spearhead that had been rammed into the wooden front. "bin Jaluwi put it there," he said, referring to ibn Saud's fierce second-in-command in the fateful battle to recapture Riyadh back in 1902. Ibn Saud and bin Jaluwi were in a hand-to-hand fight to the death with the occupying governor and some of his bodyguards before the fortress when bin Jaluwi thrust his spear at his enemy and missed, but it had been driven so deeply into the wood that it could not be withdrawn.

Ibn Saud was in his early twenties then, scion of a family that had been driven out of their tribal seat at Riyadh ten years before and into exile. Some very hard times had to be endured, but when the young warrior was ready, he got permission from his father to retake Riyadh.

He gathered up a band of about fifty cousins, retainers, desert raiders and other gung-ho types and recaptured the town in an attack that could have served as an inspiration for several Hollywood action movies. All of the elements were there; an almost moonless night, men slithering along the ground to the towering palm trees lining the protective walls, shinnying up the trees and dropping inside the walls onto adjoining roofs, jumping from one roof-top to the next until the house next to that of the governor was reached. They took over the house, then ibn Saud and a small party stole across the way and broke into the governor's house. They tied up the governor's wife and awaited his return from an inner fortress where he spent his nights for safety. The dawn broke and the governor arrived out front with his guards and ibn Saud and his cousin bin Jaluwi attacked and killed the governor while the other Saudi troops arrived to finish off any resistance.

As a dutiful son, ibn Saud presented the reconquered town to his returning father, who refused to accept it. Instead, the young victor was made emir of Riyadh and, as the sperm enters the egg, the birth of Saudi Arabia was conceived.

The wait to take back Riyadh had been hard, but now the struggle really started. It took thirty years of desert warfare, forging of alliances, tribal intermarriages, defeating Ottoman Turks, capturing Mecca and the site of Mohammed's tomb at Medina, dealing with the very devious British, plus a big, generous smile from Allah before Saudi Arabia could be called a country and ibn Saud could -in 1932- declare himself King.

What small twitch of fate's little finger had put me, along with my friends, in that palace room so that I could, in an event of consequence only to me, shake the hand of such a man. That seventy-year old grip had been much firmer once, when, in battle, he severed the head of a foe with his sword, then slashed downward with great force, splitting the headless body open so that he could see the still beating heart. Then, perhaps in gratitude for his victory, and for having been chosen to be the one to have his head and heart intact, he raised up his bloody sword and kissed it.

It seems strange that a man who could fight with such ferocity made a conscious effort to have himself looked upon as a man of reconciliation and peace. He had begun to realize it had become his lot to build a country, and he did not wish to do it with the sword alone. To help get this message across, when he had his photograph taken or his portrait made, the usual sword and dagger were nowhere in sight. Instead, he was usually shown fingering his prayer beads.

Now it was 1950, and the King, his family and his country were about to take on the central challenge of their history; to fly into the eye of the hurricane of the twentieth century. It was a flight they had to make, to take the opportunity to modernize by using wealth which was suddenly within their grasp. Up to now, if you can conceive it, the Saudis, the country as a whole, were poor as churchmice. There were almost no roads, very little electrical power, no plumbing, no hospitals, few schools, not much clean water or agriculture; the list could fill the page. The income the Saudis received from the outside consisted of a tax they collected from pilgrims to Mecca and the small royalty on the modest amount of oil which was found and pumped and owned by the American oil companies. This income belonged to the King to distribute as he saw fit.

Now, suddenly, at the time the Ambassador was paying his visit, the Saudis won an agreement for a fifty-fifty split of the oil profits, and they were about to be launched on a journey that would shake their Islamic souls. They would soon have money squirting out of their ears, so much of it that the gnawing problem got to be the question of how to spend it without ruining the world's economy.

One part of Jack Womack's duties had been to periodically fly off somewhere in his Gooney Bird and return with an installment of the Saudi royalties contained in sacks of gold coins which were arranged in rows on the cabin floor. For 1950, they amounted to 57 million dollars. If someone had to airlift the Saudi income for 1981 when it passed one hundred billion dollars for instance, one week's gold would probably come crashing through the floor of the present King's personal Boeing 747.

Meanwhile, here we were in poor but proud Saudi Arabia, having breakfast on the second day of our trip. We were in the guest house, which was a two-story rectangle of rooms around an atrium open to the sky. We were having ordinary scrambled eggs and toast with coffee, with ham, bacon or sausages nowhere to be seen. There was nothing exotic about the meal, except that when I asked for some water, the waiter picked up my empty glass and filled it from a goat skin bag which was hung from a balcony ceiling outside the dining room door. I lifted the glass to drink, and in the sunlight which poured in from a window ahead of me, I could see these strange little slivers of life, black and about a quarter-inch long, swimming around in my glass with a determined screw-like motion. I studied them for a moment, then put the glass to my lips and, thinking of the determination I would need to deal with a goat's eyeball, gulped the water down. Unlike those Libyan strawberries, the little swimmers had no discernible effect on me, at least up to now.

The events of the previous day had been exciting; the reception by Prince Faisal alongside the runway at the Riyadh airport and meeting the King in his palace were great moments for me, but there had been more. After we had returned from the palace and checked into the guest house, we had dinner and were sitting around relaxing when some cars came by and we were told we were invited to Prince Faisal's palace for some coffee and to be given some "baksheesh."

The ambassador had arrived before us and had been having a conversation with the Prince, who greeted us politely and then left for a moment. Mr. Childs took the opportunity to brief us on some of the etiquette concerning gifts; admire them but don't thank the giver effusively. Someone receiving gifts was expected to give some in return, but in our case, we could forget it.

We sat around in what seemed like a very large living room with ornate furniture and high ceilings and large glass windows. When the Prince returned, we were taken to a small room which was piled high with folded robes similar to those worn by the Prince and the King; very lightweight, dark brown cloth with woven gold edging about two inches wide which circled the collar and extended down the front from the collar to the floor. There were also mounds of soft woolen head scarves and woven-gold threaded headbands which looked like coils of golden rope.

We were each given a robe, scarf and headband and I thought to myself: I don't have to convince people I've been here; now I can show them. For good measure we were each given a wristwatch which had the King's likeness etched on the upper half of the face.

It was easy for Jack and Radio Willy to accept the gifts

without excitement for they had gone through the baksheesh business before, but when I was handed mine, my face lit up like a little boy at Christmas time.

Now it was the next day, and somewhere in the palace, the royal timekeeper watched as the twilight faded. Two threads, one black and one white were laid across the back of his hand and he glanced at them from time to time. Finally, he made his judgement that he could no longer discern the color of the black thread from the white, and he nodded. The day had ended; the evening had begun.

The party was small. There was the King, a young son who was interpreting for him, the two ambassadors, the two pilots, Willy and myself. We were up on the roof of the palace, waiting for some signal as we watched the final light fade from the purple sky.

Ibn Saud arrived and he greeted us and went over to his large, ornate chair at the head of the table. We stood behind our own massive, high-backed chairs as a retainer helped the King into his seat, and then we all sat down. The pictures I had in my mind, all of us squatting on a rug on the floor, grouped around a four foot pot with an entire, roasted sheep, eating strips of mutton rolled up in balls of rice, all of that, including visions of goat's eyeballs, had disappeared the moment we had walked onto the roof. There was a long banquet table, probably fifty feet long, with a row of ornate table lamps which shone on mountains of food on platters and in baskets and in tureens. There was a sheep, and what must have been a goat, and chickens, and fish, mysterious looking puddings and curd dishes and heaps of fruit. We did not have to attack these delights with our right hands, for before each of us lay a magnificent china service and heavy flatware, all laid out in opulent correctness.

The King's son had been given a stool and he sat himself between the King and Ambassador Childs and as they talked, a servant, dressed in a white robe with a green sash reached over the King's shoulder, took some food from one of the platters and laid it on the royal plate. I suddenly realized that each of us had a man standing behind our chairs, and they too reached out, ladled up some food and set it down on our plates.

When the King started to eat, we did too, not too sure what it was, and there was nobody to ask. There were some strange

315

sauces and textures and of course, some familiar ones like the mutton. Not long after we started, the five or six military officers who had been with the King at yesterday's reception quietly sat down a few seats away and started to eat. Each time we took a few bites, the retainer behind us would reach over and dig his serving spoon into another tureen and lay it on top of what we already had. I started to get concerned that the man was getting way ahead of me, and the food was beginning to pile up. There was no sense in trying to eat faster, the more I ate, the bigger the pile got.

And there was no way I would be able to stuff it all down, bad manners or not. I looked at Jack, and he looked back at me and shrugged. The problem was immediately solved for us when the King, who ate sparingly, said something to his servant, who reached down and took his plate away. That appeared to be the signal for our servants too, for they reached over our shoulders and took all of the plates . We sat for a while and talked and when I started to reach out for an orange, my man's hand shot out and he picked a nice one and peeled it for me.

Suddenly we were all getting up and I noticed as we moved off that a dozen or so people who had been standing in the shadows now sat down to take up where we left off. It would take the entire palace staff to finish the food that remained, I thought, and they would need to stuff themselves to do it.

We were herded to another part of the roof where a number of big, comfortable chairs were set up in a large U, with ibn Saud's seat in the middle. As at the dinner table, Ambassador Childs sat at his right, with the interpreter in between, and the British ambassador, who didn't need an interpreter, on his left. Then some high ranking officials who apparently had dinner elsewhere, sat next to the Ambassadors, and we and the Saudi military officers took the remaining seats.

The King and the ambassadors continued the conversation they had started at the dinner table and the way we were now seated, we could hear them clearly. They talked about the oil business, and ibn Saud said he trusted the Americans, and described the difficulties of doing business with the Russians and the Japanese. They also talked about St. John Philby, his old British friend who had given up his British citizenship and converted from atheism to Islam. Philby had been the go-between in the original negotiations between ibn Saud and the Americans for oil drilling rights. He was also the father of Kim Philby who was later found -in the 70's- to be a Soviet spy.

Some servants came up and brought some bowls of water to dip our fingers in and then held up small braziers with hot coals which smelled, I found out, of frankincense. We watched as the Arabs would have the brazier held up so that they could wave their hand to waft the fragrance into their beards.

What a sight this was, all of us sitting on the roof of a palace in the center of Saudi Arabia, the brilliant stars almost outshining the dim lights which bathed the King as he sat in his gold-trimmed robe and his scarf and headband. As the King and the ambassadors talked, I had an easy conversation with the officer sitting next to me who, like the few Arabs I had met, had a quick, laid-back sense of humor.

Before we knew it, the evening was over. The King said his good-byes and left, and the rest of us stood around and talked about some of the experiences the Saudis who were there had already had in England and America, and about some of the changes they expected the oil money to bring about. Then we climbed into the cars and headed back to the guest house under the starlit desert sky.

IV
BOOK FOUR

13

H PLUS FORTY- FIVE MINUTES

"**W**HAT'S HAPPENED SINCE WE'VE BEEN GONE?" I asked one of the flyboys at the McClellan BOQ as I moved my gear back in.

"Well, looks like a war has started over in Korea."

"So I heard. What else is new?"

The North Korean invasion of South Korea was another Communist move to take advantage of our obvious desire to get back to the business of peace, and followed the dismaying victory in China of the Communist Peoples Army of Mao Tse Tung, and imposition of the Soviet blockade of Berlin.

War-weary America had not quite gotten back to the pre-World War II days, where we hung signs on stove pipes that proclaimed them to be cannons, but almost. I recall something we used to refer to as "the Johnson Cut", one of a long series of military reductions in force -RIFs- that had been made when Louis Johnson was Secretary of Defense in the Truman cabinet.

When he completed this reduction in 1949, there were loud complaints that we had long ago cut away all the fat, and we were now chopping into muscle and bone as well, especially as it involved our commitments around the world which required military strength to back them up. Apparently we thought that our A-bombs would scare would-be aggressors into behaving properly and if it didn't, why, the United Nations would take care of them.

These were political decisions which were not our business

as military people, but they certainly did affect us personally. And they would certainly affect us profoundly if the decisions were not solidly based on reason. The wholesale RIFs just after World War II let go thousands of people who were pretty much standing around without much to do, but later on, the only people they could RIF were those who had a job to do involving our security.

We all read the papers and began to sweat again as we had in the past, each one of us sure that we would soon be on the street. The day before the list came out, the Adjutant, who doubled as a navigator, stopped me in a corridor and confided that he had seen the list and that I was not on it. The next day, each officer was called into the Squadron Commander's office and given the word personally: stay on or good-bye. He told me I would be kept on, but that a dozen others were being given their separation orders. I saluted and left, and as I passed the Adjutant's office he looked up at me from his desk, pointed to himself, then made a "thumb's down" sign. He had been on the list all along and didn't know it.

Twelve out of sixty or seventy officers was a big number and the effect was funereal, almost like losing an airplane and crew. And the reaction to the RIF was almost the same as to an accident; greatly relieved we made the cut, but guilty we had made it but the others didn't. It was especially hard when families were involved, since an equivalent-paying job was hard to find. But more than that, to be RIF'd was a great blow to the pride of young men who had to search within themselves to find the reason they were the ones to be let go, and could find no answer.

The Russian A-bomb was sniffed out not too long after the Johnson cut and our defensive needs began to get some scrutiny. However, in what seems like on open invitation to the North Koreans, Secretary of State Dean Acheson, in a Press Club speech early in 1950, delineated the U.S. military defensive perimeter in the Pacific in a way which pointedly excluded Korea.

Apparently Mr. Acheson hadn't told Harry Truman about the Korean gap in our defense perimeter, because when the

North Koreans crossed the border, the President's reaction was vigorous and swift. He immediately started to put a defense together, and took action so that the defense of South Korea would be made under the United Nations banner. General Douglas MacArthur, who was running Japan at the time, was appointed commander of United Nations Forces.

The reason the President reacted was his realization that a Communist victory in South Korea would encourage them to take further acts of aggression. With all of Korea in their hands, the Communists would pose a grave military threat to Japan, which was still under U.S. occupation and protection.

There wasn't much to be vigorous with in the beginning in South Korea as the U.S. had no combat troops there, just a 500 man advisory group. It is difficult to see what kind of advice would be helpful to the South Koreans, since we had taken steps to insure that they had no tanks, heavy artillery or air force. And to make sure that things were made as tough as possible on the South Korean army, as soon as the enemy hove into sight, our advisers were ordered to withdraw and leave them on their own.

It wasn't long before the North Koreans had the South Koreans and the few American combat troops we were able to send from Japan on a panic basis were bottled up in the southeast corner of the Korean peninsula, around the port of Pusan. Our troops were soft from occupation duty in Japan, and were almost as ill prepared to fight as the South Koreans. There were very dark days as we fought to hold on to the Pusan perimeter, but we held, and started to land additional forces there.

As you might expect from one of the best generals who ever lived, General MacArthur made a landing well to the enemy's rear at Inchon in what is generally acknowledged as a piece of genius, and the tide of the war, or, to name it properly, the U.N. police action, was turned. MacArthur's move was a large amphibious landing at a place considered almost impossible for such an undertaking, with extensive mud flats, a high sea wall and a thirty-five foot tide complicating the approach. The U.S. military Joint Chiefs and just about everyone else opposed it because of the risks, but the General rose to new heights in his ability to persuade and intimidate, and the President gave his approval.

The likelihood of a landing at Inchon was so remote to the North Koreans that only a token amount of their troops had been left to guard the approaches from the sea. The surprise was complete, the casualties few and the objective of severing the supply lines to the North Korean troops threatening Pusan was gained quickly. The war appeared to be over. Most of the North Korean army was destroyed, and it seemed logical to subdue the rest of the enemy and give the entire country of Korea, both North and South, the chance to hold democratic elections as stated in the United Nations resolution concerning the military actions.

The idea of chasing the rest of the North Korean armies all the way to the Red Chinese border at the Yalu River seemed logical to lots of people, but not to the Red Chinese. As South Korean and U.N. troops moved northward, Mao Tse Tung opened the flood gates and hundreds of thousands of communist Chinese rushed to meet them. We had a whole new ball game.

Meanwhile, back at McClellan, the radioactive life went on. As our troops suffered greatly through their first terrible winter under the onslaught of the Chinese Peoples Army, we found ourselves taking part in an accelerated series of nuclear bomb tests at Nevada and at Enewetak atoll in the Pacific. Our direct participation during the tests in Nevada was something new and meant that we would be flying right at the remains of the mushroom cloud within an hour of the blast.

"Countdown in ten minutes," said the co-pilot on interphone, and we all began to stir in our seats. The Superfort had already been preflighted and the engines checked and shut down again as we waited on the hardstand at Nellis. The air base was located between Las Vegas and Yucca flats, where the test sites were located. We sat there and absently listened to the burp-like drone of the auxiliary power unit in the rear end which was powering the radios.

When the five minute call was announced, most of us climbed down onto the hardstand and stood in the cold, pre-dawn desert darkness, staring toward the test site. The site was far enough away that we didn't need to worry about using dark goggles. Besides, the expected yield was "less than nominal" with nominal being the twenty kiloton Hiroshima bomb.

Suddenly, the co-pilot stuck his head out of his window and yelled," Here it is! Five, four, three, two, one, Zero!" First, nothing happened, then there was a pop of light like the one you get when a light bulb burns out and which you can feel impinge on the retina. Then the sky was lit up with this intense, white light which rose to a peak and then started to fade. The light slowly degraded from white, then to yellow, then to orange, and then it began to die out.

Countdown zero had coincided with the arrival of dawn's twilight, and as the sky lightened, we could look across the desert at one of humankind's ugliest sights: the blood-red fireball slowly ascending, sucking up a grey column of dust. Sampling rockets had been set off just before the blast and now the rocket trails hung around the rising cloud in jagged white lines. As the horrendous ball rose, the fire inside died slowly and a cloud formed on top of it like a cap of frozen steam. After a moment, we could feel the shock wave pass by us under our feet, followed by a barely audible rumbling noise. The tremor which had passed beneath us would more than likely reach downtown Las Vegas and cause some bored blackjack dealer to look up without knowing why, and then continue dealing to last night's leftover diehard who probably wouldn't have paid attention to the shock wave if it had knocked him out of his chair.

We climbed into the B-29 and the pilots started her up and taxied down to the takeoff position. As the official timekeeper, I waited until H+45 minutes and tapped the pilot on the shoulder. He smoothed the throttles forward and we took off, getting in the air quickly because of our short-flight fuel load.

Our main interest was to track the dust cloud to insure that the predictions for the direction of its drift were correct. If the wind direction forecast was right, the dust and debris would fall without immediate harm in the uninhabited confines of the test area. If not, then somebody might need to evacuate some people.

The main fireball had cooled and pushed its way into the stratosphere, its form all flattened and stretched out so that it was no longer recognizable. The radioactive debris in it which did not fall back to the ground would become part of the upper atmosphere and be scattered as it moved around the earth. The center of the stem -the part we dealt with- had also flattened out and dissipated, but the bluish-gray layers of dust were still visible in patches in the clear morning sunlight.

We were there before we knew it, and the radiological safety man in the weather man's nose position yelled, "Hard left! Hard left!" As the Superfort banked sharply he stared into his meter and waited for the needle to drop back down. "That was a little too hot!" h e said, shaking his head. "Okay, lets pull out ahead a little further to the east this time, and be ready to rack her over! Navigator, give me the position."

We did this for three or four hours; heading downwind -to the east- until the Radsafe man got a relatively low reading, then we would turn and head back toward the west, wait for the meter needle to rise, and then swiftly turn away, and do it again. Each time, he would radio the position I gave him to the command post on the ground.

The bluish-gray wisps of dust cloud had completely dissipated, but radioactivity still crackled in the air, surrounding us, getting sucked into engine and cabin air intakes. "Alpha particles," the radsafe man had said at the briefing, "are not a worry in this operation. Beta particles, well, we have to keep them from getting into our bodies by breathing pure oxygen all the time and by putting filters on the cabin air intakes. But Gamma radiation, well, " he shrugged, "when the blast ionizes the air, we get Gamma radiation which goes right through everything, the plexiglass, the skin of the airplane, right through your little gonads."

I couldn't see that anybody on the crew or anybody we dealt with was very much impressed with the personal hazards involved with radiation, once we had been in an operation or two. We were all given dosimeters to wear to keep a running total of the radioactive dosage each of us was taking, but we got to consider the little, pen-shaped gadget hung around our necks to be a nuisance. Perhaps because of this attitude, if a sampler crewmember received more than double the allowable lifetime radiation dose, nobody got excited.

After we landed, the airplane would be hosed down and

checked with a Geiger counter, especially along the leading edges, the nose and around the engines. The mechanics on the ground were probably as much at risk as we were since Boeing hadn't built the airplane to fly through a bunch of radioactive crap, and there weren't too many precautions they could take to avoid the stuff entirely.

There were, of course, people who did worry quite a bit about radioactivity when it was found outside the test areas. While I was at McClellan, our higher headquarters was located at Tinker Air Force Base at Oklahoma City and we made an occasional administrative flight there. The flight track passed pretty close to the Los Alamos Laboratory, which was situated in a large area in which aircraft overflights were prohibited. We stayed out of the area, of course, but I usually tried to lay our track right alongside the border of the prohibited airspace, to save flying time and to see what I could see, which was nothing.

After returning from one such trip, I got a call around midnight from Mike McMichaels, a major who ran the filtering operation, and he asked me to come to his laboratory building. He was standing in the doorway of his small, one-story concrete block laboratory, and even in the dim light I could see he was pretty irritated.

"Exactly where did you fly today?" he asked in an exasperated tone. He had a WAC chart -a World Aeronautical Chart- of the area between Oklahoma City and Sacramento and he held it up so that we both could see it.

"What's wrong Mike? You look a little brown around the edges."

"Its not you. I'm mad because its midnight and I'm still working in the middle of this big flap." I took the map and saw that he had already "roughed in" the track from the coordinates he had taken from the filter cover sheets. I made some refinements with a marker pen he handed me and gave it back to him.

"You're absolutely sure this is right? This thing is going directly to the White House. It looks to me like it's trash from Los Alamos and I presume they will catch hell."

I never heard another word about it. But every time I flew

past Los Alamos after that, I would look down and imagine bells clanging and sirens wailing and the Chief Scientist yelling, "There's another busybody airplane up there! Shut down the bubble machine!"

After this series of tests ended, several crews were sent on temporary duty to Hickam Air Force Base at Honolulu in Hawaii to chase fallout from tests being conducted at Enewetak and Bikini atolls. All of the bigger blasts were being set off out in the Pacific as work progressed in the development of the hydrogen bomb. We didn't chase these at close range the way we did in Nevada. Instead, we operated out of Hickam and ran filters across the forecast track of the cloud until we started to pick up radioactivity, then the crews at McClellan would be alerted to be ready to do the same.

We alternated this way between Hickam and Nevada whenever tests were in progress. In between, we flew the regular weather recon tracks up toward Alaska, or dealt with special projects as they came along.

One project which we were assigned in the late summer of 1951 involved not radioactivity, but the French, who were still in Indo-China but not for long. We had been providing the French government with various types of military assistance, including aircraft, and some of these came from McClellan. McClellan Air Base, as an air depot, had refurbished some World War II B-26 twin-engined bombers made by Douglas and had them equipped with extra fifty caliber machine guns which fired forward so they could be used for close ground support. With ferry tanks, they had plenty of range for an island-hopping trip across the Pacific to Saigon for delivery to the French Air Force. The French had asked Eisenhower for tactical nukes but he had refused, and sent them some conventional equipment, including the B-26's, instead.

It had not been practicable to equip them all with adequate long range navigation gear, and that presented a problem. The solution was to fly them in a large group which would hold loose formation, and be led by one of our B-29's, navigated by; guess who? The novelty of the trip attracted some other adventurous types and a navigator friend of mine named Jerry Post got himself assigned to the crew along with me. He was a First Lieutenant and I outranked him on that trip, but not for long because he would soon zoom up in rank, and last I heard he was a three-star general. I still tell people I taught him everything he knew, but he made three stars in spite of it.

Hal Jacobs, an eminently cheerful man, a guy who had the entire business of being a pilot put together better than anybody I have met, was the aircraft commander. He got together with the B-26 pilots on the best way to do this thing; the airspeeds, the communications procedures, the type of formation, assembly and recovery procedures and bad weather contingencies.

Everything went off without a hitch at first, including the first long leg between McClellan and Hickam, where an engine shutdown on a B-26 out in the middle could have meant a ditching. Shutting down one of your two engines doesn't mean that you cut your fuel consumption in half. It means that you have to boost the power on the remaining engine way up to keep flying; you go a lot slower and the distance you can fly is cut way back.

After Hickam, we proceeded southwest to tiny Johnston Island, which is barely more than a runway and some aircraft parking spaces, then on to Kwajelein and Guam. It was at Guam where we met our first real difficulty, because the weather had quickly deteriorated as we approached the island and the B -26's had to do some scrambling to get in.

This was August, and the Inter-Tropical front -the ITC- had moved in over Guam and sat there. The ITC is a line where two air masses meet and is marked by a semi-permanent line of large buildups which move north or south with the seasons, such as they are.

The big clouds can really dump down the rain, and since there was not a lot of active social activity on Guam and the weather was much too bad for the beach, all we could do was sit around and listen to the bullet-like rain pound on the arched, galvanized metal roofs of the transient quarters. It rained so hard you had to think twice before you braved a trip to the club or anywhere else, for once you got there, you had to sit around in your wet khakis. As the days passed, we wondered if we were going to get the full forty days and forty nights, and perhaps have Guam disappear without a trace. Hal was beginning to get a little edgy since he was a newly-wed, and had assured his beautiful bride that he was on a quick trip, out and back.

On the eleventh day, nature let her guard down and let the ponderous cumulus rain-making machines slip southward just long enough for all of us, Hal and his crew in the Superfort and all the B-26 crews to scramble around and head out for Okinawa and then Tachikawa, near Tokyo. At the big supply base at Tachi, the B-26's would be dropped off by their crews for the French pilots to pick up, and the U.S. crews would then head back for California via military transport.

As for us, we switched our recently overhauled B-29 for one that was now weary of two wars: World War II and now Korea, and needed lots of maintenance of the kind it could get only in the U.S. One engine was a little sick, which meant that the possibility of losing it had to be provided for in our fuel planning with more than the usual concern.

Hal's "quick-out-and-back trip" now became a test of the strength of his recent marriage. Unfortunately for him, as we left Japan for Midway Island to return home, the tailwinds across the Pacific were not blowing hard enough for us to make it all the way to Honolulu for a one-stop crossing. The extra stop at Midway would string things out.

Then the Superfort's war-weariness decided to assert itself, and as the flight engineer preflighted the airplane for departure at Midway, he found that the fuel tanks had sprung some leaks. Hal's good nature was able to mask the frustration he felt as the days passed, and access panels were opened and gaskets and seals laboriously checked and repaired.

We got to observe and become familiar with the strange behavior of the Gooney birds which covered the island and nested in places both logical and strange. These were the great Albatross, big, strong, graceful birds in the air; ridiculous, clumsy Gooney birds on the ground. The birds usually laid their big, ostrich-sized eggs in the sand and guarded them with hisses and squawks when humans came near.

Then, every so often, they would get the urge to return to their real element and head upwind, big wings flailing the air, webbed feet slapping the ground as they made their comical

330

take-off run. Suddenly they would become airborne and be instantly transformed into one of nature's great flying creatures, who could navigate a lot better than I ever could, and who could spread their great wings and fly non-stop to the ends of the earth without effort.

About the fourth day at Midway, I came to realize that Hal Jacobs still harbored the hope of making a one-stop crossing of the Pacific to get home. At Midway, we were already halfway across; why not bypass Honolulu and go direct to Sacramento? My first impression of this plan, as I told Hal when he disclosed it to me and asked me for my thoughts was; "Hal, nobody in his right mind bypasses Honolulu if he doesn't have to!"

Of course, I had no idea at the time that newlyweds are not exactly in their right minds, and should be humored.

"Are there any navigational problems which make a direct flight from here to Sacramento risky? The island commander tells me its never been done before," said Hal.

I studied the route carefully, and no matter how hard I tried to manufacture difficulties, Jerry and I had to conclude that it was, without doubt, a thirteen or fourteen hour piece of cake. Loran coverage was even better on the direct route than it was between Honolulu and the West Coast, which meant that I could probably read at least one book, take a few naps and spend some time swapping war stories with the crew.

But there went Honolulu, and Waikiki beach, and walking along the sea wall in front of the Halekulani Hotel, past the Royal Hawaiian and the Outrigger Club and sitting under the banyan tree at the Moana Hotel, sipping a Mai Tai or, if the company was right, maybe a Scorpion with two straws. And watching one of those gorgeous tropical sunsets.

But I couldn't tell a lie, and after all, Hal was not only the boss, but a friend with a problem. So on the fifth day, after sniffing around for residual high octane fumes, we took off and headed east for Sacramento. We flew the pioneering route without difficulty, and after we landed, everyone, especially the married men, raced for home. Nine months later, Hal Jacobs' and Jerry Post's wives gave birth on the very same day. Since Jerry's offspring arrived just ahead of Hal's, we assumed it was because either Jerry had a faster car, or Hal got stopped at a long stop-light.

Not long after, another project came along which I must admit I had to look at more than once before I volunteered my services. It appeared that an Air Force cloak and dagger organization operating B-29's, which were painted a dull black and were marked with the tiniest of USAF insignia, was having navigation problems. It wasn't that they didn't have all of the necessary long range navigation equipment; the problem was trying to use that equipment down to fifty or a hundred feet above the ground or water.

The project was being flown out of Eglin Air Force Base which was located at the far end of the western panhandle of Florida, not far from Pensacola. Eglin was not just one airport, but a complex of landing areas where they did things to airplanes that had to be done out of eyesight and earshot.

Although nobody told us as much, we came to assume that the C&D organization was involved in penetrating deeply into unfriendly territory and parachuting or even landing people at places which were inadequately served by the unfriendly transportation system. In order not to needlessly disturb the complacency of the radar stations along the route, the intruders would be flown at the lowest possible altitudes.

We were briefed by the previous project crew and they described the difficulties which had led to their lack of success. They had not been able to develop very low level navigational techniques to the point that they could, with confidence, fly from Eglin to Galveston, Texas as low as required.

"Bo" Boline, our aircraft commander and the rest of us sort of shrugged at the prospect; it didn't appear to be a big deal. But then came the rest of it. Until they could navigate to Galveston, they were even less confident they could fly the same way to Harrisburg, Pennsylvania.

Harrisburg, Pennsylvania? Our minds started to boggle a little. There were mountains in the way, and cities and high tension lines and tall broadcast antennas; the list goes on.

"And what about night, and bad weather?" we asked." "You tell us," they said.

Bo was a man who had some stories to tell. He piloted Superforts in bombing missions over Japan and was shot down and captured by the Japanese. Here he was, a tall, blonde, handsome guy who looked at you calmly and somewhat expectantly when he talked, ready to find out what you thought. And suddenly he was in the grasp of the Japanese, a perfect specimen of the Yankee aviators who were dumping incendiaries on their cities night after night. They took out some of their fury and fear and guilt on Boline and his cohorts who were not supposed to be this brave, or determined, or flying over Japan, and so they beat hell out of them.

Now Bo was cranking up the Superfort with nothing in the bomb bays except, perhaps, some leftover traces of sand from Saudi Arabia, or some spots of crackling radioactivity from Yucca Flat. We had set up a short, low-level practice flight to shake things out and after takeoff, we headed south across Choctawhatchee Bay. We crossed the spit of land at the coast and dropped down, first to one hundred, then fifty feet, playing with the radio and barometric altimeters to set up a procedure for maintaining the desired flight level.

The barometric altimeter would start lying to us as soon as we crossed into an area where the barometric pressure setting was different, but we could cope with that over water by correcting the reading against the radio altimeter. However, over land, the constantly changing terrain levels distorted the radio altimeter blip and made it virtually useless. The overland legs would be the problem; Bo would need to see obstacles to avoid them.

After wheeling around for a while, we began to get things pretty well squared away in our minds. We pulled out the short flight plan I had made up and we back-tracked across the coast, back up to 100 feet. We had determined from the project manager what types of terrain and checkpoints might be available to the intruder crew, so, with Bo's approval, I had laid out a course accordingly.

There would be lakes, the man said, and rivers and long valleys between low mountain ranges, but very few roads or railroads. Except for the roads and railroads, I began to see why the route to Harrisburg could make sense.

We didn't have any mountains to play with on this practice trip, so we headed out for the boonies to the east of Eglin. The radar man had his set cranked up and we got down to the business of knowing our position accurately enough to thread through a valley if we had to.

The ground surged by almost in a blur, faster than it had years ago on that Rhine crossing mission, because the Superfort flew faster by about fifty knots. Our first checkpoint was a lake large enough to be accurately portrayed on my chart. The lake came flashing by, just about on time, and although I couldn't confirm the sighting visually because we were too low, it showed up okay on the radar. Score one! We then altered heading a little to pick up a winding river and when a large bend came up on the ETA, I knew we had something going.

The previous crew had taken a "straight ahead" approach to their navigation. They drew a straight line course from departure to destination, which meant that they encountered a solid, unambiguous checkpoint only if one happened to be within sight or radar range of their direct course. This procedure could take them out of sight of any checkpoint for long periods of time, and they would then need to fall back on their dead reckoning. Of course, nobody but Captain Suicide is going to try to find a valley or mountain pass at low level using dead reckoning not confirmed by frequent fixes.

I sold Bo on the idea of breaking the route up into short legs which overheaded whatever good checkpoints were reasonably close to course. The slight amount of zig-zagging would add some time but, in my view, it was well worth it. After a couple of hours we reached the end of the route and were pretty well satisfied with what we were doing.

We made a one-eighty and on the way back I got myself set up to try some celestial navigation, which was on the program. The razzle-dazzle periscopic sextant had not yet become part of the weather recon navigator's gear, but the Pioneer A-14 sextant by Bendix usually worked well enough. It was a big, bulky, very well made instrument which you suspended from a hook in the center of the astrodome. The dome was only about two feet across, so there wasn't a lot of room in it for the sextant and your head at the same time.

Since we were in broad daylight I only had the sun to work with. The sun had warmed the ground beneath us and we started to get bounced around in the rising air. The idea of celestial in our circumstances seemed ridiculous, but I stuck with it. I re-checked my chronometer against the world-wide radio time signal, got out the Air Almanac and the proper volume of the Hydrographic Office tables -the H.O.-218- and got to work. The sextant bubble and the sun's shaded image jiggled and bounced in the hammering slipstream as I kept them lined up. To my surprise, the sunline worked out pretty well, within four or five miles, but it was certainly not accurate enough to be more than a backup.

I tried one more which was even less accurate so I had to put daytime celestial over land in a certain pigeon-hole in my mind.

The project movers and shakers looked at our results and shook their heads as if to say; why didn't we think of that? We got the go- ahead for the flight to Galveston and took off a few days later. It was a night flight and fortunately, there was a bright moon which glistened on the water as we reached the shoreline and headed due west. Again, we descended first to 200 feet and got ourselves squared away, then tentatively dipped down to 100 feet. The only sea surface we could see was where the bright moon cast its light toward us, but it was enough to give us some confidence. I had about a half hour to try my hand at night celestial and had no difficulty but again, the accuracy was such that it could only be used when you didn't need high accuracy to avoid higher terrain. However, the radar worked fine and we were able to keep ourselves pinpointed along the shore line.

Bo pulled the B-29 up to a few hundred feet as we crossed into the Mississippi delta area and made sure we detoured well to the south of the built-up areas around New Orleans. He did his best to avoid flying over any lights on the ground or any building he could see at all. But some individual farm buildings could not be avoided, and although the engines were pretty well throttled back, I can imagine some poor farmer suspended about three feet over his bed in sheer terror as some ground-shaking monster roared overhead.

There is no way an exercise like ours would be permitted over inhabited parts of the U.S. or anywhere else today, but that's the way things were in the summer of 1951. We motored on through the night, dodging buildings and giving tree-lines a few extra feet of clearance when we could see them. High tension power lines and tall radio and television broadcast antennas were usually marked on our charts and we were ready for them. But it took some time for new ones to appear on the chart, and these were a large worry.

After the delta, we were back out over the Gulf, and from then on, we had no further challenges to confront. We arrived abeam of Galveston, knowing that no intruder destination would be lit up like a Christmas tree as Galveston was, but we also knew we could expect to find it with radar, day or night, if it was situated on or near a coastline.

Now came the graduation trip to Harrisburg, Pennsylvania. The management apparently thought we were not altogether expendable so the flight was scheduled in full daylight. However, the weather conspired to insure that we would resolve some of the unknowns directly and without the need to simulate some of the hazards, like poor visibility.

We took off to the north, passing quickly out of Florida and into Alabama, chasing checkpoints and wheeling around unexpected obstacles. I wondered whether a navigator would be able to hold the intense concentration needed to make his judgements almost as instantaneously as the pilot, who had to turn this way or that, or lift up or drop down to find the target without being detected.

We pressed on, driving up just west of the Cumberland Plateau and west of the Allegheny mountains. The visibility started to shrink on us, and wisps of cloud began to flit by as we passed from Kentucky into West Virginia. Then came some rain showers and Bo was finally forced to climb high enough to give us more room to maneuver, and to give me more time to look at checkpoints in the reduced visibility.

We reached Cumberland, Maryland and turned northeast and found Harrisburg on our own, without the need to use the radiobeacon. But we had been unable to remain at very low altitude because of the weather, so we did not count the mission a complete success. Bo wrote up his mission report from the standpoint of the pilot, and I added my own observations concerning the navigation.

The idea of laying out the course to overhead checkpoints was the only way to go, I said. But if you throw in some bad weather or night time, you need either radar pin-point fixes or some gadget -not yet invented- which would enable the pilot to follow the terrain automatically.

I wasn't sure what the people at Eglin did with the report of our mission results since nobody in our own organization ever told us if what we did was useful. But about two years later, I opened an issue of Navigator Magazine published by USAF and there, in the centerfold, was an article by a Brigadier General in the cloak and dagger outfit describing how they had successfully used low level navigation procedures like ours.

Speaking of gratitude and recognition, when we returned to McClellan I went to my office the next morning and there on my desk was a new nameplate; 'Captain Such-and-such, Chief Navigator.' It took only a few microseconds for the little bulb to light in my mind; I had been replaced.

I knew what the Lt. Colonel who was the Operations Officer would tell me; I was never there. A Chief Navigator was a manager who had to stay home and worry about the proficiency level of the navigators in his section. He had to insure that the aircraft compasses, driftmeters and other navigation equipment were kept calibrated. And so on. I wanted to explain to him that I had all of my programs set up and run by assistants and it all worked automatically whether I was there or not. But it was too late; his mind was made up. Besides, he had some good arguments and he outranked me.

Not too much later, I got the job back when the Operations Officer and my replacement left for greener pastures. It was just as well , since the squadron ran out of special projects for a while, and I had to stay close to home.

It was not until the next spring, -April 1952- that the Nevada tests started up again. Each trip to Nevada meant only one weekday away from McClellan, so I took my turn as it came up. This time we operated out of Indian Springs Air Force Base which was situated a lot closer to the test sites. We saw big bangs, and little pops and sometimes nothing happened at all, and the cloud tracking task got to be routine.

We were occasionally informed about the radioactive

dosage we were taking, but complacency had worked its magic, and we didn't pay that much attention. We also got to know Las Vegas pretty well, both downtown and The Strip. I even got a credit rating at the Golden Nugget, with a limit of twenty five dollars. I would usually take the money and increase it a little at Blackjack. Then I would move to the noisiest crap table and get caught up in the excitement and blow it all, and that would be it for that trip. About the only thing I got out of the Golden Nugget was a calendar they sent me every year for a while, around Christmas time.

For entertainment we went to the Desert Inn, where the spectrum stretched from Noel Coward on one end to Lily St. Cyr, the stripper, on the other.

The top of the bill when Lily appeared was Joe E. Lewis, a stand-up comedian with a slash of a scar across his face which was said to have been put there by The Mob for some infraction of its rules. After the show, I walked into the bar and saw Tom Cronin, a navigator of ours just arriving. We took a table and started to nurse our drinks when Joe E. Lewis walked in and saw two servicemen -we were in uniform- and came over and sat down with us.

I was delighted and after I shook his hand I said, "Tom, you know who this is don't you?" trying to show the famous comedian how flattered we were that he would sit with us. Tom took the man's hand, looked at me and said, "No, who is it?"

14

KOREA-
THE UNFORGETTABLE
FORGOTTEN WAR

THERE WAS STILL PLENTY OF WAR LEFT IN KOREA when I arrived in Japan in September of 1952. The feeling that I was being left out of something I should be involved in had begun to get to me at McClellan after we settled into a period of routine weather recon missions during the summer. Then I got word of a job opening in the Weather Wing headquarters in Tokyo, and it sounded like just the thing for me. The Tokyo headquarters needed someone to act as an operations staff officer, and to navigate an administrative aircraft on trips to Korea and other places in the Far East. It was not a combat assignment but at least I would be on the outer fringes doing something to support our efforts.

I was, suddenly, twenty-eight years old, still hounded by those unnamed furies that had dogged me since I came back from World War II. I could now sit back on occasion and examine my wounds with some composure, and although I had no scars on my body, the wounds were there for the knowing to see. The occasional waves of anxiety still washed over me, attacks which came from nowhere, riding on some thoughts which popped into my mind and which I tried to push out. Then there were the fits of boredom, ennui so deep it could make a ten-minute bus ride seem like an eternity; and the tremors which were noticeable only when I lifted a cup to my mouth or handed a rattley sheet of paper to someone.

The toughest time was when I would try to fight off the anxiety or try to force my thoughts into some confident attitude and it didn't work. All I could do then was to try to concentrate very hard on what I was doing and where I was at the time, knowing that what was wrong had nothing to do with these two handholds of reality. I had been able to carry this burden through some horrendous predicaments; the final bombing missions, the hurricane penetrations, the emergencies which struck suddenly while we were far from any safe shore.

And now, here in Tokyo, something was happening. Either the burden had gotten a little lighter or I had gained some strength somewhere, but I now began to think that the time had come to do something about the kinks in my psyche which had caused me such torture, for torture it was.

The first thing I had to do was simple; I had to get back into really good physical condition. The shape I was in as an Aviation Cadet, when I could run the Burma Road and still do forty pushups and come up smiling were long gone. I still had the annual flight physical to pass and I never had a problem, but once in a while I would be checked for things like lung power and capacity or put on a treadmill, and it was easy to see I was not Olympic material.

First, I quit smoking. For a man who smoked two or two and a half packs a day, it was not very easy. Then, I tried to weasel my way into the task by tapering off. When I got down to ten cigarettes a day, it got so that all I thought about, all day, was when was it time for the next cigarette. I was to get a pretty dramatic example of the damage that smoking can do and the advantages that non-smokers enjoy because of my old buddy Marty Scheinkman, who I used to pal around with back in Sacramento. He could steal my girl away from me anytime, with a wink, back in California, but he usually acted like a gentleman. Now he was assigned to Yokota Air Base about thirty miles outside Tokyo and we would get together either in town or out around Yokota to have some fun.

Marty had played basketball on a scholarship in France before he was recalled to active duty and had managed to stay in athletic condition since that time. When we went for a swim at the Yokota club pool he would challenge me by diving into the pool and swimming it underwater lengthwise and about halfway back. About the best I could do, with my two and a half pack set of lungs, was to barely make it crosswise, and come up puffing.

By the time I had thrown off the shackles and had been smoke-free for only a few weeks, I could match Marty and even beat him once in a while. That, to me, was evidence that could not be ignored, and although I still don't mind the smell of cigarettes or a good cigar, I haven't taken a puff since that time.

The idea of gaining weight after dropping the habit didn't bother me too much since I could have used some, but it didn't happen. When I bumped into a Navy doctor at the University Club one evening I asked him, "Do you think there is anything wrong if someone quits smoking and doesn't gain weight?"

"At the very least," he said, looking me in the eye, "I would suspect stomach cancer." Since that time, I have hesitated to ask for free medical advice.

As soon as I stopped smoking altogether, a couple of weird symptoms showed up which lasted a while and then were gone. First, I found that my appetite did increase, but when I sat down to eat, I took one bite of food and my appetite disappeared so completely that I had to force some food down to gain nourishment. The other symptom involved my visual senses and I can recall looking down at a patterned rug or at some wallpaper and the coloration would be so intense I could almost feel them. These only lasted for a few days, and I was glad to see them go.

My quarters were located in Army Hall, a former Japanese military building located next to the Imperial Palace moat on the eastern side of the palace grounds. We were told it had been one of the headquarters of General Tojo -Japan's Minister of War and Premier- and had been spared damage from the wartime B-29 bombing raids because of its proximity to the Imperial Palace. My room was large and airy, with a high ceiling and windows that looked out on one of the main traffic arteries. The traffic noise seldom interfered with my sleep, but once in a while I would come awake, my mind suddenly attuned to some mysterious vibrations surrounding me. The bed shook, all of the furniture shook, the windows rattled, the whole building swayed a little and now here I was in the middle of a Tokyo earthquake.

I got up and opened the window and sat in the sill. The whole city was quiet except for a low rumbling sound and a strange noise, like thousands of bricks and sills and curbstones all slapping against each other. The quake would quickly taper off and except for a departing hiccup or two, it would be gone, and Tokyo would go back to bed. After a while, I didn't even bother to get up.

I had occasionally wondered what the Japanese thought about such places as Army Hall because of their links with the previous regime. A glimpse into their thinking was given to me when Professor Henry Ishikawa called me one evening and told me he had some things that belonged to me and wanted to return them. He spoke perfect English because, as it turned out, he taught English at a Tokyo school. The things of mine he wanted to return were some paperbacks and a notebook which had my name and address in it and which I had absentmindedly left somewhere.

It was past dinner time so I invited him over for a drink and he eagerly accepted. He showed up on the dot, a short, middle-aged, bulky man with a salt-and-pepper mustache, steel-rimmed glasses and a big smile. We hit it off right away because he seemed so eager to talk with an American, something he told me he missed very much.

He liked his scotch and as we talked and sipped our drinks he looked around at surroundings which first seemed to awe him a little. The Professor didn't want to talk about the war or past hardships. He only wanted to talk about the future and what his students were like, and I could see that there was nothing defeated in this man; there was too much work to do.

When I tried once more to ask about General Tojo he shrugged it off, and launched into a number of anecdotes about General MacArthur. He told them with pleasure and reverence, finishing with what must have been his favorite, about the time in the tunnels of Corregidor when the artillery bombardment was at its peak. When one of the men near the General started to bemoan his fate, General MacArthur looked at him, perhaps with a little distaste and said, "Good God, man! Do you

342

want to live forever?" I never saw the Professor again because not long after I was transferred to Yokota. But now whenever I think of MacArthur, I think of this story and of Professor Ishikawa, who had lived through the firebomb terrors and the defeat of his country but was not himself defeated.

The Weather Wing headquarters were located on the top floor of the Meiji Building in the downtown area. When the smog thinned out a little, we had a good view of the city. The Imperial Palace moat, bridges and gates to the palace grounds were just across the boulevard. The Ginza wasn't too far away, with all the noise and piled-up souvenir stalls and noodle soup carts and pushing crowds and the forest of big neon signs which shone on the streets at night in unfamiliar oriental colors. The noise came from the torrent of traffic which roared by, mostly taxies and buses whose drivers would never, on pain of losing face, step on their brakes before they honked their horn.

Driving alongside the taxies was motorized combat with a continual, nerve-wracking jockeying for position. We would have swirling dog-fights and occasionally when I pulled abreast and tried to get ahead, the taxi man would look over at me coolly, as if to say, "What we lost on the field of battle, Yankee Dog, we will regain on the streets of Tokyo!" The reason for the jockeying, one of the old-timers claimed, was that in the event of a fender-bender, the man whose front bumper was ahead of the other got off scot-free, while the other man had to pay.

Newcomers who complained about the taxies were told to tap the kamikazi on the shoulder and say, firmly and distinctly, "Hiyaku!" They would do this only once, after the driver would look around, shrug, and stick his foot further down into the carburetor. Hiyaku means "hurry up!".

The Ginza also had several great department stores, and Takashimaya was my favorite. I could spend hours wandering from one floor to another, marvelling at the simplicity of their kitchen and bathroom gadgets, the serenity reflected in their home furnishings, and the ornate elegance of things like ceremonial kimonos.

The stores were always jam-packed with people and getting from one floor to another could be an adventure. I quickly learned not be in the front rank when waiting for an elevator.

The door would open and the people in the elevator would burst out while the impatient bunch behind me would surge forward and there would be a collision. At first I made the mistake of trying to be protective of some of the smaller mama-sans caught next to me in the crush, but I was to find I unnecessarily exposed myself to attack, while they could easily take care of themselves.

If an American came to occupied Japan feeling like a conquering hero, ten seconds in a Tokyo department store elevator would be enough to adjust his attitude.

The famous Ginza was also home to bars and dance halls with gangs of young Japanese hostesses, and if you wanted one of them to dance with you and sit at your table, it cost takusan yen, which, translated, means "a lot of money." Some of them were farm girls and some were pretty well educated city girls, and most of them spoke G.I. English.

There were street girls too, not only around the Ginza, but around the main gate area of the U.S. bases. The drive back to Tokyo from Yokota passed right by the main gate at Tachikawa Air Base along a stretch of road that got to be called "The Miracle Mile."

The girls were all lined up, and as a car drove by, they would launch into their sales pitches, some of them waving or going into a pose or yelling, "Help!" to get your attention. A more memorable pitch was that of a young lady about four and a half feet tall who, as you passed, flipped open her blouse front and yelled, "I make you paralyze!"

Tokyo in 1952 was a place where a U.S. serviceman could apparently drive down the main roads in town at ninety miles per hour and not be likely to get a ticket. I don't think it ever happened; in fact the driving habits of Americans were so conservative compared to the Japanese that there never was a problem. But if one arose, the Japanese police, most of whom were mounted on bicycles, were apparently not authorized to do anything about it.

We had heard that before the war, the Japanese method for enforcing traffic rules was handled directly; If a driver ignored a stop light, for example, and was caught, the policeman ordered the driver to stick his head out of the driver's window and then bopped him-not too hard- on top of the head

344

with his club.

What a great idea, I thought. It saved everybody lots of time, the period between the infraction and the punishment was short and the driver got the point. It seemed so logical, why not try it in the U.S.? Well, we have taken much from the Japanese culture and incorporated it into our own but this idea, of course, would pose some difficulties.

First, we must get the lawyers involved. From that point on, the simple bop on the head turns into a great turmoil, with pro-boppers fighting anti-boppers all the way to the Supreme Court. And if the pro-boppers win, the concept of the "bop" would receive intense scrutiny, and guidelines would be developed which would vary slightly from state to state. The amount of force to be used would need to be carefully regulated so all traffic police people would need to go to bop school for special training. The force could not be so great as to impair the driver's ability to proceed, otherwise great traffic jams could ensue. And for speeders, thirty miles per hour over the limit would need greater punishment than a lesser amount, but this could be handled by imposing, say, one bop per each ten miles over the limit. Well, it is something to think about. But not for long.

Japan was not altogether a military motorists heaven. There were U.S. military policemen who patrolled military areas and handed out tickets, as we found out occasionally. One time, I was driving through the U.S. Army docks and warehouses near Yokohama after I arrived in Japan to check on a shipment of mine when I found myself behind what appeared to be a fire engine on call. I wasn't too sure at first, since the engine was only a jeep with a tank mounted on the rear, but it did have a flashing red light beacon mounted on top. The tank was apparently an overload for the jeep so it couldn't go very fast.

The engine was being preceded by a Military Police cruiser and we all made our way along this wide road at twenty miles per hour. After a while, we passed a sign which stated that the speed limit was thirty-five MPH, so I made the error of following logic by pulling into the passing lane and getting up to speed. The reaction from the M.P. was immediate. He swept up behind me and pulled me over since giving an officer a ticket was more fun than a fire any day. Tickets, I had heard, were a very large pain and when the M.P. came over I looked at him questioningly.

"I wasn't speeding," I said. "What did I do?

The M.P. thought for a moment, then said," Just a minute, sir," and he went back to converse with his partner. As I sat there, it suddenly struck me, that big bother or not, wouldn't it be something to get a ticket for passing a fire engine? I would have it pressed and framed to hang in a conspicuous place in my room at the BOQ.

The corporal -that was his rank- came back and I was disappointed to see he had a slightly apologetic look on his face.

"I guess you're okay to go, sir. You weren't speeding and you didn't get in the way of the fire engine. Please drive carefully, sir," and he saluted and turned to leave.

I had the strongest urge to call him back and ask him, as a favor, couldn't he, just this once, see his way clear to give me a ticket anyway? It would certainly help me, as a driver, make sure that I would not create such a problem again. But the urge passed. I started up again and left as a chance for a little bit of certified notoriety slipped from my grasp.

My trips out to Yokota to relax and escape the Tokyo smog were to be few and far between. I had never had a staff job in a higher headquarters before and I was surprised at how hard we all had to work. You were expected to be at your desk and shuffling papers at 7:30 AM and on a lot of days you had difficulty getting away at 5:00. I was also a little dismayed at how the in-box kept getting filled up, as inexorably as the tides, and how difficult it was to get the stuff into the out-box and not see it again. It was also a little unnerving at first to be required to draft correspondence which would eventually be signed by the Wing Commander and sent to other headquarters or to Washington.

We did a lot of work on reviewing new standard operating procedures to be used by the weather recon squadrons at Yokota and Guam. To make sure I was kept busy, I was also put to work on staff studies of one kind or another, and these required a lot of research and ate up a lot of time. Rounding up people with business in Korea, lining up the crewmembers and getting the C-47 scheduled also kept me occupied.

346

I had been there a few weeks before I made my first trip to Korea, in the Colonel's Gooney Bird. The war had pretty well stalemated along the original border line, so we had all of South Korea back again. The first stop was at K-l6, an airport just outside Seoul where we dropped off some people and picked up others to bring back to Tokyo.

We made other stops around the country, waiting around as the staff people we brought along did their business. We usually managed to find somebody with a jeep to drive us around to look the place over. It was a rough, hard-edged country, almost all mountainous and with a climate that was not easy to take. As we continued our trips through the winter, I came to feel that Korea had a special, penetrating cold and you couldn't put on enough clothes to keep warm. No wonder Koreans are such tough people.

The shooting war was still on and the enemy wasn't all that far away, but we never did worry about enemy aircraft as we made our rounds. The situation was different than at the start of the war, when even General MacArthur's airplane, The Bataan, was attacked by a Communist fighter on his first trip to inspect the Korean battleground. Fortunately, his flight was escorted by our own fighters, who drove off the attacker as the General watched with great curiosity.

We flew along the same route that MacArthur and everybody else did and the idea of possible enemy interception appeared so remote we never gave it a thought. The USAF F-86 Sabre Jets had cleared the skies of the Russian-built MIGs piloted by North Koreans, Red Chinese or the Russians themselves.

Many of our fighter jocks were retreads, -World War II types- who had been recalled to active duty. They had quickly gotten back their skill and aggressiveness and overwhelmed the opposition. They won the air war even though the enemy operated out of bases just across the Yalu River which could not be bombed, for political reasons.

Seoul was a city that had recently changed hands a few times and had been pretty well banged up, but not to the extent that some of the European cities were. The streets were cleared and the power, phone and water systems all seemed to be working okay. There were occasional piles of rubble where a building had been knocked own, and some of the larger buildings that remained standing were merely shells, but the place looked livable. It was difficult for me to tell whether life in the city was back to normal since I didn't know what normal was.

There was almost no motor traffic except for some trucks and G.I. vehicles, but there were many motor scooters and lots of bicycles. It was a busy city , with crowds of pedestrians in a hurry to get some where, except for the goateed papa-sans who shuffled along, hands clasped behind their backs, peering around them at the same old turmoil caused by a new bunch of people.

K-16 was a busy place, with C-54's, C-47's and the elephantine C-124's moving through all the time. They brought their cargoes in from Tachikawa and other places and took out troops just pulled off the line for their rest and recuperation in Japan. Of course, they didn't rest much and had to come back to Korea to recuperate, but it was the R&R's and thoughts of climbing into one of those 54's, or Gooney Birds or Big Shakeys -also called "eighteen thousand rivets in loose formation-" to start the trip home that kept them going.

Before the winter was over, a big, theater-wide shakeup came along intended to beef up the Korean effort. Our C-47 was drafted out from underneath us and the various headquarters, including ours, was told to slim down and put some people into combat or combat support slots. I suddenly found myself without the need to drive out to Yokota on the odd weekend anymore, because I was transferred there. It was completely without regret that I packed up and moved my gear into the BOQ at Yokota, back again with crewdogs I had been flying with since forever.

I had learned a lot, and the people at the Meiji building were great to work with, but I had had enough. Some day, I thought, I would like to try it again when I was ready for that kind of life.

The 56th Strategic Recon Squadron at Yokota must have been waiting for me, for I hardly dropped my bags before I was flying a mission designated as Buzzard Kilo. The track was flown every day to provide accurate weather forecasts to all of the military services. We flew west out into the Sea of Japan, then made a complete loop around the Korean peninsula, first turning southwest down the Korea Strait, then west again across the Island of Cheju-do. As we entered the Yellow Sea we turned due north and when we reached the vicinity of the 38th parallel with the Shantung Peninsula of mainland China clearly in our radar scope, we headed due east directly across the bomb line and continued on to Yokota. As we flew along the bomb line, we could look northward at the rough, mountainous terrain held by an enemy whose armies had been savagely mauled after we had brought in our massive firepower. He would be mauled again by the thousands before the Korean truce would be finally signed.

The battle lines had been stabilized around the original border between North and South Korea, not because we didn't have the means to move to the Red Chinese border. We halted because we had almost been to the Yalu once before and had the Chinese Communist "volunteer" army come in, and now we feared that another attempt might bring the Soviets in. But for now, as we flew along the bomb line, we could see little evidence of conflict except for an occasional flash of artillery which lit up a hillside.

The navigation on the Kilo track was easy since we had shoreline checkpoints, including the Chinese mainland, in the radar scope most of the time. But the other primary track, called Buzzard Delta which extended deep into the northwest Pacific, through the area where the evidence of the first Soviet atomic explosion was detected, could be a tough one even for an experienced navigator.

The Loran coverage was poor because of the large gap in the chain of stations along the Soviet-held Kurile Islands. Big, powerful weather systems would bulldoze their way into the Pacific from the Asian land mass and we would bump along, hour after hour, in a swirl of ice particles which, as usual, blanked out high frequency communications and whatever Loran might be available.

The same high flight level winds of a hundred or a hundred-fifty knots which had made precision bombing so difficult for the Twentieth Air Force B-29's during the war were blowing as hard as ever. Weather analyzers who got our information still distrusted some of our reports, perhaps because they knew of the difficulties a navigator might have in computing the flight level winds. So they cut the wind velocities in half before they plugged them into their equations. If there had been a more reliable means to navigate with in the area, dating back to the B-29 bombing days of 1945, the development and use of jet stream theories would no doubt have happened sooner than they did.

One day, not long after I arrived at Yokota, I found myself sitting in my quarters -such as they were- my feet up on a foot locker, leisurely reading a book. It was ten o'clock on a wintry weekday morning and the barracks was quiet. The Japanese cleanup ladies chattered and giggled down one end of the long hall, while music from a radio tuned to the Armed Forces Network drifted through the walls from the next room. The stateside music and comedy programs were intended to make us homesick, and, I presume, to keep us from going native.

I thought about my present situation, picturing in my mind's eye the troops back in the Meiji Building taking a new piece of correspondence out of the IN box and trying to decide whether to work on it or put it into the HOLD box. As for me, I had flown a grinding thirteen-hour mission the day before and I was still a little punchy. I knew it would take a while for the fatigue to drain out of my muscles and gizzard and brain, and from around the eyes, from my very bones. And there was always dehydration, which seemed to wrinkle up a man's face and make him look years older until his system got back to normal.

It seemed worth it, to endure what crewdogs endure to have the time off, to sit around on a weekday morning reading a book. Later on when the weather warmed, we could sit around the club swimming pool between flights or between training classes and drills of some kind.

There was golf too on courses which were being built next to most of the bases, on land taken from well paid but unhappy farmers. Except for the farmers, the Japanese did not object since they knew they would get them when we were gone. They built great courses and landscaped them as only the Japanese can and now, today, they are prized possessions with memberships almost impossible to obtain.

Being a crewdog again also meant that I could look around the countryside in a leisurely way. I couldn't speak the language except for what I was able to learn from my Japanese phrase book and the Armed Forces Network radio lessons, so I was limited in what I could learn about the Japanese I came into contact with. However, if they could speak some G.I. English, and I remembered enough of my G.I. Japanese, we communicated pretty well.

I liked to drive to some nearby town, then park the car and walk along the street just bumping shoulders with the crowd. The Japanese seemed to ignore your presence and seldom made eye contact, but if you made the slightest move that showed you could use some help , they gave you their attention immediately and did what they could. I never once had a Japanese become curt or impatient with me, although there were times when I gave them excuses to do so.

I got to know the best places to get a hot, steaming plate of go-han -mixed fried rice- where they would leave out the little, rubbery chunks of octopus without me telling them. And once in a while, someone would get a bright idea and we would go find a hachi-bath house, a place with a blue flame painted on a shingle out front.

There was always a small feeling of being trapped as they closed the steam-bath closet lid around your neck. Next, there was a lot of nodding to the old mama-san attendant as she turned up the heat, little by little until it got high enough, or maybe a little too high. Then, mama-san would let you out and lead you to the cold-water plunge which brought your mind right back into focus, away from yesterday's or tomorrow's long missions and back into the real world.

Feeling like a million yen, we might put on kimonos and sit around a table sunk into the floor, a grate-covered charcoal hibachi underneath. The brazier warmed up our toes as we played cards to see who would pay for the big liter bottles of Kirin beer.

Tokyo got to be a great place to go sightseeing now that I had the time to do it. There were G.I. tours to places like the Diet Building and the Asakasa Palace, where I happened to be walking into the main entrance hall just as Eleanor Roosevelt, still the inveterate world-traveler, came walking the other way. She strode along forthrightly, a guide about half her height trotting be hind trying to keep up.

The Tokyo night life was still there, with the big bands and the entertainment; the acrobats and sword swallowers and magic acts, but I didn't have to go that far anymore. The same acts were put on in our own clubs at Yokota and Tachikawa and besides, the Grand Tachi Ballroom was not too far away near the Tachikawa Air Base. This was a barn of a place with all kinds of dance hostesses and a really large "big band" of Filipino musicians. It was situated just under the approach to one of the main runways and once in a while a Big Shakey would get a little low overhead, maybe on purpose, and the vibration would rattle the ice cubes in your glass.

But there was getting to be a sameness to all of this. Fly, rest up, carouse a little, get some exercise, get some training, fly some more. Then something happened on July 29, 1953, that would force me out of my rut: the Korean war ended. After nineteen months of wrangling, with temporary truces alternating with renewed war, a permanent truce was signed at Panmunjom, on the border between North and South Korea.

It was said at the time that nothing had happened except that almost 37,000 United Nations troops, mostly American, were killed while the North Koreans and the Red Chinese lost more than a million men. And when the final truce was signed and the fighting stopped, the border between North and South Korea was approximately as before.

Looking at the aftermath now, after all these years, it can be said that the North Korean attempt to take over the entire country was stopped and her armies destroyed. The South Koreans were permitted to develop their country in peace and build one of the miracle economies of the Far East. The Red Chinese, along with the threat of Soviet intervention, had prevented the U.N. from uniting the entire country and holding free elections.

When the fighting ceased, the Chinese still had well over a million men in North Korea, but knowing the meat-grinder that would await them if they moved south again, they agreed to the final truce. The Communists had apparently been given some behind-the-scenes encouragement in deciding to sign the truce. As the masses of troops on both sides waited in their entrenched positions, a message was passed to Chou En Lai, the Red Chinese leader, through Prime Minister Nehru of India. The note was from John Foster Dulles, the U.S. Secretary of State on behalf of the newly elected President Eisenhower. It said that if the truce was not signed quickly, the U.S. would begin bombing targets north of the Yalu River, in China itself, perhaps with nukes. One wonders what the course of history would have been if the truce had not been signed.

My own particular course of history was changed by the truce; in a few weeks I was back behind a desk at the Weather Wing headquarters in Tokyo. Same desk, same IN box, some new people. Well, I thought, remembering the clearer, smog-free air I had been permitted to breath for a few months; win some, lose some.

V

BOOK FIVE

15

I, JOHN,
TAKE THEE PRISCILLA...

"**I**, JOHN, TAKE THEE, PRISCILLA for my lawful wedded wife.." I heard myself saying these fateful words in a surprisingly strong voice as I stood next to my bride. As I paused, I felt her hand gently tug mine. "Please look at me," she whispered as I continued to follow the Reverend's prompting. Now it was her turn and the world stopped for me as I watched her, trying to look past the veil into those big brown eyes.

Her voice trembled slightly as she said those words which sealed the promises we made to each other. Then the Reverend started to pray for us and as we knelt and he laid his hands on top of our heads, I sensed some great, gentle force that shone down from somewhere, through the arched ceiling, through the walls, lighting us all up for a moment. It then became a subdued glow that lingered, and lingers in me still.

There was that great swirl of energy as we came back down the aisle and stepped out into the vibrant California evening, swimming in relief and feeling suddenly different. The church bells rang as we stood in the archway atop the wide stairs, everybody shaking hands and slapping backs, kissing the bride, shouting and waving. We still had the picture-taking session to go through, but the deed was done, and done well, I thought.

We stepped back into the church as Chuck Massey, my best man, pried us loose from the well-wishers to get us a breather. I could still feel the excitement running through both of us as we looked back down the aisle into this beautiful church. It was not only a place to worship, but also a monument to the beliefs of those who built it in the classic California mission style. It would last as long as faith existed in the minds of those who walked through its impressive entrance and sat in its polished oaken pews.

The journey from Tokyo to this church, the Piedmont Community Congregational Church near Oakland, California had taken almost a year and a half. When the Korean War ended in July of 1954 and I found myself transferred back to the Meiji Building in Tokyo, I had two more years of headquarters staff duty confronting me.

The desk work was pretty well broken up by lots of trips around the Pacific in the Wing's B-17 and in a four-engined C-54 which was later assigned to us. But the urge to make some change grew stronger in me as the months passed. There was no chance of writing up a request to have my overseas tour terminated and expect to have it approved since the length of an overseas tour was fixed. But I looked at the regulations concerning transfers and found a paragraph that appeared to have been written just for my benefit. It stated that a person who had been stationed at a place in the Far East theater for two years could request an assignment "elsewhere in the theater."

It so happened that Hickam Air Force Base in Honolulu was situated within the Far East theater. Not only that, but the Air Weather Service, of which the Wing was a part, and the air transport squadrons at Hickam were all under the Military Air Transport Command. This meant that the paper trail of my request would be fairly short, with less people handling it who could say no.

It worked. I had prepared the ground with my immediate superiors, who claimed they would hate to see me go, and then the Wing Commander called me in.

He was fairly new, a non-flyer who didn't know me from a stump, and when I told him I had been in the Air Weather Service since 1946 and wanted to do something new, he shrugged and said okay.

Hickam was not a new place for me as I had been through there many times before my arrival in the autumn -which they don't have in Hawaii- of 1954. But now it would be my home base and the flight operations in which I would be involved would be those of a military air transport squadron, very similar to those of a scheduled airline. There was no such thing as flying around in your underwear, even on hot days: on passenger trips you climbed on board in the uniform of the day.

I joined the 47th Air Transport Squadron, which operated Boeing C-97 Stratocruisers, a large, double-decked airplane. They were not "airline plush," but they did have airline seats which faced backwards because someone thought they were safer that way in the event of a crash or ditching. This was unusual since aircraft designers and airline operators appear to believe that such disasters would never happen to their aircraft.

The main line was between Tokyo and Travis Air Force Base in California via Honolulu, but we went everywhere in the Pacific a C-97 could land; Guam, Kwajalein, Midway, Johnston Island and Wake Island. The crews were "staged;" they landed at a destination and turned the airplane over to a waiting crew and retired for a crew rest, then took the next airplane out. Thus, the airplane and passengers or cargo were not delayed because the crew that brought it in had run out of flying time. No more sixteen-hour backbusters; the quota of flying time per day for aircrews was controlled.

Because I had been piling up the flying time, it wasn't long before I was appointed as a Flight Examiner, a man who was assigned to flights to see if the regular crew navigator was fully proficient. I got checked the same way myself, every six months and I always sweated it out. Later on, I found myself in the Chief Navigator's seat again but as before, I flew on the regular schedule.

A few months after I had arrived at Hickam, winter arrived in the North Pacific and the jet stream, which had begun to receive careful study by this time, began to coil itself along the Tokyo-Honolulu track at our flight levels -just below 20,000 feet. Some positive-minded operational thinker at Wing headquarters began to ask; why not use the jet stream's great tail winds to enable flights to bypass the Midway Island refueling stop? The trip from Tokyo to Honolulu was just beyond the non-stop range of the Stratocruisers and the Lockheed Super

Constellations, even with halfway decent tailwinds. But if Midway could be bypassed, all kinds of good things could happen, like savings of time on the airplane and crew, less fuel, less wear and tear of an extra landing, and so on.

The navigators were sent to special classes for a week to learn more about the jet stream, which was usually situated along a line where two different air masses collided. In the operating area involved, winds at flight level of 150 knots, blowing from west to east could be found if you knew where to look.

There were some visual indications involving cloud buildups and alignments which might show that a jet stream was present, but the best and most useful indicator was the way the temperature changed along the path of the jet stream itself. It had been found that in our hemisphere, temperatures directly north of the jet stream dropped very slowly as you drifted northward . But when you crossed the stream and drifted southward, the rise in temperatures was dramatic:- there was no mistaking it.

With this information in hand, the flight could proceed along a track where the jet stream was thought to be. If the navigator thought he was north of the stream, based on the temperatures he was observing and the appearance of the sky, he would ask the pilot to make a moderate turn southward and watch his temperature gauge. As they approached the line of buildups and middle cloud, the temperature would suddenly begin to rise, and moderate turbulence would start. When all of these things came out right, the ground speed would pick up and although no one on board could feel any acceleration, the navigator who was plotting his positions would get to feel he had hooked up with a speeding freight train.

The big problem with all of this was that the track along the jet stream did have clouds and icing associated with it, along with turbulence. There was a lot of uncertainty involved too, as the wind speeds were not always sufficient, or aligned along the track for a sufficient period of time. There were also times when the diversion from the Great Circle route between departure and destination -the shortest route- was so great that no benefit was obtained.

For as long as the project lasted, I thoroughly enjoyed the

idea of chasing this monstrous force and putting it to work for us. We would look for the ZOMCOT -the Zone of Maximum Concentration of Temperatures- the area along the jet stream where the temperatures changed quickly. The job of finding it and getting the jet stream on the airplane's tail was pretty much in the hands of the navigator, and of course, I liked that.

We tried other techniques too, like the "bottoming out" procedure, where we loaded all the fuel we could, and climbing above the altitude normally flown at full gross weight, knowing that we could not hold the altitude using normal power settings with all the extra weight we had. The airplane would be permitted to settle slowly and as the fuel was burned off, we would finally reach a point where we got light enough to level off. But you could do things like this, and chasing the jet stream, only if you had plenty of airspace and a comparatively small amount of traffic.

We also tried jacking up the nosewheel a little while loading fuel before the trip to get all the nooks and crannies of the tanks filled up. Some crews even packed dry ice around the fuel cells to get the cooled gas to shrink so that more could fit into the tanks.

But it didn't last, as the problems outweighed any advantages we gained, and we went back to flying tracks planned beforehand on the ground, without the dry ice or jacking up the nosewheel. We had certainly given it a good try.

There wasn't much sense in being stationed in Honolulu and living on the base in the BOQ. So when my buddy Marty Scheinkman, who had taken my job in Tokyo and had followed the same escape route arrived at Hickam, we found a house in Waikiki and rented it. All of this was new; living in a house off the base among civilians, commuting to work, -would you believe traffic jams in Honolulu in 1955?- flying according to a schedule that didn't change much.

"So this is how normal people live!" I said to Marty on the way to work one morning, although being a crewdog in Honolulu wasn't exactly a normal situation.

Marty and I were not too much help to each other in converting ourselves into upright, well-behaved citizens. Since we were not tied down it was pretty easy after work or after a flight to shower up and head for the Moana Hotel and see what was happening under the big banyan tree.

One such evening when I was on my own I stopped in for a drink at the Captain Cook Room, a big lounge in the beachfront Surfrider Hotel adjoining the Moana, which was frequented by both tourists and locals. This particular evening the lounge was taken over by a private party, according to a sign on the entrance door, but things looked so lively that I walked in anyway.

The crowd appeared to be a bunch of professional people, and they were celebrating the departure of the Noel Coward-style lounge entertainer, who had been a favorite of theirs.

The bar was crowded but I finally managed a seat which, by the purest of chance, was next to a young lady in her early twenties who was obviously not accustomed to the power of the Mai Tai she was trying to sip. She was talking a mile a minute with someone next to her, animated and having fun and then she noticed this new person, -me- sitting on her other side and I became included in the conversation.

Big gold-brown eyes and swept-back, almost blonde hair and that great California chic, ready to surf or ski or ride horses. She was different; a little naive, certainly vulnerable. She obviously came from a place where caution involving strangers had not been drilled into her because it wouldn't be too necessary; she would stay with her own crowd.

As the evening raced on, I came to realize that a little light bulb had gone on in back of my mind when I looked at her but I had no idea what it meant at the time. She called herself Cris, but her mother, back in the slightly haughty part of Oakland, California called Piedmont, called her Priscilla Ann Park. She had made the trip to Honolulu aboard the cruise ship Lurline, in celebration of her graduation from Cal at Berkeley. She took one look at the islands; the made-for-play sunshine, the fragrant breezes, the laid-back beach life, and she decided to find a job and an apartment and stay a while.

The party started to break up and Cris announced she was hungry, so a half-dozen of us made our way through the lobby and into the street. We walked about half way down the block, toward Diamond Head and found a place that apparently stayed open all night and had tables outside in the rear overlooking the beach, and had some early breakfast. Cris had to work the next morning; she ran the telegraph booth in the lobby of the Royal Hawaiian Hotel, somewhat the same type of job I had at the Saranac Inn in the Adirondacks when I was seventeen.

After a while, it was time to go, and a few of us walked down to where my car was parked and I dropped people off around Waikiki, saving Cris for last. When we reached her place all of the usual impulses, clever dodges and fearless flyer poses passed through one side of my mind and I pushed them out the other. Her place was a low rise on the Ala Wai canal, across from the golf course and I came around to let her out.

We walked up a few flights of stairs and when we came to her door, she held out both hands. I took them and looked at her as she smiled and thanked me. Then, in a very trusting way, she held out her cheek and I kissed it and she went in and closed the door.

I didn't know, at the time, whether that moment was the beginning or the end of our time together. It turned out that it was not the end. We had dinner the next evening and just about every evening thereafter, unless I was on a trip. We also toured the islands, and I became part of her little group of friends who had a gathering place on a patch of beach in front of the Outrigger Club. Cris and her friends reminded me of the young characters in an Andy Hardy movie. They were good-looking and good-hearted young people who were primarily interested in getting into the mainstream of life by getting married and starting up a family. Cris could have played the Judy Garland parts with the same intense sincerity, the same naive sexiness.

What a place, I thought. The whole island smelled of flowers, music everywhere, a perfect breeze moving gently across the surf, making the palm trees rustle. And now there was Cris. I began to think: why can't this last forever?

But there are dilemmas even in paradise and the one I had to wrestle with started to loom very large, and the more I thought about Cris, the larger it got. My dilemma involved the same old set of excess baggage I had carried around in my mind for a long time now and I began to realize I would have to do something about it. The fits of anxiety, or whatever they were had become easier to endure, little by little. No more smoking must have helped, and I had come to realize that caffeine can have funny effects on some people, and I was one of them. I had even pretty much pushed booze off to where it was just something to celebrate with. And I surfed and swam whenever I had time off and I was getting to feel, most of the time, like the vitamin pill of yesteryear.

But they still came to me, whatever they were, sometimes more insistent than ever. They would wait for me in the shadows of the blue hour, the time when the first dim light touches the consciousness and slowly, imperceptibly, begins to bring the outlines of the room into view.

It is the time when a lover, unburdened by some haunting fear, might reach out to find some yielding, exquisite curve. I too would reach out, but then my consciousness would slowly awaken and move, past the fogged reluctance of sleep, past the hazy memories of the day before, reluctantly making me realize who I was and where I awoke. For a short moment I would be my familiar old self, idly thinking about what the day had in store. Then I would begin to stir, but before I could arise, I would suddenly feel the smothering shade of panic's wings trapping me, threatening me. I knew there was no place I could hide where this deadly shadow did not fall; it would move where I moved. It was death or me, death or me said my pounding heart and the fear and confusion would arise and all I could do was open my eyes and look around me and reach out to reality, to grasp it to me to gain some foothold so I could confront the phantoms and let them know they would soon disappear and not me. And then the dawn would come and slowly, little by little, my soul and I would be put back together and I would get up to try to act as if nothing happened.

As I shaved and brushed my teeth with trembling hands I would look into the mirror, into my own eyes, to see if there were some changes, something new, good or bad, but how could I know what to look for? And then I would turn to get dressed, trying to think about what I had to do that day, knowing the phantoms were still pressing down, waiting for some inevitable signal I would unwittingly give them.

It was during one such dreadful, waking moment that something reached through the agony and held those surging painful anxieties still and made me know I was at a crossroads; I could continue on and try to hold off those shades at arm's length, and use up my mind little by little until it was consumed. Or I could sidestep them and attack the source of their power directly, to examine the depths of my being where all those terrible, un-graspable memories had embedded themselves.

I had begun to read about anxiety; first tentatively, then everything I could get my hands on. I would feel a curious mental relief whenever I would read about someone whose experiences paralleled mine. Some of the stuff I read was useless or even ridiculous, but I read it all. Then I started to read about relaxation, things like bio-feedback and simple breathing exercises, and I knew I was getting on the right track. And so, one day, the battle was joined.

This time there was just me, and I was both defender of the grail and mortal enemy. The battleground was a house not far from the beach at Waikiki where, on a quiet Sunday afternoon, I lay back on the couch and put my feet up on the arm. I concentrated on the silky, whispering sound of the breezes flowing through the coconut palms surrounding the house. I relaxed my fingers and toes and arms and legs and the knot in the pit of my stomach; I tried to loosen the muscles in my throat and those that focused my hearing. But then I closed my eyes and the flood came, and all that black shower of terror and shame and confusion burst inside me like some exploding sewer pipe and something in me fought against it but I let it come and I thought I would drown. Slowly, it began to subside and little by little, to drain away. I lay there for a while, waiting for the flood to come over me again, but it didn't happen. I began to realize that a feeling of profound relief had settled over me and I felt it in every pore and follicle and muscle and tendon. I opened my eyes and looked up at the ceiling, then turned my head so I could look across the living room, through the windows and into the quiet street. The palms still whispered in the breeze, but their whispers came to me directly now, no longer flattened and deflected by constricted and overwrought senses. There was a sweet fragrance of plumeria blossoms from the tree on the neighbor's lawn, and that great Hawaiian sunshine filtered down, inviting and reassuring. All of these things; the sounds, the fragrance, the sunlight came to me differently, for now I seemed to be in a different, less threatening world.

It was to take years after that moment before I could truthfully tell myself that my phantoms no longer pursued me, that I summoned them to me instead. I was to go through this tortuous routine many times afterward in many different places; in the crew bunk on air planes, lying on the beach, stretched out on the couch with my feet up on the arm, wherever I had a quiet moment. It got so I would relax and when no threatening, shapeless form would some swimming along in my stream of thought I would go searching for them, squeezing through narrow, scary tunnels or slipping beneath the surface of dank pools and then -there!- I would be smothered by the old anxieties.

But the shades became paler and paler, and now I could feel the security of my surroundings as I grasped the dark form and let it take its real shape in my mind; the dozens of deaths I had died, the terrible wounds that had torn my body, the tearing blasts and consuming fires, the long, long fall and smashing into the earth, the sinking down into the terrifying deep. And there was the guilt for the things I did, or didn't do, or thought I did, or might do some time.

At one time I thought that I would try to leave no mental or emotional stone unturned, and even began to pursue the undersized goblins of adolescence. But little by little I tired of the game, for that is what it had become, and I was no longer rewarded by the relieving insight that told me I had liberated another small part of my mind. The mind being what it is, I am sure there are many more phantoms lurking just beyond the blue hour, waiting in the shadows to jump up and confront me. But a profound change had occurred in me: before, my mind had kept turning involuntarily inward as part of some self-protective impulse, and it was then that the massive worries descended. After, I could, in a quiet moment and as a conscious effort, look inward and, more and more, find assurance.

Cris and I soon became inseparable, and when we weren't on the beach, I would pick her up in my great little Studebaker Silver Hawk coupe and we would do the things tourists do, like take the drive around Oahu, or go through the orchid greenhouses, or watch the local kids dive off the dock for coins when the cruise ships came in. Cris was not too knowledgeable about the military, especially the Air Force, so I took her to all of the functions at the Hickam Officers Club so she could meet the people and learn to speak the jargon. At one of her first parties -I think it was a welcoming party for someone- the conversation had gotten pretty loud as the airplane drivers bragged about their flying exploits. I had usually referred to the airplanes we flew as Boeings or Stratocruisers, but someone nearby mentioned its military designation, the C-97, which Cris hadn't heard before. With her voice pitched up to be heard over the crowd noise, she asked; "What's a C-97?"

Unfortunately, just as she started her question, the crowd noise died as someone on the stage took the microphone to speak, and the fateful query shattered the sudden silence and hung there, naked and shameless. All of those surprised and accusing eyes turned our way as Cris started to turn pink and we stood there, both looking at the floor, waiting for the damn fool on the stage to say something. We had been talking with the squadron commander at the time, a really great guy, and he put his hand on Cris' arm and said, "Cris, when John explains to you what a C-97 is, I'm sure you'll never forget it." And so she hasn't.

I reached the point where I knew I didn't want to lose her to someone else. Not only that: I began to take some tentative, sneaky sidewise glances at the idea of marriage, which I had always looked at as a heavy bundle of responsibilities which had to be carried down a road built for other people, a road with overly predictable stops along the way. And in one of those sneaky glances, I saw that I would suddenly need to confront my own mortality, something I hadn't bothered to do in a long time. But I began to get a glimmer of what marriage really could mean. The two of you create a world of your own, shaped by both of you and your pasts, and if it is done right and you are lucky, the little world takes its place in the human universe forever. And do you have something in you that you want to last forever? If you do, then the self-sacrifices begin, and the doubts disappear and the unshakable certainty overcomes you.

Did I actually think like that, back then, in the heady days of the autumn of 1955? Not that clearly, I must admit, because the differences in our backgrounds were somewhat daunting. Her mother, Frances Hatch Park, was well known in Oakland where she founded, on her own, a school for teaching well-to-do kids the white-gloved social niceties. Her classes culminated in a cotillion, where the boys bowed and the girls curtsied, all of which was probably a sheer delight for the girls and torture for the boys.

Cris had some pictures of her mother around her place, sepia-toned photos taken in the twenties which showed a beautiful young dancer in classic modern dance poses. Her mother's forebears, generations back, had come from England and settled in Massachusetts well before the Boston Tea Party, when it was still a colony. There is some evidence that their journey took place in the century previous to that, and as they passed through Evesham in the west of England, they were reported to have rented the jail rather than stay at the local Inn where alcoholic beverages were served.

The first actual documentation of her direct ancestor's presence in America involves Abial Hatch, who was born in Massachusetts in 1755 and served as an officer in George Washington's army. Almost a hundred years later, some of Abial's progeny, who had intermarried with other old American families, got stung by the gold bug and the desire to build new lives and headed west. When I read the stories of this truly heroic covered wagon journey in letters written by an ancestor named Lucy Rutledge Cooke, the true meaning of their courage and their hardships came home to me. Months of trekking or riding in jolting wagons which sometimes broke down or turned over, dangerous river crossings by raft, abandoning wagons mired down in desert sand, poor food, voracious bugs and the ever-present, virulent Asiatic cholera; all were encountered and overcome by those who survived, overcoming one problem at a time.

The graves of the unfortunates were strung out along the wagon tracks, sometimes marked by buffalo skulls when wood for a cross was not at hand. Ten graves per mile, it was said, were scattered along the 2000-mile route, each one a family disaster as fathers, mothers or children were struck down. There was little hope of medical aid for the diseases and accidents which pursued them as they bumped along the wagon trails. There were pathetic scenes as convoys of a dozen or so returning wagons would pass by, their journey thwarted, the wagons driven by women whose husbands had had their dreams, hopes and lives terminated by one of the numerous hazards which came with the territory.

Strange to say, hostile Indians were not one of the main hazards, at least during the early 1850's, although enough incidents occurred so that full precautions were taken. Most of the men and some of the women kept guns handy along certain parts of the trail, and occasionally took some target practice to bolster their courage. They were ready to circle the wagons when some threat arose, and the cry of "Corral!" was raised.

Indians were there, of course, ready to help the travelers, usually for a price, ready to take some handouts when the buffalo or antelope hunting had come up short, ready to run off with some of the white man's livestock when he wasn't looking. Not all of the Indians fit this mold, for there were the Sioux, the warriors, who terrorized the Pawnee, according to reports of the time. Lucy Rutledge describes a visit to their camp of some magnificently dressed Sioux who comported themselves like a welcoming delegation, letting it be known they needed no charity from the white man. The men were handsomely built, thought Lucy, and the women were "quite pretty."

But the unfortunate Pawnee, apparently trying to mind their own business in coping with life on the plains, had to put up with battles with their Sioux neighbors along the tribal territory boundaries. Some of the battles took place within sight of the wagon trains, including a furious conflict between fifteen or sixteen Sioux and about a hundred Pawnees. Like U.S. Marines, the Sioux figured the odds were on their side and scattered their less-warlike enemy, killing two of them. During the fight, some of the Pawnees rode up to the wagon master and demanded he intervene in their behalf, but he would not do so.

After the battle, some of the wagons were detoured slightly so that one of the dead Pawnees could be observed, his life departed along with his bloody scalp. Later, some Pawnees were seen leading a wounded and unhorsed Sioux back toward their camp, causing him to stumble and fall as they jerked on the rope looped around his neck. The price he would have to

369

pay back to the Pawnees for the lost scalps would not be light.

The Californians, as some of the emigrants called themselves, also had to endure threats from within. There was an occasional murder and robbery as one of the wagon people tried to make his fortune without working for it at journey's end. If the murderer became known, he was strung up to the next tree that was passed. Indians, white murderers, disease, storms, whatever; all took their toll. But there was no denying the lust for a new life, to temporarily push aside the enslaving comforts and certainties of the towns and cities of the east and midwest, to move beyond the limits into a new and heady freedom and, perhaps, to find some gold.

The tough and the fortunate made it, and built the west in their image. People like Cris' "Grandpa George" Hatch, who came as far as Virginia City, Nevada and started up a general store and a stage line from there to Placerville. George Hatch became a magistrate in the fancy courthouse at Virginia City, then was elected to the territorial legislature. After that, he finished his trip westward and built a business in Oakland where, toward the end of this life, he became the president of the Oakland Board of Education.

Cris' father, who had been a cotton broker, had passed on, but her mother and her brother Warren, who had taken over his father's business, were there to guard the psychological barrier I had built in my own mind and which I had to overcome. I had come to know what to expect on bomb runs, and in the eyes of hurricanes, but now I had a new set of unknowns to face. I made up my mind to take the giant step which all right-minded mankind should eventually take. But when should I propose? Sitting on the beach watching the sunset? Dancing at the Queen's Surf club?

I came very close one evening when I went to pick her up after work at the Royal Hawaiian. She came walking across the lobby like no one else ever would in my lifetime and I found myself shaking like a leaf. The tremors passed and when she reached me I took a plumeria lei I had been hiding behind my back and draped it over her shoulders, and gave her a little kiss. "What's this for?" she asked with a pleased laugh, as I shrugged. We walked down the beachside stairs into the Waikiki dusk and made our way along a torchlit path to the edge of the beach. Cris was animated even after working through the day and she gave me a rundown of her day's happenings as we reached the surfside bar. I watched her in the flickering torch light, but before I could get up some courage, it was time to go to dinner and the moment was lost. We got up and made our way through the hotel grounds and walked across the avenue toward Don the Beachcomber's.

She had the next day off and when I came to get her for lunch, I showed up with a bouquet of flowers, which she took from me with a little smile of amusement. After she fixed them in a vase, she came around and sat next to me, her hands folded in her lap, an expectant look on her face. I am probably the very last man on the entire North American continent to do so, but I actually got down on one knee to propose. I didn't want to ask the question in some offhand way, and win or lose, I wanted her to remember the moment. Cris didn't equivocate at all; she said yes.

Now, I thought, it is white glove inspection time, as Cris announced to me that her mother would fly in for a visit in about a week and would I be sure not to be out on a trip somewhere. She didn't seem at all worried and I tried to be relaxed about it. But I wanted to make a good impression without having the slightest idea what I might do to impress her mother.

Here she comes, I said to myself as Frances Hatch Park came down the flight stairs of the PanAm DC-7. Despite her long trip she looked fresh, even a little excited as we draped her with several heavy and fragrant carnation leis. We walked into the passenger reception area and waited for the baggage to arrive as Cris got all the news about the family and Piedmont neighbors. I stood next to Cris, content to be ignored for the moment, but feeling better by the minute. My concerns began to evaporate as they talked and even let me get a word in edgewise, but not enough to let me get cocky. As they talked, I recalled some advice from the distant past, when marriage was looked at with lots of practicality and not much romance; to see your wife as she will be in twenty-five years, look at your prospective mother-in-law. In Cris' case, she got an A plus.

Whatever doubts Fruffy, as her first brood of grandchildren called her, may have had, they were either resolved in her

371

mind or pushed aside. She must have seen that there were no doubts in my mind, so when we first started to talk about the marriage at dinner that night, the only questions that came up were: when, how and where.

Fruffy and I got to be great friends over the years. She appeared to admire me as a person and laughed at my jokes, and in all the years I knew her, not one cross word ever passed between us. She generally took my side when Cris and I had some differences; now how's that for a mother-in-law? And the more I learned about her, the greater my admiration became. She must have had some tough times being on her own, bringing up two children and trying to keep up expensive appearances in a social climate where appearances were almost life and death. Fruffy was utterly feminine and every inch a lady always, even when she had to let someone know how determined and courageous she could be. But most of all, I came to admire her -and her daughter- for proceeding with all of the arrangements for a beautiful wedding as if Cris was marrying the boy next door. I never got to know what discussions there must have been about a branch of the family that might be poised to plunge down into some social abyss. Were Abial Hatch's genes being squandered? They seemed to be willing to take the chance.

As for my own family, they were so far away it was difficult to give them the full picture. Religious differences didn't count for that much anymore, for after all, my sister Kay had married an Episcopalian and had not been struck down by God's Catholic Lightning. And the bride-to-be's name was Priscilla Park. A beautiful girl with a nice name like that, what could go wrong?

I wondered what some of Cris's relatives might think but I didn't get to meet any of them until just before the wedding. When I first set eyes on Fruffy's sister Genevieve -Aunt Genevieve Hatch Stetson- I thought that she might become the focus of whatever family resistance might arise. She lived alone in a large, beautifully kept Victorian house in Oakland near Lake Merritt. Her father had built the place before the turn of the century when the area was out in the country, and had designed it with big rooms and great views from the large windows.

Genevieve's mother took pride in the English garden she had planted in back of the house, out in the sun. But by the time the house had passed to Genevieve, high rise buildings began to surround it and turn the light into a partial gloom which filtered through some of the leaded-glass windows. When I later passed through Travis Air Force Base which was not far from Oakland, and I had some time, I would pay Fruffy and Genevieve a visit and they would have some tea while I would sip some scotch if I brought some along.

Genevieve was strongly anti-communist, and we once had a few words when she brought up the John Birch Society view that President Eisenhower was a closet communist. Arguing with Genevieve was a little difficult since you had to deal with an old-fashioned grande-dame in gold-rimmed glasses and carefully coiffed white hair. She could arch her eyebrows and cut people in half with a laser-beam stare if she felt they deserved it.

One reason I got along well with Aunt Genevieve is that both of her sons were aviators. Wes Stetson had ferried airplanes during World War II as a member of the Air Transport Command. He then became a corporate pilot for a lumber company and built a house on the shores of Lake Tahoe. The lower story was a hangar for his Franklin SeaBee seaplane which he hired out and also used to make auto traffic broadcasts as the "Eye in the Sky." He gave me a ride once and as I sat in the right seat Wes got the airplane away from the ramp and started her up. We were drifting around, bouncing slightly in the waves when he announced, "Tighten up your belt! Here we go!" The problem, for me at least, was that we were not headed toward the middle of the lake but directly at the shore and the cliffs directly behind it, which seemed only a few hundred yards away. As the SeaBee got up speed, I could see Wes looking over at me from the corner of his eye, waiting for me to start to squirm or say something. But I was damned if I would let out a peep. The shore came closer and we went faster as I stared straight ahead, acting as if I knew perfectly well that this was the way seaplane drivers always took off.

As the last moment Wes, who by now had enough speed for positive rudder control, swerved the little seaplane around in a curve parallel to the shore and after bouncing off the waves a few times we lurched into the air. As we climbed he poked me with his elbow and said, "Sometimes I get guys who want to jump right out of the seat. You weren't any fun at all!"

Wes Stetson would have been a typical barnstorming pilot in an earlier time. As a teenager he had built his own airplane, with his grandmother stitching the fabric together for the wings and fuselage. He was at home with the eagles and hawks in the mountains around Tahoe and knew how to handle the cross-currents and down-drafts in the wild terrain and the blind canyons. He was a true romantic who kept a meat-eating horned owl as a pet and who loved the idea of being a flyer; a long drink of water who was never without his big hat and cowboy boots, the same get-up he wore to my wedding just to get Fruffy and Genevieve irritated.

Genevieve's other son Lincoln flew medium bombers over Europe during World War II. He too had been drawn to the flying business at an early age and it was only natural that he would join the Air Corps when the war started. I have a copy of a letter he wrote to Fruffy in between missions from France which described his flights and the flak and the fear they all felt.

"There is no glamour in it, Aunt!" he wrote, just a few days before he got shot down on the bomb run. Genevieve never got the peace of mind which might have come if some positive evidence of the death or survival of Lincoln and his crew had come to light. But the target area was overrun by the Russians after the mission and she blamed them, until the day she died, for hiding their fate from her, a fate which she believed could have included survival and imprisonment by the Communists. I think she would have been greatly pleased to learn that my daughter Holly has named her second child, a boy, Robert Lincoln in his memory.

Our wedding plans began to take shape as Cris and her mother left for the mainland to make the arrangements. We had decided on the Piedmont church for the ceremony and the Alameda Naval Air Station Officer's Club for the reception. Once those things were settled, my participation as bridegroom apparently needed no further discussion. My appearance at the wedding was set down on the list of matters already considered and resolved, like the required number of potted plants and champagne punch cups, and any contributions I might try to make in the planning was considered superfluous. This was fine with me.

Cris took a drive out to Sacramento, to McClellan Air Force Base to meet Chuck Massey, who was to be my best man, and his wife Jan. The Masseys took Cris out to dinner at the club, where they were having Monte Carlo night. As she sat there with her usual ten Bingo cards one of my old cronies, who had been at the club since the start of the attitude adjustment hour came up to her table and stared at her.

"Yes?" asked Cris, trying to track the figure of my buddy as he swayed a little bit. He finally spoke; "I just wanted to see who it was that finally shot down old Tiger Matt!" He then made his way back to his table where there was a serious party going on.

Please remember that this is an incident that happened to Cris, not to me, and I am reporting it as she described it. I have thought about this story and there must be several reasons why it should embarrass me. But I can't think of any.

The wedding, as I have related, went off without a hitch and Cris and I returned to Hickam to settle in family quarters on the base. There was usually a long waiting list for the quarters but they let us have them because I had less than a year left before I -make that "we"- would be assigned somewhere back on the mainland. The flying out of Hickam had gotten to be pretty much a "canned" operation which didn't require much in the way of exotic navigational techniques. Routine was the word for it: you crossed the same old checkpoints and gave pilots headings that didn't vary much between trips. I began to get the feeling that the pilots could easily fly the missions without navigators and do pretty well, and once in a while I got to feel like extra baggage. There were no parallel track systems with other flights alongside to worry about and the wind and weather situation at our usual flight level -around 18,000 feet- was pretty stable.

Once in a while an engine would conk out but we always loaded enough fuel on board for this contingency and it was no big deal. One time, however, one engine went out with oil pressure well down out of the green range and the pilot and flight

engineer shut it down and got the prop feathered without difficulty. We were heading westward back toward Hickam and had
passed the point of safe return, where, had we turned back at
that point, we could have made it back to Travis with enough
gas plus all our reserves. Now we were bearing down on the
point of no return, where we would have to press on toward
Hickam, no matter what. Decision-making between these two
points, if the need came up, could cause a lot of head scratching, with fuel charts and flight level and terminal weather forecast charts being passed around the flight deck for close study.

On this particular flight we had lost number three engine
and the flight engineer began to check his gauges more closely,
tapping one of them lightly in the red-lit darkness when he saw
something that bothered him. Power had been boosted on the
remaining three engines to compensate for the one that was
shut down.

Suddenly he turned from his panel and tapped the aircraft
commander in the left seat on the shoulder. "We'll have to keep
an eye on number four," he said, and all eyes were rivetted on
the engine gauges for that engine. This was pucker time again,
when you knew that you could still make it on two engines, if
the winds and the weather were right, and if everybody on the
flight deck did his job better than he normally did, and if the
pilots had been paying their officer's club dues on time. But the
idea that insinuates into your mind, when one engine is gone
and another is going, is; what if there was a real screw-up
somewhere, maybe at the engine overhaul shop, and we soon
lose them all? Then you start to look around for your Mae West
and your exposure suit, and the swimming pool ditching drills
come to mind. Number four appeared to be getting sicker by
the minute, losing power and oil pressure and obviously not
long for this world. We came up on the point of no return which
I had to recompute several times because of changes in our
speed, and then it was behind us. Then, a half hour later, the
engine gave up the ghost and the pilots and flight engineer
went through the engine shutdown checklist for the second
time. They got the prop feathered okay and you could hear the
two big Pratt & Whitneys on the left side roaring away.

The airspeed was way down even as we descended slowly,
looking for the heavier air and more favorable winds. The

radioman was giving Hickam a play-by-play account as we wallowed around in the sky, a greatly wounded bird with all those precious souls just behind us, the wives and the kids and the sergeants and field graders who made the military services work, and the young guys and gals fresh out of some G.I. training school or one of the academies, all bright-eyed and bushytailed, suddenly wondering how much world they would get to see.

The radioman told us that search and rescue was on the way but you wondered; just what could they do for us except keep things organized and maybe direct some surface vessels our way. The pilot asked that we be ready to compute a heading and ETA for Hilo on the big island of Hawaii at any time, since it was closer, but we continued on for Hickam, where all of the emergency services were alerted and standing by. We all strained to look for the red pinpoint of light being flashed by the Grimes Beacon on the Search and Rescue aircraft, and there it was, dead ahead and slightly below us. The Lockheed C-130 Hercules came up quickly, made a big, sweeping arc around us and positioned himself off to the right where he could keep an eye on us.

The dawn started to break behind us, and the thin, pink light lit up the scattered clouds below. We could now look out and clearly see the right wing, the two dead engines and the two great propellers frozen in position, the biting edges turned into the slipstream. It seemed almost impossible that the Boeing could haul all that dead weight around and still fly.

We made it to Hickam, where the pilots had to call upon every thing they had ever learned about flying the Stratocruiser. They put it down better than you might expect after a lot of tugging and hauling at the controls, and stopped it in the middle of the runway. We were quickly surrounded by about twenty crash vehicles of all kinds; ambulances, jeeps, cars, buses, behemoth foam pumpers manned by astronaut-suited men ready to walk through exploding fuel, everybody flashing their red beacons and having a big time. The base commander was there too, and he came aboard, more relieved than any of us, and suggested we all get off and climb aboard the buses and get some breakfast. The flight engineer stayed behind to supervise the tow job as they prepared to drag the

377

crippled beast to the hanger. He would also probably give some-body an earful about "now, losing one engine is bad enough, but two? Now come on! " I have deleted the creative string of exple-tives which only a long-toothed chief master sergeant might incorporate into his thoughtful debriefing.

An incident like this would be considered almost routine after the monumental feat of airmanship by Major Sam Tyson and his crew when he had to shut down not two but three engines. Sam showed what courage and genius can do when they are needed, and they were certainly needed on that day, on the same route -west coast to Hawaii- in the same type of airplane, a Boeing Stratocruiser.

The single remaining engine was not able to keep them in the air in level flight, and the rate at which they were losing altitude made it appear they would have to go through a haz-ardous ditching at sea. But Tyson knew something about ground effect, the cushioning effect of air close to surface of the ground or water. Rather than ignore the possibility that these natural effects might get him out of his predicament, he made his decision to try to keep flying, and pushed the need for a ditching aside as the second choice.

He took the airplane down almost to the sea surface, jetti-soning everything he could as the airplane descended. He kept himself ready to ditch at any time since he did not know if his idea would work. As he had hoped, the air being squeezed between the sea surface and the bottom of the airplane created more lift then they would have higher up, and he was able to maintain his altitude just above the water. Sam Tyson and his crew got the Stratocruiser to Hilo and nobody got their feet wet. He could have followed the standard operating procedures -the SOP's- and the airplane would be resting in 3000 fathoms of Pacific Ocean, with or without some or all of the people on board. He chose to view the SOP's as General Joe Smith did. The General, who was commander of the Military Air Transport Service declared that "SOP's are for idiots!" during an after-accident visit. We were all greatly shocked that a General would say such a thing, especially since his signature was on the main SOP "bible" for the USAF Military Air Transport Service. But Sam Tyson showed us what he meant.

We enjoyed our honeymoon in a place about as different from Hawaii as you can get; Sun Valley, Idaho. The biggest difference was, of course, the climate, and although the amount of sunshine was about the same, that December of 1955, the sub-zero temperatures were enough to turn my supposedly thinned-out blood to jam. We checked in after a memorable and elegant trip aboard the California Zephyr, a train with glass-topped vista-dome cars which permitted intimidating views of the of the snow-covered mountains as we wound through the Sierra Nevada.

The desk clerks were somewhat deferential when I told them my name was John Matt and we had reservations. I didn't know that Matt was a big name in skiing, and that Tony Matt, a Swiss or Austrian and not a closet Ukrainian, had been coach of the U.S. Olympic ski team and operated ski schools in Massachusetts. As he gave the bellhop our key, I asked the clerk what time the ski school classes usually started in the morning. "Nine o'clock sharp," he said, a small question in his eyes. Perhaps he thought I had come to check on the quality of the skiing instruction at Sun Valley. Little did he know that the lesson I would get the next morning would be my first, and that, for a while, I would be a hazard to myself and other skiers on the bunny slope.

Sun Valley had been built in its spectacular and very remote location as a playground for rich people and it certainly looked the part. I had seen it once before, since it was the set for a movie starring Sonja Henie, a famous Norwegian ice skating champion and Hollywood movie star. There was a heated outdoor swimming pool, circular in shape and enclosed only by a barrier to protect against the wind. It was great sport to swim around awhile and then hold up your hand in the rising vapors as a waiter slipped you a hot-buttered rum.

The train did not run directly to Sun Valley, as the tracks and noise would spoil the pristine environment. Instead, it dropped us off at Ketcham and we took a bus from there, along with several couples about our age who had just arrived from Chicago. We all sat back quietly and looked at more mountains, and I thought, well, we'll have a nice quiet honeymoon and get some skiing and plenty of rest and then we could face the real world.

It turned out that the several couples from Chicago were quiet on the bus only because they were tired from their travels. Once they got a little rest they showed their true intent, which was to have a big time every waking moment, and they readily included us in the fun. One of the men had been a fighter pilot, and I could not make him understand what it was a navigator did, or why they were necessary. He claimed we got to where we wanted to go by pure luck, while I claimed most fighter pilots got nervous flying across the Hudson River and didn't stop shaking until they got to the other side.

Between the honeymooning, the skiing and the partying, I began to run out of steam and apparently looked it. One morning when we came down to breakfast, one of the Chicagoans looked at me and my slightly baggy eyes and said, "John, I wouldn't pull down any window shades. It's liable to pull you right back up and wrap you around the roller!"

It really was a memorable honeymoon, with great surroundings and lots of nice people. When Cris and I think about it these days, we start to laugh about the antics of the people from Chicago, with their inexhaustible supply of jokes and energy. I still had some of my shell to climb out of at the time, but now I felt I was making some progress.

In the blink of an eye, it seemed, the honeymoon was over and we were back at Hickam, settled into the routine and activities of an air transport squadron. About the only serpent we encountered in this paradise was money, or I should say; the lack of it. A captain on flying pay could do all right in a lot of places, but in Honolulu it was tough. We would never again be a young married couple living in the islands, and there was too much to do and enjoy to put a priority on saving money. Although the final week of some of the months could get a little scary as we stretched out what was left of the paycheck, we made it each time.

As the end of our overseas tour approached, in the summer of 1956, we made a trip to Hawaii, the Big Island. The military operated the Kilauea Military Camp situated close to the Kilauea volcano crater, and since the volcano was resting between eruptions, we could walk to the edge and look down into the source of one of natures most violent commotions. The floor of the crater was a flat sea of cooled lava, and it seemed inconceivable that this ponderous mass would someday rise like an elevator and be blown into the sky with mighty explosions, or become molten and flow down the sides of the volcano into the sea.

We stayed in one of a group of small cabins, each named after one of the States, and built a fire in the stove to keep ourselves warm in the high mountain chill. The camp was intended to give military people a break from the sameness of the Hawaiian climate, and it was greatly appreciated by the families after being island-bound for a couple of years. There were black sand beaches to look at, with waterfalls and mile after mile of lava, and the place where an ancient Hawaiian warrior ended Captain Cook's last tour with his dagger. The ground seemed to shake a lot, and each time it did, or I thought it did, it certainly got my attention. But it was surprising how many of the locals, tourists, Park Service people, observatory scientists and technicians all spent their days as if living on the slopes of some of the world's most active volcanoes was a perfectly normal thing to do.

Getting packed to leave the islands was a little different compared to my departures from other places, as a single person. In the beginning, I could stuff all of my belongings into my val-pac-type B-4 bag and a parachute bag, get on the airplane or train, and go. Somewhere along the line, I had to add a foot-locker to hold the increasing pile of mementos, books, photos and just plain junk I couldn't do without. Now, I had to contact the base transportation office to arrange for a shipment of our household goods, which had suddenly begun to accumulate. Somehow, we had been able to afford some living room furniture, and now we had two piles of mementos, books, photos and valuable junk, along with a growing collection of framed prints and other bulky items.

As we started to get the move organized, I was asked by my friend Rod Madeiros and Gussie, his bride-to-be, to attend his wedding. I would be their witness in a Japanese civil ceremony which was held in Tokyo. I worked my way over and back on what was to be my last flight as a crewmember out of Hickam. Rod and I and Marty Scheinkman had often surfed together and Rod, who was born and grew up on Oahu, gave

Marty and me some of our surfing education by pointing out
how the shore off Waikiki was divided into several surfing
areas with names like "Queens" and "Canoes." Each area was
affected differently by a particular wind or tide condition: some
days the surfing was good at all of them, while on other days
you might have to shift from one to another to get some good
waves.

Tiger Scheinkman had also been zapped by the marriage
bug, and he and Gerry, a girl he had known for some time back
in New York were married about the same time Cris and I
were. I didn't see too much of Marty after that, this one-time
young fireman from the big city, who once tried to describe to
me what it sounded like when you were in a building getting
some water on the fire when the brick walls started to collapse.

I won't ever forget, either, the night that Winstead was
killed, and I had just returned from a fourteen or fifteen-hour
backbreaker. I got back to the BOQ and Marty met me to tell
me that the regular mission would be flown as scheduled the
next morning, even though the exact cause of the crash had not
yet been determined. To reassure the flight crews, the mission
crew would be made up of the squadron managers, like the
Operations Officer and his staff. That meant I would go too,
and I said to Marty, "In that case I better get to bed and sleep
fast."

But he shook his head. "There's no way you can fly two of
these trips in two days. I already got myself assigned to go."
That's the kind of a guy Marty is; he and I were like brothers.

While I was gone, Cris had taken charge of the packing,
and when I returned from Rod's wedding the quarters were
pretty much empty except for the G.I. items, like the kitchen
table and chairs, and the beds. I had assumed that Cris would
supervise the movers activities from a decent distance as the
old-timers did, like out on the beach. But I found her upset and
worn out and when I asked her why she hadn't just turned the
movers loose and let them do their thing, I got a wifely glare.

"I started to do just that until I went to get the parakeet to
give to the kids next door. I found him packed, cage and all, in
a box with the lamp shades!"

Looking at the empty rooms had the effect of cutting the

cord; I was ready to leave this beautiful place and start again elsewhere. It also had the effect of cutting the bond that had tied me to the single life I had lived so long. I had no regrets at all.

16

YOU'RE HOLDING HER LIKE A BOMB!

"**Y**OU'RE HOLDING HER LIKE A BOMB!" laughed Cris, as I walked out of the hospital beside her and gingerly carried our new baby out to the car. In the most astounding, most straightforward miracle of all, I had driven my wife to the hospital a few days before, when there were just two of us, and now three of us came out.

Christmas was approaching, so we named her Holly. In another two weeks we would celebrate our first wedding anniversary at Charleston Air Force Base, in South Carolina. We had left Honolulu the previous September and arrived at Charleston where we rented a house not too far from the base and settled down.

The journey from Hawaii, not yet a State at the time, to South Carolina, one of the original thirteen and so burdened with history, created some scene changes which Cris needed to get used to. She had never been east of Yellowstone Park and like most Westerners, got all of her knowledge of north versus south attitudes from what she had read. Now we were somewhere close to the heart of Dixie, where the defeats of ninety years before were still viewed with sorrow and a little bit of anger. All of the trappings of segregation were still in place, at the end of 1956; the back of the bus, the white and colored water fountains, the heavy white lid on the big, black kettle about ready to come to a boil.

The idea of a militant black upheaval was not very evident

around us, not in the eyes or the attitudes of Jane, the young black lady who taught Cris some of the tricks of the motherhood trade. It couldn't be seen in the eyes of the colored shoppers- they weren't called black or African-Americans yet- in the cash market near the house, where one of them once came over to me, holding up a quart of milk.

"Guvnuh, how much is this here milk?" said the middle-aged, keg-shaped man in a leather cap, his rheumy, beseeching eyes fixed on mine. I looked at the price tag and told him the amount. Then, in a move that still shocks me as I think of it, he held out a hand full of change to me and said, "Will you pick out the money for me so I can give it to the man?"

There was a black navigator in the squadron, and it is difficult to imagine how he and his wife were able to cope with the need to live in two worlds, the segregated outside and the generally but not altogether color blind life on the base. This navigator was a nice guy, obviously from a well-off family, who appeared to take the two separate worlds in stride. He was accepted as a crewdog like anybody else and the idea of not including him and his wife in all the squadron activities would have been unthinkable.

It came time for him to be upgraded to Instructor Navigator, which meant he would fly along with new navigators to teach them the ropes. One of my duties as Chief Navigator of the 41st Air Transport Squadron was to present him as a candidate before an upgrading board headed by the Wing Commander, a Colonel. When our turn came I made my pitch, then sat back as some of the board members asked the candidate some questions. Everything went fine, and when they were finished with him, the Colonel turned back to me and asked, "Do you think any problems might come up with other crewmembers because of his race?"

In those days that was considered to be a legitimate question, especially in South Carolina. I was naive enough to let the question surprise me, but I just blinked once and replied, "No sir, not that I can see." The Colonel looked at me, or perhaps somewhere beyond me, and I could see the slight concern in his gaze quickly fade. "The Lieutenant's approved. Let's have the next case."

The Colonel had other concerns, like the regular attendance at the Officer's Club of Governor -later Senator- Ernest Hollings and his wife, and other politicians. With people like that around, although they may have been friends of his, he very well had to be a better-than-good commander to preserve his reputation as a military man.

The journey from Hawaii to Charleston was my first change of station as a married man, and I decided that travel problems do not just double for two people, they increase exponentially. Later on, we would find that with children, the problems might further increase, but the antics of the kids often made the trip more fun than drudgery.

We didn't have any kids to entertain us when we flew out of Hickam for San Francisco, but Cris had the potential for taking care of that little oversight in her tummy. In fact, she was far enough along to require a doctor's certificate before she could travel by air.

There was a reunion with Fruffy and her family when we arrived at her home in Piedmont. Cris was obviously happy to be back on her home ground again, and after visiting with her family and friends, we made sure to go into San Francisco to pay a visit to the Top of the Mark. We also went across the street to the Fairmont Hotel where, downstairs in the Tonga Room, the floating bandstand still made it safely across the big pool on its twice-a-night trip in the violent, man-made thunderstorm. I even made a quick check, as we entered the place, to see if my favorite little statuette was still in a small showcase near the entrance. Sure enough it was there; a little six-inch high plaster rendering of two large-billed birds on a perch. A little name-plate on the base was inscribed with the words; "The Wrong Brothers- The First Birds to Walk."

When it came to maternity clothes in Honolulu, most mothers-to-be usually wore Mu-mu's, which, because of the Mother Hubbard's generous folds, meant you could barely discern they were pregnant. In San Francisco, Cris wore this chic, black velvet maternity dress when we went to dinner or a show and, of course, she looked gorgeous.

My leave time began to run out and it came time to head for New York, or I should say Yonkers, so that Cris could meet the family, and then we would continue on to Charleston. Since

Cris had only a few months to go, we decided not to get a car in California as the drive across the country would be too hard on her. To fly to Detroit and buy a car there made more sense as it would cut the driving in half and, we presumed, would be cheaper. And since Chicago was not too far from Detroit, why not stop there first to see our Sun Valley honeymoon friends?

So off we went, heading east to places I hadn't seen in a long time. When we arrived in Chicago, our friends were waiting for us, and the party started all over again. My ex-fighter pilot friend, who thought navigators decided on a magnetic heading by spitting in their palm, put us up in his big, fine home north of the city on Lake Michigan. They were an affluent crowd, and seemed to have life by the tail. When they learned we were on our way to Detroit to buy a car, a large discussion ensued as to which one of them could get us a better deal right there in Chicago. Before we knew it, we were sitting in the sales manager's office of a Chevy dealer in downtown Chicago, picking out our station wagon and signing on the dotted line.

The only problem that came up was that the dealer did not have temporary license plates that could be used out of the state, and we did not want to buy permanent Illinois plates only to have to discard them as soon as we got to South Carolina. What to do? Well, we left without any license plates at all.

It was about the time we reached Cleveland that Cris, who looked at the map and saw that Niagara Falls wasn't too far out of the way, thought it might be great to have another honeymoon in -where else?- the honeymoon capital of the world. As we left Cleveland and made our way toward Buffalo, two problems circled around in my mind. The first was money. I had planned that when we ran through the funds we had with us, I would stop in any of the many military installations along the way and cash a check. Credit cards were still only a glimmer in the eye of some financial genius, and presenting an out-of-state check at a motel or restaurant was considered an insult.

The money plan worked, but not too well, since the checking limit for transients was twenty-five dollars, and that didn't go too far, even then. So we sort of hobbled along, financially, from military base to military base, just barely getting along.

The other problem involved the damned license plates. I would begin to sweat when a police cruiser would come bearing down on us, but they merely looked at the car, and then at me as they passed, and kept on going. Then there were the bored right-seat riders in other cars, who had nothing to do but look at other people's license plates. Several times, a car driving right behind us would note our lack of a rear plate and after a while, curiosity would prevail, and the driver would pull out and start to pass. As they reached a point slightly ahead, the occupants would crane their necks to check our front bumper, and, sure enough, there was no plate there either! There would be a lot of arm waving and pointing of fingers and nodding of heads and then they would speed on, relishing the big event of their travel day.

But the big problem was that going to Niagara Falls meant crossing the border into Canada, and how would the immigration chaps, the Canadians going in and the U.S. types coming back out deal with the idea of no license plates? We would soon see. We pushed this little problem aside as we parked the car and began a walking tour of the points of interest on the U.S. side first. You could stand right at the edge of the precipice alongside the awesome torrent as it roared over the edge and down into the river below. Some of the observation points had a little brass plaque mounted on a stand marking the launching point of a not-always-successful attempt by someone to take the plunge over the falls in a barrel.

The idea of people climbing into a large barrel, however well padded, and being cast off into that overwhelming sweep of forces seemed to be part of humanity's weird streak; somewhere between sheer courage and insanity. What must it feel like just as the barrel reached the edge, suspended in space for a split second as the forward motion quit, and then the plunge down, down, down; waiting for that big, bone-jarring crash, and then the brain-scrambling shaking and spinning around as all the water in the world came pounding down on top of the barrel before it would be twirled aside into quieter waters?

We thought about all this, and walked alongside the speeding torrent for a further moment until it was our own turn in the barrel. We climbed into our brand-new Chevy wagon, still armed with false courage and outward calm, and still without those indispensable license plates, and proceeded toward unsuspecting Canada.

We were determined to make this effort because we were told that the night time view of the American Falls, bathed in powerful, multi-colored floodlights, made a spectacular sight when viewed from the penthouse lounge of the Brock Hotel just across the river on the Canadian side. We also thought that there was not much use in coming to Niagara Falls unless you could get a ride on the Maid of the Mist, which could be boarded on the Canadian as well as the U.S. side. This brave little vessel took its passengers so close to the thunderous cataract that they were usually drenched with spray despite the fishermens' slickers and hats which were provided.

So off we went across the bridge into Canada. As we pulled up to the row of customs and immigration gates I tried, in the second or two that I had, to pick out a likely candidate, an immigration officer who looked, well, good natured. I veered over toward a forty-ish, chubby type who was smiling cheerfully at the people in the car ahead as they pulled out. The smile started to fade a little as he glanced down and saw the empty license plate bracket. As we stopped in the gate, he walked around to the rear and saw another empty license plate bracket. In a gesture that could have been part of a script, he lifted his cap and scratched his head as he came up to my window.

"Do you intend, sir, to enter Canada without license plates on your vehicle?" he asked, his teeth partially clenched as he tried to control his disbelief. I then entered into a sales pitch, hastily rehearsed in my mind, about just coming from overseas, the shortage of license plates in Chicago, and trying to please my pregnant wife -and here Cris sat up so that he could not mistake her condition- and I went on and on. The whole time, the immigration man just stood there, both hands on the window sill of my car, shaking his head while looking at the ground. When I was through, he straightened up and looked at me.

"Well, now I've seen everything. You can go on through, but when you come back out, make sure to come and get me if you have any trouble." As we drove off into Canada, I looked in the rear view mirror and saw the man getting back into his booth, his head still wagging from side to side.

We took our ride on the Maid of the Mist and enjoyed it very much, even during the time when it appeared the Captain had lost his senses and was ready to take the boat right into the thundering falls. Clouds of spray billowed around us and dripped from our slickers and hats and faces and hands. "I hope this doesn't mean our new offspring will be afraid of the water," said Cris, patting her tummy afterward.

After we had checked into one of the motels, we went over to the Brock Hotel and got a table at one of the large windows in the roof top lounge so we could watch the falls which were already lit up in the late autumn evening. The motel charge had used up most of the last check I was able to cash, so we had to decide between dinner or champagne cocktails. We had our cocktails and dined on peanuts and pretzel sticks. Ah, the arrogant nonchalance of the youthful poor!

The next day we climbed into our license-less Chevy wagon and found ourselves back at the border, wondering what would happen next. As we stopped at one of the gates, I started to explain about the absent tags when the U.S. Immigration officer interrupted and said ," It's okay, It's okay. We heard about you in the new Chevrolet Wagon. Welcome back!"

Getting on the road to Yonkers was not the end of the saga by any means as we still had some hurdles in our path. I was able to cash a check in a small army post in Buffalo, but the usual twenty-five dollars slowly dissipated on the long trip down as we bought gasoline and had some food. It was about two AM when we reached the vicinity of the newly-built Tappan Zee bridge; so near yet so far, for we didn't have too far to go to get to Hank and Kay's house in Yonkers. But we were down to a dollar or two and just about out of gas, and we still had the bridge toll to pay, so what do we do next?

Gas, I thought, came first as we came upon a small service station which was closed for the night. I pulled the car up to the pumps and got out and started banging on the office door. Pretty soon a light came on upstairs and a little guy came down and turned the light on and opened the door. You can't blame the man for getting a little exasperated when I told him that not only did I need some gas, but I could only pay by check, because the dollar or two I had left was needed for the bridge fare. After some grumping around, he finally agreed to give us two dollars worth of gas, and to take a check for it. And when I wrote it out and signed it and gave it to him, he looked at me and said, "I might as well throw this away. I know damn well its no good!" Then he turned out the light and grumped back upstairs.

We got to Yonkers, to Colonial Heights where Hank and Kay lived and we had to wake them up too but they were relieved we finally made it. After telling our difficulties to Hank, who had spent a big part of his life driving gasoline tankers around New York, insisted that the very first thing after we got up we must go a few miles down the road to White Plains, the Westchester county seat, and get the car registered and have plates put on it. After all of that travelling, past dozens of police cruisers, crossing the Canadian border both ways and then completely across New York State, we just about had it made.

I left Hank's house the next morning and as I was passing through the center of Eastchester, directly in front of Hank's Gulf station, I saw a policeman directing traffic. The little hairs raised on the back of my neck, for I knew that after all of those miles, the game was up. The way he stood there, ramrod straight, spotless white gloves, shoes as shiny as the bill of his cap which was pulled down over the bridge of his nose, gave me a distinct sinking feeling. As I entered the busy crossroads, the cop looked at the front of my car and without hesitation, signalled me to stop.

"I'm on my way to White Plains to get plates for the car," I said, looking into the hard stare of a man who had heard it all before.

"Okay, but you don't go past me in a car without plates. Pull over somewhere," said this blue-suited Horatius, single-handedly guarding the approaches to White Plains, who would have drawn his sword, if he had been issued one, and rent me in twain if I had tried to get by him. It could have happened in so many other places, but it happened, luckily, where I could drive into Hank's station and borrow a car to finish the trip. Fortune seems to smile, occasionally, on people who keep pushing the bureaucratic envelope, and who take advantage of other people's good nature, thus becoming one of

391

the burdens on mankind.

I greatly admire Cris for the way she was able to enter this older and slightly different world of mine and make herself at home. I admire her even more when I think of the day we left Hank and Kay's house, in their nice neighborhood of well-kept homes and tree-lined, quiet streets and went to visit my mother. She still lived on Jefferson Street, a block down from our former house on Stanley Avenue, in a row house which had remained standing although others around it were being torn down and replaced by low-income apartments. I wondered what was going through Cris' mind as we entered the little front hall with the chipped floor tiles and the banged-up mailboxes.

I pressed the right bell and got an answering click as the hall door lock unlatched. We walked up the two flights of dark stairs and saw my mother waiting for us at the landing, ready to greet Cris as a long-lost daughter. Cris was not altogether prepared for the great emotion with which she was hugged and welcomed, and as we stepped into my mother's spotless and peaceful island in the threatening, downhill stream that was Jefferson Street, the feelings wrapped around us, and lifted us. I could see in my mother's face that she was greatly relieved and satisfied that I had brought the right young wife home with me, a beautiful young woman with warmth and intelligence. But more than the beauty and the warmth and the intelligence, my mother sensed she also possessed a trait highly prized in my own family. She knew what, in this life, was worthwhile and what was not.

We only had a few days, and as I had briefed Cris, we spent most of the time getting stuffed with food. There were roast chickens and steaks and stuffed cabbage and cheese and potato pirohi along with six kinds of vegetables and lots of drinks and beer. My mother seemed to think that the road between Yonkers and Charleston crossed an almost empty wasteland in which the few restaurants we would pass were not to be trusted and, come to think of it, she was almost right. By the time we were ready to leave, we had stored enough food energy to take us as far as Venezuela, in case we overshot. And our departure was, as it always had been and always would be, full of hugs and kisses, lots of laughing and a few tears and taking twenty minutes to move the ten feet from the front door to the car. I looked at Cris as we drove off, and I knew that whatever fears I had, were for nothing.

The Charleston of 1957 provided some pretty nice living for the older married officers and non-coms. There was no housing on the base, but living costs were not too high, and if you had saved some money and had your furniture paid up and didn't feel the need to go out much, you could do pretty well. But some of us had a bit of a struggle trying to afford some of the appearances we were expected to keep up, but we managed, from month to month.

Very few of the wives worked, but were expected to take part in club or hospital activities and play bridge or maybe some mah-jong. I recently came across my itemized budget for May, 1957, which, as part of my concise and efficient budget accounting procedure, I had jotted down on the back of an envelope. This was before Cris, who had studied accounting at Berkeley, took over and put us on the road to what could pass for solvency. The envelope list showed items like Rent; $95, Telephone; $5.84, Car Payment; $64.30, and so on, for a total outflow of $407.63. Today, of course, this seems like a pittance, but it was subtracted from another pittance which comprised my take home pay of $527.70. This meant we had $120.07 for food and all those mad, mad social activities. But I can't complain; somehow we had a great time.

Cris managed to get involved in a lot of those social activities because she had Jane to baby-sit for her. We were really lucky to find her since we got to know we could trust her completely with our very young Holly. We also managed to spend some time camping at Lake Moultrie, or sitting on one of the beaches near Charleston watching the dolphins glisten in the sun for a flashing moment as they arched into the air and dove down again, all headed off somewhere to find some current to ride. We got to Middleton Gardens at the perfect time, when everything was in bloom, and we paddled by boat through the masses of azaleas whose dazzling colors stood out against the cypress-blackened water on which we rode. And then there were the cannon-blasted remains of Fort Sumter, where the national boil was lanced when it was attacked. It let loose a shower of American blood which poured out and soaked the ground and floated on the creeks and rivers, from Bull Run to the Mississippi.

I remembered this little fort where the Civil War began when I made my first visit, some time later, to Gettysburg, that heart-breaking killing ground in Pennsylvania where the tide of the war took one of its final turns. It is one thing to read about Pickett's charge at Gettysburg, but to go there and to smell the ghostly gunsmoke floating just above the savage battle scene, the dead men's eyes glancing at you quickly to see if you were friend or foe. And then put yourself in Brigadier General Armistead's Confederate boots as he strode to the abyss that split the two sides, marching straight into the levelled cannons spewing double charges of canister shot which cut his young boys down like death rays. "Come on boys... who will follow me?" yelled the General, looking back as he came up to the guns but there was no one left to follow , and then he too was blown away. And on the other side, Union Lieutenant Alonzo Cushing, refusing to fall back from his battered artillery position at the point of Pickett's charge even though terribly wounded in the groin, and still holding his position when wounded a second time, until, finally, he was struck with his third and mortal wound. Their names are remembered in sadness and pride by their ancestors, and by those who ponder God's will in endowing some men with surpassing, self-sacrificing courage. Surely, such courage must be placed alongside faith as another of God's miracles.

We had been at Charleston a year when an opportunity came along which my instincts told me to grasp. An experienced navigator was being sought for the aircrew of a General who would be in command of classified operations "somewhere in the Pacific." The personnel chief claimed to know neither who, what, when, nor where. He certainly didn't have much information to dazzle candidates with, and only one other navigator came in to ask about the job. I told him I wanted to discuss it with my wife and he said, "That's fine but I need to know tomorrow."

My flights out of Charleston had gotten to be routine; from

Charleston to the Azores to Tripoli, to Dharan, Saudi Arabia, and return. There had been a little bit of excitement the year before, in January of 1957, a few months after we arrived in Charleston, when our squadron and others became involved in picking up refugees who were streaming out of Hungary as the Soviet tanks moved in to crush the Hungarian uprising. The refugees gathered in places like Munich and Vienna by the thousands, and we loaded them aboard and brought them to the U.S.

There were the young people, who had stood up in the streets and thrown rocks at the tanks. But the surprising aspect was the number of middle-aged and older people who made the trip, finally fed up with what had happened to their country, finally willing to take a big chance even in their later years. They made up a strange bunch of refugees; well-dressed, fussy people who acted as though they were taking a little trip to see Aunt Magda and travel at this time of year was all so inconvenient.

They complained about the heat, or the cold, or the hard seats, or the tea was too hot and the box lunches, of course, were a grievous insult. We made a refueling stop at the U.S. air base in Prestwick, Scotland on the way home, and as the refugee-passengers came down from the airplane and waited for buses to take them for a meal at the G.I. mess hall, some of them walked up to the civilian air terminal restaurant and looked into the large windows. The refugees looked at the elegantly laid tables, the diners sipping coffee or wine, and they started to look for the entrance door.

I thought there would be another uprising when some Scottish immigration men came out and barred their way and led them back to the waiting area.

We went to other places like Bermuda, Casablanca and Trinidad once in a while, but the main destinations were Dharan and Tripoli, to deliver the goods that kept the bases going. On the leg between Tripoli and Dhahran, we had to fly around Egypt, to the south, because the Egyptians would not permit us to overfly their country. This added enough distance to the flight so that we had to make a refueling stop along the way. The only place that was suitable and available was Khartoum in the Sudan, well to the south of the Egyptian border on the Nile. There was a large dining room on the second floor of the air terminal at the Khartoum airport, and we would all order Covina, a nice perch-like fish which the local fisherman pulled out of either the White or the Blue Nile rivers, which converged near Khartoum to form the Nile itself.

The currents of history also converged not too far away at Omdurman, a few miles to the north, where the young Winston Churchill observed what came to be called "the last great mounted cavalry charge." British General "Chinese" Gordon had been killed there while on a mission and Lord Kitchener was sent down to straighten things up, British style. His forces confronted the Khalifa and his tens of thousands of fierce Whirling Dervishes on a September day in 1898 and the desert silence was shattered as the battle was joined. By the time the desert silence had once again returned, the Dervishes had been conquered, and British rule was reimposed. To make sure there was no doubt who won the war, Kitchener began to redo the city of Khartoum, which was to be laid out in the form of the crossed stripes and bars of the Union Jack. As the British like to say, once in a while, that was a bit much.

History had swept all of this aside by the time I began to make trips through Khartoum in 1956, which was the year that the Sudan was formed as an independent republic, the same year that Nasser, up in Egypt, had taken over the Suez Canal. But up at 18,000 feet we could only imagine the screams of mortally wounded men or impaled horses in the battle which happened a half century before. There was only the pale-yellow moonscape below, prostrate under the unattenuated sun.

Tiny groups of humanity were scattered here and there in places with names like Bir Salala and Tundubal, settled long before there was a Sudan or a Suez Canal, and in all the years, had left their surroundings so little disturbed they were almost invisible from our height. You had to stare at the ground until the rock outcroppings and the dry river beds got sorted out in your mind and then there; there it was, a little blob of huts and alleys, but with all signs of activity too far below for us to see. There might have been some barefoot young girl slowly making her way down the path to the well to fill the big jar she balanced on her head, or some goats and sheep dozing in the sparse shade of the stunted trees at the edge of the village. But if the sound of our engines reached them as we passed overhead, they probably noticed it less than the buzzing of the pesky flies that had bedeviled them since the dawn of memory.

Like most of Africa, there wasn't much navigational information available and you had to do some artful terrain interpretation to come up with halfway accurate headings and ETA's. However, we did have The Navigator's Friend, which was Jebel Uweinat, the tallest of a group of mountains which rose suddenly from the desert floor directly on our route, right at the place where the borders of Egypt, Libya and the Sudan met. It appeared to be a sawed-off volcanic peak with an unmistakable shape, a lot like Diamond Head, so when we passed by, in daylight or when there was a bright moon, I didn't need a map to tell me where we were. And as long as we stayed to the south of it, we would steer clear of Egypt and not give that country further excuse to be angry with us.

Cris and I talked about whether I should take the new assignment in the Pacific. I couldn't be told where I would be based, or how long I would be gone, or who the General was, or who the other crewmembers were, or what the type of airplane was, or exactly what I would be doing. But the idea of being a General's navigator sounded like a good idea.

I was told that Cris and Holly would not be able to come along, but as we talked, we began to conjure up this picture of flying some General around the Pacific with lots of trips back to the States. Cris could let go the house near Charleston and move in with her mother back in Piedmont, and I could drop in whenever we landed on the West Coast. The clincher was the thought of a possible rendezvous in Honolulu, to have a Mai Tai under the big Banyan tree at the Moana, or sit on the beach and watch the sun go down.

Well, that did it. The next morning I went to see the personnel man, a major, and when I told him I volunteered for the assignment he looked at me with his eyebrows arched up. "Are you sure?" he asked, "because once I send your name in, and you decide you don't like the assignment, I can't change it even if you shoot yourself in your big toe!" He was some recruiter.

The big manila envelope was stamped Confidential; and I

took it over to an empty desk near one of the windows, sat down and opened it. The sets of orders, a list of instructions, certificates I had to sign and a sketchy information circular all told me what I would be doing the next nine months. The orders were effective on the first of January, 1958, which meant Cris and I had only a couple of weeks to get ready. My slot as Chief Navigator was easy to fill, since all three of my Flight Examiners had experience running the shop while I was gone, which was quite a bit, and they were all Number One.

I was assigned to Bolling Air Force Base, just outside Washington, for administrative purposes, with further assignment to Arlington Hall Station, a former fancy girls school in the nearby Virginia suburbs. It was now a double-fenced, heavily guarded place where, as someone said, "You need a secret clearance to listen to somebody clear his throat."

Arlington Hall Station was the home of Joint Task Force Seven which was responsible for running the nuclear bomb tests at Enewetak, formerly spelled Eniwetok. The series of tests with which we would be involved was called Operation Hardtack, and the JTF commander for the operation was USAF Major General Alvin R. Luedecke. General Luedecke was a calm, quiet man whose pleasant half-smile hid any concern or awe with which he may have regarded the task he was about to undertake. He was in his forties, a medium-sized man who was a rated pilot himself, and who spoke with a disarming drawl which probably come in handy in dealing with some of the prima donnas which Hardtack would attract. I could imagine, if I had been sent back to his compartment on the airplane and tell him we were running out of gas and couldn't make it to Enewetak, that he would look at me with that bemused smile. And after a pause, he would probably say, "Well, we better get ready to ditch this thing."

This thing, -the General's airplane- was a Douglas C-54, a World War II four engined transport that came from the small fleet of such planes at Bolling. The base's runways have now been replaced by administrative buildings, housing and the like, but back in 1958, it was still active. Airplanes which were used to haul military brass around were based there, including the Sacred Cow which Presidents Roosevelt and Truman had used. When I first arrived at Bolling and went to Base

398

Operations, the Sacred Cow was pointed out to me and I walked out to the ramp to look it over. No one was around but some stairs were pulled up to the door, which was open, so I climbed up and stepped aboard. When I entered the main cabin, the idea of it hit me; here is where Presidents Roosevelt and Truman spent some time, discussing world-shaking decisions with advisors, their well-being placed in the hands of a picked aircrew and maintenance men. The compartment wall coverings were faded and yellowed with age, and a foot-square, not very distinguished landscape painting was still on the wall where it must have been for a long time. There was no sense of great power left; in fact, it was somewhat quaint compared to the latest Presidential aircraft. But it was the fore-runner, the first rendering of the idea that the President of the United States should be able to travel by air in complete safety and reliability as a matter of routine.

It was very quiet in the Sacred Cow; there was nobody taking off or landing or running up an engine outside. I walked up to the President's chair, a big, padded thing next to a large, square window and sat down and thought about this man who had to be loaded aboard in his wheelchair on a special, built-in elevator. And I thought about the tremendous burden he carried during the Depression and then the war, a burden which squeezed the life and vitality out of him and made him look ten hard years older than the age of sixty-three when he died. History may judge that presidents who have come after him may meet or exceed his greatness, but they will not be someone who wore a dramatic opera cape and big fedora hats with the brim turned up and who smoked cigarettes in a long holder.

Major Amin George, the General's Aide -also known as "Flamin' Amin" because he was a fireball who got things done- was to the be Aircraft Commander. He was a scrappy fighter pilot type who never stood still very long because he had a lot to do.

But the day-to-day worries about keeping the airplane in shape, complying with all the right regulations, supervising the crew and looking after the several million details that had to be dealt with, were assigned to another pilot, Bill McKenny, a Captain and a crew dog just like me. I was to find he could play the C-54 like a virtuoso cellist, who could gather all of its wings and engines and various parts and assemblies and accessories and make them heed his firm but gentle commands. Bill was a lot like the General; calm and soft spoken, but of course he could not sit around giving bemused smiles to people because he was only a Captain and had to please a lot of customers. And please them all, he did, for he was the typical old pro who could be depended on.

One of the first things we learned from Amin was that we would not move out to the Pacific right away, but would spend a couple of months flying out of Bolling while JTF-7 got fully organized. Cris and Holly's trip to the West Coast was therefore postponed and we found an apartment on a bluff overlooking Bolling's main runway. The first night we went to bed we were awakened about midnight by a set of headlights which lit up the bedroom like daylight. We both thought some madman in a car was about to drive right through our wall, but it turned out to be an airplane with his landing lights on for his final approach to the Bolling runway below us. He roared on by and let us know why it had been so easy to get this apartment so close to the airport on such short notice.

The General's airplane had the usual VIP configuration; a standard flight deck, then a galley with stainless steel cabinets and sinks with a stove and a fridge, then the large VIP compartment with a fold down table and bunk, and beyond that, seats for the staff and other peasants. Bill and The Flame and I took the airplane out to give it a careful compass swing, where we took accuracy readings every fifteen degrees around the dial to make sure the instrument was within tolerances. We also gave the other navigation gear a checkout because the entire Pacific was to be our operating area, and there were vast, empty areas of that ocean where we would need every navigational break we could get.

The pilots were more interested in the condition of the engines and whether all the controls and instruments worked okay, and if the landing aids like the ILS, -the Instrument Landing System- worked or if the fuel system leaked anywhere. We also took long flights at the C-54's usual operating altitude, -around 9000 feet- and checked the fuel consumption to make sure we could believe the fuel charts we used for flight planning.

There wasn't anything new I had to learn about the navigation in the area since it had been my "back yard" for a number of recent years. So I used some of the waiting time to study some of the non-classified manuals available at Arlington Hall concerning the effects of nuclear testing, especially with regard to radioactive fallout. The business of fallout was not that new either, and I could remind myself that, for a time, there weren't too many people in this world who had watched more nuclear detonations than my colleagues and myself as we waited to take off and chase the radioactive cloud.

Meanwhile, General Luedecke and his staff wrestled with the planning for Operation Hardtack: the ships, the aircraft, the people, the scheduling, the nuclear devices, the scientific and operational procedures for each detonation and on and on, all done on a gigantic scale. Little by little, General Luedecke got his Task Force put together and he let us know that departure time was approaching. Bill got together with the Flight Engineer to decide on the spare parts to take along on the C-54, some to carry with us on the airplane at all times, others to store at Enewetak. Before we knew it, we were ready to go.

17

SUDDENLY, THE TALLEST
THING ON EARTH

THE COUNTDOWN WAS RUNNING and it was too late to stop it now, ...five, four, three, two, one," -then that heart-stopping instant, and then Whammo! The stupendous light, the light beyond the power of the sun, the molten white light filling the corners of the universe, getting brighter as the pure energy smashed outward into the millions-of-degrees fireball two miles across, vaporizing the air, the sea, the guileless piece of atoll on which the threatening-looking machine had sat. And then the shock of this great insult to the earth surged outward from the yawning, white-hot crater, and heaved and rolled the atoll so that the firing party in the bunker twenty miles away, caught unawares by the greater than anticipated force of the ther-monuclear blast, had to hang on. The giant thunderclaps of sound spread across the Bikini lagoon as the fireball rose and the light, imperceptibly, began to slowly dim. The vaporized residue of coral, sea-water and the device itself was dragged upward with the great ball as it rose ponderously to burst through the tropopause into the stratosphere. As tall as Mt. Everest, then twice as tall, then three, then four times, sudden-ly the tallest thing on earth; this great deadly mushroom loomed in terrifying majesty over the dawn-lit sea.

A feathery, white mantle of ice crystals lay draped over this eminence, whose symmetry held together for a moment. But even this monstrous force had to finally give way to other forces of nature; the movements of the atmosphere, the cooling of the thermonuclear fires. The symmetric shape of the cloud began to distort, and the crater at surface zero became a mile-wide, 200-foot deep cauldron of boiling ocean as the water surged in to cover the wound.

It was some of the other forces of nature that caused the problems which slowly, surely, began to drop from the sky and coat the test fleet, the sea, the nearby islands, the natives, the sailors, outlying weather observers and the Japanese fishing boat Daigo Fukuryu Maru, -The Fortunate Dragon No. 5- with a silent, deadly, ionizing grit. Inhabited areas and the test fleet had been dusted before, very slightly. But this time the unexpectedly high yield and upper air winds which moved differently than had been forecast caused heavy fallout to come down outside the designated danger area.

The test fleet of work ships had been pulled out of Bikini lagoon and positioned to the east and southeast, generally 50 to 80 miles away. The fallout was expected to move to the northeast, sliding past the fleet and clearing the inhabited Rongelap atoll, 105 nautical miles to the east. Rongerik Atoll, another thirty miles further east and manned by 28 U.S. weather and scientific personnel was also considered not endangered. But the great size of the explosion -15 megatons instead of an expected 7- and the unexpected movement of the upper air in the direction of the work fleet and the inhabited islands put a lot of people at risk to the dangers of fall out radiation.

This was Test Bravo of the Castle Series which was held at Bikini Atoll in March of 1954, four years before we arrived in the area for Operation Hardtack. The accident was to have a profound effect on the public's attitude toward nuclear bomb tests, and began to change the somewhat relaxed attitude which test personnel had, from the top scientists to the test-site ditch diggers, toward radioactive fallout's hazards, both to themselves and to immediate bystanders.

Bravo had been the first real U.S. test of a large, air-deliverable H-bomb using a design by Dr. Edward Teller, who had used some input from a mathematician named Ulam. The flawed success of Bravo put us ahead of the Soviets once more in the see-saw battle for nuclear supremacy, but the demands to halt testing were getting louder and coming from all sides.

The U.S. versus Soviet thermonuclear box score up to the

time of Bravo had gone like this; after their success with the A-bomb in 1949, the Soviets set off a nuclear device two years later which was thought to have a "fusion component." Then in 1952, U.S. exploded the Mike shot, a thermonuclear device -not a bomb- on the island of Elugelab at Enewetak which yielded 10 megatons. It wasn't called a bomb because it had to be cooled down to minus 250 Centigrade; was as big as a building and weighed 65 tons. But it proved out the Teller-Ulam configuration and set the stage for the Bravo bomb test.

Meanwhile, just before our 1954 Bravo shot, the Soviets exploded an air deliverable bomb called "Joe 4" which, as H-bombs go, was a little on the puny side, probably less than half a megaton and smaller than our biggest A-bomb. The Soviet success with Joe 4, which , like Bravo, could be labeled a bomb rather than a "device," has led some people to claim that the Russians were the first to develop an H-bomb.

The year after Bravo, in 1955, the Soviets exploded what was considered to be a genuine Soviet H-bomb, which they dropped from an airplane. After that, you might say that we both stood with equal stature in Lucifer's shadow.

The death of one of the fishermen aboard the Fortunate Dragon, apparently as a consequence of test Bravo is considered by some to be the first human fatality of the H-bomb. The fishermen had apparently ignored or had not received the publicly disseminated warning to mariners and had been 85 miles east of the blast. They had been missed during the pre-shot air and destroyer sweep always made before each shot to guard against such eventualities. The crewmen were heavily coated with fallout as they processed their catch above deck and were soon affected by radiation sickness. They were able to make it back to Japan, where Aikichi Kuboyama died six months later.

The natives on Rongelap and the U.S. service personnel on Rongerik were evacuated after what appears today to be some leisurely decision-making. Even after it was decided to take the people off the affected atolls, the "let it wait till morning" rate of urgency was applied while the natives and G.I.'s sat, ate, played and slept amidst the clouds of radioactive particles, and had their body tissues, along with their genes and chromosomes bathed in the invisible, penetrating gamma radiation. The main thing that was wrong with Bravo was that it had gone forward with the radiological safety aspects partly dependent on a fallout prediction system that was good but not great. Much of it depended on forecasting the high level wind direction, and even today , with the big Cray super computers at the National Meteorological Center at Suitland in Maryland and the razzle-dazzle satellites, we still cannot predict some of the major curls and whims of the atmosphere.

Bravo was the largest nuclear explosion we had ever set off. But the limit on the size of an H-bomb is open-ended, and a proposal had been made after that test to make an even bigger one. President Eisenhower decided enough was enough, and vetoed the idea. The Russians, however, pressed on and in a show of nuclear macho, exploded a 58 megaton behemoth - almost four times the size of Bravo. After that, all they had to do was find a target big enough to use it on.

Meanwhile, back at Enewetak, the Hardtack series of tests proceeded. The list of projects was amazing in its diversity: it appeared that the two competing U.S. weapons development facilities; The Los Alamos Scientific Laboratory and the University of California Radiation Laboratory had studied their project lists and combed their files, and even gave the kitchen sink an appraising glance, then chose the experiments they wanted to tinker with before the atmospheric testing moratorium closed things down.

There was a shot suspended from a balloon at high altitude, a couple of underwater tests, two more to be mounted on rockets and set off above the atmosphere and the rest on barges or on one of the atolls at either Enewetak or Bikini. Thirty-five shots in all, more than all previous ocean detonations combined.

Yucca, the balloon shot came first on the 28th of April. Looking back, this exercise seems the scariest of the 35. Balloons had been used before, in Nevada, but they were tethered and they could be cranked down if something went wrong. And if the tether broke? Well, I presume the balloon could be shot down within the confines of the test site. This time the large, helium-filled balloon was untethered and the whole apparatus was launched from the deck of the aircraft carrier Boxer by a specially trained crew. The scary part was the launching of a free balloon which could carry a nuclear weapon up beyond our reach and perhaps not respond to any of the radio commands intended to control it. The nuclear device -the size is still classified- was therefore fitted with a number of gadgets to insure that it went off or came down without endangering anybody.

First, there were explosive squibs which could be fired to cut the device loose from the balloon rigging if necessary. Then there were pins which had to be removed at launch to make sure the explosive squibs didn't fire prematurely. Then there were more pins to insure that the device didn't fall out of the big forklift which held it in place for launch on the deck of the Boxer. More pins had to be removed at launch which prevented electrical power from reaching the arming circuitry too early, and also prevented the baroswitch system -which armed the device after it reached 40,000 feet- from operating prematurely. The baroswitch, if it had armed the device at 40,000 feet and sensed that the balloon was drifting back down below that altitude, would set off a timer which ran for 190 minutes and then gave signals to fire the bomb and explode the release squibs at the same time. This meant that if the command radio signal didn't set the thing off, then the timer would give it a try. And if that didn't work, then the thing would drop down into the ocean.

Wait, we're not through yet. If the radio firing signal or the 190-minute timer switch didn't set the thing off and the weapon dropped down into the ocean, there was a possibility that seawater could provide electrical conduction paths to complete the firing circuit and set it off as it floated on the surface. Therefore, two saltwater-activated probes were installed which would operate to cut off the voltage to the arming circuit.

Finally, if the gadget had remained intact after all of these indignities, there was the "good riddance" device, consisting of plugs which dissolved in seawater and, after four hours, let the damned thing sink.

On launch morning, the Boxer steamed out to the northeast and when it reached a point somewhat more than halfway between Enewetak and Bikini, it started a run downwind. This was intended to zero out the wind across her deck by moving with the breeze. The balloon was inflated with the calculated amount of helium and it rose to its full stature of 80 feet. The device was armed, the launch party took a few nervous swallows, and they let the thing go. Except for a small initial delay caused when one of two B-36's orbiting near the detonation point was out of position, the exercise went like clockwork. The two B-36's -lumbering giants with six propeller engines mounted pusher-wise on the trailing edge of its wings- were loaded with instrumentation and situated only 12 miles from the zero point. They must have had quite a display.

But to all of us on the ground at Enewetak, approximately 150 miles away, the event looked like a tiny pin-prick of bright light which lasted for only an instant. Well, I thought; one down and 34 to go. When I observed the pin-prick of light, I did so, I'll have you know, not as a casual bystander, but as an official member of the Radiological Safety office. On the flight out to Enewetak, I had discussed with Amin and Bill the idea of my having an additional duty on the ground, in between flights, so that I could keep busy. Bill and the flight engineer would be occupied keeping the airplane healthy and ready to go, but there wouldn't be much for me to do except, perhaps, get rock happy.

Bill didn't mind, and neither did Amin George, provided my first priority as the General's navigator was not interfered with. The General bought it too, so Amin found me a slot in the RadSafe office which was run by Lt. Colonel Frank Richie. Since that office was busy just before, during and after an exercise -times when the General wouldn't be flying anywhere- the assignment seemed just right.

Frank Richie was like all of the staff I came into contact with, intelligent and highly aware and, fortunately for me, easy to get along with. He was in his thirties, medium height, with a hairline that was surrendering with dignity. He was not only my supervisor now but also my teacher and he would answer questions about my new job with forced patience, mulling over the answer in his mind, taking a puff on his cigar.

He had a big job to do and training me would be an extra chore, but I tried to make him feel the effort would pay off in the assistance I might provide. I had already had some training in the rudiments, like "there is no such thing as good gamma"

407

and other important principles. But I had to absorb some of the detail so that I could speak the language convincingly since we were expected to brief some of the transient big shots on radiological safety when they arrived to witness an exercise. Richie's job was to keep radiation away from people as much as possible, from fallout or from direct effects. Someone else worried about radiation already on the ground or in the water, so that beaches might be closed down or hot areas placed off limits. Richie took part in the operational planning for each shot, along with the Fallout Plot Unit and gave the General a picture of the risks involved and precautions that needed to be taken.

There was another job the RadSafe Office did which involved the actual tracking of the movement of the nuclear cloud immediately after the detonation. This was done, on one hand, with the weather radar, since the cloud showed up on the scope as it moved across the lagoon or out to sea. The Radsafe Office tracked it too, using a more close-in approach by directing U.S. Navy P2V Neptunes toward the general vicinity of the radioactive particles, invisible to both radar and the human eye, raining down at the edge of the moving cloud. They would nip in and out of the edges of this moving curtain at a few thousand feet -just as we had done in Nevada- until we could say that the lagoon was clear, and the instrument retrieval crews could move in by helicopter and boat. These somewhat risky measures were taken because the quicker the instruments could be retrieved, the more worthwhile the quickly decaying data they recorded would be.

After the lagoon was cleared, the P2V's would take up a course along the edge of the fallout area, on barrier patrol, to keep the uninformed or overly complacent mariners out of danger. The procedure was cumbersome; first Richie established contact with the weather radar people immediately after detonation to get the picture of the general cloud movement. Then he would get the control tower on an open phone line and pass instructions through them to the P2V which had come up from Kwajelein and would be orbiting on standby.

The instructions Richie passed through the tower required that the P2V fly a particular course or head toward a particular island on the atoll until his gamma meter started to climb. Then he would turn off and Richie would vector him to get him behind the retreating cloud so he would know when it cleared the lagoon. It took some time to get accustomed to the procedure, but after I watched a few times, Richie sat me in the seat and I inherited the job. Before long, I would sit in the seat and listen to the countdown, and when the thing went off, I would step outside for a moment to gaze at the mushroom in feigned wonderment, and to no one in particular, I would make mad scientist motions and say, "Its mine! Mine! All mine!" And then I would get back into my chair and get to work.

There were also ground stations with radiation monitors scattered throughout the test area, and readings from them were sent to the Radsafe Office to help track the cloud.

We were now running through the list of shots, all shapes and sizes, big and small, on barges, on atoll islands, under the water. In between exercises, I was able to make myself at home in the aluminized metal barracks, with air conditioning provided by sea breezes which came through the large openings under the eaves. We weren't very crowded, with one or two people per enclosure -you really couldn't call it a room- and you put up with it with the idea that it wouldn't last forever. There were two islands on the atoll that housed most of the military and scientific people; Enewetak, where the main airfield and most of the barracks, administrative buildings and recreational facilities were located; and Parry Island, just north of Enewetak, where the Commander of JTF-7 had his headquarters. As a member of the Radsafe Office, I was billeted on Parry Island, along with the other big shots, while the rest of our crew was put up at Enewetak.

The food on both islands was surprisingly good; apparently the idea was that there wasn't too much you can do to keep a bunch of bright and hard-working people happy on an atoll that wasn't illegal, immoral or imperiled discipline, but food might keep up the old morale. It is not that we had chefs who carved little flowers out of carrot slices to dress up the mess tray, but we did have steaks and prime ribs occasionally.

Once in a while, Richie would get the urge to wander out among the coral outcrops along the beach just after dark to collect sea-life specimens for radiological examination, and he would take me along with him. With rubber-soled shoes, heavy rubber gloves and five-celled flashlights, we would plod through the shallow water, heads down, intent on our prey. We ignored the small eels, the minnows, the starfish and sea urchins until there it was, the reddish-blue outline faintly visible in the flashlight's glow. You had to keep the light still and straight on top so that the prey would not surge backward and away. Then you positioned your free hand over the outline and paused, then plunged it down to grasp the creature around the main body and pin it to the bottom so that its spiny legs and slashing tail would not cut you. The strength of it surprised you as it squirmed and tried to shake itself free, but you learned to hold on tight and lift that gorgeous spiny lobster out of the water and work it into a sack you brought along. Three pounds, four pounds; they were all a perfect size for the process they would soon undergo.

The best place to perform this process was the Admiral's mess, which was called that because it was built during a previous test series when the JTF commander was a Navy man. Once Richie and I had passed a Geiger-Muller probe over the specimens -which seldom turned up more than a few pops in the earphones- the experiment was placed in the hands of the mess cooks, whose eyes would light up at the sight of our catch.

We made sure that a decent specimen was laid aside for the General, then Richie and I and the cooks and mess boys all took our pick. After that, they were up for grabs, but the Admiral's Mess membership -which certainly did not include us- was small enough so that there were enough to go around. We never did find a lobster that flunked the test.

There were other entertainments, like an occasional flight down to Kwajelein to do some shopping at the Base Exchange or, back at Parry, the nightly movies on a screen outdoors not far from the water's edge. The same films were occasionally repeated due to a lapse in logistics and, once in a while, the program was called off because a slight dusting of fallout from a cloud that had failed to move out completely made it wiser to stay under roof.

Now here came Dr. Edward Teller himself, his head bobbing up and down as he gimped along the duckboards down the headquarters street on his artificial foot. He seemed greatly pre-occupied, certainly not thinking about the time when he was twenty years old and a student in Germany when he jumped from a still-moving street car and slipped under its wheels. There was a lot more to think about than that accident, for now he was once more at the proving grounds, anxious to see if the tests would provide answers to new questions which had arisen.

An old question -whether America had the will and courage to continue testing and not leave the field to the Russians had been answered earlier at the urging of Teller and others like him. Looking back, it seems as though Teller, for a moment, carried the entire burden of man's demand for freedom on his shoulders. What if he had failed ? What do we owe this man?

Teller had been greatly disturbed concerning the fallout accident which had muddied the success of BRAVO, the bomb with "too much paprika." But he had not been deterred and had, in fact, continued in his efforts to increase human control over the thermonuclear beast. And so, at Enewetak, he peered over people's shoulders, asked penetrating questions, and came to his conclusions. He stayed there for some time and found answers to many of his questions. The solution to one problem, however, eluded his grasp. It was an experiment in mathematical probabilities called Liar's dice which was conducted in the Admiral's Mess before dinner and in which the loser bought the drinks. He diligently applied his brilliant mind to the task, but apparently never won a game.

There were other well known scientific and political figures, and even the occasional celebrity who showed up at Enewetak, or had to be picked up at Kwaj or Honolulu. One time, most of the Atomic Energy Commission arrived, and since they were designated in legislation as the body responsible for nuclear weapons development, rose petals were strewn in the paths they walked.

After they had observed an exercise, the General piled them into his C-54 and we took them down to the atoll of Majuro. The trip was obviously intended as an R&R outing for people who had been grappling with weighty matters for a long time. So we flew for about four hours to the southeast, deep into the central Pacific Ocean, overhead Kwajelein, past Namu and Ailinglapalap atolls and then to the destination in the southern Marshall Islands. Majuro was about halfway down to Tarawa, which is almost on the Equator, where the U.S. Marines wrote the book on bloody amphibious landings when their landing craft got hung up on reefs on the way in, and where the survivors prevailed over the Japanese defenders.

Amin and Bill made their approach alongside an east-west line of towering cumulonimbus which marked the seasonal position of the inter-tropical front. Although it was early afternoon, the looming clouds blocked most of the sunlight and we landed in the damp, brooding gloom. I expected to see some hula dancers, but as the flight steward swung the door open, the oompah band sound of Ach du Lieber Augustin came wafting up from the flight line. They certainly cheered things up; a bunch of bright-eyed young boys in white shirts and black slacks, their cheeks puffed out as they piped the Commission and the General down to the ramp.

We were met by the island dignitaries and were given a bus ride to a picnic area which had been cleared of some of the island's lush vegetation, under some towering palms. There were tables set up with food and lots of cold beer. The Commissioners looked a little like fish out of water for they hadn't brought along the official picnic uniform, which was short pants, a Hawaiian shirt and go-aheads. They managed to unbend enough to take off their suit-coats and ties and roll up their sleeves in order to pitch some horseshoes or just sit around with a beer.

The flightcrew had to be satisfied with Cokes and ping pong, and when we were challenged by some of the locals, we were wiped out so badly I began to get this exasperated look on my face. One of the victors, a wiry little guy with lightning reflexes looked at me as he paused, his racket held up ready for the serve. "Hah! Maybe you guys get too much fallout!" he said.

The General said he wanted to get back to Enewetak before dark so we climbed into the bus and rode back out to the airport. Without benefit of the oompah band we climbed aboard the old reliable tub and we took off and headed northwest. The ITC had firmed up and we couldn't find a hole to slip through on the climb-out so we plunged in and were thrust upward and then down, the big raindrops splattering against the windshield. We popped out the other side into a bowl of Pacific emptiness, the faint tracings of the scattered atolls below reaching toward the horizon where the red sun hung, poised, ready to drop down for the night.

I doubt if the oompah band had anything to do with it, but there must have been something about the General and the way he ran JTF-7 that impressed the Commissioners. Not long after Operation Hardtack was over and we had all returned to the U.S., they appointed General Luedecke General Manager of the Atomic Energy Commission.

The sandbags were being piled up around buildings which had a lifetime requirement beyond the Hardtack series, like the LORAN navigation transmitter, and other facilities. Large cables were strung in a great web from the top of the water tower to anchoring points around it, and valuable equipment was moved around out of the reach of a possible base surge tidal wave across the lagoon which might be caused by a large detonation. Barracks roofs which were broadside to the blast direction had anchored cables attached to the eaves to keep the roofs from flying off into the ocean.

The expected big blast was exercise Oak. The chief scientific personage in JTF-7, Dr. William Ogle, who was the General's deputy, apparently was confident that another Bravo overshoot would not happen. In fact, sufficient confidence had been built so that Oak was to be detonated at Enewetak rather than Bikini, which had previously been used for the big megatonners. The device was assembled in a building in a super secure area not far from the Radsafe office where I worked. It would be installed on a shot barge which would be towed out and anchored to the reef directly across the lagoon from Enewetak and Parry Islands, about twenty short miles away. When the thing went off, the shot barge would go with it, along with some of the ocean and a chunk of the reef.

There was not much sense in setting off such expensive, powerful and dangerous mechanisms unless every bit of information possible was recorded in a usable form during and after the detonation. First priority was placed on the data concerning the experimental aspects of the test which was needed by the AEC. The data would confirm whether or not some scien-

413

tist's or engineer's idea had worked or not. Then there were the diagnostic tests which involved the way the nuclear event developed from the first instant of the detonation, through the intricate, much-quicker-than-a-blink millionths of a second firing sequence, through to the horrendous blast and fireball.

Some of the diagnostic data-gathering used simple means: they often ran a long pipe right into the bomb case, with the other end attached to a recording device located beyond the crater area, buried and protected so that it would survive. Then they got the air sampling crews -crewdogs of the first order- briefed on where and when they were to enter the mushroom cloud to bring back some of the deadly debris.

Finally, the military aspects were considered, which involved the way in which the heat, blast and radioactivity would affect any conceivable aspect of military operations. But although the military were last in line, it seems obvious that the thousands of men and all the intricate machinery would not have been sent to these small atoll islands far out in the Pacific Ocean, with all the risk and expense involved unless the security of the country would be greatly improved as a result.

Now the detonation of Oak came closer as the shot barge was tethered at a carefully surveyed point, about four miles southwest of Bokoluo Island. As in the past, very ingenious methods were used to install the instruments so that they could get the necessary information without being destroyed themselves, and so that they could be located and retrieved afterward.

Measurements of the power of the explosion were not automatically easy to get. It wasn't the amount of noise, or the way the ground shook that mattered. An important indicator was the size of the fireball that gave an idea of the yield, along with measurements of the optical and thermal energy which blasted outward from the detonation. Very high speed cameras on strategically placed photo towers were aimed toward surface zero to record the size of the fireball and the speed with which it developed. We got to look at some of these films, and after a while, as we watched the pinpoints of light expand, in slow motion, into perfectly round orange discs you got to thinking, "You see one fireball, you've seen them all."

414

Now came the countdown, and at 730 AM, Oak was detonated, all 9 megatons of it, and even now, after all of the shots I had witnessed before, the thing held my mind in its grip. The white light exploded into being and rose in intensity until even the almost opaque goggles we were wearing could not hide the brilliance. You could feel the force of it on your face as it held its peak for what seemed like forever. But once more the Archangels triumphed over Lucifer, who had, again, challenged the sun with his ungodly morning light.

"The world is still here," I thought, as the light faded so that we could take off the goggles and watch the fireball as it rose grandly and inexorably upward to around 80,000 feet in perhaps two minutes, and tower over the world. The Fallout Prediction Unit had predicted that the cloud and all of the fallout would move to the northwest and harmlessly out to sea. As I returned to the RadSafe office and the P2V's and I began doing our thing, we could see that they were right.

The Neptunes took some nips at the rear end of the curtain of fallout as it moved off, and, just to make sure because of the size of Oak, some extra sweeps were made. Then the lagoon was reopened and the choppers moved in to take readings near ground level around some of the data-gathering sites and then the instrument retrieval process began. What a sight it must have been that greeted the pilots of Hotshot ll, or 12, or one of the others, or the sampler controller in call-sign Opium as they climbed their twin-jet B-57's higher and higher alongside the stupendous mushroom.

As the great ball rose, the grey-white cloud that surrounded it roiled upward and outward as it began to slowly flatten out. Now Opium and the Hotshots, along with the people in Watchdog, a big B-52, could survey the entire grand and terrible scene from their own great height; the still roiling mushroom cloud, the white veil of ice crystals which capped it, the great, fat stem through which the debris was sucked upward. The size of it; everything was measured not in feet, or in thousands of feet, but in miles.

Then Opium gave the word and the Hotshots peeled off and headed in, not directly at the fireball's heart where they would have been burned to a crisp, but at the lower bulge where much of the airborne debris collected. Once in, they scooped up the radioactive particles into their wingtip pods and opened up evacuated bottles mounted on the fuselage to suck in some of the air. Then they came back out, no doubt wondering how effectively their cockpit shielding was protecting them. Some of the B-57's, the F-models, were specially modified with extra-long wings to get them to high altitudes, up above 60,000 feet. The wings were so long that they drooped almost to the ground when they were parked. But give it a little airspeed on takeoff, and the wings straightened out like an awakened eagle, eager to haul the pressure-suited two-man crew up to where the daytime sky begins to turn dark.

The Hotshots would come back down to land and taxi to the decontamination area to get washed down. When the gamma got down to a reasonable level, the aircrewmen would be lifted out of the cockpits with a cherry-picker and the retrieval ground crew would move to a point not closer than 25 feet from either pod. Then, one of the crew would gingerly approach the wing pod with a four-foot long clipper and cut a retaining wire on the sample compartment. Then he would move back, and another man would approach with a nine-foot pole and lift the filter assembly out and deposit it into a shielded holder. He would move back and a third person would move in and insert another long pole into the filter assembly and roll the filter paper around the end of it. Then he would take the roll of filter paper to a lead-lined pig and shove it in to be carried away for analysis.

The hot sample was handled like a big, poisonous snake for good reasons. The radioactive dose which the retrieval crew was permitted to receive was 10 Roentgens, after which they had to be relieved from that duty. The sample usually drove a meter placed within a foot of it to 100 Roentgens per hour, which meant that the usefulness of a man who got that close would be wiped out in six minutes. Of course, it wouldn't do his health a lot of good either. As for the air sampling crews, they were permitted to accumulate a dose of 20 Roentgens, because they were so brave and handsome.

Not long after Oak, Richie checked out one of the L-20's, a light single-engined courier plane and we went out for a low-altitude survey of the atoll. We flew around it clockwise, and

416

we noted that there wasn't much to see in the way of effects on the ring of islands, most of which rose hardly ten feet above the surface of the ocean. We were approaching surface zero for the Oak shot when suddenly Richie spotted something. He brought the L-20 around and down a little further as we peered into the hole in the reef where Oak had detonated.

"There!" he said, pointing slightly forward, and then my eyes too caught the movement of some giant sea turtles as they flippered along just underneath the surface. We had no way of knowing whether they were just passing by, or were revisiting a slightly rearranged playground. You might think they would be scared off permanently, but perhaps it worked the other way. Maybe they knew that after each blast they could expect to find tons of food which they could leisurely pick off, food which had showered down from the sky after being boiled, fried, x-rayed or neutron-bombarded to a proper turn. I can imagine them, today, sitting around on some sandy spot on the bottom of the lagoon on a lazy Sunday afternoon, talking about the good old days when, after the big boom, all those delicacies would come raining down and keep them busy eating for weeks.

One day, Bill called me from the main island and told me that a Special Air Missions flight was due to arrive with some VIP's and he thought it would be great to have lunch with the crew. I told him I would meet him at the Enewetak mess hall and I took the ferry over. The Special Air Missions crew was part of the 1254th Air Transport Group which was located at the Washington National Airport. The Group had two flight squadrons, one of which flew twin engined aircraft around the U.S., and the other which operated four-engined long range aircraft anywhere in the world. The crew we were to meet was assigned to the latter organization.

To be assigned to SAM as a pilot, navigator, maintenance man, whatever, you were considered to have arrived at the top of your profession. The presidential aircraft was attached to the Group and the crews were almost always drawn from its ranks. If you can think of a world figure in the era from World War II to today; the Eisenhowers, Churchills and so on, the squadron or one of its predecessors more than likely had them aboard, or brought someone to meet with them.

417

For some time I had the idea in back of my mind that assignment to the SAM squadron would be a great way to finish up my twenty years. But it was a difficult organization to get into. The Military Air Transport Service, the parent Headquarters had an application procedure, but the 1254th didn't pay too much attention to it. Instead, when a vacancy was expected to come up, they looked around at crewdogs who had plenty of flying time and had worked their way up to become a crewmember for some General or made a reputation in some other way. The selection process was that simple; the few people who ran the operational end of the squadron found somebody they thought was suitable and offered him the job. I didn't know it at the time, but Joe Sheehan, the Major in command of the crew we would meet, who was also the SAM operations officer, could find a man he thought was qualified and give him a job on the spot.

We met Sheehan and his crew and had a pleasant lunch which was a little hurried because they would be heading back to the U.S. in an hour or two. Bill and I did manage to nudge the conversation over into the matter of SAM vacancies without seeming too eager and after a few minutes, Sheehan looked over at me and asked, "If we get to need a navigator, would you be interested?" It was no time to be nonchalant.

"You're damn right!" I said. Then they got up and left.

The winds at the proving grounds kept blowing in the right direction most of the time and we were running down the list of detonations; Oak, Hickory, Sequoia, Cedar and so on. The two underwater shots had gone off sometime before Oak, and had provided data on the effects of underwater detonations on destroyers, submarines, mines and surface ships. Both shots were conducted not too far from us near the southern edge of the atoll, and a lot of the pre-shot work normally done by workers on the surface had to be done by scuba divers. On one of the shots -Wahoo- a manned submarine was submerged to periscope depth and positioned a mere 18,000 feet -a little more than 3 miles- from the detonation site.

As operation HARDTACK was nearing its end, the Task Force began to make preparations for the two rocket-mounted shots, Teak and Orange, originally scheduled for Bikini early in the program. The launches had been postponed when the General received a report from Los Alamos with an estimate of hazards to natives on the surrounding atolls which caused him to change his plans. This time the dangers, if the shots went off as planned, involved not fallout, but eye damage. The fireballs would be too far from earth to stir up a radioactive dust cloud; however, both shots were in the megaton range, and the intense light from the high altitude shots could cause a serious problem. A number of inhabited atolls in the area were found in the study to be within the circle of hazard in which permanent retinal damage could occur to an unsuspecting observer. Disciplined Hardtack people could be ordered to take the necessary precautions to protect their eyes, but locating all of the natives and getting them to cover their eyes at the right instant seemed impossible. The decision was made to move both shots to Johnston Island, a tiny spot of land at a distance from Honolulu -more than 700 miles- which would put the entire hazardous area at surface level over open ocean.

A Redstone rocket had been used earlier in the year to launch the first U.S. satellite, Explorer I. Two of those rockets had originally been set up at Bikini for Teak and Orange, megaton range warheads ready to be installed, the launch crew trained, drilled and ready to light the fuse. Now, with the decision to move the launches to Johnston, they would be delayed. Teak and Orange were put on the back burners of our minds as the Task Force ran through the rest of program.

July on the Pacific atoll of Enewetak. Doesn't that conjure up a mental image of blue sky, sandy beaches and ocean breezes? Well, it shouldn't. We had the blue sky and the breezes all right, but beaches for swimming, except for one on the main island, were off limits. Sunbathing was okay anywhere, but at Enewetak or Parry in July, just walking from the office to the mess hall could get you some suntan, along with a little bit of gamma thrown in. The prohibition was caused not by the slight radioactivity in the water, but with things like Stonefish, which were difficult to distinguish from a rock on the sea bottom and which flicked a poisonous barb from its back if you stepped on it. There were also turkey fish, which could brush you with highly poisonous stingers on their dorsal hump. Most of all, we

419

worried about a small, innocent-looking conical shell which contained a creature which could inflict a sting with some of the most deadly natural poison known to man.

With threats like these, we didn't have much time to think about the Moray eels and barracuda which had been spotted from time to time. Because of these dangerous creatures, and because there were uncharted undertows and unexpected drop-offs, all swimming was limited to one patrolled beach on the main island of Enewetak. We all had swim fins and snorkel tubes and we all used them mostly, I presume, to make sure we had the means to see and avoid the hazardous beasts.

One day, like a bolt out of the blue, Amin George called and told us to get the airplane ready to take General Luedecke and some of the staff all the way across the Pacific, via Honolulu, via San Francisco, across the U.S. to the Kennedy Space Center at Cape Canaveral in Florida. We had to get there in time for a scheduled launch of a Redstone rocket, and although Bill and I were not told of the reason for the trip, it obviously had some important bearing on Teak and Orange.

Cris was waiting at the Travis Air Force Base air terminal as we all trooped in and we had a big welcoming scene. I introduced her to General Luedecke and to Dr. Ogle, the JTF-7 Chief Scientist, who was standing next to the General. "Oh, you must be the flight surgeon..." she started to say, assuming his title was the medical kind. He picked up on it right away and put on a serious scowl.

"Yes, and I'm sorry to say we can't give John any time off in San Francisco. This long trip has given him flight fatigue and he won't be able to get any rest here." She looked shocked but then we all laughed as I explained the joke.

As I found my bag and we walked out to the car, I told her that we were not scheduled to leave Travis for three days and I was on my own until then. I had a happy reunion with Holly and that great mother-in-law of mine, then Cris and I spent some time poking around San Francisco.

Then we got into Fruffy's car and took off to spend a few days in a cabin on the north shore of Lake Tahoe. I had forgotten about that curious aspect of Lake Tahoe's water, that even in summer the water temperature could be cold enough to chill your wine in short order. I stepped up to the dock in front of the cabin and dove in, failing to notice that I was being watched with some curiosity. You may recall one of Walt Disney's cartoons where Pluto dives from a diving board into ice-cold water, and as soon as his nose hits the surface, he does a U-turn in midair and leaps back onto the board and stands there with his teeth chattering. Of course, I couldn't do a U-turn, but I was back up on the dock just as quickly and with my teeth chattering just as hard. "My blood is thinned out from Enewetak," I claimed, wrapping myself in a big towel.

It didn't take long, however, to get used to the mountain air and the gentler sun, whose rays were not avoided as they were on the atoll. We stretched out on beach chairs on the dock dozing, drinking it all in. Cris looked better than ever to me after my several months of monastic existence at the proving grounds, where women could be landed only if the aircraft in which they travelled encountered some emergency. And then they had to leave on the next airplane so that they would be exposed to the area's radioactivity as little as possible.

The days passed by in a blink, and before I knew it, Amin and Bill were landing us at Canaveral. The crew had no function to perform this time except to sit around and wait for the General to finish his business. There wasn't much to do in the way of sightseeing then since Canaveral was in a primitive state. Today's tour is a wonder, from the great Titan rocket mock-up lying on it's side, to all of the launch pads for the now historical departures for earth orbits and then the moon. You can see the pads today, many of them abandoned and decrepit, derelicts left behind in a frantic effort to catch up with the Russian space effort. Most of those pads were not even a glimmer in some engineer's mind when we came there for the Redstone launch.

I have said before that if you get around enough and get involved in what's going on in the world, you will, usually by accident, bump into the people who are making things happen. And so, on the day of the launch on our way down to breakfast in our elevator, the door opened on the way down and who was standing there, big as life, but Wernher von Braun, the rocket scientist. He was a large man, with square-cut, Germanic good looks, and he looked hesitant when he saw that the elevator was crowded with passengers, but we pressed back to make room. I was standing in the way and he looked at me, then at my necktie, approvingly, I thought.

When I was able to move over he stepped in and as I deftly pressed the "door close" button, we made our journey together, Wernher and I, down to the lobby where a crowd of colleagues and reporters awaited him. He strode out into the admiring multitude to answer questions and receive congratulations on the recent progress he had been demonstrating concerning the next generation of U.S. rockets after Redstone. It had been less than six months since a Redstone had launched the first U.S. satellite but now von Braun likened it to a Model T Ford when compared to the Cadillacs which would be launched soon.

The Redstone went chug-chugging off into space that same evening and it demonstrated the launch reliability which the Atomic Energy Commission, the Department of Defense and the General all thought were needed to hurl some H-bombs into high altitudes. All we could see after the launch was the quick, periodic blink of a strobe light mounted on the rocket as it rose and then programmed itself downrange, and was quickly gone.

There were still some shots left to be completed at Bikini and Enewetak when we returned and we settled back into the routine to get them over with. One of the last tests, Pine, had gone off with apparent perfection and I had just completed a little sketch of the cloud's movement across and away from the atoll which was to be included in the record. General Luedecke came walking in and quickly put us at ease and sat down across the table from us. He was making the rounds to thank the troops for their good work, but there seemed to be a little bit of apprehension in his manner.

Pine was the last detonation which, if the winds didn't blow as predicted, could result in a fallout incident involving natives on the surrounding atolls. "If we can get through this one we'll be home free," he said, shaking his head. The movement of time and the disappearance of the last fallout problem was not happening fast enough for him. It was obvious that, of all the things the General had to think about, the possibility of dusting the natives or his own people nagged him the most.

I knew he had already gotten the cloud tracking report from the weather radar people, but he was still sweating it, so how do you cheer up a General? Richie wasn't there so I had to do the talking. I passed my sketch over to him and said, "General, this has been the least threatening shot of all. The winds at all the levels have moved the stuff straight out to the northwest. It'll all be down before it could get to Siberia." He looked at the sketch for a moment, then put it down.

"Yes, I know it looks good. I just hope it stays that way." We all got up when he did. "Are you and Bill ready to take me to Johnston Island?" he asked. "Yes sir. Anytime you say."

Johnston Island is about as small as an island can be and still have a runway big enough to handle large aircraft. "You can spit right across it if the wind's right!" said somebody as Amin and Bill lined up the C-54 on the approach and then put it on the ground.

The place certainly looked different than it had the times I had arrived there before. The Redstone gantry loomed up not too far off the runway on one side, and a series of sample collecting rockets were lined up and ready to launch along the other side. It had a greatly crowded look, as you might expect with more than a thousand people milling around, tending to the various projects which operation Teak involved. Some of them were billeted aboard some of the ships, but to this day, I can't imagine where they put all of those people.

Except for 175 men, everyone would be evacuated the day before the launch with most of them being lightered out to the aircraft carrier Boxer, which would take up a position about 60 miles northeast of the island, toward Honolulu. The stay-behinds would spend launch-time in the launch bunker, 350 feet from the launch point, or under ground level in the basements of the Headquarters and hospital buildings about a 1000 feet away. Some of the hardier souls would tough it out in small shelters also about 1000 feet away or on Sand island, a minute spit of land a mile away. The radar tracking ship Acania would remain anchored just within the reef and not far from surface zero, its big dish ready to swivel up to follow the rocket.

423

General Luedecke decided that the place for him during this very momentous event was not on the Boxer or in Honolulu, but in the launch bunker. It must have taken surpassing trust in the reliability of the devices with which he had been provided and in the competency of the people who dealt with them to take his position, along with the launch personnel, only several hundred feet from the Redstone. Concrete walls or not, the bunker seemed to be almost within touching distance of a skyward-pointing vehicle full of explosive fuel and topped with a device which had the power to instantly transform Johnston Island and the living bone and flesh on it into a number of radioactive isotopes and chemical components.

The Redstone and the sampler rockets were not the only vehicles to be launched. Two Lockheed P2V Neptunes also remained behind, with one expected to take off at launch plus 30 minutes and the other kept behind as a spare. The crew was underground and would need to scramble to get to the primary P2V and get it off within the allotted half-hour. Then it had to begin to locate an instrument pod which the Redstone would release just before detonation, about 3 minutes after launch. The Neptune would also try to track down the sampler rocket nose cones which, like the instrument pod, would be equipped with radio beacons, flashing lights and, if the search dragged into daylight, marker dye. Once they located the pod or the rocket cones, they would direct surface vessels to retrieve them.

Before we left Enewetak, Col. Richie briefed me on how the radiological safety problems were being viewed, and this is what they looked like. First, it was a foregone conclusion that if the megaton range warhead went off on the launch pad in compliance with Murphy's Law, there wasn't too much to talk about. A good part of Johnston Island, the Acania and all of the 175 people would be gone. A substantial problem concerning fallout might also have to be dealt with in this case, so the wind had to cooperate to blow the cloud anywhere but towards the Hawaiian Islands. However, given the installation of safety devices on top of safety devices, the possibility of such an event was considered negligible.

Next was the possibility of a simple launch failure, where nothing happened except that the rocket fizzled out. In this case, all that was needed was to fix the Redstone or get another one and try again. Another notch up the ladder was a catastrophic launch failure on the pad, where everything detonated except the nuclear material. This would result in a radioactive mess of the first order, with highly dangerous debris scattered around that had to be cleaned up before most of those at Johnston could move out of their shelters. Then there might be a launch that got off the ground and went partially or all the way on its flight, but the warhead was a dud. This posed an interesting problem, like when we were kids with big firecrackers on the 4th of July that failed to go off. In the case of a rare fizzled cherry bomb or one of the gigantic 5-inch salutes the older kids threw into the street, you waited for a while and looked for signs of activity in the fuse, then you poked it with a stick for a while until you overcame your good sense and picked it up. The idea of a dud megaton range warhead in the local waters or on the island itself sounded pretty wild, but the experts appeared to consider that to be a manageable problem and not too big a fuss was made over the possibility.

Finally, there was the possibility of a launch that went off course. The launch crew was fully trained to handle a problem of this kind, which involved pushing the rocket destruct button and then having someone go looking for the pieces. The Redstone, of course, could be destroyed in flight without detonating the warhead. None of these problems had any real potential for endangering anyone except those involved in the launch process. The Redstone had only enough fuel for a 3-minute ascent to 250,000 feet -about 50 miles- so if it did go off course, it couldn't go very far.

But the problem which had caused the launch to be moved to Johnston Island -damaging retinas in the eyes of people who unknowingly looked toward the high altitude blast when it went off- was studied one more time by Richie. The radius of the circle in which damage could occur expanded with altitude, so we looked for points of higher elevation on the Hawaiian chain which might be populated even temporarily and be at risk, but no real problems were found. As a precaution, however, residents on the big island of Hawaii living at the higher elevations were issued dark goggles.

There was one more problem, one which the planners

agonized over as much as any other. It involved not people, or radioactivity or eye damage, but birds. There was a flock of terns which inhabited Sand Island, a tiny spot of land in the lagoon. After weeks of study, it was decided to rig up a series of of pipes, pumps and spray heads over the small area. A few seconds before detonation, clouds of water would be sprayed above the terns to attenuate the intense light and whatever heat that might reach the ground. To further reduce these effects, the Redstone was programmed to veer away to a point several miles from Johnston to increase the atmospheric path between the explosion and the Island.

Since the C-54 would be in the way on Johnston Island, we brought it to Hickam. I must admit that Bill and I didn't have any real feel for the problems that were being overcome at the launch site as we sat on a hotel balcony at Waikiki Beach, our feet up on the rail and sipping on a beer.

We were waiting for midnight on the 31st of July and watching for some effect of the first megaton range warhead to be detonated aboard a rocket. A small device had been exploded aboard a low altitude rocket at the Nevada proving ground some time before, but this was the big stuff. Would it work? And what if it didn't and the Russians, who were ahead of us in rocket development, succeeded?

Thirteen minutes before midnight the rocket was launched and three minutes later, the warhead was detonated. People on Honolulu with good vantage points could see a great yellow flash and then a reflection of the fireball that persisted for many minutes. There were reports of a strange phenomenon involving a reddish bubble that expanded from the detonation point and became larger and larger, and after forty minutes, passed its edge over observers watching from the island of Maui, more than 800 miles away from ground zero.

What I myself saw was sort of an auroral display, nowhere near as bright as those I had seen over Iceland or northern Greenland, and not in quite the same form. There seemed to be pale violet arcs which spanned a great reach of the sky and persisted for many minutes, then faded into the darkness.

As expected, the dispersion of a layer of highly radioactive debris from the device itself at high altitude interacted with the ionized layers of the upper atmosphere. These layers normally reflect radio waves and bounce them outward in ever-increasing circles from the transmitter, so that radio communications can be carried great distances. The interaction screwed up this process so that radio communications with Australia were blacked out for 9 hours, and air traffic control communications between the U.S. and Honolulu suffered a lesser outage.

The view of the Teak shot that Bill and I and the people on the Hawaiian Chain had was of a remote event, a not very threatening curiosity. At Johnston Island it was a little different. For those in the launch bunker, there was a very tense moment when, a short time after lift off, it became obvious that the programmed path would not be followed. Instead, the rocket went straight up, and in the few seconds available for the launch crew to make a decision, they decided to go ahead with the detonation. As the time quickly wound down, the General and some of the crew stepped out of the bunker for a better view. Most of the immediate peril had passed by as the Redstone gained height and there was only the light and heat to contend with.

As General Luedecke reached up to make sure his nearly opaque goggles were on tight, the H-bomb went off. There was the intensity of light like no other, but then the heat reached them, from fifty miles away. Scattered pieces of trash on the ground around them ignited and started to burn. He felt something on his bare arms, and was amazed, as he was able to remove his goggles, to see that the hairs were singed off. And in the fading light, he could look over to Sand Island and see that the spray system was working as planned. Fortunately, the terns escaped unharmed.

The detonation of the Orange warhead, another megaton range device, took place eleven days later, this time at a half hour before midnight, at the height of about 25 miles. For the observers in the Hawaiian Islands, the resultant display was a disappointment, as only a weak yellow flash was visible.

With Teak and Orange, we had crossed the threshold into the never-never land of pushbutton annihilation. And what did

427

a man like me, one of the worker bees at the nuclear weapons proving grounds think of all this? First, I could look around me at the people at Enewetak and know they were not a bunch of mindless robots like those jump-suited zombies in a James Bond film, working to blow up the world. They were a dedicated and patriotic group who knew what the stakes were if they failed. They all knew that the nuclear struggle had started many years before, not with the Soviets, but the Germans in World War II.

The struggle included, as one of its early milestones, an attack by British and Norwegian commandos on a heavy water plant at Rjuken, Norway. The factory in the German-occupied country was the only source of such material available to the Germans for their A-bomb research. The commandos parachuted into the mountainous site and blew up the heavy water storage tanks. But the plant was quickly rebuilt and in November 1943, 160 Eighth Air Force B-17's and B-24's, including 18 Liberators from Wendling bombed the place and put it out of action for good.

The Germans were able to salvage some of the already-produced heavy water and tried to ship it back to Germany, but the Allied derring-do persisted, and it was sabotaged when a ferry boat on which it was being carried was sunk. They never got the heavy water and never got their program going. What if......

VI

BOOK SIX

SAM FOX

*Previous Page: SAMFOX is the radio call sign for the
USAF Special Air Mission Wing.
This wing transports the President of the
United States around the world.*

18

CARAMBA! ITS THE SAMBA!

I LOOKED AT THE ENVELOPE with unbelieving eyes. The return address of the 1254th Air Transport Group was printed on the upper left hand corner of the white, legal-size envelope and my name had been printed in blue ink across it's face. Was this a request for information of some kind, or perhaps instructions for an interview which could lead to my joining this famous organization? I had just arrived at Bolling Air Force Base after severing connections with Joint Task Force Seven at Arlington Hall Station. I had turned in my Top Secret badge, dosimeter, flying equipment receipts and had jumped through all the other bureaucratic hoops required to be cleared to leave one station and travel to another.

The Adjutant at Bolling, a harried Major who sat in the middle of a stream of paperwork which he tried to control as it swirled around him looked up at me. "Matt? Matt?" No, I don't have any orders sending you back to Charleston," he said. "I'll have to call them to see what they want to do with you. Could you come back in a couple of hours?" The poor guy had just taken a six-inch stack of papers out of his In-Box and he was checking the routing symbols on each document as his Tech Sergeant assistant stood by. I turned to leave and was halfway to the door when he called out, "Wait a minute! I do have something for you! I just remembered! You were on the road so I held it here." He pulled open his desk drawer and took out the envelope which he handed to me.

It was this envelope which I opened with quivering hands, and which I found to contain not just a request for information but an actual set of orders assigning me to the 1254th Air Transport Group in Washington, at National Airport. I was further assigned to the 1298th Special Air Missions Squadron, effective immediately. I walked out of the big Bolling Headquarters building into the afternoon sunshine, my mind bouncing back and forth between shock and euphoria.

"Do I really want this?" was the first thought that settled on my mind. I had always worked very hard at being the best navigator I could be and now I would have to work even harder. Then my mind calmed a bit and I knew what the answer was; Yes, I certainly wanted it and I felt ready for it. But what had I done, I wondered, to cause this nice surprise to be dropped into my lap?

The flights I would now take part in would seldom involve routine military or diplomatic business. Instead, I would be part of a crew flying movers and shakers around the globe to take part in important events, all to the delicate minuet of protocol. We would bring the great, the near-great and the would-be great to occasions where history might be made. The squadron had a phenomenal safety record; it had never had an accident, or even scratched a customer, and I would join those who dreaded the idea of being the person responsible for cutting the string.

I climbed into the Chevy and drove over to the transient family quarters to give the news to Cris. She and Holly were taking an afternoon nap and I had to awaken her to give her the word. She was too groggy to have much of a reaction at first, but then it started to sink in that we would not be going back to Charleston, that we would stay in Washington instead.

I decided to wait a few days before I checked into the new organization so that Cris and I could do a little sightseeing. Once I signed in, there was no telling how much spare time I would have for such things. Cris had already visited some of the attractions in town so we made the trip to Mount Vernon, and poked around some of the other outlying tourist sights. On the way back, I told Cris I wanted to visit the Pentagon in the next day or so to look at my personnel file, particularly the evaluations of my performance, and she asked to come along.

I had been to the Puzzle Palace a number of times and had always gotten the same reaction when I visited this brooding Gibraltar of a building. It was not quite a fortress and certainly not an ordinary office building, perhaps a combination of both. As a military man, the place made me nervous because it was full of people who had firm control over my activities and my well-being. Some one there could send me to war or promote me or turn my promotion down or put me on the street in the blink of an eye.

The Pentagon visit took place while we were still at the transient family quarters at Bolling, before we found a place of our own. I learned that a motor launch was operated by the Air Force on a schedule between the air base and the Pentagon, both of which border on the Potomac. Presumably, the boat was operated to keep some means of transportation available in the event the Potomac bridges were blocked, which happened frequently. The Woodrow Wilson bridge further south was still on some bridge designer's drawing boards.

We climbed aboard the launch in the hazy sunshine of a late summer morning and headed northward up the Potomac, enjoying the breeze and looking at the sights as the boat sliced through the slightly rippled water. Hains Point fell astern as we sailed between National Airport and East Potomac Park and followed the course of the river as it angled to the northwest. Before we knew it we were passing underneath the bridges to the city, and the Jefferson Memorial and other landmarks came into full view. The young crewmen, who looked a little strange in Air Force uniforms topped off with sailor hats, made a quick left turn, or I should say came hard a-port and threaded their way through the passage under the George Washington Memorial Parkway and into the Boundary Channel lagoon. A crewman jumped off onto the Pentagon dock as we eased into it and the launch was made fast.

Cris and I followed the other passengers up the pathway to the River entrance, the one the big shots generally used. Up the wide stone stairs we climbed and passed through the big, oaken doors into the small lobby. The other entrances opened into wide, dark pedestrian ramps which were full of people, mostly in uniform, bustling in and out with attache cases and intent, purposeful looks on their faces. But the River entrance led to a quiet, sunlit, marble-floored lobby with not a hint of hustle; in fact, after the other passengers disappeared down the hall, there was no one in the room except Cris and me and the receptionist.

You might think that an entrance to the premier military headquarters of the free world would be manned by hard-eyed guards and Frisk'em machines and ever-watchful TV surveillance cameras. But there was only this sweet-faced, middle-aged lady with graying hair and rimless glasses on guard, back in 1958. If the idea of keeping watch on such an entrance, where the offices of the Chairman of the Joint Chiefs of Staff were just down the hall made her nervous, she gave no sign.

My plan was to make a quick check of my personnel records, which would take about twenty minutes, then I would came back for Cris for a stroll around the building. The lady had a sheet of instructions for me, and pulled out one of those floor-plan cards and traced my route on it in red pencil, through the rings and wings and ramps and stairwells, down into the bowels of the building.

Cris had been next to me at the counter as I went through this, and as I turned to leave, the lady reached out and grasped one of Cris's hands with both of hers and said, "Would you mind very much taking my place behind the counter while I go to the ladies' room?"

When she saw the look of uncertainty on Cris's face she continued, "It will be all right. If any one comes just tell them to wait and I'll be right back."

I shrugged and Cris moved behind the big, impressive-looking counter as the receptionist went somewhere down the hall. I started down the hall too and as I looked back, Cris was making herself busy, straightening out some of the papers on the desk, acting as if, well, this is just another event in the life of Priscilla Park. I took a few more steps and turned again and as I watched, a Lieutenant came through the doors and stopped at the desk. I expected that he would have a few words with Cris and then sit down to await the real, bona fide receptionist. But I should have known better.

The Lieutenant was apparently another records checker, and I watched as she handed him a copy of the same list of procedures that was given to me, and then she got out a floor plan card and after some discussion, they got the route traced on it. Then he left. The receptionist had entrusted the protection of the River entrance to the Pentagon to capable hands.

But could it be possible that today, after all these years, there is a bearded, haggard Lieutenant staggering through the lower level labyrinths of the Pentagon, existing on survival rations stored in dark corners, searching for the right combination of stairwells, corridor turns and exits that would get him out of the building?

Or what if he had been trapped only a few years, and had emerged, blinking and dazed during the sixties, only to come face to face with a group of strangely attired people with painted faces and a spaced-out look in their eyes, who might dance around him and put flowers in his hat. And some of them might even spray-paint anti-war slogans on the walls near the entrance as he watched. He would, no doubt, stagger back to the River entrance reception desk to see if Cris was still there to direct him back to the subterranean corridors from which he had just escaped.

Cris didn't know at the time what the Special Air Missions squadron was, or what they did, so she turned her thoughts to some of the practical matters we would now have to deal with. It wasn't long before we were out looking for a house and we found a nice little brand new brick rambler in North Springfield in the Virginia suburbs. Three little bedrooms, two baths, no basement; a perfect starter house for a young couple with one child and another on the horizon. The young salesman assured us that no down payment was necessary, but we insisted on putting down twenty-five dollars to show him that we were not just anybody off the street.

Just to get out of the G.I. quarters, we moved in before the power was hooked up and we spent the first night in candlelight, a couple of happy morons enjoying the idea of the first house we had bought. We also had to borrow things like beds, dishes and other paraphernalia until our stuff was shipped up from Charleston, but since all of the necessary appliances came with the house, we didn't suffer too much. The house was part of a development which directly adjoined a massive road building project which was to become the Washington Beltway. A barrier of trees protected us from the sea of mud which was to become two four-lane roads separated by an island.

We hadn't been in the house very long when one of those weird and terrifying coincidences occurred which still shakes me today, more than thirty years later. I had started my commute to the airport one morning by driving along our street until I came to a new underpass under the future Beltway. I passed underneath the Beltway, then doubled back along the new road toward my commuter route.

As I reached a point across from our house, I saw this little creature up ahead, just stepping onto the road where I would pass by. I looked again and couldn't believe my eyes; It was my daughter Holly. Clothed in nothing but a diaper, little legs all muddy, dragging her stuffed dog Morgan by the ear, she was headed west in response to some irresistible urge. Of course I stopped and put her in the car and took her back home. She had climbed out of her crib, pushed open the screen door in back of the house, toddled through the tree barrier, across eight muddy lanes of future Beltway and onto the road on which I drove and arrived there precisely at the time I was passing by.

I have often thought about what could have resulted if any aspect of the timing had been different, or if I had changed any small part of my normal routine on that particular morning. Some times when I want to torment myself, I think of this.

A few days after I had opened the fateful envelope, Cris and I went to the Bolling Officer's Club to celebrate. We had dinner and were headed for the lounge where they had a small band and a dance floor when I saw General Griffith having dinner alone. I brought Cris over and introduced her and he asked us to sit for a while. Brigadier General Perry Griffith had been General Luedecke's chief of staff at Enewetak, which meant he was responsible for keeping the day-to-day activities of that massive enterprise running smoothly. Like Frank Richie, he occasionally flew one of the liaison airplanes on a tour around the atoll and took me along to get some stick time, and I told him how much I appreciated it.

General Griffith -who later became a three-star general- was a West Pointer, the son of a churchman who helped found Wichita, Kansas. He had been a champion diver at the Academy, and during his first assignment with the cavalry at the Presidio in San Francisco he won the all-around equestrian championship of the entire cavalry in 1939. A background like that conjures up images of the military good old days between the wars, with young cavalrymen playing polo or idly slapping their britches with their riding crops as they watched the new-fangled tanks and airplanes. They all moved along with the technology, and Griffith turned in his riding crop and went to flying school. I can imagine him in a Boeing P-26, a stubby little open-cockpit pea-shooter with a couple of teensy-weensy little machine guns, flying patrols out over the water to protect the Panama Canal and our bases in the Philippines.

I told him about my new assignment and he knew what that meant to me and he congratulated me warmly. His own reassignment was to return to the Tactical Air Command where he was given command of an air division in TAC's Composite Air Strike Force. They were having problems getting the bugs out of the newly developed twin-jet close air support bombers, a situation which was no secret to anyone who read the papers. One of the bugs managed to kill Lorin Johnson, the young Colonel who had been commander of my World War II bomb group.

"We're also having a problem with the navigation which I've got to get solved," he said, looking at me. "But with that new assignment of yours I guess you won't be available." I'm not sure if he was actually putting out a feeler of some kind, but I didn't say anything. He could have had my orders changed with one telephone call and I would be back in the trenches again, doing weird things with airplanes at places like Eglin Air Force Base and loving every minute of it. But I didn't bite and the General said good-bye and left.

Before the year was up he was sending his squadrons of light bombers along with aerial tanker support to the middle east to get the Lebanon crisis of 1958 resolved, which was accomplished without a lot of bloodshed. While his units were in the Middle East, he had to send a similar force to Formosa- now Taiwan- because of threatening moves by the Red Chinese.

In some countries, military officers had found it difficult to shake the horse manure from their boots, to avoid the horse cavalry mind-set which made them resistant to new ideas. But General Griffith was able to move from horseback to pea-shooters to jet bombers, managing two powerful forces in two different places 13,000 miles apart.

As for General Luedecke, his assignment after Hardtack as General Manager of the Atomic Energy Commission was the start of a highly distinguished civilian career. After six years with the AEC, he took an important position in Cal Tech's Jet Propulsion Lab and had much to do with the success of such programs as the Ranger and Surveyor series which involved Moon landings and orbiting Mars. Then came the time to bring his knowledge and wisdom to bear, not on immediate problems, but on the education of our youth, specifically those at Texas A&M. After some time as a Department Director, he was appointed interim President of the University.

Were it not for the presence of General Luedecke and others like him, we might not yet have landed on the moon, and the Berlin Wall might still stand.

The time came for me to report to my new organization and as I drove down to National Airport I got my first taste of what the Washington commuter situation looked like. The back roads from North Springfield weren't too bad, but then I got out on Shirley Highway and got stopped cold and the following traffic quickly filled in behind me, giving me a trapped feeling. After a few minutes, the mass of cars up front would move a few feet and I would fill in the gap, then everything would stop again. A drive that had taken me twenty minutes during the day now took an hour of stop and go, jockeying for position, ramp cheats trying to wedge into the line, all of the things that cause you to show up at the office ready to tackle a tiger. It quickly got to be a training course in self-control, in learning how to keep your teeth unclenched, to loosen tightened stomach muscles, to relax your death grip on the steering wheel.

On my first morning I checked in at squadron headquarters and had to track down Lt. Col. Roy Parnell, the squadron commander, who apparently spent most of his time where the action was rather than in his office. I found him in the operations section, a big, hearty type with wavy grey hair and a mischievous twinkle in his blue eyes.

"If you're all through setting off those bombs out there in the Pacific we'll get you settled down and get some work out of you." He smiled when he said this, a laid-back, comfortable guy who obviously enjoyed his humor. He took me in to see Colonel Grover Dunkleberg, the 1254th Group Commander, a man about my size with a grey fringe of hair, a slightly flattened nose and a relaxed, friendly attitude. Then Parnell took me in to see my immediate boss, the squadron chief navigator and left me with him.

Lt. Col. Joe Smolenski was his name, otherwise known as the Polish Eagle and he, too made me feel at home. Joe took me around to meet some of the crew members who were not flying or on crew rest, then he took me into his section and showed me the roster of navigators printed on a large board hung on the wall.

My name had already been grease-pencilled in about halfway down on the alphabetical list. Alongside some of the names on the list were notations like: Navigator for the Secretary of the Air Force, Navigator for the Secretary of Defense, Navigator for the Chairman of the Joint Chiefs of Staff. At the bottom was the name Lt. Col. Vincent Puglisi, Presidential Navigator.

The President's crew, it turned out, was attached to the Group rather than assigned, an artifice which permitted Colonel Bill Draper, President Eisenhower's pilot and aide to bypass some of the Air Force's bureaucratic entanglements. The rest of the navigators, about ten of us, were free for use on missions to transport cabinet members, congressional super-stars, Kings, Queens, Emperors, Prime Ministers, senior generals and other travelers of exalted rank whose station required that they be buttered up when they moved around in our midst.

I was to later find that assignment to a particular important person's crew required that all of his crewmembers spend long periods of time on close standby both at home and on the road. On one trip when we had some sort of gathering of the clan in Paris and we had four or five crews and aircraft there, I bumped into Bill Draper, the President's pilot at the Hotel Monceau, where we were all staying. We chatted for a moment while he looked around him nervously and finally he said, with some exasperation, "Dammit, I haven't seen that co-pilot of mine for at least twenty minutes!"

Smolenski gave me a few days to run my clearance and get settled into the house in North Springfield. Then I started to take some local flights; some test hops which were required after major maintenance, and pilot proficiency flights on which two or three pilots practiced instrument approaches and landings. The pilot who bounced the aircraft had to buy the beer after they landed, but before that, he had to listen to some comments intended to extract vengeance for some of his own previous sarcasms. Little by little I became familiar with the equipment layout in the airplanes, both in the Constellations and the Douglas DC-6. I also got to know the operations counter and the flight line routines which were used to get an airplane off the ground.

Sooner than I thought, I was scheduled for my first trip, a flight to Rio de Janeiro to pick up the Brazilian Air Minister, Francisco de Mello, and bring him to Washington. I would have an instructor navigator on board to look me over and let Joe Sheehan know if he had made a mistake in getting me on board.

We would transport some Air Force middle-shots on the way down and remain on the ground at Rio for seven days. When I told this to Cris I had to add that somebody has to do the boring, tedious jobs in the military, and that although I had objected strongly to being stuck in such an out-of-the-way place for such a long time, no one would listen. She wasn't listening either.

Before we ever left the ground, I began to believe that the toughest part of the trip was the planning of it. Unlike regular transport missions involving military passengers or cargoes of, say, mixed loads of weapons and PX supplies, our trips were almost always outside the protective envelope of the U.S. military air transport system. Airfields with runways of adequate length and load-bearing capacity, aircraft parking space, navigational and landing aids, proper fuel supplies, oxygen resupply carts and ground electrical power units with compatible connections all had to be dealt with.

Other countries demanded to know well in advance what time you intended to cross their borders on an overflight, and if you couldn't make it within the prescribed time limits, you had to scramble around to get the change approved, or fly around it if you could. Landing permission at some foreign civil airports for our military aircraft was sometimes slow in coming, and there were times when we departed before the reply to our request was received, fingers on both hands firmly crossed to help the decision-making process along.

Then there were the inoculation requirements which had to be determined so that the passengers could be informed; when it came to the crew, the problem was bypassed by shooting up each man with the entire world-wide anticipated requirement. There were times when five or six shots came due at the same time and you had to use both arms to take them all. There just weren't too many disease germs around that could exist for long in our bloodstreams.

After these details were taken care of, it came time to plan the operational aspects of the mission, like best altitudes, enroute flight times, possibilities of icing or turbulence, weather effects on takeoff and landing and all of the things the aircraft commander would need to know to get the passengers to destination on time and in one piece.

After I had gone over the details over and over again and had flown the mission in my mind six or seven times, I came to believe we were ready to go flying down to Rio. The instructor navigator and the aircraft commander both looked over my paperwork and asked me some questions and seemed satisfied, so off we went.

Today's intercontinental jets, like the Boeing model which carries lots of fuel but less passengers than other models, can make spectacular non-stop flights like New York to Tokyo on a daily, routine basis. They can also easily make the New York or Washington to Rio de Janeiro flights the same way, with no refueling stops. But our Lockheed Constellations, which were the state of the art for long range propeller transports at the time, had to stop along the way for refueling on the way to Rio. We chose the Piarco airport in Trinidad which was on the route and had all of the facilities we needed. The flight down to Piarco, which I had become familiar with on my trips from Charleston to Belem and across the South Atlantic to Africa, was routine. The track passed within airborne radar range of

441

Bermuda, which made the navigational job easier, and we arrived at Piarco on time. I had begun to feel the physical burden of the all-day flight we had already had as we departed Piarco and headed southeastward toward Rio. We had travelled about 2000 nautical miles and had 2300 more to go. I could not expect to be spelled by my instructor, who was there to see if I could handle such long flights, and not to do my work for me when I got tired. The two pilots and the flight engineer could rotate their shifts and get some rest.

The equatorial night fell as we made our way across parts of Venezuela and Dutch Guiana and into the Amazon basin of Brazil which spread underneath us. As for the navigation, I was doing okay until we passed abeam of Manaus, the Brazilian city that rubber built and then betrayed. I could pick up the distinctive curves of rivers in the radar, which, on the Constellations and the DC-6's I operated myself. Then we were flying over the great Amazonian jungle, an ocean of teeming life with no distinguishing features at all for a navigator to identify, and I had to dig out my sextant and start shooting fixes on stars in the unfamiliar southern latitude constellations. And then came red-eye time as we waited for the sun to come up, when the drooping eyelids felt like sandpaper sliding across already abused eyeballs. Just to lay my head down on my curled-up arm on the desk seemed like such a reasonable thing to do, so tempting and so harmless. My head felt as though it weighed a hundred pounds but had to be held up at all costs despite all the lies which fatigue was whispering in my ear.

It was a relief, when the time came, to get up to the astrodome to shoot my three-star fix and make all the complicated computations and plot the damn thing on the chart, and forget about the battle to keep my eyes open. But then my guardian angel showed up in the form of one of the flight attendants, who laid a plate of bacon and eggs down before me.

The food was on an actual china plate inscribed with the U.S. Air Force insignia which he turned with a practiced hand so that the shield and wings were at the top of the plate as it faced me. The coffee that went with it brought me back to life and little by little the fatigue slipped back into the shadows of my mind, ready to emerge later, when the need for concentration had passed.

We flew toward the blood-red sunrise, which began to light up the endless, unbroken carpet of vegetation beneath us. The future city of Brasilia was on our course, and as the earth around us was once again fully lit by the sun, I could make out a great white scar on the hazy, dark green horizon. We came upon the mammoth project, a big national capitol being built from scratch on a high plain in the center of nowhere. From our altitude, we could see that the new city had already taken form, with the streets laid out and many buildings, large and small, already erected. In a year's time the city would be officially opened and the bureaucratic apparatus along with the bureaucrats would begin to function after moving, somewhat reluctantly, from Rio de Janeiro.

I made a trip there a year or two after the opening and it seemed like a beautifully built, futuristic, well organized ghost city. A lot of people hadn't moved in yet and those that were there would tell you that it was an empty city, a city without a soul. To build a city all at once, rather than have it grow at the whims and desires of the people who are born there or emigrate to it is obviously a great gamble. The new inhabitants would have their architecture, their movements, the places where they worshipped, dined, danced, or played all decreed beforehand. What if nobody, nobody at all wanted to stay there? Well, the gamble has obviously paid off. Brasilia, which was designed for 300,000 people, now contains about four times that number in the city itself and in satellite areas and the inevitable shanty towns. Many government workers who came to work there and later retired now refuse to give up their government housing and go back to where they came from.

By the time we landed at Galeao Airport we were all wide awake and ready to see what gave Rio its great reputation. As we were driven into town we had the usual discussion after an all-night flight as to whether to go to bed for a while and have trouble sleeping the first night, or tough it out until fatigue drew big circles under our eyes and made us drag our rear ends into the sack after dinner. But the hotel was right on Copacabana Beach and as we drove along the elegant curve of that famous playground we knew that bedtime could wait.

In no time at all our baggage was unloaded and we were checked in and on the beach, banging around in the surf and then stretching out on the warm sands. It took about two sessions on the beach to make us whole again and to get us ready for the walking and hill climbing needed to see the sights in and around Rio. We had been left pretty much on our own except that the Aircraft Commander had to check in with someone by phone twice a day.

We had just come back from the trip up Mt. Sugarloaf and waited in the coffee shop as the A/C returned a phone call from someone at our Embassy. When he returned, he informed us that the crew had been invited to a party. Not just any old party, but some great social extravaganza which broke friendships and started family feuds in the battle for invitations. Black tie was specified but uniforms were okay so we called some taxies and arrived at this large ballroom at midnight, when Brazilians apparently wake up and start feeling their oats. We had a large round table right in the middle of things and I started to have a good time right away, looking at the crowd of happy, handsome Brazillionaires and their gorgeous wives. "Don't spill a drink on anyone," the A/C said," It might be the President." "The President of what?" somebody asked. "The President of Brazil, you moron."

Everyone was friendly to us because, as I understood it, the U.S. Air Force, on behalf of Uncle Sam, was in the process of doing some nice things for the Brazilian Air Force. Sometime during the evening, or I should say morning, a distinguished looking dark haired lady sat at our table and introduced herself. She was Perle Mesta, the famous Hostess with the Mostest who had achieved fame giving parties in Washington.

"And what is it you are doing here," asked one of the military wives seated next to her. Mrs. Mesta didn't bat an eyelash.

"I am the American Ambassador here," she said sweetly, and I thought the politely curious lady would slide under the table. To be generous, perhaps she hadn't caught the name.

The morning wore on, and everyone seemed to be drinking lots of champagne and having fun. We had to behave ourselves so that the USAF image would not be tarnished but we also had to show the hosts our appreciation by appearing to have a good time. The second part was easy. There was a big band which played mostly sambas, including "Caramba! Its the Samba! Its the one dance I can't do!"

They must have watched me try to dance the samba for a while and then played that song in my honor since I had never been able to get the hang of it no matter how hard Cris, the daughter of a dancing teacher, tried to teach me. We got through the party without doing damage to the USAF reputation and arrived back at the hotel about the time the sun was coming up. We were faced with the same decision we had to make when we arrived; should we stay up and go to bed early in the evening, or go to bed now. This time I didn't think about it very long. I went to bed.

Our VIP passenger, Brazilian Air Minister Francisco de Mello, made it obvious that he would rather be known as a pilot than as a bureaucrat. He was a tall, lanky guy with greying hair who enjoyed sitting up front talking with the crew. He watched the Constellation's gauges and blinking lights as the various levers were pulled and knobs were turned and switches flicked on or off as the big bird made its way back north-ward toward Washington. He told us about a high point in his younger life, when Ernst Udet, a famous German stunt pilot visited Rio some time between the wars and put on his spectacular show. He was considered by many to be the best in the world at the time, and one stunt for which he was known was to swoop down and, with a hook on the wingtip of his plane, snag a handkerchief suspended between two short poles stuck in the ground. Udet performed this stunt perfectly, as usual, and de Mello, one of the young pilots who was watching, took the occasion as a personal challenge. He had a wingtip of his own stunt plane rigged up with a hook and accomplished the difficult feat with the same success. "Madman Mello, that's what they called me after that!" he told us with a laid-back satisfaction, chuckling and shaking his head as he savored the memory.

But like other aviators around the world who rose up in the ranks, he had to bridge the mental gap between picking up hankies with his wingtip and operating large aircraft whose functions were becoming more and more automated. Pretty soon, with the arrival of the space shuttle, the distinction between aircraft and spacecraft would begin to blur, and the pilots would begin to be looked upon mostly as managers of the on-board computer systems. And who knows, but some day an astronaut, somehow touched by the spirits of the Udets and the de Mellos and our own superb aerobatic pilots, and disenchanted with all the automation, might return from orbiting Mars, and climb into his tiny Pitts Special and swoop down on some beach, his lightning reflexes responding to the burbling thermals and quickly shifting cross-winds. Instant death could await him here on the beach as it did on his trip to Mars as one slight misjudgment could dig his wing into the sand and slam him nose-first into the ground.

But he would keep his concentration and snag that little white square of cloth from the poles with a hook on his wingtip and then vault upwards in a victory roll, ignoring the G-pull on his guts, free from mortal cares, free from the fear of death, free to rub shoulders with the Gods.

Madman Mello must have thought we were okay, because a week or two after we brought him to Washington, I came home from the airport one evening to find Cris waiting for me, an envelope in hand. It was an invitation, stating that the Embassy of Brazil would be eminently pleased if Captain and Mrs. John Matt would attend a reception given by the Air Minister of Brazil for the U.S. Secretary of the Air Force. As for myself, I couldn't see how we could turn it down. Cris, of course, had already decided on the dress to wear, her hairdo, shoes and the shade of her fingernail polish, since she loved parties, especially when you had to dress up a bit.

"Is something like this going to happen every time you go out on a trip?" she asked. The whole idea of it sort of frazzled my mind.

"If it does," I said, "I'm going back to Charleston."

Cris and I and the other members of the crew and their wives started out feeling like little fish in a big pond as we walked into the embassy ballroom and went through the reception line. But the feeling wore off and we started to enjoy ourselves as we looked around us and found that the natives were friendly.

The dress that Cris wore was made of a beautiful, flaming red brocade that I had brought from Tokyo. It came from the same place I had found the pristine white brocade that had been made into her wedding gown. The reason Cris and I remember the dress is because Gwendolyn Cafritz, the famous hostess, complimented her on it. Mrs. Cafritz had made a practiced entrance, regal and elegant, and as she circulated through the crowd during the evening, she joined a group that Cris was part of. She obviously liked Cris's dress and when she asked where it came from, she seemed a little shocked when Cris told her she made it herself.

They had a band there too, which played, you guessed it, sambas, along with enough other kinds of dance music so that I didn't have to spend the evening watching my feet as Cris explained the steps. When it came to music you could jitterbug to, and I found ways to do this when others might not, I required a certain amount of dancing room around us which, after some bumps and jabbing elbows, was usually provided. They even played rumbas and an occasional tango , that perfect dance rhythm which, when it is done right, should be danced only by married couples or others who are willing to make long term commitments.

Cris and I had such a good time that we were still there when most of the other guests, who had paid attention to diplomatic party protocol, had left. The party got bigger and noisier as the embassy lesser ranks and hired help arrived. They looked at us and wondered why we were still there, but then they got used to us and even started to give me some pointers on the samba.

"Loosen Up! Loosen up!" said one boisterous dance-master, who was fairly well into his rum, "Your knees are too stiff!" I got the impression that if I didn't loosen up those knees he would consider it an insult to Brazil. I tried, but all I could do was fake it a little better than I had, and wait for another rumba.

My second trip, again with a watchful instructor navigator aboard, came up very quickly. It was an Atlantic crossing which was set up to drop off some middle-level military and State Department people who would make preparations for a big

NATO meeting the following month. NATO Headquarters was in Paris at the time, but would later be forced to move out by General DeGaulle, who apparently wanted to restore French pride by insisting to the world that France didn't need any help in defending herself.

There was no sightseeing or partying this time. We had our crew rest and took off for home, our flight time lengthened by the winter headwinds which were already blowing in early November. They blew hard enough so that we had to land and refuel at both the Azores and at Argentia, a U.S. Navy base at the southeastern tip of Newfoundland. We were gone somewhat over eighty hours and had spent thirty-three hours in the air, and the rest of it at crew-rest or on the ground refueling. But now I had my required ocean crossing out of the way, and the instructor told me he would report that I was ready for my graduation ride with a navigator flight examiner.

My checkout ride came up about three weeks after we returned from the last one, and as before, it was to Paris. This time we had some of the heavy-hitters involved who would attend the top-level Nato meeting. Secretary of State John Foster Dulles and other high-level attendees departed a few minutes before we did. Our own VIPs were a contingent from the Department of Defense Office of International Security Affairs, headed by Lt. General Clovis E. Byers.

Sometimes the fates forget to conspire, or they are busy cooking up trouble elsewhere in the universe and everything happens according to routine and previous planning. Then everyone can sit back and relax; the pilots with their feet up on the bar above the rudder pedals, taking an occasional glance at the flight instruments and the flicks of light on the autopilot control panel, talking about a great thick steak they had somewhere, or about some rich, stunning, sex-crazed blonde they had met in their youth who just wouldn't stop harassing them.

Then there was the engineer, nodding in appreciation as he listened, thinking about his own steaks and blondes, his ear cocked to the sound of the machinery, his eyes casually sliding across the engine and fuel gauges, the scheduled time of the next manifold pressure and propeller RPM adjustments in back of his mind.

The fates apparently got finished with what they were

doing elsewhere and turned their attention to us. They decided to fiddle not with the airplane or the weather or the crew's ability to perform, but on the health of one of the ladies on the General's staff. About halfway between Newfoundland and landfall on the French coast, one of the flight attendants came back and reported that a woman, who had been airsick for some time, suddenly developed a difficulty in breathing. We were at the normal east-bound cruising altitude for a Constellation, about 19,000 feet, which meant that the atmospheric pressure inside the airplane was about 8,000 feet.

Back went the power and down we went, after being cleared by Oceanic ATC, to 9,000 feet where the flight engineer could run the cabin pressure almost down to sea level. Bottled oxygen had helped somewhat, but we alerted Orly Airport at Paris to have an ambulance standing by.

As the drama in the passenger cabin unfolded, I had to deal with a bit of drama of my own. "We'll arrive when we get there," the old saying goes, but navigators can't say that, especially with the suddenly increased scrutiny on our progress caused by the medical emergency, and with the Flight Examiner looking over my shoulder.

So what could I do but scramble around, in what seemed like a calm, orderly way to the Examiner, to deal with an entirely new navigational picture. Different altitude, different flight level winds, different outside air temperature with resulting change in true air speed, different drifts, new headings, new ground speeds; everything was changed as we levelled out at our new altitude. As you proceed along at a particular flight level, you get the feel, after a while, of how the actual navigational picture is comparing with the forecast. You can then project your estimates forward with confidence, knowing what changes to make to the forecast further along your flight. But when you make a large, unexpected change in altitude, all of this is suddenly lost and you must start over again to get the feel of the shifting winds, to picture in your mind the new pattern they will assume.

It wasn't long before the radio operator received a request for our revised ETA for Orly. I worked up my new estimate and passed it forward to the Aircraft Commander, who looked at it for a minute or two before he called the radioman on interphone. Then he turned around and looked back at me as if to say, "You better be right, buddy!" letting me know that SAM ETA's were expected to be right on the minute.

Well, I lucked out again, and although the minor detail of an ETA that was right on had no further interest to anyone once our wheels hit the ground, it loomed large between me and the Flight Examiner. He didn't say much but when we got back to Washington, he gave me a nice write-up and turned me loose. The lady's illness turned out to be temporary and she recovered quickly. Paris can do that to people.

Suddenly, here I was, a fully qualified Special Missions navigator, ready to go wherever Joe Smoe sent me. In between trips I would pull duty in the navigation briefing office, where we updated the operational information, answered lots of questions and helped other navigators plan their trips. But it was the trips we thought most about. All of the places in the world we could go to, exotic or mundane; all of the VIP's we might carry: some of them always in the news or on television, taking them to events which could become part of history.

The most desirable trips were those to London or Rome. The people and the scenery were great, and if you managed to get a few days on the ground, it was easy to have a pleasurable time. Strange to say, Paris at the time was not high on the list. The people were as snotty to strangers as they were to each other, and the city itself was still somewhat dog-eared from the effects of the war. And the language barrier was almost impenetrable: few Parisians would admit to knowing any English, and if you tried to use some guide book French, they would roll their eyes skyward and sigh in exasperation. As for me, I learned to pronounce a number of useful questions with a passable accent, but when the answers came flying back at me I was lost. Now, of course, I love the place.

When the list of proposed trips for the following month came out, London or Rome trips were usually snapped up by the Examiners so that they could administer check rides. The missions were usually short and provided most of the necessary challenges which the examinee needed to overcome. Besides, how was a new man like me going to argue with an Examiner over a trip to London?

To tell the truth, this situation didn't bother me. There were too many other places to go that I had not yet seen, and I looked forward to walking around in places like Bamako and Niamey and Ouagadougou and other cities south of the Sahara; and in revisiting places like Bangkok and Tokyo and Hong Kong and Djakarta. If there was any place on this earth that was served by a runway big enough to take our aircraft, it was possible we might someday land there.

My trips as a navigator on my own started with missions which were considered routine, or I should say routine as far as SAM was concerned. The first involved the transport of Army General Lyman Lemnitzer, who would become Chairman of the Joint Chiefs of Staff, to a meeting at Wiesbaden, Germany, with side trips to Turkey, Pakistan and Madrid, Spain. While in Pakistan, we made a trip to Peshawar so that the General could have lunch with the Khyber Rifles, the legendary regiment. The best I could do was to get a jeep ride up to the Khyber Pass so that we could look down into this historical choke point and imagine invading armies trying to make their way to some conquest or other in the looming mountain shadows of the Hindu Kush.

The next trip went the other way, out to the far reaches of the Pacific to New Zealand, where the meetings of the of the Australia, New Zealand, United States -ANZUS- Treaty Organization were held. Our VIP was C. Douglas Dillon who was travelling as a senior State Department official to represent the U.S. at the meeting. I would later be part of a crew which took John Foster Dulles, the Secretary of State to the same meeting. On the Dulles trip, rooms in the major hotel were scarce so the crew was put up in a small place in the downtown area. The regular habitues appeared to be the horse racing crowd, a very lively bunch who welcomed Americans as long lost brothers. Fortunately, hotels in Wellington closed their bars and public rooms at a decent hour. But while they were open, we re-fought World Wars I and II, scrapped and remade treaties, and began to look at one another with newly appreciative eyes. All of this was done while partaking of what seemed to be gallons of beer, which the locals seemed to consider as a necessity before food.

The next morning we came down to breakfast about nine

o'clock in the same room where the bar was located. The racing crowd was already there and as we awaited the eggs and bacon a misunderstanding arose. Somehow they thought, based on our actions the night before, that we could be expected to start having a few drinks to start the day. And we, as well, thought the same thing of our new friends, so before we knew it, we were fighting the wars and scrapping treaties all over again. New Zealanders, I became convinced, had two hollow legs.

The hotel proprietor insisted on showing us his basement beer storage room, an immaculate place which, instead of rows of kegs as we had expected, contained a row of large, refrigerated tanks. These tanks, he explained, were refilled by tank trucks which funnelled the brew through large pipes which had outlets at street level on the side of the building, just like those for heating oil. When you ordered a beer, the bar tender took up his "beer gun" which was attached by a long, thin hose to the tank, and squirted the suds into your glass.

The New Zealanders attachment to their beer is well known, since they are usually reported as having the world's largest per capita consumption. Imported hard liquor was so heavily taxed that beer became the alcoholic staff of life. When the tax on beer was raised with the approval of the Prime Minister just before we arrived, there was a general negative discussion any time two or more people met.

I had joined a crowd for a flag raising ceremony in front of the set of buildings where the meetings were being held, and as Prime Minister Nash came out with Mr. Dulles and the other representatives, a distinguished-looking gentleman stepped out of the crowd of the generally polite onlookers and shook his fist in the air and yelled, "Damn you Nash and your damned beer tax!"

Mr. Dillon and his wife were frequent travelers with our squadron, both as a member of the State Department and later as Secretary of the Treasury. He came across as a kindly, dignified man who was thoughtful of the crew and who would keep his cool at all times.

Mr. Dillon met my own test for VIP cool on a trip which was returning him from Europe when he made one of his rare visits forward to talk with the crew. He entered the flight deck, ducking his head as he passed through the passenger cabin

452

doorway. As he straightened up his head bumped into a strange object suspended from the astrodome. I could see his eyes as it happened; "It can't be, but yes it is! By Gosh, it actually is a Salami I just bumped into!" But his expression did not change. He continued forward as if he would have found it unusual if some navigator had not hung this beautiful Genoese Salami from a hook in the astrodome. In fact, I think he thought it was a great idea.

Cool had to be in plentiful supply for our VIP passengers who were appointed by the President to act in his behalf during the numerous independence celebrations held throughout Africa at the end of the 50's and early 60's. Independence was breaking out all over and there were plenty of celebrations for the Presidential reps to attend.

The Europeans had to pull out of their former colonies somewhat gingerly since, in some of the countries, there was no predicting what would happen when they left. There were so many countries in Africa in and around the Sahara becoming independent in 1960 that they had to stagger their independence celebrations to insure full international representation at each such event. Senegal, Mauretania, Mali, Ivory Coast, Upper Volta, Togo, Dahomey, Nigeria, Niger, Chad, Cameroon, Central African Republic, Congo/Brazzaville, Belgian Congo - which became Zaire- the Somali Republic and the Malagasy Republic on the island of Madagascar, all took the plunge within a few months of each other.

What happened was nothing less than a political revolution of an entire continent. It would not be accurate to call it a bloodless revolution. They turned out to be revolutions whose normal series of events were reversed; they got their freedom first and had the bloodshed afterward, and, in some cases, ended up with even less freedom than before. After attending several of these celebrations it seemed that they were all working from the same script, with a spectacular cast of characters. In places like Mali and Chad and the Central African Republic, causes for celebration came few and far between, so the people in the towns and the wandering Bedouin, who liked to whoop things up whenever they got the chance, made sure that the celebrations would be something to remember.

There was always an unforgettable parade in which the

tribal chiefs throughout the surrounding area demonstrated their respect for the new turn of events by making an ostentatious show. Each sheikh rode at the head of his haughty bodyguard of burnoosed and scimitared warriors, preceded by camel-borne drum beaters and trumpeters, and followed immediately behind by his richly dressed harem. Then came the acrobats, dancers, strong-men and jugglers doing their act as they passed in review.

The lean, spike-bearded sheikhs rode astride magnificent stallions with imperiously arched necks and flaring nostrils, and passed by with obvious pride. The powerful beauty of the horses matched the splendor of the accouterments in which they were dressed; gold and silver chased leather with which they would be burdened only on occasions such as this. When the spirited, excited horses reared up or tried to swerve onto a parade path of their own, the riders reminded them who was man and which was horse without effort and without a change in their bemused expressions. The sheikhs and their retinue were figures I had imagined many times before and now they rode before me, not disappointing in any way . They were like tigers wrapped in silks and brocades and fancy bandoleers and pistol belts and the indispensable jewel-hilted dagger and scimitar.

Then came the mysterious Tuaregs, in one of the parades I witnessed. They were the supremely arrogant desert raiders from the central Sahara who treated even Allah with some indifference, and who needed no fancy raiment to enhance their imperious image. Tall, fine-boned and lean, they wore simple robes and swathed their heads and faces with a blue-dyed cloth which stained their faces and caused them to be called the Blue Men. The opening in the blue cloth was only large enough to permit them to look out at their surroundings with dark, intent eyes.

During one parade, a troop of Tuareg warriors swept by, hooded and mysterious, hut-hut-hutting at their camel mounts to keep up their shuffling gait. Suddenly, one of the camels slipped on the unfamiliar pavement and quickly recovered but the rider was gone in a flash, headed for the ground. As he fell, his flowing burnoose snagged against some part of his saddle and he was dragged along upside down by the heaving, terrified animal. The cloth finally parted and he scrambled to his feet, his mystery stripped from him along with his veil and his pride. He was no longer an imposing man of mystery. The Tuareg had become a tall, thin guy with a scraggly beard, shaking with frustration and rage, running after the camel that had betrayed him. If a simple matter of life or death had been involved, he probably would have taken a death-blow against his neck without a whimper, but now he was forced to scramble around before a derisive crowd, trying to remount his camel. The embarrassment would probably dog him to his grave.

As long as the new countries to which we brought our VIP's were comprised of sand dunes, wadis, a few isolated towns and not much else, whatever violent problems might arise because of their new freedoms would take a while to develop. But when a rich colony declared its independence, one with minerals and copper mines and uranium and other valuable attributes, then the predictable internal upheaval would already be simmering by the time we got there. The freedom ceremony had better be held in a hurry and the participants would be wise to participate and get out before the lid blew off.

In one such situation we brought Ambassador Robert Murphy to Leopoldville in the Belgian Congo -now Kinshasa in Zaire- and in the belly cargo compartments were cases of tear gas and concussion grenades for the U.S. Marines who would guard our future embassy in Leo. The atmosphere in the city was a strange mixture of impending violence and anticipating joy as the people began their celebrating. The soon-to-be U.S. embassy let us have a car with a driver who spoke pretty good English to do some sightseeing and we were impressed with the place. Large, modern buildings lined the streets, along with elegant shops and restaurants, and I had a difficult time realizing that we were not in some European capitol, but in the heart of Africa, five degrees or so south of the equator.

We stopped at the monument to Henry Morton Stanley, his arm raised against the sun as he peered into the distance, still looking for Dr. Livingston. Then we drove alongside the banks of the Congo River which was at flood stage. The river's surface was covered with large, green leaves and broken tree branches which appeared to have been torn off in some great storm upriver and sent floating in the swift, roiling current toward the sea. The scene seemed to fit right in with what was going on around us.

The driver, a black man who apparently was not a full time chauffeur but a bureaucrat in the Foreign Ministry, dropped us off at a swimming club which had a membership limited to the diplomatic corps and other mostly-white groups. As we thanked the man for driving us around, he looked toward the large, inviting pool and said with determination, "Pretty soon I will be swimming there."

There was a large parade in the afternoon, with platoons of well-drilled troops and constabularies, brass bands, fraternal organizations, trade groups, masses of colorfully dressed school children, some of the same types of people you might see parading in any big city. There were also tribal groups with shields and spears, with faces and bodies painted for battle. Some of these groups were brought in from the bush and they looked it, while others appeared a trifle too chic in their feather head dresses and lion tooth necklaces. I suspect that when the celebrations were over, they would wipe off the spectacular body and face paint and go back to their jobs in shops and offices in town.

Paraders in other cities would not be likely, in a few days time, to be at war with one another, in a country that was beginning to come apart at the seams. Congolese troops at the head of the parade would soon have their hands full with the smart-looking constabulary from Katanga marching behind them, called the Katanga Cowboys because of their flamboyant, Aussie-style hats. They would also have to cope with a mutiny in their own ranks and with large numbers of mercenaries who would be imported to assist in the revolt. Katanga was where the mineral and other riches were, and an effort would be made to carve it out of the new republic so that the carvers could keep it all themselves, and let the less prosperous part of the new country shift for itself. The weapons they would use would not be shields and spears.

We walked among the dancing, celebrating groups on the field of the Sports Stadium, trying to get some pictures in the fading, evening light. Painted up, dolled-up, juiced-up men and women danced and sang to pounding drumbeats that slammed into you and made your solar plexus jump. It was all so easy, something they had been doing since they could stand, something they could do for hours or days on end.

It almost seemed as though everyone was waiting for something to happen and finally, as night fell, there came a great, tense moment. King Baudoin of Belgium, dressed in his royal regalia, was making his farewell speech to the massed thousands in an outdoor ceremony when a man from the crowd jumped up on the podium and tore the King's sword from his waist. There was a stunned silence, after which anything could have happened, but then a great cheer went up and the moment for further violence passed.

Today, you might look at that act as a perfect symbol of the occasion, as the true moment of birth of Zaire. But that night, with all kinds of rumors flying around involving mistrust of Belgian intentions, the crowd could have been set off into a conflagration.

But the celebration was able to come to its high point without further major incident the next morning, when the long limousines pulled into the stadium and the newly made big shots were eased out and led to the flagpoles. First the old anthem was played as the Belgian flag was lowered, then the band took up the new, unfamiliar refrain as the new banner was run up to the roars of the crowd.

We left just before the real violence erupted, only to return a few months later to a city and country in disarray. Struggles for power were causing the beautiful capitol to become unglued. Threats and rumors of threats against the remaining Belgians caused them to leave precipitously, leaving behind memories and belongings accumulated for generations, and deserting their autos at the airport by the hundreds as they boarded Sabena jets for the strange newness of Brussels.

This second trip to the Congo was part of a journey across Africa by Ambassador Loy Henderson, who was making an inspection tour of the new embassies, and appraising sites for embassies not yet built in the newly independent countries.

On our return trip to what was still called Leopoldville, we landed across the river at Brazzaville in an adjoining new country that had once been part of French Equatorial Africa. We had been on the road for a while and the Ambassador hesitated going into Leo without updated information regarding the security situation.

We waited for a day, then the Ambassador decided that we -the crew- would take the airplane without passengers into Leopoldville and then he and his party would follow by boat across the river. I jokingly told the State Department coordinator that by sending us in first it sounded like they were throwing a hat beyond the swinging doors into the hostile bar room so see if it would be shot full of bullet holes, and he thought that was pretty funny.

Our passengers made their way across the Congo River into Leopoldville and conducted their business. We were put up in a small hotel outside of town on the way to the airport, where the manager advised that we sit tight until it was time for us to leave. But after a few days, the embassy sent us a car and we drove into town to check our instructions for the departure.

Leopoldville was no longer the chic, immaculate European capitol city. In a few months time, the continuing conflict had begun to wear the place down and signs of neglect were beginning to show. Downtown was beginning to look a little shabby, and the rows of big villas on the outskirts of town were getting a seedy look with lawns un-mowed, hedges un-trimmed and wash hung out on ropes strung between portico columns.

Violence had washed through the Congo and still ebbed and flowed, rising whenever there were colonial spoils to fight over. Troops, both loyal and mutinous; imported mercenaries; United Nations peacekeepers; anybody with a gun joined in and it was not always easy to discern where the immediate dangers lurked.

Leo itself seemed quiet enough for us to linger awhile and look for some dinner. Some of us returned without incident to our hotel in the outskirts, but Ken Mayo, our flight engineer, and others in the crew riding in the other car took a wrong turn somewhere in town and found themselves halted and surrounded by soldiers.

First there was a silence, then they could hear safety catches clicking off and rifle bolts sliding home. "Nobody say a word!" ordered the embassy driver. "Let me do the talking!" The driver assured the officer at the roadblock that he had only American tourists on board, and they all waited as this information was digested by the nervous troops. An eon passed, and finally the officer demanded that the car be turned around, and that the turn be made slowly and with care.

It turned out that the driver had somehow blundered into the area where Joseph Mobotu, who would eventually win all the Congolese marbles, was being held under house arrest. Ken and his colleagues made it to the hotel okay, but with the sound of those clicking guns, of rifles being made ready to fire very fresh in their minds.

The time came to leave and the crew made it out to the airport without incident. I had computed my navigator's flight plan and given it to the pilots, who went over to the operations desk to file the clearance. As I looked out of the large glass windows which over looked the flight line, the embassy cars with our passengers aboard pulled up at the gate in what seemed to be a big hurry. As I watched, the people in the first car trotted over toward the airplane, and I noted that one of the men had his suit jacket off and there was a stripe of what appeared to be blood down the back of his shirt.

I quickly made my way out and followed the group up the flight stairs so see if they needed help. The wounded man, a young member of the embassy staff who had been driving one of the cars, had taken off his shirt and was being treated by the doctor we had on board. There was a stab wound high up on one of his shoulders near the neck which the doctor worked on rapidly.

It turned out that the embassy cars were being driven from town to the airport with passengers and baggage when a boy on a bicycle swerved in front of the lead car and was instantly killed. When the line of cars stopped to see what assistance they could give, a hostile crowd quickly gathered and started to push the American group around.

The embassy people, including a large security type who had been a U.S. Marshal, got the passengers away from the crowd, "using lots of knees and elbows" and back into the cars. As this was being done, the embassy staffer was somehow identified as the lead car driver, and was attacked by a man with a knife.

As the doctor patched the man up, I decided to go back to operations to make sure the pilots realized what was going on. I got down to the bottom of the flight stairs and found a Congolese soldier armed with a rifle about to make his way up. I held up my hand and he stopped, but he swung his gun up and pointed it right at my nose. All I could do was gulp as I looked down into the rifling of the barrel. Then I looked into those buck private's eyes and saw some dangerous confusion, and I realized he didn't know what to do either. I pointed somewhere behind the soldier and said, "Officier! Officier!" giving the words my best Belgian accent and mustering as much authority in my voice as I could. We stared at each other for a moment longer, then he brought his gun down, backed off a few steps, then walked off to find his officer.

I went back up the stairs, taking two at a time, and found the two Air Police guards who were part of our crew watching the doctor sew up the embassy man.

"Don't let any Congolese come up the stairs unless the A/C is there and he says it's okay," I told them. The guards put on all of their police paraphernalia, picked up their carbines, set their caps at the proper angle, and took their position at the base of the flight stairs. Meanwhile, the Congolese officer showed up and after some discussion which, by this time, included Ambassador Henderson, the patched-up embassy man was handed over to the Congolese authorities.

The embassy man apparently survived his period of temporary captivity without damage and managed, over the years, to make a rapid climb up the government ladder until he became head of the National Security Agency and then Secretary of Defense in President Reagan' s cabinet. His name was Frank Carlucci.

Around this same time one of our USAF transport crews had landed at Stanleyville -now called Kisangani- with a load of relief supplies as part of the United Nations effort which was raised to stop the fighting. They were met by thousands of locals, all shouting the Congolese version of Kill! Kill!

A rumor had spread among them that the USAF crewmembers were some of the mercenaries who were fighting on the wrong side of the insurrection. They pulled the crew out of the Big Shaky -a Douglas C-124- and mauled them as they handed them overhead from one part of the mob to another until they finally decided that they were not mercenaries after all, and let them go.

An Italian relief crew was not so lucky. When the mob seized them they hacked them to pieces with machetes and threw what was left into the Congo River.

We were pretty well spooked by incidents like these by the time we reached Lome, further along the south coast of the African bulge, in Togo. The passengers had left for town, and we sat underneath the wing of the airplane away from the afternoon sun, waiting for our taxi. We heard some singing, and watched as a large group of natives headed directly toward us. They were swinging machetes at nothing in particular, their singing getting louder as they approached.

"This is it!" I thought, and so did some of the others, all of us looking on helplessly. When they reached us they suddenly stopped singing, and we all stared at each other for a moment. Then they began singing again, and flowed around us, happy and smiling as they made their way home after a day's work in the cane fields adjoining the airport.

Our trip through Africa with Ambassador Henderson had started out as one of those I went out of my way to get. As usual, we stopped at Dakar, did some beach time at the N'gor Hotel, picked up our Evian water and took off across the Sahelian plain.

The Ambassador wanted to visit the whole string of newly independent countries along the sandy underbelly of the Sahara, starting with Bamako, the capitol of Mali, where French Foreign Legionnaire Beau Geste had become a legend. Our next stop was Ougadougou, in Upper Volta, which seemed even more remote than Timbuktu. Like most of the places we were to visit, there was an adequate hotel built by Air France. But in Ougadougou, the place was full, and although the passengers were able to get rooms by doubling up, the crew was put up in what could only be described as the camel drover's quarters.

Of course it was called the Annex, but it had an honest-to-god dirt floor, and a musty, ancient smell which made me suspect that not only did the drovers stay there, but their camels as well. Well, as we say in the trade, we can put up with anything for one night, so we did. I still have a slide of Dick Teufel, one of the pilots and me leaning up against a fence in front of our quarters which was decorated with the skulls of desert creatures impaled on the fence stakes.

Mel Schmit, the other pilot, was pushed a little too far, he thought, when he found that his room had half a ceiling, with the rest of the room open to the sky.

Ouagadougou was the place where, as I walked around the market place, I noticed an airport service truck pulled up under some trees. They were unloading meat which had arrived by air and as I watched, two men on the truck picked up what looked like part of a hind quarter of beef and carefully positioned it on top of the head of a porter standing by the tail gate. The porter tested the balance for a moment, and then slowly began to walk off, carefully turning to set his proper course toward somewhere. As he walked by me I could see and hear the flies buzzing around in a frenzy, and several trickles of blood from the meat began to drip down the side of his head and down his naked back.

There were a number of other stops on the trip like Abidjan, on the Ivory Coast, where the hotel seemed okay, except that the shower was installed directly over the water closet. Now that was a peculiar arrangement, with several tough decisions to be made when you got up in the morning.

Then there was an unexpected stop at Fort Lamy, where we landed because we had to make an extremely rare in-flight engine shutdown. If Ougadougou and Timbuktu are considered remote, then Fort Lamy in Chad is at the end of the world. I am sure there are thousands of natives who are born in the area and live their entire lives surrounded by the burning sands and the great shallow stretches of Lake Chad who think that Chad is heaven on earth.

There is a great natural beauty in the land which might not be appreciated by a casual visitor who could not help feeling trapped in the middle of nothingness. But a Chadian who survived to adulthood looked at a familiar landscape; he or she knew where the water wells and the camel caravan trails were.

They dealt with the blowing sands as part of their nature and if they tired of the place at which they set up their hide-covered tents, they folded them and gathered their goats and camels and moved somewhere else. Once in a while they might hear a strange droning noise and look up and if the sands were not blowing, they might see the tiny dot of an airplane against the sky and wonder; who are they and what is the meaning of their journey?

The local Chadians had probably become accustomed to airplane noises over the past few weeks as there was a surprising amount of traffic in and out of the Fort Lamy airport. They were mostly French military aircraft who had come to take most of the garrison home to France, we learned, and I presumed there would only be some advisors left.

A small bus was sent out to our airplane to take us to get billeted, and as we drove toward the barracks area I noted that the driver, a young blond private who was dressed in fatigues, was having a tough time keeping the vehicle on the road. We came upon a white-burnoosed native padding alongside the road and the driver grasped the wheel and swerved toward the man, who jumped away just in time.

"Sauvage!" snarled the young driver, who really had a snoot full, and we all looked at each other. As we came into the barracks square and went around to the rear of the bus to get our bags, we could hear derisive, drunken singing coming from some of the buildings. At first it seemed the whole base was drunk, but it was just one group celebrating their imminent departure, and apparently the driver was one of them.

We couldn't find anybody who spoke English, but our flight engineer, Ken Mayo, spoke French he had learned in parochial school but which he hadn't used for years. When he asked a question, the Frenchman would knit his brows, shake his head and make him repeat it two or three times before he gave his answer.

"My accent is so bad I guess they just can't believe it," said the F/E.

It would take several days for a new engine cylinder to be flown down from Frankfurt so we had some time on our hands. Meanwhile, a replacement airplane and crew were sent down, also from Frankfurt, to take the passengers to the next few stops until we got our Constellation fixed. The replacement crew had been dispatched on such short notice that they didn't have time to find some tropical uniforms. They looked obviously unhappy as they disembarked into the furnace that was Fort Lamy wearing their itchy, sweaty blue uniforms.

We went into town late the next afternoon and found the hotel which seemed to be empty except for the desk clerk. He doubled as the bartender in the lounge and brought us some bottles of beer, which were passably cold. As we sat and sipped, two young French officers came in dressed in immaculate Foreign Legion uniforms. They had a beautiful young girl with them, about seventeen or eighteen years old, truly, a desert princess. There was that vibrant olive skin again and the fine, straight features, just like the girl who sold shirts in Asmara. The two men ordered some drinks and appeared to ignore us, but the girl, who sat very close to one of the Legionnaires and kept her hand on his arm, stared at us with curiosity, and I presumed we were the first Americans she had seen. She was dressed in a cool, gauzy outfit of some kind, in turquoise to match her eyes.

It would have been great, I thought, to meet some French Foreign Legionnaires on their own ground and get some insight as to what the Legion was all about, to find out what it was that made them among the best in their profession. But they appeared somewhat aloof and besides, we didn't see how we could have much of a conversation, given the language barrier we were certain to encounter. So after a while, we moved into the dining room and as we passed the Legionnaires' table, we all nodded politely, and that was the last we saw of them.

Fort Lamy was named after a French military man, a major who was co-leader of an expedition which left a jumping off point at Ourgla in northern Algeria, for a two thousand mile journey across the Sahara, to Lake Chad. The lake had come to be considered one of the goals of the French conquest, although it was more of a swamp than a body of water, a 40 by 160 mile shallow depression in the earth in which the water level rose and fell with the seasons.

Lamy's expedition reached the lake and proved that the Sahara could be crossed by Europeans, and that a trans-

Sahara railroad from Algeria to Lake Chad could be considered slightly less than impossible to build. Unfortunately for Lamy, the area around the lake was in the hands of a formidable foe who had to be conquered, and although the French forces prevailed, the Major was mortally wounded in the final military engagement.

He died after gazing at the decapitated head of his adversary, Rabih, a competing invader from the Sudan. The encampment south of the lake which was given his name became a city, and sixty years later -around 1960- when the new country of Chad became independent, the name of Fort Lamy was changed to N'Djamena.

The conquest of the Sahara had not been a Boy Scout camporee. There was heroism and sacrifice along with savage murder and massacre, the highest and lowest forms of military endeavor. It is probably too early to accurately assess what would have happened to the Sahara civilizations, such as they were, had they been left completely alone. They were their own worst enemies, fighting each other for what few riches the desert had to offer. But the French came, in the person of soldiers like Major Lamy, and the lives of everyone there were changed for a while. Sixty years from now, except for his family and French military men interested in their own history, who will remember the name Lamy?

The last time I saw Dick Teufel, the Fort Lamy trip came up in our conversation. "Ah yes, Fort Lamy," he said as he shook his head in wonderment, remembering the drying desert heat. "It was a great place to do your laundry!"

I have described trips eastward to Africa and Madagascar, westward to New Zealand and southward to Rio de Janeiro. Just to make sure I had all directions covered, Smolenski also sent me northward. But before that happened, I found myself assigned to a round-the-world trip to take the Director of the International Cooperation Administration around the other side of the world to Djakarta, Indonesia. We would then continue on around the globe to come home.

The original plan was to start eastward, through Europe, the Middle East and India and then to destination. The planning was extremely complicated as the trip was routed through a number of countries with complex overflight or landing clearance procedures, and who were generally reluctant to issue clearances in the first place. I worked on the itinerary for weeks and sent out dozens of messages, a number of which had to be chased down with second requests. About a week before departure I was finally able to brief the aircraft commander that we were all set except for a few clearances.

The next day, someone from the VIP's office called to say that the trip was still on, but that some changes were necessary.

"Oh?" I thought, "perhaps they want to change a few enroute stops or some departure times." "It is nothing complicated," the man said. "We still want to leave on the same date, but instead of going around the world eastward, we want to head out westward." He was very nice about it.

The trip northward involved the Panel on Geophysics of the Air Force Scientific Advisory Board. Some of the matters this board was involved with were the way missile operations and related equipment would be affected by the arctic environment. There was a meeting which the passengers attended in Fairbanks, Alaska, then we went further north to Point Barrow where there was a Distant Early Warning site -a DEW line radar station. I was surprised to find that the commander of the station was a friend of mine, Major Harry Shaw, a transport pilot whom I had last seen at his station in Honolulu. He seemed to have taken the change in climate in stride, but I got the distinct impression that he would rather be back in Honolulu.

Point Barrow is the northernmost point of the United States and was, in 1960, a desolate place. There was a tarpaper shack village, acres of fuel oil drums, both empty and those waiting to be emptied and a rocky shoreline blown clear of snow even at the height of winter. There was also a monument near the shore to commemorate the crash of Wiley Post, a one-eyed, black-eye-patched advance copy of Chuck Yeager and Scott Crossfield and the astronauts, who had tried to outwit Mother Nature. Trying to land in bad weather because there was no place else to go, he smashed into the rocks with his great friend and world famous humorist Will Rogers in the back seat.

Even at Point Barrow we had not yet finished our northward journey. There was Ice Island T-3, a large chunk of primeval ice floating in circles in the Arctic Ocean, which was on the itinerary. T-3 was used as a scientific station during winter when the ice was firm, by the Russians when it was on their side of the 180 meridian, and by us and our allies when it was on our side.

The long, flat ice island was only about 60 miles offshore when we headed out from Point Barrow. It was easy to find because of its aeronautical beacon flashing clearly in the arctic dusk. Colonel Tom Collins, who was the A/C and our deputy Group commander, made contact and was told to be on the lookout for some bulldozers which were smoothing out the icy runway as he approached. The ice looked smooth, but we rollercoastered up and down after we touched down and Tom let the speed bleed out since brakes weren't too useful in the ice.

There was no such thing as air stairs to get the passengers off; instead, somebody on the island had banged together a set of stairs of just the right height out of boards, and this was pushed against the main cabin door. There was a ridge of ice which prevented the stairs from being moved flush against the airplane fuselage, and a gap of about two feet remained between the top of the stairs and the threshold of the door.

Because of the cold, the welcoming ceremony was reversed; instead of the visitors climbing down the stairs and meeting the greeters, the visitors stayed on board and the greeters came up to meet them. As the visitors came up the stairs, they would extend their hand in welcome, step over the two-foot gap, and enter the airplane. One scientist, an oceanographer burdened with thick bifocals, came up the stairs, extended his hand and plunged through the gap down on to the ice below. Fortunately, he was not injured and he picked himself up, came up the stairs and carefully stepped across the gap.

He had taken the plunge with such perfection, that had he been a friend of mine, I would have accused him of having rehearsed the maneuver until he got it right.

T-3, sometimes called Ice island Bravo, had also been called Fletcher's Island, in honor of the weather recon pilot who

got the brilliant idea to use this large chunk of ice as a scientific outpost for oceanography, meteorology and other sciences. It
floated around at about one knot and by agreement, when it
came closer to the U.S.S.R. they put their people on board, and
when it moved closer to Alaska or the Canadian shores, they
got off and we got on.

The scientists learned that no matter whose backyard it
arrived in, came the summer, everyone got off. The surface
became puddles and rivers of water and slush, which made life
pretty much unbearable. They also learned that the modular
buildings they used to live and work in could not be placed
directly on the ice, but had to be placed atop mounds of snow,
otherwise they would melt their way down into the ice. Every
so often, new snow mounds had to be piled up by bulldozers
and the buildings lifted off the melted down piles and repositioned on top of the new mounds. There were places where you
could look down into the ice and see oil drums, crates and an
occasional piece of machinery such as a pallet loader, perhaps
six or eight feet below the surface, trapped like prehistoric
relics.

Polar bears were a problem, but on the occasions where a
man met a polar bear coming around the same corner, the man
was able to duck in somewhere quickly enough to escape. The
bears seemed to be more interested in the garbage pile than in
humans except once, when the island commander, a USAF
Lieutenant Colonel was out on a walking tour with his dog, a
mongrel, the only one on the island. The story, as I heard it,
was that a full size bear rose up from the snow and as the
Colonel turned and ran, the bear came after him. There is no
way a man can outrun a polar bear, and since he had some distance to go before he could reach shelter, it would have been
the end of him. But the courageous dog nipped at the bear's
feet and distracted him enough so that the Colonel escaped.
The dog was unharmed too, and was regarded as a canine hero,
and rightly so.

Despite the threat polar bears posed to humans, they were
certainly not hated or despised, but just treated with a healthy
respect, and looked at as if they belonged there and we didn't.
There were people like the Inuit -the Eskimos- who hunted
them because it was in their culture, but there were others who

hunted them so they could hang that big, beautiful pelt on the wall or lay it before the fireplace. On this same trip, at Anchorage, I admired one such skin on someone's office wall. It was edged in red felt and had a perfect head with snarling jaws and fierce, fake eyes. He offered to sell it to me for a hundred-fifty dollars but I wasn't interested.

Later, at Point Barrow, I was in the operations hut getting the latest position of T-3 for my flight plan. A pilot, dressed in an arctic orange flying suit, was sitting on a crate putting on a pair of mukluks, which you might call arctic overshoes. He had the ruddy complexion and rugged build of a true out-doorsman. We struck up a conversation, and it turned out he was a bush pilot who was getting ready to fly a hunter -up from the lower forty-eight- out on the ice to find him a polar bear.

He had a ski-equipped, single-engined Canadian airplane designed for the climate, and he would take off from Point Barrow and look for a bear, then sit the airplane down on the closest ice floe large and smooth enough to land on, then he and his hunter client would stalk the victim down.

When he was finished with his mukluks, he got up and started to gather up his gear, including two large-bore rifles.

"This is my last trip," he said, his eyes idly studying a map on the wall before us. "They're just like humans, good human beings. You fly around slowly and watch them playing with their cubs, and when you land and come up on them and get in your shot, they'll keep coming at you with a bullet in their heart just to let their cubs get away." He fell silent for a moment, then looked over at me.

"Yeah, I've had enough," he said, then he was gone.

The ice island; the string of distant early warning stations that stretched along the coasts of Alaska and Canada to Greenland; the radar stations sitting on top of the Greenland ice-cap; the BMEWS -the Ballistic Missile Early Warning System- with radar so powerful that the moon rising over the horizon could cause a false alarm; all of these comprised one of those separate worlds like the Sahara and other remote places, peopled with special types of humans that make up this earth. But, as some unfeeling people remark about the still fascinat-ing Big Apple, this world was a great place to visit, but I wouldn't want to live there.

I know I am not alone in this opinion. There was a graffiti, in some men's room up there somewhere which said, "Kilroy was here -but not for long!"

19

THERE WAS NO PEACE
IN LA PAZ

THE EISENHOWER ERA WAS ENDING and, although we didn't know it at the time, so was the feeling of relative tranquility which the country enjoyed during his two terms. As 1960 wore on, the presidential campaigns of Ike's vice president, Richard Nixon and the young senator from Massachusetts, John F. Kennedy began to monopolize the news.

We had seen more of Mr. Nixon on our flights than you might expect for a vice-president, because of Eisenhower's several serious illnesses including a heart attack and an intestinal disorder called ileitis. Nixon made his trips at a time when the cold war was starting to cycle up again and Third World expectations continued to rise. Vice-President Nixon was sent to Moscow to lend a high-level U.S. presence to a Moscow trade fair and found himself with his hands full as he took Soviet Premier Khrushchev on a tour of the U.S. exhibit.

When Khrushchev intimated that the kitchen was a ringer, that there were few like it back in America, Nixon felt the U.S. had been insulted, and the famous "kitchen argument" took place right on TV. Mr. Nixon was also involved in a serious, touch-and-go incident at Caracas, where he was trapped in his car by a big, hostile, spitting crowd. The crowd was somehow prevented from turning the car over and he came through the long ordeal without a scratch and with his reputation for courage intact.

I was not along on any of his trips, but it was always interesting to get first hand accounts from the crewmembers when they returned. I did get to watch Nixon at close hand during several foreign VIP arrivals during rainy weather, when the arrival ceremonies had to be moved indoors. At such times, a podium with microphones was quickly set up in our hangar or in our terminal building.

As I watched from a few feet away, I could see Mr. Nixon go into his act in welcoming some premier or other, an imperturbable smoothie who seemed to be able to whip up a perfect little speech with no effort at all. The interpreter was usually the brilliant Vernon Walters, a U.S. Army Lieutenant Colonel soon to be a four-star general, later to rise even higher to the top levels of our government. He made things easy by translating both ways; English to whatever for the Vice-President, and whatever to English for the visitor. He seemed to be able to handle any language that came along.

My African trips had not yet run out their string, although by this time I had seen so many camel races I guess they began to get to me. I could visualize, somewhat reluctantly, six or eight of the funny-looking but fast creatures being led around the paddock at Belmont or Pimlico or Santa Anita. Then, instead of the dramatic call for "Jockeys up!" the announcer demands "Camels down!" and instead of getting a leg up, the riders stand aside while the ungainly beasts collapse themselves down onto their knees so that the rider can mount. Then they sort of see-saw themselves back onto their feet and are led out to be paraded along the track in front of the stupefied bettors in the stands.

Meanwhile, Sheikh so-and-so is being interviewed on TV by Jim McKay with regard to the favorite who, he notes, has had two wins at Bamako and one at Ouagadougou in his last three outings. He also points out that these are racing camels, not your ordinary ships of the desert; more like Chris Crafts of the sand dunes.

Then comes the big moment and they are loaded into the starting gates and Wham! the gates fly open and they all go hut-hut-hutting around the turns and along the backstretch, big, bony legs stretching out in their great strides, then come rounding the last turn and surging down the homestretch,

472

rider's burnooses flying in the wind, the crowd yelling like crazy, wishing they had muskets to shoot into the air. What a way to pump new life into the racing industry!

It wasn't only Africa that had gotten into the independence game, but the island of Madagascar as well. The Malagasy Republic had been formed there and President Eisenhower appointed William P. Rogers as his representative at the cere-monies. Mr. Rogers was Attorney General at the time -he would later become Secretary of State for Nixon- and the pilots and I were asked to come to his office to talk about the trip. He enjoyed the idea of his trip so much that the ten minute time allotment stretched to forty-five minutes as we described our services and discussed possible enroute stops.

Tananarive, the capitol of the new republic was a poor, beat-up place, and constant rain or threat of rain gave the event a gloomy air. Mr. Rogers did his duty and we returned as we had come, back across the Mozambique Channel and the country of Tanganyika, across what would soon be Zaire and then toward the African bulge. Nigeria was about the right dis-tance away for an enroute stop and we would normally use Lagos, the capitol because it had all the facilities. But during our discussion in Mr. Rogers office, I nudged along the idea of using Kano since it was a much more exotic place and besides, I had never been there. The distance to both places was about the same. Kano is in the far northern part of Nigeria, a desert city astride the caravan trails, not far from Fort Lamy. Most of the buildings and homes were the thick-walled mud kind and were painted with decorations and prayer symbols.

We were met by the Emir and his retinue who padded along on their camels alongside his vintage Rolls Royce as they came down the airport road. Giant bicycle horns were mounted on the sides of the car, and we could hear their loud blast as they approached.

The Attorney General paid his respects and as we got ready to leave in the evening, Mr. Rogers brought the Emir on board to show off his Constellation. The Emir was a little man dressed in his tribal clothes, seeming almost happy-go-lucky as he peered in wonderment at our luxurious machine through campfire-reddened eyes. Through an interpreter, we explained

473

who did what, and how the airplane worked and he nodded vig-
orously as we bragged about our communications, and navigating by the stars and controlling the powerful engines. I'm not
sure if the Emir had been around as a very young child when
the French took a short cut through his neighborhood, which
was supposedly British territory at the time, and had to hide
from the marauding troops. He may have survived then, but he
didn't survive independence too long, for he was soon to be
swept away in the Nigerian turmoil that came after our visit.

William P. Rogers public image has always been one of,
well, intelligence and consideration -a perfect gentleman. In
person, this image was translated into reality. But he also
seemed to me a friendly, accessible person, ready to laugh or be
impressed but without letting go his sense of propriety. And,
because of this air of propriety, I was surprised to catch Mr.
Rogers, as his limousine passed by Cris and me loading the
Chevy after we returned, with his eyebrows arched and a silent
whistle on his lips as his eyes happened to fall on Cris. I didn't
think Republicans did things like that.

The end of my second year with the Special Air Missions
squadron came around as 1960 was drawing to a close. I had,
somewhere in that time, passed my ten thousandth flight hour
as a navigator, and although that is a lot of flying time for a
military navigator, Joe Smoe and one of the other navigators
had more than that. My flight rating had been upped from
Senior Navigator to Master Navigator which meant that the
little star on top of my navigator's wings would now be surrounded by a little silver wreath, like those of a Command
pilot. When unsuspecting persons asked us what the star and
wreath meant, we told them it indicated that one of our parents was a member of Congress.

Neither of these events had any effect on my position within the squadron. But I was also appointed as Flight Examiner
which meant that I not only flew missions on my own, but also
on trips to pass judgement on some of my colleagues, to check
out new navigators and to administer periodic checks to experienced navigators. It also meant that I had somehow wormed
my way into the confidence of the management and was placed
in the ranks of those who could be trusted. As a result, I was

now being scheduled as navigator on the Presidential aircraft Columbine. This did not mean that I was the President's navigator, since he now used one of the three new jets which were flown out of Andrews Air Force Base across the river on most of his flights.

My trips in the Columbine were either back-up flights for the Presidential jet, or they involved missions we called "State Department Specials," which had an itinerary specially designed for royalty. On the back-up flights we were required to prep for the flight just as though the President was on board, then sit on the ramp, ready to take the trip in the event the presidential jet did not check out. The State Department Specials usually took the royal party to Williamsburg, Virginia to look at some of our past history. Then we would head for places like Chicago, the Grand Canyon, San Francisco and Los Angeles. Los Angeles was visited because Hollywood and Disneyland were there and Chicago because "it was so American" and, I suspect, because the visitors halfway expected to see some gangster bullets fly. Of course, today, you don't have to go all the way to Chicago to experience that.

Crown Prince Akihito -now the Emperor of Japan- and his beautiful, doll-like bride made this tour and I vividly remember his shyness. As we sat in the airplane ready to go and waiting for the passengers to board, I suddenly realized there had been some change in procedures and the Prince and his bride were boarding by way of the crew entrance on the flight deck instead of by way of the main cabin door.

I had been tuning up the radar at my position just across from the entrance when I looked up directly into that shy stare, and his eyes slid away as he made his way to the rear. At the time of Admiral Perry, had I done the same thing, I no doubt would have been instantly beheaded.

King Frederick of Denmark and his Queen also made the trip and we were all settled down on the long, evening leg to the west coast. I sat hunched over the radar scope when suddenly, Bang! and I felt a big thump on my back. Startled, I looked up to see the King, smiling away, and he said, "That's it, Captain! Keep up the good work!" Then, clasping his hands behind him, he went forward to give the pilots similar encouragement.

After we landed at Los Angeles, I made my way to the rear to watch the arrival scene as if unfolded. The King and his party were standing near the main cabin door, waiting for it to be opened. He was pointing to the big Presidential seal mounted on the door which, when swung open, exposed the seal to the outside, waiting world.

I got there just in time to hear him say, "Now the sergeant tells me that is the President's seal," he said, looking around and demanding our attention. "If that is his seal, where does he keep his elephant?" We all roared with laughter, because when a king expects you to laugh, you better do it, G.I.!

Ike spent his summers at Newport, Rhode Island and we learned that he would make one last trip there as President. Bill Draper was to take him there in one of the jets while Don Billings and Bill Thomas were assigned as pilots on the stand-by Columbine, which would also make the trip. Since the Columbine carried a full crew no matter where it went, I was to go along too.

Our job was to sit around on close standby in the event the President had to go somewhere in a hurry and didn't have time to wait for the jet to come back to pick him up. The jet, of course, was too expensive to sit around on standby for a long period of time, so it was used on other trips. I was pleasantly surprised to hear from Don Billings that families were not only permitted to come along and stay, but were encouraged to do so. The idea of spending a summer up in New England in the Newport area not by myself but with Cris, Holly and the recently born Jill seemed like a great, unexpected gift. Not only that, but there was room on the Columbine for family members, which made the whole thing almost too good to be true. With this news in hand, I went home to tell Cris.

"Guess what," I said to her. This opening was intended to put her on alert, and to tell her that she should remain calm.

"We're getting transferred?" she offered.

"No. Just another trip for a month or two. Pack your bags."

"Me too?" A little bit of surprise was beginning to show.

"You. The kids. The dog might be a problem."

"Can we fly?"

"Of course. On the Columbine."

476

"That's nice. I hope Ike doesn't mind."

After we talked about it for a while, we decided that for all those weeks, it would be more fun to have our own car along. Since I was pretty well tied to the airplane, Cris was stuck with the task of bringing it from Washington to Quonset Point Naval Air Station, where the Columbine would sit on alert.

But there was no way she could be denied a trip on the presidential aircraft, so we concocted a complicated plan. First, Cris, Holly and I would make the flight to Quonset Point, near Newport and spend a weekend while Jill stayed behind with neighbors. Then Cris and Holly would return on the Gooney Bird shuttle operated by the Navy several times during the week between Washington and Quonset Point. Then she would pack up the girls, put the dog in a kennel and drive back up.

For the first time, Cris and Holly were passengers on an airplane on which I was a crewmember. While we were getting the airplane preflighted, they came on board with the other passengers and as they settled into their seats, Holly became convinced that since she couldn't see me, I was being left behind. One of the flight attendants noticed her alarm and assured her that, yes, I was on board and up front, "playing with his Chinese television set." He took her by the hand and brought her up to the flight deck where I was tuning up the radar. She climbed up into my lap and watched as I went through the checklist, flipping switches and twirling knobs.

When the weekend was up, Cris and Holly got a ride back to Washington National on the Navy shuttle, a Super C-47 which was modified with bigger engines and other improvements. John Eisenhower, the president's son was one of the few other passengers on board and he appeared obviously accustomed to the perks which were forced on him.

When the airplane landed at National, several chauffeur-driven cars pulled up to the airplane, and one of the drivers approached Cris as she stepped down onto the ramp with Holly.

"To the White House, Ma'm?" he asked.

If it was me, I would have said "If you don't mind," just to take the ride and get the feeling not too many people get, of wheeling up to that perfect mansion and going through those

477

well-guarded gates in a White House car.

But Cris had her mind on getting things together and returning north, and all she wanted to do was to get to the Chevy and get home. So she had the car take them to the Base Operations parking lot, and the chance was gone.

Being on standby can get pretty boring if all you can do is sit around the motel we had found near the main gate and wait for a telephone call. That's the way it was for the first few days at Quonset Point, but then the situation loosened up after Cris returned and we were able to head for the beach. Sometimes I dropped Cris and girls off and went out to the base to sit around operations, or climb into the Columbine and prowl around, sitting in Ike's seat, trying to imagine lesser moments of history, like Soviet Premier Khrushchev when he was on board, loudly complaining about not getting enough Scotch in his drink. Other times I would stay at the beach and help Cris and Holly look for starfish or unbroken shells, while baby Jill, who was nine months old and had gotten to be a lot of fun to watch, wiggled around in her portable crib.

We rode the ferry over to Newport and took some of the tourist tours through the twenty or thirty-room beach cottages along the shore and had great seafood lunches at restaurants which overlooked the water. The weather was really great; cool, breezy and dry with a few fluffy good-weather clouds floating across the water.

On some mornings we would sit on the motel lawn and help Holly with her coloring book or watch Jill discover the outside world. One such morning as we sat sipping our coffee, we heard some loud popping noises and some yelling which came from a tree-covered hillside behind the motel. I went around back to get a better look and began to realize that what I heard was firing from perhaps a couple of dozen rifles.

Suddenly, a group of Marines in fatigues and helmets entered a clearing from one side, in a crouching run, each man stopping to rise up and fire, then crouching down and running again. In a moment, another group entered from the other side, also running and firing the same way. The second group was helmet-less and bare above the waist, to mark them apart from the other group, and I concluded that one bunch were the intruders and the other, the defenders.

They came within about twenty yards of each other and fired their blank cartridges, still yelling loudly between shots. I don't know if there had been an agreed number of mock casualties who were required to fall down or leave the action, but no one budged; they all stood their ground. Suddenly, one of the bare-chested marines threw his gun down and ran toward the uniformed group and two or three others followed. Five or six of the uniformed marines also threw their guns down and they collided in the clearing, flailing away with their fists, with epithets floating to us on the morning air that were unique enough for me to file away for future study. Nobody tried to stop the fights, but the surging lust to prevail soon died and the action came to an end.

The fist-fighters staggered back toward their groups, looking around in the grass for their weapons, some of them wiping bloody noses. It wasn't long before the groups came together again, this time with lots of raucous laughter and back-slapping, and then they all formed up into skirmish lines and walked back into the trees, toward the base. Apparently they were just working off the plate of rusty nails and broken razor blades they had had for breakfast.

One morning we got the word that Ike would interrupt his vacation and go to Denver on the jet -Air Force One- to make a speech. Since the Columbine would also head west to back up the flight, Mamie, the First Lady decided she would take the opportunity to head west also, on the Columbine, to Arizona, where we would drop her off and rendezvous with Air Force One at Denver. We all knew that Mrs. Eisenhower had to gather up all of her courage to overcome that cold fear of flying that many people have, and that Don Billings and Bill Thomas and the flight attendants would need to do what they could to make things easy for her.

The First Lady managed to endure the flight nervously as she always did. Some subterfuges were used to satisfy her belief that there was safety in flying low and slow. The airspeed and altitude indicators on the forward wall of the VIP compartment could be phonied up to disguise the true height and airspeed, and this was done whenever she was on board.

After we dropped her off we went to Denver to meet with Air Force One and act as backup for the Presidential aircraft. When the President was through, both aircraft went back to Quonset Point so that he could resume his vacation.

The end of Ike's vacation came with the autumn chill, and was marked by a fancy clambake at a Newport country club given by the Governor of Rhode Island. The crew was invited and Cris and I had a long conversation with Jim Haggerty, the President's press aide. Haggerty was a powerful figure in the Administration, since he was not viewed merely as a representative from the press who was assigned to make news gathering more convenient for reporters. Instead, he was a member of the President's staff whose views on the impact of a proposal on public opinion were part of the decision-making process.

Some years later, I was taking the air shuttle from Washington to New York, and as we took off, I looked over at my seat mate and it was none other than Jim Haggerty. He had been on friendly terms with Ike's aircrew and recalled incidents from some of the trips with a chuckle. It was obvious he was enjoying his life outside the political arena, outside the pressure cooker.

Now came presidential election day, and, of course, John F. Kennedy was elected. Suddenly, nothing happened in the lower key anymore. Everything began to take on an increased urgency and excitement, generated in equal measure by the domestic political situation and by the activities of our foreign adversaries.

Kennedy's victory certainly had a direct impact on our squadron, since a new president meant a new Presidential aircrew. Colonel Bill Draper had been not only the Presidential pilot, but Ike's Air Force Aide as well, and there was not a chance he would stay on. So most of the 1254th Group flyboys sat around wondering if they might be struck by the presidential lightning and gain one of the ultimate pinnacles of crewdog status, that of permanent crewmember on Air Force One.

I'm not certain who had the power to make the decision, but the chosen few were certain to be scrutinized at the highest Air Force level. I did not count myself among these few since I was certain the pilots, navigator and flight engineer would be chosen from the jet contingent at Andrews. Nevertheless, it was a time of tension for us all, and the rumors flew, including one which was obviously concocted at Happy Hour, which would have us believe that since Mr. Kennedy was a Catholic, only members of that persuasion would be chosen and that the aircraft, in keeping with the same attitude which gave rise to the name "Sacred Cow," would be called "The Holy Mackerel."

As I surmised, the crew was chosen from among the Andrews group, including the new Presidential pilot Jim Swindal. Bill Draper looked around for a command assignment and found one up in Alaska, while the other pilots in the Presidential Pilot's Office stayed with the organization.

I didn't get the chance to mope around too much because about the time all of this was happening, I was promoted to the rank of Major and given a supervisory job in the navigation section. We had a promotion party on our patio with some of the other new majors and with the neighbors. I had laid by some bottles of French champagne which I had brought back on my trips and we drank it up like it was going out of style. For weeks afterward, when I mowed the lawn, the mower would snag up one of the foil-capped corks and..Zing!..the missile would shoot off like a bullet and bang into a tree or the side of the house. A major's pay still wasn't all that great, but it was certainly a definite improvement. It permitted us to live in what you might call "elegant poverty."

Up to the time I made Major, I really hadn't worried much about my long term goals. Suddenly here I was, in my middle thirties with a wife and two kids, in a career with a dead end. I had been a reserve Air Force officer for eighteen years, and I could expect only two more years on active duty. It was very unusual for a reservist to get this far but once I reached this point, twenty years and retirement at half pay was pretty much assured. The problem was that half pay retirement for a Major with twenty years was peanuts.

One thing I had done was to attend after-hours college classes along the way, and this was not an easy thing to do. Along with people in my same situation, both officer and enlisted, we would sign up for courses and give it the old college try, sometimes bleary-eyed after a long work day, sometimes having to deal with an instructor who wasn't that crazy about the military. The University of California, University of Maryland, Florida State University, Georgetown University; all had a chance to number me among their alumnae, but I just wasn't around in one place long enough.

Once I retired as a reservist, it would seem wise for me to find a university that suited me and get my degree. But a degree in what? I had come to believe that becoming involved in some endeavor outside the flying business would be an act of desperation, no matter how well it paid. So what did I do? While I attended college classes, I also joined the 1254th Group flying club to start on my way toward all of the FAA pilot tickets; private pilot, commercial, instrument pilot and the top of the pile; the air transport pilot certificate.

When I had the time, I would check in with Master Sergeant Magee -I have already described his success in getting me to solo- and we would climb into the club Piper Tri-Pacer, right there at National, and head off somewhere to teach me all over again why airplanes stall, and to do some of the less violent maneuvers. Then we would go to some small airport like Croom, in Maryland, which was just a grass strip marked off with white-painted auto tires, and shoot landings.

One very windy day, Magee had me trying to put the little bird down at the right spot between the tires. The approach to the runway, such as it was, took us over a bare spot, then over some high trees, maybe sixty or seventy feet high, then we came to the approach end of the grass.

I was able to put the Tri-Pacer down with some difficulty three of four times, then just before Magee was satisfied, I made one more approach, and as I cleared the open spot and came up on the trees, a downdraft sucked us down. The high trees rose before us, not looking as deadly as they really were, and I slammed the throttle forward, and nothing happened. I pulled it back once and slammed it forward again and the engine caught in full power, and we shot upward barely clear of the trees.

"Let's go home," Magee said, and that was good enough for me.

Flying a little airplane out of National Airport presented more than the usual number of challenges; I got to feel like a small winged bug flitting around in a sky full of hawks and eagles who could gobble me up and spit me out. Propwash was a big concern and we had to avoid flying behind and slightly below the big airliners where the effect was the greatest.

Whenever we returned to National, the traffic procedure was to have us hold over Georgetown reservoir and circle until the tower felt there was a break in the traffic flow large enough to accommodate us.

"Okay, Tripacer number so-and-so, take up a heading to the field and squeeze in between the TWA Connie and the Delta DC-7 now on the downwind for runway three-six," the tower would call, just as though there was nothing to it.

As we came down the final approach, the man in the tower would usually call, "Okay Magee, how about giving us a slip so you can clear the runway at the first turn." Magee would then give it left aileron to put that wing down and give it opposite rudder to keep the airplane on heading and we would slide down like an elevator, with our forward motion greatly slowed. Just at the right time, he would kick and roll everything straight and put the Tripacer on the concrete just right. I liked the maneuver so much I practiced it to perfection and sometimes used it even when I didn't need to. It also came in handy later because a modified form of it can be used during normal crosswind landings.

I owe the Old Sarge a lot. Your first instructor who leads you to success, especially the one who gets you to solo, stays with you. He was with me in spirit, years later, at the FAA Academy in Oklahoma City when the Examiner ran me through the list, not omitting a single requirement in a flight check which highly experienced pilots sometimes failed. And he was with me when the Examiner, after my successful 145 knot no-flap landing, the final item, looked over at me and said, "Okay Captain, that's good enough for me."

Despite the continuing changes in the 1254th, including preparations to move all of us to Andrews, business was still brisk for us at National. For one thing, we still had a few remaining African independence celebrations to deal with, and we took Arthur Goldberg, Kennedy's new Secretary of Labor to one of them. As the Goldbergs were packing for their return trip, they found that a snake was trying to stow away in their luggage. And Mrs. Goldberg's instincts as a Jewish mother were evident as she let us know we were working too hard and not getting enough to eat. On one occasion, she came up front herself with some extra plates of dessert.

It didn't take long for the Presidency to catch up with JFK. He had his first few months of the usual re-organizational turmoil and then, in April, 1961, disaster struck. The Bay of Pigs invasion was launched. The invasion of Fidel Castro's communist Cuba by a U.S.-trained army had been hatched during the Eisenhower administration. The army consisted of about 1500 young Cubans from families who had been forced to flee because of Fidel's revolution. The time was not opportune during Ike's second term so it was handed off to JFK, who had the go, no-go responsibility when the time came. It become obvious right away that the operation was a planning and decision-making fiasco. The invasion force got into big trouble right from the start, and they were abandoned to complete defeat. If only he hadn't let it happen, the young President must have thought, over and over again. If only! If only!

The Bay of Pigs event was the beginning of a new era for us at the 1254th Air Transport Group. Before that time, we were able to spend our alert periods at home. After the Bay of Pigs, if we were on alert, we had to pack a bag and move out to the base, close to the airplane. The way it all started for some of us was a call around midnight as the invasion attempt was going forward, and failing. The caller had alerted me for a flight and I arrived about forty-five minutes after receiving the call to find an unaccustomed amount of hubbub going on. Mechanics and refuelers who normally kept their cool regardless of the pressure were scurrying about in the glare of the flight-line floodlights.

We were briefed quickly for a trip to Miami where the pilots, who had just landed at National from another trip, would rest while the passengers, who were not identified to us immediately, accomplished their business. We were told to expect a return to Washington in the early afternoon. Little bits and pieces of information were picked up here and there, but the big picture escaped us. As for me, I had no idea what was going on.

As I walked up the flight stairs I passed by Colonel McHugh, the president's new Air Force aide who had evidently left a party in a hurry and was attired in full dress uniform. He was shaking his head and anxiously checking his watch. I walked through the stateroom on the way to the cockpit and had to brush by a gentleman I thought I recognized from newsphotos I had seen as Adolf Berle, the president's Latin Affairs advisor, who looked like a man who had been kicked in the stomach, yet he nodded and politely wished me good evening.

By the time we headed south, we had learned that an invasion of Cuba by Cuban exiles had been attempted and would certainly fail, and that we were bringing Berle and Arthur M. Schlesinger Jr. of the White House staff to meet with the top anti-Castro Cubans involved. The Cubans comprised the Cuban Revolutionary Council, who had planned to come ashore right behind the landings and set up a provisional government.

Apparently, the operation had not yet been screwed up enough and we, in our small way, were given the chance to screw it up a little further. But like Buster Keaton, who ducks just in time to be missed by the custard pie, we missed the chance.

The plan called for us to deliver Messrs. Berle and Schlesinger to Miami International and wait there until they were ready to return to Washington. They would proceed by car to nearby Opa Locka, to console the Cubans who were being held incommunicado, for some reason, at an abandoned airport.

We arrived at Miami just as dawn broke and Trusty Whitehead, the aircraft commander and his co-pilot Dick Twining, the Air Force Chief of Staff's son headed for bed. We had agreed, I thought, on the Skyways Motel and as they left I told them I would be along later since I had already had enough sleep and would wait at the swimming pool for a call from the contact man. The arrangement was real convenient since the motel was just a short walk from the flight line and I was able to persuade the manager to open the pool early.

At about nine AM I heard them page my name for a phone call, and the caller announced that there had been a change in schedule and that we were to depart immediately for Opa Locka. It turned out that a decision had been made to have Berle and Schlesinger bring the Revolutionary Council back to Washington with them to meet with the President as soon as possible.

I hurriedly dressed and walked to the front desk. "Captain Whitehead or Captain Twining please."

The clerk checked through his card file, then checked again. "Sorry, nobody registered here by those names." I thought I had taken leave of my senses. "You mean they've checked out?"

"No, I have no record of Whitehead or Twining." I began to get a little panicky, but since I hadn't actually seen them check in I realized that they must have been sidetracked and gone elsewhere. But where? With an increasing sense of doom, I headed out to the airplane. Whatever hopes I had left were dashed when the rest of the crew, who hadn't needed sleep either, said they hadn't seen the pilots since we landed.

With a nonchalance I didn't feel, I usurped the A/C's prerogative and asked Ken Mayo, the flight engineer, to get the airplane ready, then walked over to operations to get the paperwork done. When I got to operations, there was a call waiting for Trusty Whitehead from the mysterious trip coordinator, who I think was a CIA big shot. All he wanted to know was if there generally was some liquor on board for the passengers to drink, and I got the impression they would need it. We hadn't brought any down, so one of the flight attendants had to run off somewhere to find some.

The pilot always files the clearance but I was able to perform this chore, wondering as I did it how to enlist the aid of the man behind the counter without letting him know the predicament we were in; we had an airplane, passengers to pick up, fuel on board and a place to go, but no pilots.

"Has Captain Whitehead been around?" I asked.

"No, he hasn't. You want me to call his hotel?" Sure, what have I got to lose, I thought, and gave him the name of the motel I had just left. The pickup time was getting close but I tried not to look too desperate. The man dialed once, spoke to someone and waited for a while, then hung up and dialed again. After a moment's further conversation he handed me the phone and said, "Here's Captain Whitehead on the line."

The man behind the counter smiled at my bewilderment. After I talked with Trusty, he said, "There is an Airways Motel and a Skyways Motel here. If you don't find them in one, they're usually in the other.

We picked up our angry and sorrowing passengers, who not only had to deal with the failure, but also had sons who were missing in the action, along with other young Cubans they themselves had recruited for the mission. As we flew northward to Washington, they could only hope that their sons and the other invasion force members were captured and not dead.

The failure at the Bay of Pigs and the surprisingly popular support which the Communist revolution was enjoying in Cuba prompted President Kennedy to re-examine our policies in Latin America. An apparent outcome was a decision to help upgrade the Latin American economies to counter the rising tide of Communist agitation in the region. A program was put together and called the Alliance for Progress. Adlai Stevenson, the Democrat candidate for president who had been defeated twice by Eisenhower was given the task of visiting every country in South America to sell the program. He was to make the trip in one of our aircraft, and I was assigned to the crew.

At one time, a chief of state or his emissary could make an official visit without creating a massive, sometimes dangerous uproar regardless of the political implications of his trip. To be sure, assassins have always lurked as they did at Sarajevo; some of them successful, some of them bunglers, and who knows how many who turned chicken at the last minute. But they were usually elements of a small nut fringe who thought that the only way they could become a person to be reckoned with was to perform some spectacular act.

Just a year and a half before, President Eisenhower was able to make a full-scale state visit to countries like Greece, Turkey, Iran, Afghanistan, India and Pakistan, all of which were politically volatile, without being subjected to unfriendly acts. He rode in open cars through massive crowds and without the need for overwhelming security precautions. The only incident where he could have been harmed occurred in New Delhi, India where his car was surrounded and stopped by a surging crush of Delhians, part of a crowd of a million people, who threw flowers and wanted merely to touch him.

The crush was getting to the point that the President and his host, Prime Minister Nehru might be injured and the people themselves trampled. Nehru was able to calm the crowd in front of the car so that a space could be opened, then he jumped out onto the road. The crowd parted before him like the Red Sea before Moses, and the slightly damaged car was again able to proceed. The incident had happened not because of hatred, but because of adulation.

But how quickly things changed as visits by top level dignitaries became pivot points around which mass political demonstrations were turned. Friendly, cheering crowds waved small flags of the visitor's country while unfriendly elements rioted and sometimes burned a large version of the same flag. Acts came to be committed and passed without too much notice which would have caused severe diplomatic traumas or even war in the past. The change in status of the VIP traveler from a manipulator of public opinion to one who is manipulated was beginning to raise some of the trips from routine to memorable, especially if the trip was intended to involve some degree of exposure of the VIP to the public. Adlai Stevenson's trip to South America was one of these.

It seems strange to recall now that we -the crew- received no security briefing although I presume Governor Stevenson's party knew what the various threat levels were. With expectations beginning to rise all throughout Latin America, the potential for trouble existed everywhere; in most places it could be controlled, but in other places, we would have to wait and see.

Our aircraft commander was Jim Conover, an old pro who was to have his coolness tested on his arrival in Saigon, some years later by the Viet Cong's launching of the Tet offensive. I can imagine his feelings as he crouched in his quarters in town as tanks maneuvered and fired in nearby streets and fighter-bombers released rockets overhead.

The Governor -he had been governor of Illinois- had us meet him in Buenos Aires, where he had arrived by commercial airliner after starting his tour at Caracas, Venezuela. We had to sweat out some low ceilings because of the seasonal rains in the Platte delta. The situations at Buenos Aires and again at Montevideo, Uruguay were both under full control, as they had been at Caracas. We headed inland, and the rains fell intermittently as we taxied up to the waiting nabobs at Asuncion, Paraguay. A lesser man would have slapped his forehead in dismay as he surveyed what seemed to be the whole Paraguayan army strung out in single file, awaiting inspection.

Stevenson resolutely locked step with the officer of the guard and took off over the horizon, trying to ignore the occasional shower . He eventually returned, no doubt a better man, but with his awareness dulled by fatigue. He let himself get too close to his escort, and had to pull back quickly as the officer, his sword held at the salute, just missed Stevenson's nose as he wheeled around to notify his visitor that his services were no longer required.

So far, the flashing sword had been the extent of our immediate security problems, but possible troubles were expected at Santiago, Chile, our next stop. To get from Asuncion to Santiago, you have the Andes mountains to cross. The Chilean Andes pose no problems for today's jets, which can vault the twenty thousand-foot-plus peaks with altitude to spare. Our Connie, however would have been somewhat abused to operate at an altitude high enough to clear 22,834-foot Mt. Aconcagua with a few thousand feet extra for grandma as needed under instrument conditions.

The mountain stood guard at the entrance to a relatively narrow pass which, when the skies are clear, can be negotiated at medium altitudes for a direct descent to Santiago. But when the airplane is flying on instruments at altitudes lower than the mountain tops, the pilot must follow an airway marked with radiobeacons which is routed over low terrain. The route proceeds northward across the mouth of the pass, then turns westward across the Andes where the mountains are lower, and finally, southward to Santiago on the descent.

Both Jim Conover and I could see the city of Santiago through occasional gaps in the clouds and knew it was possible to take up a heading and take the plunge, assuming you were directly over the pass and not too close to Aconcagua.

"Nah, that's no way to run an airline," said Conover after we discussed it, and he pressed on along the airway. But Mr. Stevenson had seen it too, and he sent his aide up to ask why we hadn't slipped through the pass and save some time. If he had been a man we could have bantered with, we could have told him we did not want to make the mountain-top statue of the Christ of the Andes, also visible through gaps in the cloud, a monument to our foolhardiness. But Jim just shrugged. "Just tell him we're required to stay on the route we've been cleared to fly. Its for his safety." The word safety usually ended the discussion, and it did this time too.

Nothing happened at Santiago. The rumblings were there and there were some minor outbreaks of unrest which were kept away from the center of the city. Those who wanted to turn the government firmly leftward would have to wait almost ten years. In 1970, the people of Chile, who generally preferred ballots to bullets, voted a Marxist candidate, Salvador Allende into office as president, the first time such a candidate had been freely elected to the top office anywhere. A few years later, the economy was in a shambles, Chileans were rioting in the streets and eventually, Allende was overthrown.

Meanwhile, Adlai Stevenson met with the leaders of Chile, made his speeches, appeared on the front pages of the local newspapers sometimes caricatured as an American Superman, sometimes as the Yankee Devil. Then we headed northward for our next stop, Lima, Peru. As we flew up the snow-capped Andean backbone the first tangible evidence of trouble which concerned both the VIP and the crew alike confronted us.

Our routine position reporting communications were interrupted by a message from Lima. It advised that a hostile demonstration could be expected at Lima International Airport or on the roads leading to it and advised us to land at another airport on the other side of town. The alternate landing was made without difficulty and we were all whisked into town and into the safety of a well-guarded hotel. Some of the members of the welcoming delegation who had waited at the originally chosen airport were not so lucky and their cars had to run the gauntlet as they were returning from their wild goose chase. The Spanish ambassador to Peru, who was riding in an impressive-looking limousine that was apparently thought to contain

Mr. Stevenson, had his car heavily damaged.

We heard reports of scattered acts of rioting and violence, but the Governor was able to make his way around town to conduct his business. Then we headed northward once more, for Ecuador, where we would stop first at Guayaquil for a quick speech, then proceed to Quito, the capitol of the country.

The airport crowd at Guayaquil was the first one we had met so far that seemed genuinely friendly. They had draped welcoming banners from the airport terminal observation deck and cheered as Stevenson came down the stairs. He launched into a speech before the flight engineer could shut down the auxiliary power unit, a gas-engine driven machine in the rear of the aircraft that had been quitting with a loud pop when the fuel was shut off. Conover had to decide which was more bothersome; the steady drone of the APU, or the loud disturbing noise of the backfire. Jim had the engineer shut it off and sure enough the thing went off with a bang like a pistol shot and suddenly you could hear a pin drop. Nobody breathed, and I could see Mr. Stevenson's eyes, those bright, amazingly blue eyes swivelled around to the source of the sound and opened wide as if to say, "Is this it? Is now the time?"

But now was not the time, and we proceeded to Quito where we were put up in a very plush hotel with a super-size swimming pool and a gambling casino. As usual, I made a little money at Blackjack and took it over to the crap table where I was sure to lose it. I got there as Conover had the dice, and listened as he had to explain a slightly complex hedge bet to the croupier. The croupier, a local man, seemed to be getting on-the-job training from a Chicago type standing beside him who looked skyward and shrugged helplessly.

The honeymoon was finally over when we got to La Paz, perched on its twelve-thousand-foot-plus Bolivian mountain top. There was no alternate airport at which to land and the reports we received were all ominous. The tin miners had been up in arms for some time as were the students and the Indians. The hostile demonstrators had been faked out somehow and there was no waiting crowd at the airport or along the route into town. We made it to the hotel to find it guarded like a fortress, with streets cordoned off by troops and with a platoon of young, determined-looking military cadets guarding the hotel itself. They were armed with bayonet-tipped rifles and appeared ready to give up their lives if they had to. There were also several squads of firemen who stood by across the road with tank trucks and high-pressure water cannons.

Mr. Stevenson had to leave this sanctuary several times and proceed directly into the lions mouth as the rest of us sat around to await reports. In the evening the Governor would return with deep fatigue etched in his face, his breath coming in gasps because of the rarefied air.

As we sat and waited for the visit to wind its course, I attached myself to newsman Charles McCarthy, a correspondent for the New York Daily News who had commandeered a telephone and had stationed himself in a small lounge just off the lobby. He had used the telephone to deploy his leg-men to strategic locations, and then sat and waited for the reports to come in.

Mr. Stevenson left to attend a function on his last night in La Paz and this was the signal for whoever was in charge of riots to give the word, and hell broke loose. McCarthy's phone started to ring and excited voices on the other end gave him blow-by-blow descriptions of the rioting. Most of his conversations were in Spanish, but he took the time to tell me what was going on. Reports of casualties started to come in; first injuries, which were mounting rapidly, then deaths.

McCarthy, trying to stay calm in the mounting tension always asked, " How many bodies did you see with your own eyes?" and, "Were they shot in front or back?"

Of course, it didn't make much difference to a dead rioter whether he was shot front or back but it did to McCarthy, who wanted to report on the legitimacy of the anti-riot measures being taken. If the rioter was shot "in the front" it was presumed he was killed or wounded while attacking the police or riot troops. If he was shot in the rear, it was presumed that he was shot while retreating and that force had been over-applied.

The number of deaths climbed to twelve, all of them "shot in the front," with many more injured. Mr. Stevenson returned to the sudden bedlam in the hotel, his eyes stricken with tragedy and disappointment, his lungs again gasping for breath.

"Do you have anything to say about the dead students?" he

was asked by one of the reporters, and what the hell do you say to something like that? But he groped for the right answer, expressing regret and not blame, and sadly stating his own bereavement.

We got ready to leave the next day and Mr. Stevenson thanked the young cadets, who had been billeted in the basement of the hotel. Everyone seemed to be affected by a sense of loss as we drove past the university where the students had barricaded themselves and it stayed with us as we took off from the mountain-top airport. La Paz means The Peace, and Adlai Stevenson had found no peace there.

After La Paz, the rest of the trip was pretty much an anti-climax. First, a short hop northward to Bogota, Colombia where I once sat on a river bank and idly wondered if a piranha would bite off my toes if I stuck my feet into the water; and watched a sloth suspended in a tree laboriously shift position from time to time as he waited for night, and feeding time, to fall. Then we doubled back to the southeast, to Brazilia, almost completed, still waiting for someone to touch it with a sense of life. And finally we arrived at our last stop, Rio de Janeiro, Brazil.

It was by the time we reached Rio, I think, that the depression of La Paz started to wear off and the world seemed to return to normal. Otherwise, I would not have so clearly remembered our arrival there -which, thankfully, was friendly-when the VIP's climbed into their big Cadillacs and Mercedes and swept grandly away, surrounded on all sides by a squadron of helmeted and gauntleted motorcycle escort. When they were gone, I could observe a single motorcycle policeman left high and dry when his machine had stalled in the excitement.

I can still see him completely alone and astride his machine on the suddenly deserted ramp, his chance for glory lost. His forlorn backside hiked up in the air and came down with a thump as he jammed down the foot-starter to get the infernal thing started again, up and down, up and down...

20

THE PRESIDENTIAL HAT

THE KENNEDY ADMINISTRATION, which started out with a bang and a whimper at the Bay of Pigs, was quickly handed another basket of snakes to deal with by the Soviets a few months later, in Berlin. Almost overnight, in August 1961, the Soviets and East Germans built the Berlin Wall.

The Wall, which has now been dismantled, caused a great shock of dismay to be felt around the world. There was even some tough talk about knocking it down with American tanks at the time, but that didn't happen. Instead, the barrier remained for adventuresome or desperate East Germans to pole-vault over it, tunnel underneath it and find other, not always successful ways to escape.

The East Germans have jack-hammered parts of the wall that have been imaginatively painted with graffiti and political murals into sections and have sold them as works of art. Perhaps they can earn additional hard currency by staging thrilling re-enactments for tourists of the more clever and daring escape attempts. They could use barb-less barbed wire, ketchup blood and stage one-way shoot-outs between guards firing blanks and escapees armed with, well, maybe a toothbrush and a burning desire for freedom.

After the Berlin Wall problem arose, more brush fires, conflagrations and suspiciously smoldering situations kept popping up all over the world. The Congo had come apart as predicted and some action was required to keep the Soviets out.

494

Laos, in Southeast Asia was a problem from the start and 5000 U.S. Marines had to be placed just across the border in Thailand to intimidate the communist Pathet Lao into a truce with the weak Laos government. Viet Nam was in a similar situation, but it was obvious that 5000 Marines would not be able to do the trick as they did next door in Laos. Vice President Lyndon Johnson was sent there on a survey trip a few months after JFK's inauguration, and when he recommended a military buildup, General Maxwell Taylor was sent to take another look a few months later. The Red Chinese were massing troops on their coast adjacent to Taiwan and appeared ready to invade Chiang Kai- shek's island stronghold. Meanwhile, Chiang Kai-shek was pounding on the table for American assistance for an invasion of Red China by his army.

Poor JFK: the list goes on. The Red Chinese were apparently not fully occupied by the threat from Chiang Kai-shek so they launched a small invasion of disputed territory on their border with India. And when the President decided to send military aid to India, India's next-door neighbor and mortal enemy Pakistan got angry and people had to be sent there to hold their hand. All of these events required that high-level emissaries, firemen, experts, negotiators, apologizers, intimidators and seekers of the truth be dispatched to where the action was, and our squadron carried a good share of them.

New President, new cabinet members, new White House staff: the new administration brought with them a different atmosphere. The old crowd had been in office for eight years and had become confident Special Air Missions travelers and were easy to deal with. The new bunch seemed a little less sure of themselves, at least in the beginning, and apparently not quite as well organized. Short-notice trips had been rare in the past, and now they did not seem unusual. For a while, at least, the new travelers seemed awed by the political status they had attained, and by some of the perks to which they were now entitled. Our airplanes were roomy, uncrowded and spotless on the inside, and so shiny on the outside the finish could hurt your eyes when the sun was bright. And when they landed, there was a lot of bowing and scraping by the welcoming party and, for the biggies and their aides, limousines and fancy quarters. The flight attendants really knew their stuff; they had that practiced, ego-enhancing air you might find in a first-class hotel or restaurant.

There were, of course, more luxurious ways to travel, like first-class on some of the major international airlines, with caviar and lots of champagne and French brandy after a pretty good dinner. But "G.I. plush," based on a lot less money than the airlines had to work with, didn't do too bad. The meals, which the passengers paid for out of their travel allowance, were generally "roast beef basic" but often with some fancy touches, and I could get into trouble with Cris when I returned from a trip and suggested we have some melon and prosciutto for appetizers, which I had managed to sample.

There was less ceremony in the departures and arrivals for a while, and the VIP's and their entourage would be whisked on and off the airplane. But somebody like JFK had to pay his ceremonial dues every time, except for his trips to Hyannisport. As a student of such matters, I would make it a point to watch JFK from our terminal windows as he moved through the departure choreography. First, the arrival in the bubble-top Presidential car, with smiles and waves to the crowd along the flight line fence. The car is stopped at the foot of the line of official greeters, high level well-wishers and relatives.

The limo door is opened and he and Jackie step out with big smiles and waves to the cheering crowd. The Presidential couple makes their way along the reception line quickly, yet not seeming to be in a hurry, Jackie hanging back slightly, a bouquet of flowers in her arms.

JFK holds his hat along his left side as he shakes all the proffered hands, then he and the First Lady mount the platform. The President steps up to the microphones and faces the flight line scene spread before him. He avoids a direct gaze into the massed TV cameras set up on a separate platform just off to one side, until he begins to speak, and then he looks straight into America's TV eyes. He informs America and the world what he expects to accomplish on his trip, thanks them for their support, then, as he finishes his short speech, he steps back slightly and waves again to the crowd as they cheer loudly.

Then he turns toward the airplane, shakes hands of all those on the platform with him, and slowly makes his way toward the air stairs, followed by Jackie. They climb about half way up, turn and wave to the applauding crowd around the airplane, then they finish the climb to the top of the stairs. One final wave to the entire assemblage, another big smile as they all cheer, then they turn, duck their heads as JFK follows his wife into the airplane, and it is over.

I came to the conclusion that JFK still had some rough edges that needed work, like what to do with the hat. He could have taken some pointers from Eisenhower, whose arrivals and departures were always masterfully done. And Ike looked as though he, once in a while, actually wore the hat he carried. JFK looked as though he wouldn't put his on in a thunderstorm, and only carried it to have something to do with his hands.

When the president arrives somewhere, the ceremony is usually a reverse replay of the choreography I have just described. But when visitors come to Washington to see the President, things are done differently. The Prime Minister or whatever is whisked away from Andrews in the Presidential helicopter and landed on the Ellipse near the White House. A limousine then picks up the party for the short ride to the rear portico of the Mansion, where the President and First Lady await them. There are booming cannons if the VIP rates a salute, with fanfares, a snappy parade and serenade by the Marine or Army Band, and then the speeches. It was, and is, memorable theater.

After some years in the business, I noticed we all had a tendency to get somewhat jaded about the proceedings and some of the VIP's involved. Most of my trips were now sort of zipping by without registering very much on my memory, except for a few. There was a trip on which we took Secretary of Defense McNamara to Puerto Rico so that he could attend a hemispheric defense conference. Since the Bay of Pigs, the military establishment and the Secretary were reported to regard each other with mutual disdain. When we arrived at Puerto Rico, it was interesting to note that he stood alone waiting for his helicopter while the generals and their families greeted each other like old family members. Some time later, I happened to hear McNamara reading the citation for an award of a military decoration for bravery. When he reached the part describing the courage and the sacrifice of the recipient, his voice trembled so badly I thought he might not be able to finish, but he did. He was, and is, a very complex man.

And then there was Lyndon Baines Johnson once more. After his trip to Saigon, he seemed to disappear from view, obviously due to the wishes of JFK and those close to him. For a man like LBJ, this was very hard to take, and he must have come to agree with an earlier Vice President from Texas -John Nance Garner- who had decided that the job "wasn't worth a bucket of warm spit." In between some of his un-publicized ceremonial trips, he would apparently vent some of his frustrations by using our aircraft to take joyrides.

Ralph Albertazzie, who was his pilot on most of these trips, wasn't always sure what the destination would be right up to take-off time, and what time the Vice-president would show up for the next leg of the trip. All of this uncertainty was good training for Ralph. When he later became Richard Nixon's presidential pilot, he was given the task of flying Henry Kissinger around on those highly secretive trips to set up President Nixon's visit to Red China. He was, of course, the pilot on Mr. Nixon's momentous trip.

I only had one experience with Mr. Johnson aboard an aircraft while he was still the V.P. We picked him up in New York after he had attended what must have been a dressy affair at the Waldorf, for he came on board in white tie and tails. His destination was San Juan and by the time we arrived there, he had changed into a suit. They were leaving by way of the crew entrance, and he came out of his stateroom fuming, a hapless Army sergeant at his heels. As they passed by me they stopped, and the sergeant put a suitcase on the table at which I sat and they both started to rummage through it for what seemed to be a missing cuff-link. LBJ's impatience and frustration billowed out from around him like flames from a flame-thrower, but the sergeant took it like a man.

They finally found the damn thing, and LBJ stood there with his arm out-thrust like some Pedernales version of Julius Caesar while the sweating sergeant found the holes in the imperial cuff and snapped the cuff-link shut. Then LBJ turned toward the exit and hurtled forward and I thought that if he didn't hit the doorway, he would make one of his own.

There came a time, later on after I had retired and was working for the FAA, I had a chance to revisit the Special Air Missions organization, still at Andrews Air Force Base, now designated as the 89th Military Airlift Wing. My visit had to do with the Air Force One of the moment, the same Boeing 707 put into service for President Eisenhower. Broadway Bob Morrison, a fellow FAA Inspector and I would take a flight in it to determine if some new inertial navigation systems -the same ones I looked at on the Speckled Trout trip to the North Pole-were compatible with FAA requirements.

The airplane was now more than twenty years old, but it still had that great Never-Dull shine, that immaculate, pampered appearance. But Bob and I had been involved in the 747 and other programs and we got the feeling that technology was passing the President by. The Presidential aura was still there, but somewhat diminished in our eyes. I didn't get the same feeling I had gotten once before when I sat in FDR's seat in the Sacred Cow, that the airplane had had its day, but almost.

We watched as the crew operated the new inertials and could find no fault. As we flew, we learned that the technology and prestige gap would soon be closed, that Boeing was building two specially configured 747's to be used as Air Force One and its backup. The new airplanes would have all the latest gadgets. Moreover, the showmanship factor would be catered to by installing built-in air stairs, which would permit the President to make dramatic entrances right there at the edge of the red carpet. And now, today, those promises have come true. The first of the 747's has been in service for some time, and the pride of SAM has been restored.

Meanwhile, here I was, back in 1963, soon to be thirty-nine years old, looking forward with a little bit of concern about the future. My military career would end soon, along with my Major's salary and my ticket to adventure. I didn't get too worried about supporting my little family since we could scrape along on my retired pay along with income from some job or

499

another. But I had gotten rid of my phantoms, and I was in better physical and mental condition than I had a right to expect. I was actually ready and anxious for a change of some kind, yet there was something I was afraid of losing. I couldn't put my finger on it at first, but after a while it came to me. What I had always wanted, even when the well-placed 88 might threaten, or the hurricane might be getting ready to shake us crewdogs to pieces, or the penetrating gamma might be having some profound effect; what I had always wanted was to avoid the smothering clutches of an ordinary life.

So far, I had been able to do so. But now, what was in store for me?

EPILOGUE

"**T**HE LORD WATCHES OVER IDIOTS AND NAVIGATORS!" some
exasperated instructor once exclaimed for one reason or another at navigation school, and now I thought that maybe he was
right. I couldn't believe my ears as Marv Besch, one of our
Boeing pilots explained to me that his next door neighbor, a
USAF major attached to the FAA -the Federal Aviation
Administration- was looking for four fully qualified navigators
who would be retiring from the Air Force soon.

"Its part of something called Project Friendship..." he started to explain and I said, "Project Friendship? It sounds like
some foreign aid program..."

"Look, John, are you interested or not?" When I assured
him that I was totally interested and that I would keep quiet,
he wrote down the Major's name and phone number on a card
and handed it to me.

"Can we see this guy right now?" I asked, and Marv
laughed. "No, I'll give him your name, and you can call him in
the morning."

The FAA needed the navigators to navigate two beat-up C-
54's for some interesting work up in Iceland, Greenland and
arctic Canada, and in other places around the North Atlantic,
like the Azores and Bermuda. The airplanes were being handed
over by USAF and given civilian registration numbers. They
were marked officially as N-84 and N-85 but I came to know
better: they were really known as Old Smuggler and Old
Struggler.

Marv's news had come not long after I had received an
expected letter from the Air Force reminding me that my allotted twenty years would soon be up, and that I should begin to
make other plans. Now, my plans were made. In January,
which was almost upon us, I would be transferred to an FAA
office at Idlewild Airport in New York, and some months later, I
would be retired from USAF and become a temporary FAA
employee. There was no way of telling how long the job would

501

last. But there was a good chance that after one year, I could have my civil service status made permanent, and I would have a whole new career ahead of me, extending beyond my navigating days.

As Christmas approached, I made one more trip out of Andrews Air Force Base and when I returned, I began to get ready for my new job. I made arrangements to stay with my family in Yonkers until we could sell our house in Virginia. Then Cris and the girls would move up with me somewhere near the new office at Idlewild, which would be renamed after the soon-to-be-martyred JFK.

And when the day came for me to leave, I said good-bye to Cris in the pre-dawn winter morning. Then I moved quietly into the girls' room, timing my step to freeze the moment either one might stir, but they slept. As always, at such a time, my mind was calmed and my difficulties dissipated in the peaceful silence. The night light near Jill's bed was still on and I turned it off, and as the light went, I caught a glimpse of a tiny, chipped-eared ceramic dog, put carefully to sleep next to the lamp in a match-box bed. It was the last thing she had seen before she slipped off and would be the first thing to greet her eyes when she awoke.

Then I looked down at Holly, and in the winter moon's half light, I could see her arms were flung out by the tumbling forces of her journey through the sugar-plum galaxies. Her tumbling must have been gentle, however, for she slept in quiet serenity.

An involuntary smile overcame me as I leaned over and gently kissed those two innocent brows. I had known for some time what my smile meant. It came from the deepest recesses of my being and I had no control over it. It meant that, for me, the riddle of existence was solved and, at the moment, I had pressing questions for neither God nor Man.

I straightened up and quietly left the room.

BIBLIOGRAPHY

BOOKS:

A Thousand Days:- by Arthur M. Schlesinger, Jr.
Houghton Mifflin Company, The Riverside Press,
Cambridge, MA

The Advisors:Oppenheimer, Teller and the Superbomb
by Herbert Frank York W.H. Freeman and Company,
San Francisco CA

Air Force Spoken Here:- General Ira Eaker and Command of the
Air:- by James Parton.
Adler & Adler, Bethesda, MD

Arabian Peninsula:- Library of Nations,
Time-Life Books, Inc. , Alexandria, Virginia

Assault in Norway:- by Thomas Gallagher
Harcourt Brace Jovanovich, New York, NY

Conquest of the Sahara, The:- by Douglas Porch
Alfred A. Knopf, New York, NY

Lucy Rutledge Cooke Papers, MS 443
California Historical Society, San Francisco, CA 94109

Destruction of Dresden, The:- by David Irving
William Kinscher & Company 46 Walton Place, London SW1

Doolittle, A Biography:- by Lowell Thomas and Ed. Jablonski
Doubleday & Company, Garden City, NY

Eisenhower at War, 1943-1945:- by David Eisenhower
Random House, New York NY

Fighter Aces of the Luftwaffe:- by Col. Raymond F. Tolliver
and Trevor J. Constable Aero Publishers, Fallbrook, CA 92028

Fighter General:- by Col. Raymond F. Tolliver
and Trevor J. Constable Apress Publishers, Irvine, CA 92715

Flying White House, The:- by Col. Ralph Albertazzie
and J. F. terHorst. Coward, McCann and Geohagan, Inc.

Harry S. Truman:- by Margaret Truman.
William Morrow & Company, 105 Madison Avenue,
New York, NY

*Hurricane Hunters:-*by Ivan Ray Tannehill
Dodd, Mead & Company

I Could Never Be So Lucky Again
An Autobiography by Jimmy Doolittle with C. V. Glines
Bantam Books, New York

The Kassell Mission Reports:-
Kassell Mission Memorial Association P.O. Box 413,
Birmingham MI

Kennedy:- by Theodore C. Sorensen
Harper & Row, Publishers, New York NY

The Kingdom-Arabia and the House of Saud:- by Robert Lacey.
Avon Books, Madison Avenue, New York

Korean War, The:- by Max Hastings
Simon & Schuster, New York, NY

The Life and Times of Edward Teller:- by Stanley A. Blumberg
and Gwinn Owens. G. P. Putnam Sons, New York NY

Log of the Liberators:- by Steve Birdsall
Doubleday & Company, Garden City, NY

Marshall Cavendish Encyclopedia of World War I
MacDonald and Company

Mighty Eighth, The:- by Roger Freeman,
Orion Books, Crown Publishers, New York NY

Mission Failure and Survival:- by Charles C. McBride
 Sunflower University Press, 1531 Yuma, Manhattan KA

One Last Look:- Philip Kaplan
 Abbeville Press, New York NY

Saudi Arabia, A Country Study:-
 Department of the Army, 1984

The 1000 Day Battle:- by James Hoseason
 Gillingham Publications, 89 Bridge Road, Oulton Broad,
 Lowestoft, Suffolk

Thor's Legions:- by John F. Fuller
 American Meteorological Society 45 Beacon Street, Boston, MA

Washout:- by Charles A. Watry
 California Aero Press, Carlsbad, CA

Warplanes and Air Battes of World War II:-
 edited by Bernard Fitzsimons Beekman House, New York NY

PERIODICALS AND REPORTS:

Air Weather Service Bulletin No. 6, 1949
 HQ Air Westher Service, Andrews AFB MD

Air Weather Service: Our Heritage:- Historical Office
Military Airlift Command, Scott AFB, IL

Back-Issue Files, Herald Statesman
Yonkers, NY

Castle Series- A Report of DOD Participation:-by Edwin J.
Martin and Richard H. Rowland
Defense Nuclear Agency, Washington DC

News, 392nd Bomb Group Memorial Association
 5 N. Columbia Street, Frankfort, IN

Operation Hardtack:- by F. R. Gladeck et. al.,
Defense Nuclear Agency, Washington DC

Organizational History, 1254th Air Transport Group
89th MAW History Office, Andrews AFB, MD

Organizational Histories, 53rd, 54th, 55th, 56th, 57th, 373rd, 374th, 375th Weather Reconnaissance Squadrons
    Air Weather Service History Office Scott AFB, IL

Second Air Division Association Journal:-
    P.O. Box 627 Ipswich, MA

Yank Magazine, April 3, 1945.

Song: Caramba Its the Samba! (c) Kiss Music

INDEX

A

A-Bomb, First Soviet, 290-293
Acania, USS, at Johnston Isd., 423-4
Acebedo, Bruce, Capt., 230
Acheson, Dean, Sec. State, 322
Admiral Scheer, Battleship, 185
AFN, Armed Forces Network, 351
Air Weather Service, 358
Airborne-101st, 169
Akihito, Crown Prince, Japan, 475
Akureyri, Iceland, 238
Alameda Naval Air Sta., 374
Albertazzie, Ralph, Col. Presidential
    Pilot, 498
Aldrich, Wm. Capt., 236-7
Andrews, Dana, 216
Angra, Azores, 241
Aramco, 298
Arlington Hall Sta. VA., 398, 431
Armistead, BGEN CSA, 394
Army Hall, Tokyo, 341-2
Arnhem Annie, 198
Aschaffenburg, 182-83
Atomic Energy Comm., 411, 438

B

Balbo, Marshal Italo, 33
Barnes, Leonard J. Maj., 159
Bastogne, Belg., 169
Battle of Britain, 87
Battle of the Bulge/Ardennes, 167-70
Battleship Admiral Scheer, 185
Baudoin, King of Belgium, 457
Bay of Pigs, 484, 487, 494, 497
Beau Geste, 461
Berchtesgaden, Germ., 199
Berle, Adolf, 485
Berlin Wall, 494
Besch, Marvin, Maj. 501
Bikini, 403
Billings, Don, Maj., 476,479
Boeing Stratocruiser, C-97, 359, 367,
    375-8

Boline, Laurel, Capt., 332-3, 334-6
Bolling AFB, D.C., 398
Bosnia, 10
Bloody Hundredth-100th BG, 122
    193-4
Bluie West One/Narssarsuaq, 218
Bluie West Eight-Sondrestrom, 94,
    231-34
BMEWS, 469
Bohlen, Chas., Gen., 202
Boswood, Jas., Sgt., 287
Boxer, USS, aircraft carrier, 405-6
von Braun, Wernher, 421-2
Bravo/Castle Nuclear Test, 402-405
Brazilia, Brazil, 443
Burg Rueland, Germ., 175
Buzz Bombs, V- 1, 87
Byers, Clovis E. LGEN, 448

C

Caffritz, Gwen, 447
Californians, The, Covered Wagon
    Travelers, 368-70
Canaveral, Cape, FL, 420-1
Carden, Alva F, 247, 249, 252, 264
Carlucci, Frank, 460
Castle Series Nuclear Tests, 403
Caesar, Sid, 20
Chamberlin, Neville, PM, 35
Charleston AFB, SC, 384
Chiang-Kai-shek, 495
Childs, J. Rives, Amb., 301, 309-311
    313, 315-18
Chou en Lai, 354
Churchill, Winston, 178, 201, 204,
    395
Clarion, Operation, 180-2
Cochran, Jaqueline, 2
Collins, Tom, Col., 467
Columbine, Pres. aircraft, 475
Compass Swing, 400
Connell, Royal, Col., 286-7
Connors, Larry, 229

Conover, Jim, Maj., 488, 489-91
Cooke, Lucy Rutledge, 368-70
Coward, Noel, 338
Cray Supercomputers, 405
Cronin, Tom, Capt., 338
Cuban Revolutionary Council, 485
Cushing, Alonzo, Lt., 394

D

DeGaul, Charles, Gen., 448
deMello, Francisco, Air Min. Brazil, 440,445
Dempsey, Jack, 17
Dhahran Airfield, Saudi Arabia,Wea Recon activ.,294-317
Dillon, C. Douglas, 451-2
Don the Beachcomber's, Waikiki, 371
Doolittle, Jimmy, Gen., 123, 134, 152, 193-4
Double Drift, Descr., 220
Douglas C-54/DC-4, 398
Draper, Bill, Col., Presidential Pilot, 439, 476, 480-1
Dresden, Bombing of, 178, 185
Duckworth, Joe, Col., 254-5
Dulles, John Foster, Sec State, 448, 451-2
Dunham, "Dingy",Lt Col., 265
Dunkleberg, Grover, Col., 439

E

Eaker, Ira, Gen., 189
Earhart, Amelia, 2
Eastburn, Mack, Capt., 261
Eglin AFB FL, 332
Eielson AFB, Alaska, 268
Eisenhower, Dwight D. Gen.,162, 202, 354, 405, 439, 471, 479, 487-8
Eisenhower, John, 477
Eisenhower, Mamie, 479
Elder, Alan., Capt.,231
Ellsworth, Richard, BGen, 278
Emir of Kano, Nigeria, 473-4
Empire State Bldg, accident, 207
Enewetak, 324
Euskirchen, Germ., 171

F

Fallout Plot Unit, Enewetak, 408

Faisal, Prince, 310, 314
Fatiuk, Professor, 22
FDR, 4, 17, 49, 398
Fidel Castro, 484
First Air Force, 77
First Bomber Command, 77
Fletcher's Island-Ice Island T-3, 467
Fort Lamy, Chad, 462-5
Fort Sumter, 393
Fortunate Dragon #5, 403-4
Fox Able One Mission, 263-7
Franklin SeaBee, amphibian, 373
Franz Ferdinand, Archduke, 10
Franz Josef, Emperor, 6, 10, 11
Frederick, King of Denmark, 475-6
French Air Force, 328
French Foreign Legion, 464

G

Galeao Airport, Rio de Janeiro, Brazil, 443
Galicia, Aust. Hung. Emp., 6, 10, 13
Galland, Adolf, Gen. Luftwaffe, 123
Gaggenau, Germ., 124
Gander Airfield, Can., 93
Garner, John Nance, V.P., 498
GCA-Ground Controlled Approach 226-7, 291
GEE Box, 147-8, 187, 189
George, Amin, Maj., 392,420
Gettysburg Battlefield, PA, 394
Goebbels, Josef, 197
Goering, Heriyiann, 197
Goldberg, Arthur, Sec Labor, 484
Goodman, Benny, 4
Gooney Birds at Midway Id. 330
Goose Bay Airfield, Can., 93-6
Gordon, "Chinese," Gen., 396
Grand Central Station, 80
Graves, Jack Lt., 157
Grenier Field, NH, 219
Griffith, Perry B. BGEN, 436-7
Grosvenor House Hotel, 138

H

Haggerty, Jim, Press Secretary, 480
Hamburg, Germ., 127
Hamm, Germ., 114-15
Hardtack, Operation, 398
Hatch, Abiel, 368

Henderson, Loy, Amb., 457,461
Henie, Sonja, ice skater, 379
Hindenberg, dirigible, 34
Hiroshima, 35
Hiryu, Aircraft Carrier Japan, 35
Hitler, Adolf, 35, 139, 165, 167,
    197-8
Himmler, Heinrich, 197
Hollings, Ernest M. Gov. SC, 386
Hummel, J. R. Lt., 192
Hungarian Refugee Airlift, 395
Hunsaker, Capt., 199

I

ibn Saud, King of Saudi Arabia,
    310-13, 315-17
Ice Island T-3/Bravo/Fletchers
    Island, 467
Inchon, Korea, U.S. Landings, 323-4
InterTropical Front-ITC, 329
Ishikawa, Henry, Professor, 342
ibn Saud, King of Saudi Arabia,
    310-13, 315-17

J

Jacobs, Hal, Capt., 329-31
bin Jaluwi, 311-12
Jebel Uweinat, Sudan/Libya, 397
Jet Propulsion Lab, CalTech, 438
Jet Stream, 350-351, 359-60
Joe 4, Soviet Nuclear test, 404
John Birch Society, 373
Johnson, Leon, BGen., 122, 184-5,
    198
Johnson, Lorin, Col., 106, 127,
    149,184
Johnson, Louis, Sec Def, Reduction
    in force, 1949, 322

Johnson, Lyndon B., 495, 498
Johnson, Robt. C. Lt., 289-93
Johnston Island, 419, 420, 423-4, 427
Joint Task Force Seven-JTF-7,
    forming of, 398, 401
Jones, C. B., Lt., 256-7
Jones-Burdick, Wm. Lt., 255
Jolson, Al, 19
Jules Club Hotel, 137-8

K

Kaiserslautern, Germ., 170
Kassel, Germ., 112, 119-22, 129-30,
    150
Katanga Cowboys, 456
Kennedy, John F., Pres., 471, 480,
    484, 487, 496-7
Kennedy Space Center, FL, 420
Kepner, Wm, Gen., Big Dog, 122
Ketcham, Don., Lt., 264
Khadafi, Mouamar, 270
Khrushchev, Soviet Premier, 478
Kilauea Military Camp, Hawaii, 380
    volcano, 380
King ibn Saud, 310-13, 315-317
Kissinger, Henry, 498
Kitchener, Lord, 396
Korea, South, 347
    siege of Pusan, 323-4
Korean War begins, 321
    war ends, 352
Kougias, Geo., Lt., 256-8, 263
Kuboyama, Aikichi, 404
Kurile Islands, 349

L

Laguardia, Fiorello H., 4, 5
Lam, August, Lt., 230
Lamarr, Hedy, 303
Langley Field-AFB, 91
Lay, Bierne, Col., 123
Lear, Ben, Gen., 53
Lemay, Curtis, Gen., 123, 179, 277-8
Leinnitzer, Lyman, Gen. USA, 451
Lewis, Joe E., comedian, 338
Lindbergh, Chas A., 1, 254, 282, 284
Lockheed Constellation, 359-61
Lockheed, P2V Neptune, 408, 414
LORAN, 217, 220, 349
Los Alamos Scientific Laboratory,
    327-8, 405, 412
Loy, Myrna, 216
Luedecke, A.R. MGEN, Commander,
    JTF-7, 398, 401, 413, 420, 422-
    4, 427, 429

M

MacArthur, Douglas, Gen., 6, 323-4
    342-3

Madeiros, Rod, Lt., 381
Magdeburg, Germ., 185
Magee, MSGT, 58-60,482-3
Maginot Line, 35
Maid of the Mist, 389-90
Majuro, 412
Mao Tse Tung, 321
March, Frederick, actor, 216
Marshall, Geo. C. Gen., 276
Martens, B. Henry, 247, 249, 264
Masefield, John, poet, 7, 8
Massey, Charles E., Capt., 282, 290, 357
Matishowski, John, 6, 8, 9, 15, 16, 19
Matt, Holly, 384
Maxwell Field, AFB, Ala. 45-47
Mayo, Ken, MSGT, 458, 463, 486
Mays, John Chambliss, Capt., 257
McAuliffe, Anthony Gen., 169
McCarthy, Charles, NY Daily News 496
McClellan AFB, CA, 283-4, 375
McConnell, Jos. Capt., 279
McDonagh, Chaplain 392nd BG, 160
McHugh, Col., Pres.Air Force Aide, 485
McKay, Jim, 472
McKinney, B. B. Lt., 301
McNair, Lesley J. Gen., 162
McNamara, Robt., Sec Def, 493
Meeks Field, Iceland, 98-9
Meiji Bldg., Tokyo, 343, 350
Messerschmitt
    ME-163 rocket plane, 177
    ME-262 jet, 177
Mesta, Peric, Ambassador, 444
Midway Island, 330
Mike Nuclear Test, 404
Milchak, Sgt., at Wesel, 192
Military Air Transport Service, 358
Miller, Glenn, 138
Miracle Mile, Tachikawa, Japan, 344
Mitteland Canal, Minden, Germ. 151-2
Mobotu, Joseph, of Zaire, 459
Morrison, Robt., FAA, 499
Muldoon, Jas. Lt., 132-3
Murphy, Robt., Ambassador, 455

N
Nagasaki, Japan, 35
Nasser, Gamal, 396
National Met Center, Suitland MD, 405
Nehru, Jawaharlal, PM India, 354
Niagara Falls, NY, 387-390
Nicholas, Czar, Russia, 11
Nixon, Richard M., Pres., 471-2, 489
Novik, Albert, Lt., 156-9, 180

O
Oak Nuclear Test, 414-15, 417
Ocean Station Bak-er-Bravo, 97
Ogle, Wm. Dr., 413,420
O'Hair, Ralph, Lt., 254
O'Hara, Maureen, actress, 300
O'Keefe, Wm. Gen., 298, 307
Omdurman, Sudan cavalry charge, 396
Operation Clarion, 180-82
Operation Varsity, 185
Oppenheimer, J. Robt., 293
Orange Nuclear Test, 418-20, 427

P
Pacusan Dreamboat Project., 231-2
Park, Frances Hatch, 368
Parnell, Roy, LTCOL, 438
Parry Island, Enewetak, 409-10
Path Finder Force-PFF, 91
Patton, Geo. C. Gen., 35, 153, 166-7
Pawnee Indians, 369
Pearl Harbor, 38, 41
Peary, Robt. C., Adm., 287
Pentagon, The, 433-4
Philby, Kim, 317
Philby, St. John 316-17
Piccadilly Commandos, 106
Pickett, L. J. Maj., 265
Pidgeon, Walter, actor, 303
Pilsen, Czech., 199
Ploesti Raid, 88, 122
Point Barrow, Alaska, 466, 469
Post, Gerald, Lt., 328-331
Post, Wiley, 2,466
Pres. Pilot's Office, 481
Princip, Gavrilo, 11
Prohibition, 15

Procak, Anna, 7
PT-23, Fairchild, 54
Puglisi, Vincent, LTCOL, Pres. Nav. 439
Pusan, Korea, siege of, 323-4

Q

Quirk, Chief of Police, Yonkers, 16

R

Radio Bomb Release-RBR, 118
Radsafe Office, Enewetak, 407-09
Redstone Rocket, 419, 422-5, 427
Regensburg Mission, 88, 125
Reykjavik, Iceland, 99, 238-9
Richie, Frank, LTCOL, 407- 10, 416-17, 424-5
Rjuken, Norway,
    Commando Raid, 428
    Eighth AF raid, 428
    Heavy water plant, 428
Rogers, Will, humorist, 466
Rogers, Wm. P. Atty Gen., 473-4
Rooney, Andy, war correspondent, 86
Roosevelt, Franklin D., 4, 17, 49
Roosevelt, Eleanor, 351
Royal Hawaiian Hotel, Waikiki, 363
Rub-al-Khali desert, 302
von Rundstedt, Gen., 170
Russell, Harold, 216

S

Sacred Cow Pres. Aircraft, 398-9
Salzburg, Germ. 197
Salzbergen, Germ., 156, 176
Sampson and Hercules Club, 106
Sarajevo, Bosnia, 10, 14
Saranac Inn, NY, 37, 51, 363
ibn Saud, King of Saudi Arabia, 310-13, 315-17
Scheinkman, Martin, 340-41, 375
von Schlieffen, 13
Schilling, Dave, Col., 264-7
Schlesinger, Arthur M. Jr., 485
Schmeling, Max, prizefighter, 17
Schmit, Mel. Maj., 462
Schultz, Dutch, 17
Schweinfurt Raid, 88
Sextant, Bendix A-14, 334
Shaffhausen, Switz., 132

Shaw, Harry, Maj., 463
Sheehan, Joe, Maj., 418
Sinatra, Frank, 4
Sioux Indians, 369
Smolenski, Jos., LTCOL, 439-40
Sonderkommando Elbe, 196
Sondrestrom Fiord, Greenland, 94, 231-34
Soviets
    first A-bomb, 289-293
    first H-bomb, 293
    rocketry, 294
    58-Megaton test, 405
Spaatz, Tooey, Gen., 178, 193-4
Speckled Trout, USAF Boeing jet 287-8
St. Cyr, Lilly, 338
Stanley, Henry Morton, 455
Stars and Stripes, newspaper, 192, 194-5
Stephenville, Can., 221, 222-25
Steinmetz, John, 238
Stetson, Genevieve Hatch, 372
Stetson, Lincoln, Lt., 374
Stetson, Wes, 373-4
Stevenson, Adlai., 487-493
Stewart, Jimmy, actor and combat pilot, 121
Sturmgruppen, 120, 122
Sun Valley, Idaho, 379-80
Surfrider Hotel, Waikiki, 362
Swangren, Roy, Capt., 149, 159
Swindal, Jas., LTCOL., 481

T

Taylor, Maxwell, Gen., 595
Teak Shot, 418-19, 420, 423, 427
Teller, Edward, Dr., 403, 410-11
Teufel, Richard, Capt., 462, 465
Thomas, Bill, Pres. Pilot, 476, 479
Thompson, Gus, Capt., 247-50, 264
Thrower, Tom, Sgt, 249
Thule Airbase, Greenland, 288
Tibenham Airdrome, U.K., 119-121
Trans-Arabian Pipeline, 295
Travis, Col., 276-7
Travis Air Force Base, Cal., 373
Truman, Harry S., President, 293, 322-3, 398

Truculent Turtle, Navy P2V, 231-2
Tuaregs, the Blue Men, 453
Tunney, Gene, pugilist, 17
Turner, Bulldog, Maj., 47
Turner, Roscoe, aviator, 2
Twining, Dick, Capt., 485

U

Udet, Ernst, stunt flier, 445
Ukraine, 30
Ulam, Teller-Ulam Config., 403
Univ. of Cal. Radiation Lab., 405
USAF Scientific Advisory Board, 466

V

V-1 "Buzz Bomb", 87
V-2 Rocket Bomb, 87
V-E Day, 202-3
Vercelli, Edw. Lt., 275
Verny Forts at Metz, 113-114
VLF-Very Low Frequency, 287-8
Volstead Act, 15
von Braun, Wernher, 421-2

W

Walters, Vernon, LTCOL, 472
Wheelus Air Base, Tripoli, 270, 273
Whirling Dervishes, Sudan, 396
Whitfield, H.H. Col., 298
Wilhelm, Kaiser, 11
Winchell, Walter, 17
Wendling Airdrome, U.K.,102,104-5
Whitehead, Trusty, Capt., 485-6
Wilhelmshaven, Germ., 195
Williams, Eldon, MSGT, 301-305,
        311, 314-315
Winstead, Leonard, Lt., 229-30
Womack, Jack Capt., 301, 309-11
        313-14, 315-16

Y

Yeager, Charles, B.Gen., 254
Yonkers Statesman, Yonkers Herald-
        Statesman, 21
Yucca Nuclear Test, balloon, 405-7
Yucca Flats, Nevada, 324, 333

Z

ZOMCOT, 361